Cambridge Studies in Social Anthropology
General Editor: Jack Goody

39

THE FISH PEOPLE

For other titles in this series turn to page 285

The Fish People

Linguistic Exogamy and Tukanoan Identity in Northwest Amazonia

JEAN E. JACKSON

Associate Professor of Anthropology
Massachussetts Institute of Technology

CAMBRIDGE UNIVERSITY PRESS

Cambridge
London   New York   New Rochelle
Melbourne   Sydney

Published by the Press Syndicate of the University of Cambridge
The Pitt Building, Trumpington Street, Cambridge CB2 1RP
32 East 57th Street, New York, NY 10022, USA
296 Beaconsfield Parade, Middle Park, Melbourne 3206, Australia

© Cambridge University Press 1983

First published 1983

Printed in the United States of America

Library of Congress Cataloging in Publication Data
Jackson, Jean E. (Jean Elizabeth), 1943–
The fish people.
(Cambridge studies in social anthropology; no. 39)
Includes bibliographical references and index.
1. Tucano Indians – Social life and customs.
2. Barasana Indians – Social life and customs. 3. Indians
of South America – Colombia – Social life and customs.
I. Title. II. Series.
F2520.1.T9J3   1983   306'.08998   82-23564
ISBN 0 521 23921 4 hard covers
ISBN 0 521 27822 8 paperback

For my father and in memory of my mother

Contents

List of figures, maps, and tables   x
Preface   xi
Acknowledgments   xvi
Note on orthography   xviii

1   Purpose and organization of the book   1
Social identity   2
Regional perspective   5
Fluidity   8
Ideal and real   9
Final remarks   11

2   Introduction to the Central Northwest Amazon   13
Ecological setting   13
The population   17
Language and linguistics   19
Ethnic history   21
Early explorer and missionary efforts   22
Early and recent ethnographic descriptions   23
The Makú   24
A note on acculturation   24

3   The longhouse   26
The setting   26
The people of Púmanaka buro   26
The longhouse structure   30
Outside the longhouse   31
Inside the longhouse   33
Significance of the longhouse   36

Contents

4 Economic and political life   39
   Daily patterns   39
   The river   42
   The forest   46
   Cultivated foods   50
   Exchange in general   59
   Property   62
   Leadership   65

5 Vaupés social structure   69
   The settlement   69
   The sib   71
   The language group   77
   The phratry   86
   Regional integration and
      interaction between settlements   96

6 Kinship   105
   Kinship terminology   106
   Expectations and behavior   108
   Specific kinship roles   117

7 Marriage   124
   Principles of marriage   125
   Marriage behavior   138
   Conclusions   147

8 Tukanoans and Makú   148
   Background to the Makú   148
   Tukanoan attitudes toward the Makú   151
   Interaction between Tukanoans and Makú   154
   Makú as symbol to Tukanoans   158
   Conclusions   161

9 The role of language and speech in Tukanoan identity   164
   Vaupés language and speech as badges of identity   165
   How Vaupés languages assume features
      of the nonlinguistic environment   171
   The importance of language in
      Tukanoan culture   177

Contents

10 Male and female identity   179
    Relations between men and women   181
    Conclusions   192

11 Tukanoans' place in the cosmos   195
    Shamanism   195
    Festivals   202
    The Tukanoan world   204
    Conclusions   208

12 Tukanoans and the outside world   211
    Extractive industries   215
    Homesteaders   217
    The Colombian government   217
    Missions   218
    Mitú   223
    Conclusions   224

13 Conclusions: themes in Tukanoan social identity   227
    Types of comparisons   227
    Themes associated with social identity   231
    A note on types of evidence   239

Notes   243
Glossary   256
References   259
Index   273

Figures, maps, and tables

Figures

1 The longhouse setting 27
2 The inhabitants of Pǔmanaka buro 29
3 Ground plan of longhouse interior 34
4 Traditional Vaupés social structure 73
5 Marriage distance between language groups 95
6 Marriages during three generations at Pǔmanaka buro 139
7 Two conflicting models of language distance 172

Maps

1 The Eastern Colombian Vaupés 14
2 Membership of settlements by language group 80
3 Locations of settlements intermarrying with Pǔmanaka buro 140

Tables

1 Language group affiliation of Tukanoans in sample 82
2 Names of language groups 85
3 Estimates of populations of language groups 87
4 Zero generation terminology at three levels of inclusion 90
5 Phratries listed by three informants 91
6 Marriage between selected language groups 94
7 Bará kinship terminology 109
8 Simplified Bará kinship terminology 112
9 Language distance as measured by cognates 173

Preface

In November 1968 I arrived in the Vaupés territory of Colombia planning to study beliefs and practices related to disease and curing in a Northwest Amazon tribe. I originally intended to work with the Tikuna, south of the Vaupés, but conversations with anthropologists Gerardo Reichel-Dolmatoff and Alicia Dussan de Reichel after my arrival in Colombia convinced me that the Tikuna were too acculturated for the study I really wanted to do. I turned to the Vaupés region, which had the additional advantage of being the focus of a number of ongoing research projects, including Reichel-Dolmatoff's own work with the Barasana and Desana.

After arriving in Mitú, the airstrip town on the Vaupés River that is the administrative seat of the Vaupés territory, I spent about three weeks making canoe trips and flights in small airplanes to various settlements. Realizing I had to locate myself quite far away from Mitú and the Vaupés River, I then took a missionary plane south to Monfort on the Papurí River and soon after went on a ten-day visit with some Desana Indians to a small, nucleated village on Caño Virarí, which, however, was still too acculturated for my purposes. It became clear during this frustrating but valuable period of orientation that I really did not want to compromise in terms of acculturation level, and I reconciled myself to the inevitability of settling in an extremely isolated community reachable only by a long canoe trip.

During my stay at Monfort I met Samuel, a Desana who spoke Spanish and understood why I wanted to stay in the most traditional settlement possible. Samuel agreed that a longhouse community was the only answer to my requirements and even listed a number of characteristics still applicable to longhouse communities but absent in nucleated villages. He said that later I could live in a mission town, once I understood where Tukanoans had started from in their journey toward the Colombian–Brazilian and Christian worlds. He suggested I live with his Bará in-laws on the Inambú River, assuring me they would be delighted to have me, and I decided to trust this indirect invitation. First, however, I returned to Bogotá to buy such necessary equipment as an outboard motor and gasoline. I then returned to the Vaupés, meeting Samuel in Mitú and traveling with him to his wife's parents' longhouse, Púmanaka buro ("hill of many leaves"), where I was to spend the next eighteen months.

The longhouse was the home of about twenty Tukanoans: Bará men, their non-Bará wives, and their children.[1] These people had heard via the Vaupés grapevine that I was coming, and undoubtedly were as anxious about my liking them as I was about their liking me. (They later told me some of the worries they had had during the beginning of our acquaintanceship.) For my part, I desperately hoped things would work out because it seemed as though I had already wasted an inordinate amount of time.

My first two days in the longhouse were a confused jumble of talking to people via Samuel and making attempts to begin learning Bará; a puppy I had acquired in Mitú provided a conversation topic of sorts. Disoriented and anxious, I was also extremely excited, reactions shared by virtually all anthropologists upon entering the field but perhaps heightened by several factors in my situation.[2] One, I was completely alone. Two, by then I had spent almost three months and was extremely impatient to begin "real" fieldwork. And three, living in a Tukanoan longhouse involves an intensity and exclusivity of contact with one's fellow residents unmatched in the vast majority of residence arrangements found in the world. For periods of a week or more a settlement's residents see only one another. Púmanaka buro, like all longhouses (at least at present), is remote from other settlements; a two-hour canoe trip separates it from its nearest neighbors downstream, a Tuyuka longhouse community. Still, although I felt terribly cut off from virtually everything familiar to me, I adjusted, and over time a very deep attachment formed, both on my part and, I believe, on theirs. The intensity of feeling has been only partly diminished with time.

Over the months I would come to realize just how dependent I was on these people, a dependency that made me euphoric at times and depressed at others. At the beginning, I only dimly realized some of the psychological adjustments I would have to make; these demanded more of me than any other aspect of fieldwork, far more than physical discomfort. It is one thing to learn to cope with new routines, to eat strange foods, to survive wasp massacres and fungal invasions. Much of it, in fact, I enjoyed, and the challenge posed by the rest suited my romantic side very nicely. But my feelings of loneliness and incompetence were hard to deal with, heightened as they were by my belief that anthropologists should not become "too involved." I tried to remain objective, not to take sides in arguments, and in general to monitor my behavior so as to avoid permanently alienating people. Straddling the fence of emotional involvement and expression (saying and feeling neither too little nor too much) was perhaps the most difficult of requirements in a setting like the longhouse, because these people, how they felt about me and I about them, affected my life and work in the most profound way. Of course I failed to keep my supposed objectivity. I did take sides in disputes, and I have come to accept the inevitability of this involvement far more than I did then. Certainly at times my role as anthropologist conflicted with that of coresident, but I believe that in general whatever value my research has derives to a considerable extent from the relationships I shared with my fellow members of Púmanaka buro. I am *not* making the obvious observation that the longer one lives and interacts with a group of people, the better one understands them. True as that is, I mean to suggest here that a process of emotional attachment must occur in order really to understand a culture but that at times it works against one's desire to be detached, objective, scientific. The best emotional stance to take when carrying out fieldwork must, of course, be an individual decision, but to believe in one's total objectivity and detachment is naive and self-deceptive: A great deal can be gained in crossing emotional boundaries along with the cultural ones.

These rather lengthy remarks are intended not only to express my deep feelings of appreciation toward the people of Púmanaka buro but also to call attention to the fact that I did spend much of my time with one particular group of people in a rather isolated location, a fact that bears directly on the avowedly regional perspective taken by this book in portraying Tukanoan social identity. How I came to reorient my research plan from a local to a regional perspective is important information for a number of reasons, and thus a discussion of it follows.

Soon after arriving at Púmanaka buro I began a study of the Bará language, in preparation for carrying out the cognitive ethnosemantic part of my research. It quickly became apparent that the proposed research could not be done, because it depended on an implicit research assumption that the members of the subject group all spoke the same language. I found myself in a region with more than sixteen languages, several of them represented in each longhouse. Although I had been aware of this fact before, its implications did not strike me until I was in the field. The rule of exogamy required that all inmarrying women at a settlement be from other language groups. Every Tukanoan I talked to was at least trilingual, and children began acquiring two languages almost from the beginning of language learning. Most conversation was in Bará, but the women with whom I spent much of my time also spoke in Tuyuka and occasionally in Tukano ("just for a change").

Furthermore, the same problem arose when I contemplated research on decision making about disease and curing and the degree of fit between normative pronouncements and actual behavior. Other settlements of the region were at least half an hour by canoe from each other. Worse, there were no other Bará longhouses on the river or in the immediate vicinity of Púmanaka buro, all its neighbors being Tuyuka, Tukano, and Desana. How could I, then, by working with one language, claim to say anything about how these people think about and classify disease terms and behaviors, or anything else, for that matter? This situation, which fortunately confronts few fieldworkers, seemed to discourage every possible avenue of research until I decided to capitalize on it and begin an investigation of the social structure of Tukanoans, in particular those of the Papurí drainage region, concentrating on the relation between multilingualism, kinship, and marriage.

If I had begun with a well-thought-out research design, complete with hypotheses to be tested and so forth, my fieldwork would have conformed to current standards more closely than it did. My progress toward understanding the various linguistic and marital mysteries of the Vaupés has in fact been much more serendipitous, full of dead ends and interesting side paths that, unfortunately, incomplete data have not allowed me to explore thoroughly. I offer these remarks to explain some of the gaps in the data; I simply was not aware of the complexity and reach of the system while researching it. The conclusions given here have evolved during a ten-year period and are the result of many struggles with the data and many conversations with fellow Vaupés specialists and other anthropologists.

Although I spent much of the field period at a single site, I traveled frequently; sometimes I accompanied the residents of Púmanaka buro when they went to rituals at other settlements but more often I traveled in order to get in and out of the region. The canoe trip from Púmanaka buro to Mitú never took less than six days, and one memorable trip during the dry season took ten days. As I came and went I changed boat crews frequently and slept at a different settlement each night. I gathered as much information as I could at each stop, especially on demography and settlement locations; by the end of my fieldwork, when I had grasped at least in part the extent of the marriage system, I came to see this information as extremely valuable. In every settlement some of the inmarried affines came from distant places, making it possible to find out about communities well off my route. Furthermore, Tukanoans displayed a great interest in the physical and social geography of the Vaupés, and they seemed to see it as a single region. Their interest in answering my questions or finding others to answer them gradually convinced me that I was investigating a true cultural focus, equivalent to the interest of highland Chiapas Indians in corn or Dobuans in sorcery.

Thus, I eventually broadened my study as far as possible, because neither I nor Tukanoans could see any clear-cut boundaries between Tukanoans and "other people." Even my goal of a complete census of marriages of living individuals of the upper and mid-Papurí and its tributaries, which I eventually achieved, did not mark off a socially bounded unit. During my trips I drew sketch maps, which, crude though they were, demonstrated in combination with the census data the extent to which marriage unified subsections of and, less so, the entire Vaupés region. Thus those canoe trips that I often dreaded, greatly envying other anthropologists who were able to fly into and out of their sites, proved to be the source of much essential data.

It must be borne in mind that my research strategy evolved during fieldwork and that I spent most of my time in a single longhouse community, circumstances that have led to my taking the Bará language group and, more specifically, the residents of Pűmanaka buro as representative of Tukanoan society. Although I have been careful throughout the book to point out all the discrepancies and exceptions of which I am aware, it should be remembered that in general we shall be looking at Tukanoan society through the spectacles of the Bará living in the Papurí drainage region. My approach has also necessitated striking a balance between ethnographic specificity and systemic overview. The balance here seems to me a good one, but because the work deals with both local and regional data I have had to make many decisions regarding the amount of material to include from either perspective. I obviously cannot, when describing an open-ended system like the Vaupés, describe and analyze how every person, every local group, every language-affiliated group differs from and resembles every other one. A serious attempt to combine both a regional overview with a comprehensive ethnography of every group encompassed within the overview would require more years of research and more volumes than even the most forgiving granting agency or publisher could conceivably tolerate.

Thus, this book represents a point – I hope a high but not a final one – in a long process of investigation and analysis of Tukanoan social identity. I hope to return to the Vaupés and continue research; indeed, this monograph was completed before another sojourn only when it became evident that one planned for 1976 would be impossible.[3] Many of my intentions for future research will become apparent in the following pages. I am confident in the essential accuracy of my portrayal of the form of the Vaupés social system; by adding content, admittedly largely from Bará/Papurí sources, I believe I have sketched a reasonable portrait. It is hoped that this book will inspire others to comment on the picture I have painted or attempt their own interpretation of this fascinating system and the people who have created it.

Acknowledgments

Many, many people have helped me in the various stages of preparing this book. Of the numerous people at Stanford who offered their advice and support before, during, and after fieldwork, special thanks go to Benjamin Paul, George Collier, and members of my dissertation committee, Charles Frake, Bernard Siegel, and Renato Rosaldo.

Many Colombians assisted in the research, and I would like to thank the Colombian government and its representatives in Bogotá and Mitú for permitting and facilitating my investigations along the way. The many individuals attached to the Prefectura Apostólica del Vaupés gave generously of their time and hospitality, in particular Monseñor Belarmino Correa and the missionaries at Monfort and Acaricuara. Betty Welch, Birdie West, and Janet Barnes of the Summer Institute of Linguistics, Colombia, also offered encouragement during my stay. The warmth and laughter of Don Tito Vargas and his wife, Doña Alix, of Mitú made my stops there far more pleasant than they otherwise would have been.

My thanks also go to the many people of the Universidad de los Andes and the Instituto Colombiano de Antropología in Bogotá who aided the research, in particular Alicia Dussan and Gerardo Reichel-Dolmatoff.

During the years spent writing this manuscript, various sections of it were sent to people or used in lectures. Many people responded generously with comments and criticism. I will simply list them alphabetically, because to do otherwise would be very cumbersome: Kaj Århem, Joan Bamberger, Ellen Basso, Patrice Bidou, Roy D'Andrade, Gertrude Dole, Steven Fjellman, James Fox, Nina S. de Friedemann, Hugh Gladwin, Irving Goldman, Joseph Greenberg, Thomas Gregor, John Gumperz, Robert Hahn, Raymond Hames, Dell Hymes, Judith Irvine, Pierre-Yves Jacopin, Theodore Johnson, Joanna Kaplan, Kenneth Kensinger, David Kronenfeld, David Maybury-Lewis, Wick Miller, Jerry Moles, Naomi Quinn, Howard Reid, Peter Rivière, Kimball Romney, Benson Saler, Gillian Sankoff, Judith Shapiro, Joel Sherzer, Peter Silverwood-Cope, Janet Siskind, Carol Smith, Arthur Sorensen, David Thomas, Katherine Verdery, and Norman Whitten. I also acknowledge the many other people who gave assistance.

Acknowledgments

Research in Colombia during 1968–70 was supported by the Danforth Foundation and the Stanford Committee for Research in International Studies. An Old Dominion fellowship and a grant from the Dean of Humanities and Social Sciences, MIT, supported work on the manuscript.

For encouragement and, at times, forbearance, I thank my colleagues at MIT, especially Martin Diskin and James Howe. Jim's contribution, in the form of painstaking editing of parts of the manuscript, I and all future readers of this book have reason to be grateful for.

As is evident from the many references to their written work and various communications to me in the following pages, my debt to Stephen and Christine Hugh-Jones is immeasurable.

I also thank the people at Cambridge University Press, in particular Jack Goody, Walter Lippincott, and Susan Allen-Mills.

Finally, the people at Púmanaka buro, in particular Juanico Escobar and his wife, María Tamaño, and family, took me in and helped me in countless ways.

Juanico, María, Lois Paul, Michelle Rosaldo, and my mother, Mary Elizabeth Gaines Jackson, have all died since the research began. I regret they cannot see its final form, because they were all instrumental – in very different ways – in bringing it about.

I gratefully acknowledge permission from Academic Press to reproduce Tables 1 and 2, Figures 2, 3, 5, and Map 3 of my chapter in C. Smith, ed., *Regional Analysis, Volume 2, Social Systems*. I also thank Cambridge University Press for permission to use material from my chapter in Richard Bauman and Joel Sherzer, eds., *Explorations in the Ethnography of Speaking*. Mouton Publishers kindly permitted reproduction of Chart 1, p. 121, of Nathan Waltz and Alva Wheeler's article in E. Matteson, ed., *Comparative Studies in Amerindian Languages*, which appears as Table 9 in Chapter 9. And Seminar für Ethnologie has permitted reproduction of part of the material on "Ethno-linguistic groups of Colombia" in W. Dostal, ed., *The Situation of the Indian in South America*, which appears here as Table 3.

Note on orthography

The orthography used in this book is a phonetic transcription of Bará, simplified to make it accessible to and convenient for English-speaking readers. The kinds of simplifications chosen do not confuse the particular lexical items dealt with in the text, that is, they would not reduce phonetically distinct forms to homonyms. For a more comprehensive treatment of Bará (as spoken in the Pirá-paraná, a separate dialect from Inambú Bará), see Stolte and Stolte, 1971. For example, tone (Bará has two) is not indicated in my transcription, and stress has been simplified (high tone and stress co-occur): Stress falls on the penultimate syllable unless shown elsewhere. Aspiration is not phonemic; I have indicated preaspiration where it occurs with the voiceless stops /p/, /t/, and /k/ as an aid to pronunciation (e.g., *mehkó*, "father's sister").

Vowels

Unnasalized		*Nasalized*
a	as in f*a*ther	ã
e	as in *e*ight	ẽ
i	as in ped*i*atrics	ĩ
o	as in *o*val	õ
u	as in f*oo*d	ũ
ü	similar to German ü	ü̃

Consonants

p	as in *p*ut	ñ	as in o*n*ion
b	as in *b*ut	m	as in *m*an
t	as in *t*ub	r	alveolar flap, as in Spanish pe*r*o (between *r* and *l* in English)
d	as in *d*ub	w	as in *w*ater
k	as in *k*it	y	as in *y*awn
g	as in *g*ot	h	as in *h*at
n	as in *n*ot	ng	as in si*ng*

Note on orthography

In order to distinguish the linguistic stocks from which cited forms derive, I have used *italics* at the first occurrence of Bará and other Eastern Tukanoan words (as well as for scientific names, emphasis, and metalinguistic references) and **bold face** for the first occurrence of Spanish, Portuguese, and Tupian loan words.

1.

Purpose and organization of the book

The social system of the Tukanoans of the Central Northwest Amazon has intrigued virtually every scholar who has come into contact with it. Each of the more than sixteen languages spoken there is identified with a named descent group. Although these groups have sometimes been called tribes, they are rather strange tribes. For one thing, with a few exceptions, they are exogamous. This book is intended as a general introduction to the Vaupés, the Colombian sector of the Central Northwest Amazon, and more specifically to Tukanoan social identity.

To a considerable extent, the book's conception and organization reflect the way Tukanoans organize their social world. Most of the chapter topics derive from categories and distinctions Tukanoans themselves make among kinds of people and among other kinds of beings in their universe. By providing clues about the essence of being Tukanoan, these categories offer a logical starting point for discovering the content and organization of Tukanoan social identity, as Tukanoans conceptualize it and as they reveal it in their behavior. The general progression of chapters can be understood if we imagine ourselves to be looking at Tukanoan society through a series of lenses, each successive lens of lower power than the preceding one and thus encompassing units and categories of increasing scale and magnitude. The geographical scope of an image increases chapter by chapter, beginning with the traditional local unit, the longhouse, and ending with the entire Tukanoan universe. The first chapters serve to distinguish kinds of Tukanoans by such characteristics as kinship or language affiliation, whereas later chapters take up contrasts of wider scope, such as those between Tukanoans and Makú (the other indigenous inhabitants of the Vaupés), between Tukanoans and nonhuman spirits, and between Tukanoans and whites. The field of view does not increase evenly in every chapter: For example, discussion of the male–female polarity comes toward the end because it is a distinction of great scope, even though our starting point, the longhouse, includes both men and women. In addition, other considerations have in places supplanted the progression from small to large scale: The book ends, for example, with the contrast between Tukanoans and whites, because it is white society that is destroying

1

traditional Tukanoan culture. Among other things, this final chapter deals with some of the unhappy transformations Tukanoan identity will undoubtedly undergo in the future.

The time reference of this book, unless otherwise noted, is the ethnographic present of 1968–70. This means that some of the discussion, particularly concerning acculturative influences, is now somewhat outdated. Rather than alter the picture to adjust it to the changes I know have taken place (for example, those caused by the penetration of the cocaine trade into the area) I have decided to maintain consistency and hold to the time period of my fieldwork. Not having returned to the Vaupés since then, I would otherwise skew my descriptions toward aspects of recent change that have reached my attention, neglecting others that have not.

A discussion of some of the theoretical and methodological issues addressed in these pages follows.

Social identity

This book takes as its focus and orientation those components of identity that derive from a Tukanoan's membership in various social groups, categories, and positions. It analyzes the various social roles Tukanoans play throughout life and how these affect the way the people are conceptualized and categorized by themselves and others. The stage on which these roles are performed – the Tukanoan world – is described as well. As already indicated, emphasis falls here on social rather than strictly personal identity, that is, on those components of a person's identity that are acquired through relations with other people. These components include relatively abstract analytical relations, for instance those of similarity and contrast as well as others embodied in relatively concrete relations of genealogy, location, or language. Gender is by this definition an aspect of social identity, whereas sex, if defined strictly in genetic, anatomical, or physiological terms, can be seen as a feature of personal identity. (Transsexuals, whose gender and sex diverge, exemplify this distinction. Even for transsexuals perhaps, the two types of identity are not unrelated, but they *are* analytically distinct.)

A number of authors have stressed the social constitution of identity. For Peirce (see Singer, 1980), because the self is both a product and an agent of semiotic communication, it is both social and public. Individual identity, in his theory, is "also a social and cultural identity and is not confined to the individual organism" (Singer, 1980, p. 485). Similarly, Hallowell, while acknowledging the universality of the concept of self, notes that the cultural form this concept takes is highly variable: "the individual's self-image and his interpretation of his own experience cannot be divorced from the concept of the self that is characteristic of his society" (1955, p. 76). G. H. Mead has also stressed the social nature of concepts of self, and Kaplan goes so far as to say: "action is not to be understood as some by-product of the real characteristics of the person but as being the only means of constituting reality itself. The person, in effect, creates himself by what he does" (1961, p. 310). Given that human beings do not spend their lives in a closet (or the Tukanoan equivalent, alone in the forest), such an existentialist position implies that the action that constitutes social identity is interaction with others.

Although I basically agree with these statements, my use of "social identity" is narrower. This book concentrates on the crucial features Tukanoan society highlights when assigning its members to different groups. Kinship, marriage, age, sex, humanness – identity components of this sort are in large part created and refined by the actual relations between individuals and groups. The Tukanoan version of this essential interconnection between social identity and social structure, in particular between identity and regional and linguistic organization, will emerge as the book progresses. Of course, identity components not comprehensively treated here, such as ideas of conception and growth, anatomy and physiology, are extremely important and do influence social identity. Space does not allow a thorough treatment of these and other topics such as the effects of Tukanoan socialization patterns on personality or the feelings Tukanoans have about their individual selves. Still, in my opinion, the areas of life and culture stressed here – the assignment, symbolism, and performance of social roles – although they do not provide a complete picture of Tukanoan identity, do fill in a large part of the canvas.

Of course, my information on Tukanoan social identity comes from individuals with distinct personalities living in unique slices of space and time. My goal is to understand what Tukanoans have in common without hiding or ignoring those things that make them different from each other, to transcend individual variability so as to see the logic of Tukanoan identity as a system. This goal demands that in a number of places throughout the book I wrestle with the slippery issue of how one distinguishes individual idiosyncrasies from other sorts of variation, such as regional differences.

As a concept, "identity" defies easy definition. Erikson simply considers it to be a person's "name . . . and what station he occupies in his community" (1968, p. 61). If we broaden this a bit to include all the names and labels by which Tukanoans are known and all the statuses and roles they play in life, we have a fairly adequate initial definition. Given the quintessentially Western nature of the preoccupation with identity as linked to *individual* identity and individualism (for recent examples, see Burridge, 1979; Macfarlane, 1978), one runs quite a few intellectual risks in extending the concept to small-scale non-Western societies. To begin such an undertaking, therefore, perhaps what should be discussed first is how the Tukanoan self differs from its more individualistic Western counterpart. It should be noted that the Western notions of self, other, and identity as

3

presented here may seem simplified and almost stereotypical without the nuances and contradictions we know to be there. But as a foil for Tukanoan identity, stereotypes are sufficient.

Basically, Tukanoan notions of self and other are more relational, contextual, and evanescent than those of many Western societies, in that the more individualistic Western notions place greater stress on the permanence of differentiation between self and other. Bará or other Tukanoans in contrast, although they certainly could speak of an individual in terms of a unique intersection of characteristics that occurs in no one else (i.e., in terms of space, time, genealogical position, gender, language, etc.), seldom seem motivated to do so. When they distinguish X from Y or X group from Y group, they usually make the contrast in terms of only one or two characteristics relevant to the situation at hand, leaving other features of X and Y in abeyance. In Western society, we too make context-specific distinctions that lump people into broad categories at the same time they distinguish them, but as a general tendency, we are more ready than Tukanoans to conceptualize people as distinct individuals and to make much of the complete bundle of characteristics that makes each person unique.

Further discussion of the Tukanoan-Western contrast is saved for Chapter 13, after the necessary ethnographic foundation has been laid. In the meantime, however, the themes of permanence versus transience and relationality should be kept in mind, along with the notion that the Tukanoan self, like the Bororo self, "is created, defined, and systematically transformed by other selves; the person does not exist except as it is reflected by these" (Crocker, 1977, p. 144).

In this book I try to show that although we can analyze Tukanoan social identity in terms of features and dimensions, identity is both structure and action. The abstract qualities and dimensions I have listed take on meaning only within a contextualized action that is simultaneously moral (e.g., I am a human Tukanoan rather than an animal if and because I continue to behave in a moral manner), instrumental (e.g., I am able to do this because I am Bará, and would not if I were Makú), and relational (e.g., I am Bará, which is in part defined by what I do and am vis-à-vis Tuyuka) action. At times, contradiction results, a paradox best seen in Tukanoan terms as a necessary outcome of sets of principles that, when acting concurrently, overlap in incongruent fashion. Many examples of this incongruity are given later. Of course, Western notions of self also embody paradox and contradiction but in a somewhat different fashion, which follows from differences in the roles played in the two systems by morality, instrumentality, and relationality (a theme also discussed further in Chapter 13). Tukanoan society, although full of oppositions, does not oppose the individual *qua* individual against others nearly as much as we might expect. Instead, it transforms oppositions into continua and it allows individuals to slide back and forth between different positions on these continua according to the context at hand. With the emphasis on self and other as a process, an identity to be maintained rather than something absolute and eternal, self and other become even more flexible

4

concepts and are often literally and figuratively linked together in conceptualization and action. Although all of this occurs in the West, I argue that it does so to a lesser degree; we tend to see ourselves more in terms of being effectively and permanently separated. Many markers of distinct identity exist in both systems (among Tukanoans, the system of language identification is a prime example), but in the West the markers tend to distinguish us as separate individuals in a unique and more permanent manner.

The Bará (or other Tukanoan) self is indeed a distinct self, but to a greater extent this self is constantly merged with other selves through participation – cognitively and behaviorally – in various categories. Oppositions can involve the self as an individual, but these are transient, and more often oppositions involve collectivities of people. In sum, although without doubt a Bará has at his or her disposal any number of clearly specified reference points with which to contrast himself or herself with others as a distinct individual, I argue that the opportunity and motive for doing so occur far less among Tukanoans than in many other societies.

Regional perspective

Whenever possible, this book stays with the regional perspective introduced in the Preface. As noted there, in certain respects a single Vaupés settlement is anything but a microcosm of the larger social system. A settlement, although often equivalent to other like units, sometimes stands in complementary, antagonistic, or other kinds of nonidentical relationship with other settlements. Furthermore, settlements are also internally divisible along a number of structural dimensions; they do not always stand as homogeneous, whole units. As settlements are nodes in a regional network, so are their individual members and subdivisions. Regional interaction involves, for example, marriage, residence and visiting patterns, ceremonial and trade relationships, and, in the past, warfare. In addition, it soon becomes obvious that Tukanoans themselves see the Vaupés as a single system. Linguistic evidence also supports this view. Although structurally differentiated along several dimensions, Tukanoan groups display a remarkable degree of cultural homogeneity, using many of the same rules for conceptualizing and participating in a single system, although at times occupying different positions in it.

The unity of the Vaupés social system, moreover, has been at least conceded or implied in previous works on the area, even when they take a more particularistic approach. Goldman, although confining his monographic study (1963) to a single group, the Cubeo, notes the cosmopolitanism of the region, and in his article in the *Handbook of South American Indians* (1948), he treats the Vaupés as a unified culture area. Brüzzi Alves da Silva (1962, 1966) concerns himself with the integration of social units in the region, emphasizing their underlying similarity; the same is true of Fulop (1955) to a lesser extent. Reichel-Dolmatoff

5

(1971), although more impressed by differences than similarities, also examines the relations between language-affiliated units (see the discussions in Jackson, 1972, pp. 16–17, and S. Hugh-Jones, 1979, p. 22). Sorensen's well-known article on Vaupés multilingualism (1967) emphasizes how apparent diversity can sustain integration and regional unity. Århem (1981) also demonstrates the existence of a complex territorial organization linked to descent and marriage systems for Makuna in the Pirá-paraná.

In the last few years two new books on Tukanoan culture, by Stephen and Christine Hugh-Jones (both 1979), discuss the importance of focusing on a region, in this case the Pirá-paraná, in addition to looking at a single exogamous group (the Barasana). Their books complement this one because they pay more attention to symbolism than to the sociological concerns emphasized here. Nonetheless, the Hugh-Joneses and I find ourselves in substantial agreement on the form of regional integration in the Vaupés, if not on all details of its content. In general, almost all the ethnographers of Tukanoan peoples have acknowledged the unity of the Vaupés and grappled with the implications of that unity. I do feel that mine is the most full-fledged regional approach; I am not castigating other investigators for any neglect on their part but rather extending an already established tendency (see also Goodenough, 1981, pp. 1–3).

Often it seems difficult to communicate to nonspecialists what characterizes the Vaupés system and the lessons, both methodological and theoretical, that can be learned from it. The kind of approach I am espousing here is discouraged by the size of the area in question, roughly that of New England. Indeed, as pointed out in the Preface, extremely difficult issues relating simply to size of the unit of study must be dealt with constantly, at times in the form of rather unsatisfactory compromises. Regions characterized by thick forest cover, no roads, frequent rapids, and unreliable communication and transport do put obstacles in the way of regional studies. Still, we must not allow these admittedly important considerations to lead us into ignoring the reality of extralocal, and often long-range, interaction and its symbolic significance; Tukanoans overcome such obstacles and so must we.

Indeed, such interaction among widely dispersed local groups characterizes virtually all low-density populations around the world, especially hunter–gatherers such as the Shoshone, Montagnais-Naskapi, San Bushmen, or Australian Aborigines, who ipso facto form regional systems because local groups are not self-sufficient in every respect and because they exploit extensive territories.[1] Dispersed hunter–gatherers, with their local group interdependence, fluidity in territorial boundaries, and fluctuations in local group membership, offer a model, I would suggest, for understanding the Vaupés. Although Tukanoans affiliate with groups and categories in less flexible ways than many hunter–gatherers, and Tukanoan institutions appear to be less amorphous and malleable, they still preserve considerable freedom of choice within the framework of these more

6

rigid institutions and their rules of membership. This flexibility, operating out of a rigidity at a more abstract and idealized level of Tukanoan social structure, is a central concern throughout the book.

When one takes into account the Tukanoan view of the Vaupés as an unbounded system (that is, a large geographical area in which people are basically similar and distance and differentiation are seen in terms of degrees rather than absolutes), one can understand why the ubiquitous term *tribe* does not fit anywhere in the region. This label has been applied most often there to the language-affiliated units encompassing a number of local settlements, but this usage leads to so much confusion that I have substituted *language group* in its place. The substitution brings its own difficulties, as we shall see, but they pale in comparison with the confusions of *tribe*.

Anthropologists have not been able to agree on a single definition for the word *tribe,* although many of the same definitional criteria turn up repeatedly (see Fried, 1975; Godelier, 1977; Helm, 1968). These include (1) a shared territory with discrete boundaries, (2) statuses and organizations for the tribe as a whole, (3) more interaction within the tribe than without, (4) more marriage within than without, (5) significant cultural differences with neighboring units, (6) a shared tribal language. Singly or in combination, these criteria do not work for Tukanoan language groups.

By definition, the members of a language group share a patrilineally inherited affiliation with a language, but the problems encountered when trying to use language as a criterion of tribal membership are manifold (Hymes, 1968). Very infrequently do all members of a language group occupy a discrete territory that is considered theirs and to which they have exclusive or almost exclusive rights. This state of affairs is most closely approached in the Pirá-paraná region (see Århem, 1981; Bidou, 1976), but in general we may speak only of segments of language groups occupying continuous stretches of rivers, and even in the Pirá-paraná, where occupation of a continuous territory by *all* member settlements of a language group may be said by them to be the ideal, "in practice there is considerable overlap between descent-group territories" (C. Hugh-Jones, 1979, p. 25).

The criterion of statuses or organizations whose point of reference is the tribe as a whole (with the implicit assumption that the tribe, at least to that extent, is a corporate body), does not work any better in the Vaupés. Activities involving everyone in a language group, or an individual or group selected to represent all the others, are conspicuous in their absence. Language groups may perhaps have acted as political units in the past, but they certainly do not today. Although roles in ritual often incorporate aspects of language group identity, this identification does not make them "tribal" roles.

Because language groups are exogamous, the criterion of tribal endogamy, of course, works not at all. And, given language group exogamy and settlement

7

exogamy, people deal almost as frequently with members of other language groups as with members of their own. Indeed, the role of language group exogamy, more than anything else, dooms the concept of tribe from the start.

The last distinction, which assumes relative cultural uniformity within tribes and sharp cultural differences between them, runs up against the homogeneity of Tukanoan culture pointed out earlier. Settlements and language groups do differ culturally, and I will spend a good deal of time describing and accounting for such differences, but they do not produce tribes. Many of the most obvious and frequently mentioned differences are emblematic and superficial; they fulfill the need for social markers differentiating the units in the regional system, and as such they point toward social and cultural integration and underlying homogeneity rather than heterogeneity. This is not to say that true cultural differences cannot be found in so vast an area, variations that can be ascribed to disparate origins, to cultural drift in different directions, to the effects of diffusion from neighbors outside the system, and to different degrees of acculturation. None of this variation, however, coincides in any simple fashion with the language-affiliated units traditionally called tribes.[2]

Fluidity

One of the central theoretical concerns in this book is the interplay between fluidity and apparent rigidity found in many Tukanoan social institutions. The effects of choice and manipulation show themselves in household composition, political organization, and almost every situation in which seemingly inelastic and unchanging principles assign people to groups and categories. I argue that this paradoxical juxtaposition is inherent in many small-scale societies. Variability and invariance, operating at different levels, support and play off each other, and in the long run probably allow societies to adapt to fluctuations in their ecological and demographic bases.

General conclusions on this interplay must wait until the concluding chapter, after the material showing its importance has emerged. At this juncture I need only point out that the issue of fluidity and rigidity cannot be separated from others already introduced: the nature of Tukanoan social identity and the utility of a regional perspective on the Vaupés.

Fluidity also applies to the issue of the boundaries of a system like the Vaupés. I have stated that the Vaupés is regionally organized into an open-ended system that cannot properly be called a society in the sense of a bounded social unit (C. Hugh-Jones, 1979, pp. xv, xvi). I am not merely saying that at places the boundaries are fuzzy or even nonexistent but that the system presupposes no boundaries except single-dimensional, and therefore quite arbitrary, ones (for example, at times Tukanoans use the criterion of language exogamy to exclude the Cubeo but clearly include them – and properly so – in the system most of the time).

8

A big challenge I faced in writing this book was to describe the fluidity of the system comprehensively and yet also to account for why the Vaupés, as a system, works. And work it does: Its social structure "does" things such as assign roles, get people married properly (or show why they have married improperly), and point out the way to each generation on its journey to full-fledged adult status. This is accomplished with varying combinations of the opposites of fluidity and rigidity and difference and equivalence, but this is very difficult to describe. Tukanoans share many cultural and social traits: related languages and speaking patterns, intermarrying settlements, basic subsistence patterns, similar kinship terminologies (as well as virtually all other semantic domains), a common mythology, and so forth. Some features, moreover, normally associated with cultural and social cleavages are not to be so viewed in the Vaupés case; examples are territorial dispersal and language differences. Finding out what these differences, equivalences, and identities "really" are is not only a problem, it is *the* problem. Confusion seems to reign at times, not all of which is trivial and easily cleared up by acquiring more information or by increasing one's awareness of one's anthropological or ethnocentric assumptions or by some other similar scholarly operation. Confusion, when explained, is of course no longer confusion, but I do not believe that the Vaupés system – capable though it is of being described, explained, and formulated into models – can ever be reduced to a coherent, logical, unitary system. Confusion gives way to paradox, and this paradox, along with the dynamism existing between levels in the model (i.e., fluidity and manipulability) remain. The process of discovering the Tukanoan system, incidentally, teaches us much about our firmly built-in epistemological constraints, in both language and modes of conceptualization, which will become more apparent when examples of such fluidity in action are given.

Ideal and real

The polarity between rigidity and fluidity resembles and sometimes overlaps another dichotomy, one between ideal models of society and culture on the one hand and so-called on-the-ground reality on the other. Although ethnographers and informants deal in both commodities, and almost every interpretation or piece of data inevitably mixes the two together, cultural accounts tend to emphasize one or another. According to an anecdote narrated by Napoleon Chagnon,[3] Lévi-Strauss likened society to a chambered nautilus. This mollusk combines a beautiful structure – its shell – with a singularly ugly and slimy creature inside. Some choose to study the shell, whereas others prefer to examine its inhabitant. The trick is to keep oneself aware of one's preferences and of the reality of both parts of the animal, without deluding oneself into thinking that only one part is real or important. Seeing the two together, so interconnected and yet so contradictory, is not always easy. The ugly little creature inside is responsible for the

9

existence of the sublime shell, yet the shell far outlasts its creator and has a logic and structure – an identity – of its own, separate from its occupant's.

As little as we may like seeing ourselves as mollusks, the societies and cultures created by human beings embody the same duality. Structures, abstracted at one level or another of analysis from the behavior that generates them, deserve the absorbed attention given them by many anthropologists (including, of course, Lévi-Strauss himself). Yet social structures do not create themselves nor myths think themselves, any more than shells generate spontaneously; it is individuals and individuals in collectivities, by engaging in discrete bits of behavior that often are so seemingly lacking in logical structure, who do. When formalized into descriptive or explanatory models, some of the empirical validity of these behaviors is lost. That the sublime structures created are separable from and outlive their creators, be they cephalopods, Tukanoans, or anthropologists, may be our pleasure or our sorrow, but it is always our frustration to some extent, because some of the richness and detail of the reality that produced the structures is lost.

Chambered nautiluses, however, cannot, so far as I know, have false consciousness; they create their shells, each one distinct from all others in some minor respects but all of them basically to type, because that is what they are genetically programmed to make. Human beings, on the other hand, create various kinds of structures that can be hidden by conscious models, models that tell us little about the structures because they are intended to perpetuate certain phenomena rather than explain them (Lévi-Strauss, 1962, p. 324). The Vaupés illustrates the problems encountered in this regard par excellence. We might prefer to study the equivalent of the shell *or* of its occupant; but the two are far more interconnected than those of the chambered nautilus, and we perforce must study both when encountering Tukanoans. For example, the fact that structures outlive the individuals creating them, be they mollusks or human beings, is extremely important: If the word *dialectic,* surely the most overused word at present, applies at all to this problem, it does so in terms of the way in which individuals and structures influence and even create behavior and idealization (both native and ethnological). Paradoxically, whatever exists and can be found on the ground is impermanent, whereas what is unreal in this sense – what is structure or idealization and derived from the real – is permanent, or at least more enduring. Here we run the risk of falling into a positivist (perhaps the second most overused word) trap, because we are not looking at shells or organisms but at behavior that has no meaning without explanation. The trap is a trap because it assumes that somewhere there is reality without idealization. Still, idealized structure continually influences the behavioral system (which is why we cannot talk about "reality" versus idealized expressions of that reality even when we use the most precise of measuring instruments or statistical tests), a system that is always both being and becoming.

In addition to the relative permanence of structures and behavior, the ideal–

"real" dichotomy implies another temporal question – how one deals with variation over time. Change can be cyclical or directional, and a short-term observer often cannot tell whether a particular phenomenon or range of phenomena represents variation around some relatively stable standard or is a harbinger of the new state a system is moving toward. (Nautiluses take much longer in changing the shape of their shells than societies do.) The analysis presented here depicts Tukanoan society at one particular moment. My model is, I believe, an understandable, accurate, and tolerably sophisticated depiction of the system, and I do not think that huge amounts of historical research (particularly given the state of documentary sources available) would change the basic parameters given here. But to the extent that it takes account of change, the analysis treats it as a disruption or modification of a synchronic system rather than as part of a diachronic process. We know a good deal already about such forces of change as missionization and the rubber boom and about their highly variable impact on different populations in the region. Although I try to keep such change in mind throughout the book, and in some places speculate about earlier developments in the evolution of the regional system, my concern with depicting a traditional culture in terms applicable across the region makes it impossible to encompass change and local variation as thoroughly as a more diachronic or a more localized model would certainly do.

Final remarks

In addition to these broad concerns, the following pages bear on a number of familiar issues of slightly narrower scope, such as descent and alliance, genealogy and category, the position of women in horticulturalist societies, and similar topics. Although I sometimes push hard for a certain interpretation or stance on an issue, the book does not in any comprehensive way represent a particular school or tradition in social anthropology. My general assumptions and approaches obviously derive from the schools of thought current in recent years, but when I come out on one side of an issue, I am not necessarily aligning myself with the school identified with that interpretation. More often I have latched on to it in an eclectic manner because it makes sense of the data at hand.

This book tends less toward a particular interpretative stance than toward a generally sociological approach. As a consequence, although I use myths to illustrate some of my points about marriage or genealogy, I pay relatively little attention to symbol, cosmology, and ritual. In recent years the ethnology of lowland South America has come to the fore in precisely these areas. Structuralist and symbolic approaches do not, however, fall in my areas of specialization, and the appearance of several works of this sort on the Vaupés by Århem, Bidou, Goldman, Langdon, Reichel-Dolmatoff, and others, and especially the excellent recent works by Stephen and Christine Hugh-Jones, convinces me that I can safely leave this domain to my fellow ethnographers of the region.

11

To keep publishing costs down, I have included only the quantitative material absolutely necessary to the arguments presented in this book. Readers interested in fuller discussion of, or quantitative data about, a particular topic (for example, names and locations of sibs – the localized patrilineal descent groups in the Vaupés), should consult my other writings, listed in the References.

2.

Introduction to the Central Northwest Amazon

Ecological setting

The Vaupés region, roughly the size of New England, lies approximately between the equator and 1° north latitude, and between 69° and 71° west longitude (see Map 1).[1] It is bisected by the Colombia–Brazil border, and in terms of political boundaries its territory forms part of the Brazilian Territorio Nacional do Amazonas and the Colombian Comisaría del Vaupés. The latter comprises 90,625 square kilometers (Instituto Geográfico "Agustín Codazzi," 1969). Humid, tropical rainforest covers the entire region. This vegetation is typical of the whole western extension of the interfluvial Guiana Highlands (Moser and Tayler, 1963, p. 440), of which the Vaupés forms part, being more densely wooded and shorter than the canopy forests typical of the Amazon basin itself. The **cerros,** or flat-topped and domed hills that dot the landscape, date from the Guiana Shield epoch (Reichel-Dolmatoff, 1975, p. 64). Visible from far away, these cerros stand out in an otherwise largely undifferentiated extent of forest, river, and smaller hills. Their prominence makes them important landmarks for Tukanoans, as are the swamps dominated by the **mirití** palm (*Mauritia flexuosa*). The land generally slopes eastward, and high open lands and exposed rock and caves are typical of the western sections. Savanna is found both to the south and north but not in the region itself.

The major rainy season lasts from April to August, the lesser for a few weeks in October or November (Instituto Geográfico "Agustín Codazzi," 1969, p. 67). Because the dry and rainy seasons differ largely in terms of volume of rain – great versus enormous – river height most obviously distinguishes dry from rainy periods. The rivers, however, also fluctuate a great deal from day to day, and river height correlates only roughly with time of year. The effects of this fluctuation are extremely important for Tukanoan travelers, especially when canoeing with cargo. When rivers are at their lowest, crossing from one to another demands extra skill and endurance. Not only must travelers portage canoe and cargo overland, but at each end of their portage they may find the river reduced to a succession of shallow puddles. Under such conditions, they can proceed only by raising the water level with a series of earth dams, difficult and tedious to do.

13

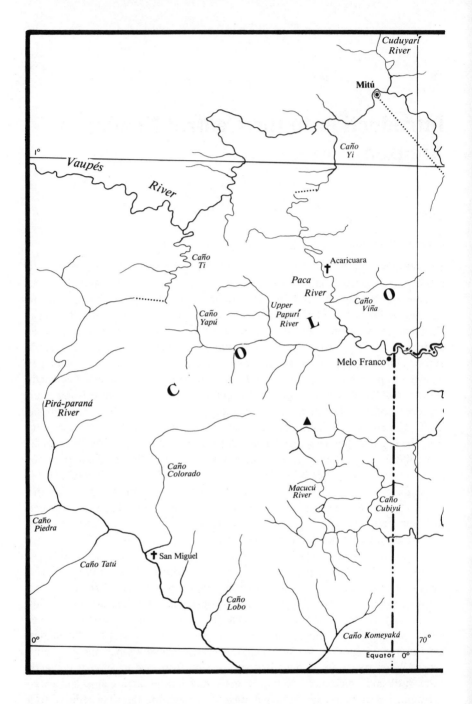

Map 1. The Eastern Colombian Vaupés. The sources for this map include discussions with Tukanoans during fieldwork in 1968–70 and the *Mapa Físico–Político de la República de Colombia* (Bogotá: Instituto Geográfico "Augustín Codazzi," 1968).

14

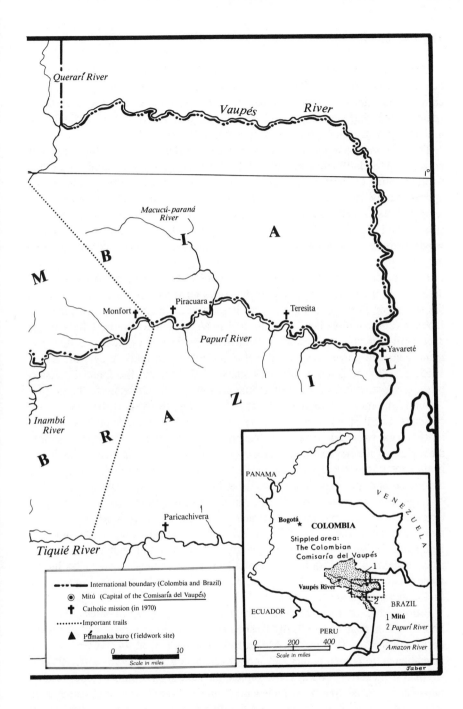

Querarí River

Vaupés   River

Macucú-paraná
River

M

B

A

I

1°

Monfort

Piracuara

Teresita

Papurí River

Yavareté

L

I

Z

A

Inambú
River

R

B

Paricachivera

PANAMA

V E N E Z U E L A

Bogotá   COLOMBIA

Tiquié River

Stippled area:
The Colombian
Comisaría del Vaupés

1

Vaupés River

2

BRAZIL

ECUADOR

1 Mitú

2 Papurí River

PERU

Amazon River

— ·· — International boundary (Colombia and Brazil)
◉ Mitú (Capital of the Comisaría del Vaupés)
✝ Catholic mission (in 1970)
········ Important trails
▲ Pumanaka buro (fieldwork site)

0   10
Scale in miles

0   200   400
Scale in miles

Jaber

The section of this map depicting the Pirá–paraná region has been derived mainly from
C. Hugh-Jones 1979, maps 1 and 2, and Århem 1981, map 1. Because these maps are not
in agreement, representation of the area is approximate.

15

The fish people

Other seasonal markers are position of the constellations, availability of various wild fruits and other forest products, harvest time for certain crops such as corn (manioc itself is not seasonal, but the preparation of fields is certainly geared to the yearly calendar), and animals and animal behavior, in particular the availability of fish and game (S. Hugh-Jones, 1980).

The minimum temperature varies between 10° and 20°C and the maximum between 34° and 40° (Reichel-Dolmatoff, 1971, p. 4). A rather strange period of weather called the **aru** or **friagem** (S. Hugh-Jones, 1979, p. 19), occurring for approximately four days at the height of the rainy season, consists of cold temperatures, a drizzling and distinctly untropical rain, and in some cases a strong wind (Moser and Tayler, 1963, p. 440). This phenomenon, caused by winds forming in the Atlantic and traveling westward, occurs every year throughout the Amazon.

The Vaupés is one of the headwater regions of the Northwest Amazon River drainage; in the north and northeast the rivers form part of the Orinoco system. Some Vaupés rivers join the Amazon directly to the south via the Caquetá and Japurá rivers, but most flow east into the Rio Negro and do not meet the Amazon itself until Manaus. The crystalline beds over which rivers of the region flow give them their well-known inky black color and relatively acidic water (M. Bates, 1965, p. 178); as a result they lack much of the aquatic life found in slower-moving rivers with deep beds of sediment, such as the Guaviare to the north.

Surely the most impressive characteristic of Vaupés rivers is their rapids and cataracts. Local Spanish and Portuguese words for these features of the landscape (**cachiveras, raudales**) invariably take on powerful associations for any visitor to the region. Travelers, rubber gatherers, missionaries, and Tukanoans alike share a healthy respect for the hazard and obstacle to travel that these rapids present, and those who have not experienced accidents involving injury, death, and total loss of cargo invariably know others who have. All of the major rivers in the region have several major and minor cataracts, although the Vaupés River is free of them upstream of the Yuruparí Rapids. As may be expected, rapids are important landmarks for Tukanoans, who frequently choose them as longhouse and village sites, except in the Pirá-paraná region, where settlements tend to be hidden some distance from rivers. Also as may be expected, rapids have great significance in Tukanoan myth and cosmology.

Petroglyphs, or rock carvings, are found at some rapids sites. Goldman observed Tukanoans periodically freshening the etched-in figures and geometric designs (1963, p. 8), although Moser and Tayler (1963, p. 442) discerned little resemblance to contemporary Tukano art (cf. also Reichel-Dolmatoff, 1967).

Apart from cerros, swamps, and rapids, the natural environment tends towards homogeneity. Clay, quartz, and a few other materials are scarce or absent in some areas, but a trade network evens out the distribution of both raw materials and manufactured items. Local differences in such ecological variables as the presence or absence of leaf-cutter ants or the fertility of soil affect each settlement's

16

adaptation, as do the size of the river on which it is located and its relative position upstream or downstream. By and large, however, the land supports agriculture everywhere, and the overall homogeneity of the environment does not encourage much local specialization or social differentiation.

The population

Population density for the Vaupés is quite low; one approximation is 0.2 inhabitants per square kilometer (Instituto Geográfico "Agustín Codazzi," 1969, p. xiii). Recent population estimates vary between 7,000 (Reichel-Dolmatoff, 1975, p. 64) and 13,403 (Instituto Geográfico "Agustín Codazzi," 1969, p. xi). The latter figure includes non-Indians, approximately 1,000, mostly in Mitú and its environs.

Because most Tukanoans live on the rivers, the region appears to be more densely populated than it is. Missionary efforts have increased nucleation by encouraging both the merger of longhouse settlements and movement to mission towns. This intervention has disrupted the traditional social organization of the region and degraded the environment near all mission towns.

The rubber boom earlier in the century devastated the indigenous populations of the region. Rubber gatherers "recruited" labor through the most viciously coercive techniques, scattering the settlements of those who managed to avoid them. When given advance warning, Tukanoans sometimes chose to flee into the forest during the recruiting season as certain rubber gatherers came into the neighborhood. Often hiding for months at a time, refugees experienced great privation camping in the forest, with their gardens inadequately tended. The police and armies of both Brazil and Colombia frequently helped the rubber gatherers recruit Tukanoans and apprehend runaways; however, the authorities of one country could not cross into the other, and Tukanoans became adept at border-hopping. Quite a few of the family and sib (localized exogamous patrilineal descent groups) histories I collected spoke eloquently of this disruption and dislocation. It is also true, however, that Tukanoans sometimes sought out whites, including rubber gatherers, as sources of trade goods.

Any settlement map of the region graphically illustrates Tukanoan awareness of the international border, which has continued up to the present. The stretch of the Papurí between Melo Franco and Yavareté serves as the boundary between the two countries. Except for three mission towns, all Tukanoan settlements are on the Brazilian side, where Colombian Catholic missionaries, Javerians, have no jurisdiction. The closest Brazilian mission is the one at Yavareté, run by Salesians. Although this might be taken as evidence of a Tukanoan preference for Salesians over Javerians, the preference in fact is probably for the mission most removed from Tukanoans' daily affairs. Howard Reid (personal communication), an anthropologist who in his studies of the Brazilian Makú has had prolonged contact with Salesians, feels they pit themselves against traditional Vaupés culture more than the Javerians. He points out as evidence the complete lack of longhouses in the Brazilian Amazon – Salesians burned out the last one, on the upper Tiquié, in the late 1960s.

Some Tukanoans have emigrated permanently from the Vaupés, although just how many is hard to say. A decision to leave the region permanently usually follows a period of work at a rubber camp, where the potential out-migrant acquires a taste for the rural Colombian (non-Indian) lifestyle. Some of these men move as far as San José de Guaviare or even Villavicencio, towns experiencing moderate booms, although even there the chances of finding work are slim. Mitú is closer but prospects are even worse.

Goldman (1963) reports a higher population density for the Cubeo during his period of fieldwork in 1939 than is the case now. If this decline holds for all of the Vaupés, it is difficult to be sure what causes are most to blame, although epidemic disease, the depredations of the rubber industry, out-migration, and the loss of people to mission towns have obviously all contributed.

Whether the Vaupés environment could at present sustain the large populations reported for the floodplains by such early writers as Orellana (Goldman, 1963, p. 2) is an open question. Certainly land is not a limiting factor for Tukanoans at present. Nor was it for the Cubeo of 1939–40, although Goldman does state that available land for manioc plantations was a decisive factor in choosing a longhouse site, because sibs had to retain their traditional boundaries (1981, p. 3). Still, he notes that "from terrain alone there is no doubt that the Vaupés could have supported far greater Indian populations than it did at the time of first contact" (1963, p. 36). On the other hand, the concentration of population in mission towns has created real land shortages there; some women have to canoe and walk a substantial distance to reach their fields.

Epidemic diseases introduced by whites, which include influenza, measles, and whooping cough, have undoubtedly contributed to the depopulation of the region. Tukanoans have a horror of all three, and with reason. A single epidemic can ravage the population of a large area if it lacks immunity. For example, *boa,* the Bará name of the river on which the longhouse I stayed at was located ("rotten," "putrid"), refers to an epidemic early in this century that killed or seriously sickened everyone living on the river. Those who could do so fled the area. Even today only five local descent groups survive on the river, half the number present before the epidemic.

Reid, reporting on the health and nutritional status in the eastern Vaupés in 1974, reports malaria and tuberculosis as the only major chronic endemic diseases (1976, p. 20); he notes, however (personal communication), that onchocerciasis (African river blindness) was confirmed in the Brazilian Vaupés in 1975. The endemic eye, skin, and internal conditions caused by fungal, helminth, nematode, and insect parasites, although not classified as major illnesses, can last for years and cause intense and disabling pain. Any sore heals slowly in so humid an area, increasing the likelihood of infection and spread.

18

Conjunctivitis can cause excruciating pain and near-blindness for weeks at a time, and fungus infections affecting the feet are especially hard to cure, because it is impossible to keep the feet dry or clean. Everyone plays host to a variety of intestinal worms.

Speaking in the most general terms, one can say that population size has declined from its levels during earlier periods; virtually all early reports lead one to this conclusion. Beyond this, the paucity of hard data makes it impossible even to speculate about specifics such as rate of decline. It is also clear that although overall population and settlement size have decreased, cultivation has relatively increased. Further discussion of some of the issues related to the matter of population size is found in the treatments of subsistence patterns in Chapter 3 and acculturation in Chapter 12.

Language and linguistics

Language families represented in the Vaupés include Eastern Tukanoan, Arawak, Carib, Makú, and, in a limited way, Tupian. **Lingua Geral** (called **lingoa Geral** in Portuguese and **nheengatú** in Tupian) is a Tupian trade language used throughout the region in the past. It has been almost entirely replaced by Tukano, the traditional lingua franca of the region. Lingua Geral was introduced by Jesuits and other missionaries coming into the region from Brazil. Some Tukanoans spoke it, though few fluently. No one speaks it in the region any more, although some older men remember words and phrases. Its only continuing importance is as the source of names of places, plants, and animals in the local Spanish and Portuguese dialects. Undoubtedly the presence of two national languages rather than one increases the importance of Tukano as the unifying language of the region (Sorensen, 1967, p. 680).

The Eastern Tukanoan language family, which is identified with the Central Northwest Amazon, appears to be the oldest in the region. Apart from Lingua Geral itself, Tupian cultural influences go back many years (Goldman, 1963, p. 14). Arawakan languages and cultural influences, on the other hand, have arrived more recently, as have Carib languages.

Specific named linguistic varieties presently spoken in the Vaupés include: Carib (Carihona [Umaua]);[2] Arawakan (Baniwa, Cabiyeri, Curripaco, Tariano); Eastern Tukanoan (Bará, Barasana [Paneroa], Carapana, Cubeo, Desana, Uanano, Makuna, Piratapuya, Siriano, Tatuyo, Tukano, Tuyuka, and Yurutí). Waltz and Wheeler (1970) also mention twenty speakers of Pápiwa (possibly known in Bará as *Wahüná*). Named linguistic varieties spoken directly to the south of the Vaupés include Yukuna and Matapí (Arawakan), and Letuama and Tanimuca (Tukanoan).[3] Other linguistic varieties named in the literature are almost certainly dialects understood by speakers of "languages" on the list; Taiwano (or Taibano) for instance, is mutually intelligible with Barasana (S. Hugh-Jones, personal communication; see also Waltz and Wheeler [1970, p.

120], who note that the Barasana intermarry with Taiwanos "whose language is almost identical with their own"). Sources disagree on the status of certain varieties. Linguists (see note 3) of the Summer Institute of Linguistics (SIL) consider the languages in the primary list just given to be mutually unintelligible, as does Sorensen, who states that the most closely related pair in his list of thirteen Tukanoan languages is "considerably more distant . . . than Jutish is from Standard Danish" (1967, p. 674). He adds that Tukanoan languages in general seem to be less closely related than Central Algonquian or Romance languages. Areas of differentiation include grammar and lexicon and, to a lesser extent, phonology. Close relationships obviously link several pairs on the list, such as Barasana and Makuna (S. Hugh-Jones, personal communication), Desana and Siriano, which share 98.9 percent cognates in sound correspondence tests carried out by Waltz and Wheeler (1970), and Piratapuya and Uanano, with 99.2 percent cognates. Obviously the multilingualism of all Tukanoans except some Cubeo complicates efforts to determine mutual intelligibility.

To sum up, the linguistic situation in the Vaupés is enormously complex; linguists disagree about the number and identity of languages in the region and the criteria to be used in identifying them. Some of the causes of this complexity are already apparent: the presence of multilingualism, the cultural–semantic equivalences shared by all the languages, and linguistic exogamy. Others will be discussed in Chapter 9. It might seem presumptuous to call into question conclusions drawn from comparative linguistic research without having done such work myself, except that the experts also doubt one another's conclusions. Problems are bound to arise when attempting to enumerate linguistic varieties in a situation of 100 percent multilingualism, in which, moreover, the native speakers have their own nonlinguistic reasons for treating all the named varieties as mutually unintelligible. In this respect the concepts "language" and "tribe" present similar difficulties. There is a sense in which closely related linguistic varieties should be considered discrete units (regardless of whether an omniscient observer would call them languages or dialects), so long as native members of the system consider them so. It is also true that the languages of the Vaupés form a regional system in terms of phonology, grammar, and lexicon, with regular sound shifts (the subject of the Waltz and Wheeler article), inversions, and transformations that are very like those of the social system. Thus, we also have to look at everyone's (again, Tukanoans, ethnologists, linguists) assumptions about just what a language is and what purposes or motives lie behind a concern with such questions in the first place. Tukanoans are concerned because they marry people identified with different linguistic varieties. SIL needs to know in order to fulfill its goal of translating the Bible into all the languages of the world, as the title of an SIL publication by Wallis and Bennett (1959), *Two Thousand Tongues to Go*, indicates.[4]

Ethnic history

It should be apparent by now that one could hardly ask for a more demanding and frustrating task than to attempt to piece together the linguistic and ethnic history of the Vaupés. The apparent ease with which traits and languages are picked up and dropped only makes the problem more difficult. This cosmopolitanism is discussed by Goldman (1963, p. 15), and Koch-Grünberg (1909–10, vol. 2, pp. 65, 66, 81) provides evidence for exchanges of cultural traits and languages. The multilingualism and linguistic exogamy among all groups except the Cubeo also illustrate this.

Information on the cultural and linguistic history of the region is extremely limited, however, and although a plurality of discrete cultural traditions and languages characterizes the region, no assumptions can be made concerning isomorphisms between linguistic or cultural units and the actual populations that have maintained these traditions over time. Cultural and linguistic traditions can be easily learned or just as easily forgotten (in favor of what may be radically different ones) over a generation. Around the world, cultures vary greatly with respect to their conservatism or openness in their willingness to accept intrusive ideas and customs. This is undoubtedly an important area of research in the Vaupés, given what Goldman, Koch-Grünberg, Reichel-Dolmatoff, and others say regarding the cosmopolitanism of the region, and it is obvious that any attempts to piece together the histories of ethnic groups in the area will never reconstruct the complete picture.

Reichel-Dolmatoff (1975, p. 66) finds a "kernel of historical truth" in the various Tukanoan origin myths, which invariably trace a particular group's history as one of westward, upstream migration from downriver sites in Brazil. On the basis of these histories, he suggests that Makú, "a substratum of band-based hunters," were the earliest inhabitants and were followed later by Arawakans, who were subsequently invaded by Tukanoan speakers. This Arawak–Tukanoan sequence is the reverse of the scheme proposed by Goldman (1963, p. 14), yet such differences of opinion must inevitably occur when working with oral histories. I collected quasihistorical accounts, concerned with both the original peopling of the region and more recent migrations; these too undoubtedly contain "kernels of truth." The migrations described, although telescoped in the narratives, were almost certainly spread out over a number of years and even generations. The often epic accounts of war, treachery, and invasion also undoubtedly depict to some degree what actually happened.

The few general historical trends that we can be certain of are the following: (1) Population density and settlement size have declined markedly over the past hundred and fifty years, and at one time, some settlements may have consisted of two or more rather than single longhouses (S. Hugh-Jones, 1979, p. 25); (2) the ancestors of some present-day inhabitants migrated upstream from the east into the region; (3) raiding and feuding, a general though intermittent fact of life in the past, had largely died out by the time the oldest Tukanoans alive today were born. The cessation of raiding and the population decline undoubtedly came about in part from white influence in the form of introduced trade goods (among which machetes and axes very probably had a substantial impact on subsistence productivity), disease, and the appearance of an external enemy. The rubber boom, in particular, severely disrupted every aspect of Tukanoan life. All of these developments will be discussed further.

The diffusionist or acculturational model of change, characterized by a pattern of regularized and gradual accretion of foreign traits, will not work for the Vaupés. Indeed, the inadequacy of such passive models as explanations of either stability or change in language and culture is one very clear lesson of this book.

No archaeology has been carried out in the Vaupés, and travelers in the nineteenth and early twentieth centuries who might have been far more informative about the earlier situation (albeit post-contact even then) did not concern themselves with such issues. Consequently, the available information is scant, imprecise, and highly conjectural.

Early explorer and missionary efforts

Doubtless the paucity of information on the Vaupés from early explorers can be attributed to its inaccessibility and hostile landscape. The territories to the north, in contrast, which consist of open **llanos** (savanna) and unobstructed slow-moving rivers, were penetrated by explorers much earlier, as were the forested lands to the east, where the rivers, although subject to flooding, could be navigated more easily than those farther upstream. Along with the climate and terrain, national boundaries contributed to the region's isolation. Much of the Vaupés falls within the borders of Colombia, but access from the west over the cordillera is nearly impossible. The Brazilian Vaupés, although more accessible, lies at the extreme periphery of the country, hundreds of miles from the nearest major town. Thus until the introduction of the airplane in about 1935, exploration of the area was full of risk and demanded large, well-organized expeditions originating far downstream. Examples of the difficulties encountered can be found in accounts written by H. W. Bates (1864), Coudreau (1887), Spruce (1908), A. R. Wallace (1889/1972), and Whiffen (1915), some of the better-known explorers and naturalists who traveled to the region. In general, the Vaupés is and always has been peripheral to Colombia and Brazil, both geographically and (with a few short-lived exceptions) economically.

The earliest explorers were the conquistadors looking for the famed ''Dorado de Los Omagua'' in the first half of the sixteenth century. Their expeditions left little in the way of documentation, apart from passing mention of ''Gaupé Indians.''[5]

Although the Dominicans and Franciscans founded missions in neighboring areas, the first mission (set up by the Carmelites) did not appear in the Vaupés until 1852. Neither this nor subsequent attempts took hold until 1914, when the Dutch Catholic Monfortian Congregation built two missions on the Papurí River at Monfort and Teresita. Later, in 1929, the Salesians established a mission at Iauareté (Yavareté). The political unit encompassing the region, the Comisaría del Vaupés, was created in 1910. In 1949 the Order of St. Javier founded the Prefectura Apostólica de Mitú, which has since administered all Catholic missions in the Colombian section of the region. Almost all the clergy of this order are Colombian, and many come from a single region, Antioquia. This domestic domination of mission staffing contrasts starkly with the foreign flavor of Catholic missionization throughout most of South America and even with early missionization of the Vaupés. In most South American countries a lack of native-born priests and nuns forces the Catholic orders to import missionaries from other, mostly European, countries. (Italian Salesians, for instance, oversee the missionary effort in the Brazilian Vaupés.) Colombia, however, even exports missionaries.

Protestantism has had a great impact on the Vaupés since its appearance in the late 1940s. One source estimates that as many as a third of the inhabitants of the combined **comisarías** of the Vaupés and Guainía are at least nominally Protestant,[6] a result attributable to the enthusiastic efforts of the Summer Institute of Linguistics, and the years of work of the near-legendary New Tribes Mission evangelist, Sophia Muller.[7]

Early and recent ethnographic descriptions

One of the earliest commentators on the Vaupés was Humboldt (1822). He was followed later in the nineteenth century by the naturalists H. W. Bates (1864), Coudreau (1887), Spruce (1908), Stradelli (1890), and A. R. Wallace (1889/1972). The first systematic work by an ethnologist came from Koch-Grünberg (1909–10), who visited the Cubeo on the Cuduyarí. as well as various groups on the Vaupés and Tiquié rivers. (He did not enter the Papurí region.) His work is voluminous and impressive, particularly in its comprehensive surveys of language, material culture, and some of the more visible customs and technologies. He is an especially valuable source on customs and manufactures now abandoned. Other explorers and ethnographers who were in the Vaupés during the first half of this century include Nimuendajú (1950), Rice (1910, 1914), and Whiffen (1915). McGovern (1927) and MacCreagh (1926), primarily explorers, provide many valuable and interesting pages of reading.

Modern ethnography in the Vaupés begins with Irving Goldman, who carried out fieldwork among the Bahúkiwa sib of the Cubeo on the Cuduyarí River in 1939 (1948, 1963, 1964). He returned in 1970 to study the Cubeo of a much higher-ranking sib (1976, 1977, 1981). Gerardo Reichel-Dolmatoff, among his numerous ethnographic and archaeological publications on different peoples and regions of Colombia, has written two monographs (1971, 1975) and a number of articles on the Vaupés (1967, 1976). His first book, based on information acquired from Antonio Guzmán. a remarkable Desana informant, deals with Desana cosmology and symbolism. The second analyzes Tukanoan cosmology and symbolism in terms of the use and meaning of hallucinogens, primarily *banisteriopsis (Banisteriopsis inebrians; Banisteriopsis rusbyana)*. Two Colombian anthropologists, Marcos Fulop (1955, 1956) and Alvaro Soto Holguín (1972), have published on the Tukano and Cubeo, respectively. Rodriguez Lamus has written on Tukano architecture (1958). Biocca (1965) and Moser and Tayler (1963, 1965) have also published in recent years on the Vaupés. Missionaries who have published studies include Brüzzi Alves da Silva (1962, 1966), Giacone (1949), and Kok (1925–26). Recent studies based on long-term field research in the area include Århem, 1976, 1980, 1981; Bidou, 1972, 1976, 1977; C. Hugh-Jones, 1977, 1978, 1979; S. Hugh-Jones, 1977, 1979; Langdon, 1975; Silverwood-Cope, 1972; Sorensen, 1967, 1970; and Torres Laborde, 1969.

The Makú

The peoples I call Tukanoan share the Vaupés region with another native population, the Makú. In contrast with the riverine Tukanoans, Makú generally live in the forest away from the rivers and lack the elaborate longhouses, canoe and fishing technologies, and ceremonial patterns characteristic of Tukanoans. They do not follow a rule of linguistic exogamy, and they tolerate settlement endogamy far more than Tukanoans do (Silverwood-Cope, 1972).

Once classified as an isolated language, Makú was placed by Greenberg (1960) in his Macro-Tukanoan family. Since Greenberg, it has become clear that there are actually at least two Makú languages (Silverwood-Cope, 1972; Cathcart, 1973).

The Makú, who are considered inferiors by their riverine neighbors, frequently form temporary servant–master relationships with Desana, Cubeo, Uanano, or other Tukanoan communities. In such arrangements, Makú provide game, manufacture items, and perform odd jobs in exchange for cultivated foodstuffs and white trade goods. Makú, however, do grow their own crops, and it is unlikely that they were ever completely nomadic or nonhorticultural.[8] Makú are further discussed in Chapter 8.

A note on acculturation

Visitors to the Vaupés as well as Tukanoans cannot help noticing the highly divergent goals of outsiders resident there. Individuals and organizations not only compete with each other, they often slip into outright hostility. Because the primary discussion of the effects of outside intrusions does not come up until Chapter 12, I offer a brief sketch of this subject here.

Mitú, an airstrip town of approximately 1,000 inhabitants in 1970, forms the administrative center for the Colombian Vaupés. Catholic mission towns never have more than a resident priest and a few nuns and brothers, and thus Mitú is the only settlement in the eastern Colombian part of the region with a substantial nonindigenous population. Agencies in Mitú affecting indigenous life include (1) the clinic, with a dispensary and about ten beds; (2) the **comisariato**, the government-run store; (3) the various representatives of the Colombian government, such as the **comisario**, or governor, who play an increasing role in Tukanoan affairs; (4) the Prefectura, the administrative seat for all Catholic mission activities in the Vaupés; (5) the Caja Agraria, the government-run agricultural cooperative that buys all rubber and makes loans (occasionally to Tukanoans) for setting up a rubber-camp operation; (6) the police garrison, which has only minimal effect on Tukanoans but indirectly serves as a deterrent to the more violent and blatant abuses of Tukanoan labor and schemes to capitalize on their ignorance; (7) the general stores (**almacenes**), which although having higher prices than the comisariato, extend credit to Tukanoans and buy artifacts from them, such as baskets.

By 1970 a number of Tukanoans had permanently migrated to Mikú and its environs (see Map 1). These individuals are fairly well acculturated. They speak reasonably fluent Spanish, wear ironed clothing, and display such status symbols as shoes, watches, and transistor radios. Household composition among them follows affinal lines to a greater degree than elsewhere in the region.

I did not travel much in Brazil and thus cannot report firsthand in depth about how the effects of white influence differ from those in Colombia. There are no centers of non-Tukanoans comparable to Mitú in the Brazilian Vaupés, but in general Indians are more acculturated. The Brazilian government was in greater evidence in the Brazilian areas I visited than any comparable Colombian government Indian agency, first through the Serviço do Proteção ao Indio (SPI) and after 1967 through SPI's replacement, the Fundação Nacional do Indio (FUNAI).

3.

The longhouse

The setting

Pǔmanaka buro sits on a hill overlooking an oxbow turn in the Inambú River. Like most settlements, it takes its name from a particular feature of the local landscape, in this case the "hill of many leaves." Settlements are also known by the headman's Spanish or Indian name. The Inambú (tinamou bird – *Tinamus* and *Crypturellus* spp.) is a small river on which five local descent groups – one Bará, four Tuyuka – live at present.

It is difficult to convey how radically the character of a river in this region changes over the course of a year. At low water no English speaker would call the Inambú anything but a creek or stream, and huge logs, debris, and sand dominate the landscape far more than water. Yet at high water the stream grows to a raging torrent. The Inambú's height and volume alter its every aspect: its appearance, its aquatic life, and the amount of time necessary to travel its length.

As is the case with most settlements, on arriving at Pǔmanaka buro one barely sees the longhouse.[1] The canoe landing, however, always shows various signs of human activity. One or more canoes, usually small one-man fishing craft, will be tied to a tree or beached, depending on the shoreline and season. Baskets of soaking manioc tubers may be visible in the water. A woman may be washing clothes, cleaning an animal carcass, or scaling and gutting fish. Women and children, or perhaps a lone man may be bathing. (Adult men usually bathe alone, although young men bathe together at dawn.) The landing is often the scene of social activities: Children play there several times during the day, and women come in groups to fetch water; wash clothes, dishes, or manioc; and bathe with their babies. The canoe landing is kept clean; poor maintenance is a sign of low morale (Goldman, 1963, p. 38). Stairs and sometimes a railing are installed when needed. See Figure 1.

The people of Pǔmanaka buro

The people and units composing the settlement I lived in are briefly introduced at this point because they so clearly illustrate a number of important features of

26

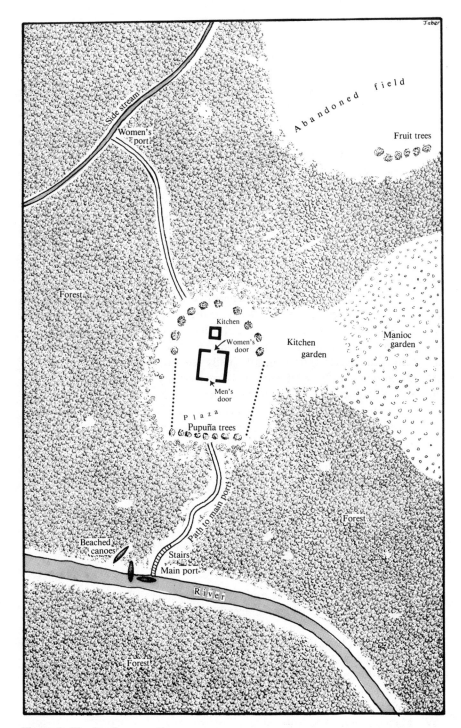

Figure 1. The longhouse setting.

27

residence patterns and longhouse life. Figure 2 shows how the residents of Pǔmanaka buro are related to one another (although not all consanguineal links are shown); any discrepancies between it and the following list of who was actually present when I arrived are due to marriages and births occurring after my arrival.

In January 1969, five family groups resided at Pǔmanaka buro; I call these hearth families, after Silverwood-Cope's (1972) "hearth group." Although not a translation of a Bará term, *hearth families* labels a tacit native category (A. F. C. Wallace 1961; see also Berlin, Breedlove, and Raven 1968), because Tukanoans treat the people who share a hearth as a unit. A hearth family shares a fireplace, eats together, and hangs its hammocks on the same four posts making up a compartment (which may or may not be screened off with mats), with the exception of unmarried initiated men, who sling their hammocks at the front of the longhouse. The hearth family always contains an adult man and woman, most often a husband and wife with their unmarried children. In many cases it contains other unmarried kinsmen as well. Because it suggests that somehow such relatives belong elsewhere, the term *nuclear family* is inappropriate for the hearth family unit. If, for example, a brother and sister are both unmarried and have lost their parents, they might constitute the core couple in a hearth family at that stage in the domestic cycle. Thus, a hearth family requires one adult couple, closely related consanguineally or affinally, and may have any number of other relatives attached. Two married couples, however, never share a hearth. The variety of possible arrangements is illustrated by the following list (names are pseudonyms; except where necessary to place other relatives, dead members are not mentioned; members absent in January 1969 are listed in brackets):

I   Mario, the headman
    Juana, his Tuyuka wife
    Sons: Estribino, [Lina], Berto, Pedro
    Daughters: Maximiliana, Francisca
II Pedrina, Tuyuka widow of Firbino
    Josefina, Bará mother of Pedrina (a very old widow)
    Sons: Juanico, Angelino, Marto
    Daughters: Armanda, Horacia
    Others: Luisa, daughter of Emilia (dead daughter of Pedrina and
        Firbino), who had been married to Emiliano, a Tuyuka who later
        remarried.
      Casimira, born three weeks after my arrival, to Armanda whose Tuyuka
        husband, Mario, was away in a rubber camp.
III Anastasio, married to Joaquina, a Desana
    Sons: [Cándido], Bonifacio
    Daughters: [Lina, married to a Desana], Luciana
IV Manuel, married to Esmeralda, a Tuyuka

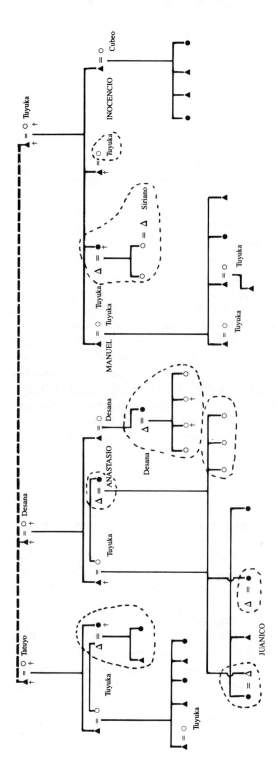

Figure 2. The inhabitants of Púmanaka buró. Not all consanguineal links are shown; only the name of the oldest living male is given for each hearth family. Individuals within circles are not residents of Púmanaka buró.

† Died
▲ ● Bará
△ ○ Not Bará

Sons: Mariquino, Nazario, Paulino
Daughters: Magdalena, Cándida
V   Inocencio, married to Bibiana, a Cubeo
Sons: Amelio, Líjio, Eugenio
Daughters: Micaela, Sabina

These families illustrate several stages in the life cycle of a local descent group. At the time of my arrival the members of the younger generation in three families (I, IV, V) had yet to have any marriages or births. This changed during the next two years with three marriages (one unsuccessful) and two births (one the product of a mating between a daughter in IV and a son in II). On the other hand Anastasio and Joaquina (in unit III) had lost their two oldest children: Cándido was far away in San José de Guaviare, and Lina had married and moved to the village of her husband (a Desana). Finally, family II shows some of the arrangements that can result from prolonged absences and deaths. Both Pedrina and Josefina were widows and kept each other company, although Josefina spent part of her time at her dead husband's Tuyuka longhouse downriver with her grown son (Pedrina's brother). Armanda, properly speaking, should have been living at her husband's longhouse (although she was due to give birth, and some women choose to visit their mother for the birth of their first child), but because her husband was in a rubber camp she was living with her agnates. Similarly Luisa, also a Tuyuka, was at Púmanaka buro being raised by her grandmother and mother's sisters rather than with her father and stepmother at his settlement. A number of the children present when I arrived were on vacation from the mission school they attended in Acaricuara; they returned to school the next month.

The longhouse structure

Any Tukanoan longhouse is an imposing sight. The one at Púmanaka buro is almost square (41 ft. × 47 ft.) but appears far more rectangular than these dimensions would suggest owing to the height of the roof and the slope of the eaves, which almost touch the ground at the sides. At the time of my arrival it stood alone in the clearing except for a flimsy kitchen structure at the back. A year after my arrival a hearth family moved out of the longhouse and built a mudwalled house approximately twenty yards from the main structure. All longhouses I saw were rectangular, although I was told that some on the Pirá-paraná River have rounded ends at the back to accommodate extra people.

Longhouse roofs, thatched with leaves of paraná or other palm, are supported by a framework of large posts, expertly lashed together with vines. The center posts are enormous, and finding and bringing back tree trunks long and straight enough demands herculean efforts. Walls are of bark, and the spaces between the eaves and walls in the front and rear of the house are most often covered with matting. The practice of painting the outside front walls still continues in the Pirá-paraná region but has been abandoned in the Papurí region.

The headman plays the greatest part in selecting a site and organizing long-house construction, and his role in this process identifies him as the "owner" of the house. Construction of a longhouse testifies to his success as a leader, because it would not have been finished without the willingness of his housemates to follow his direction. In particular, because it requires unusual amounts of labor and communal spirit, the transitional phase in the life of a community (between the decision to rebuild and the completion of the structure) is an important and demanding stage in a headman's career.

The decision to move a longhouse and the choice of a new site are influenced by a complex mix of factors. Considerations related to agriculture, notably the presence of suitable soils and terrain, most influence site location and the extent of initial field clearing. A number of places may fulfill these key requirements, however, leaving room for the influence of other considerations. These include preferences for (1) proximity to a river; (2) higher ground, higher even than needed to avoid flooding; (3) nearby arable land served by branch streams; (4) distance from the nearest mirití swamp. Other seemingly idiosyncratic factors – "There are a lot of such-and-such songbirds there," "They liked it there" – also seem to influence decisions. On the other hand, a factor mentioned by Goldman (1963, p. 36) in reference to the Cubeo, the pressure to maintain discrete sib territories along the river, does not hold much importance along the Inambú, because population densities are lower than among the Cubeo.

Outside the longhouse

The size of the clearing around a longhouse varies from one settlement to the next. From the examination of drawings and photos from earlier periods, I have the impression that as a general rule Tukanoans clear more now than they did formerly. If so, this increase in clearing size possibly follows the lead of mission towns, which are separated from the forest by extensive open ground. This style of landscaping exposes mission towns to the torrential rains, leading to serious erosion. Longhouses, moreover, can afford to clear more widely than they did in the era of active warfare, when encircling vegetation offered some concealment from enemies which sometimes included rubber gatherers. Before pacification, longhouses also tended to be situated some distance from the river, as they still are in some parts of the Pirá-paraná region.

Some settlements clear fields almost abutting the longhouse clearing, but the normal pattern is to put even the nearest ones out of sight. In the past, I was told, fields were always kept at some distance.[2] Here again, missionary influence may account for this change.

The plaza in front of the longhouse, kept scrupulously clean, is in most respects a male area. Men congregate there in late afternoon, sitting on stools, smoking, talking, and working on various crafts such as basketry. Curing ceremonies are carried out there, and during festivals the plaza turns into a dance ground.

The area behind the longhouse, in contrast, is predominantly female, although men appear there more often than women do in the front plaza, perhaps because the rear area is more family oriented and informal. Ostensibly out of the sight of visitors, it tends to be much messier than the plaza. Unlike Goldman (1963, p. 233), I did not see female guests being received at the rear during a festival. Children and dogs congregate behind the longhouse, and women process food, either outside or in separate kitchen structures sometimes found there.

Although no one voluntarily sits outside in the midday heat, late in the afternoon activities needing light take place in front of or behind the longhouse. Women gather in the rear, sitting and talking while mending clothes, polishing newly made pottery, or feeding pet birds. Occasionally a lone woman will be found in the front area, chatting with the men or working on some project – particularly if it is one involving the labor of both sexes. Activities that occur outside include basketry, plaiting, mending clothes, pounding tobacco, plucking coca leaves, and various kinds of food processing.

Before a festival, outside activity increases greatly. The front plaza is meticulously swept. The cane crusher is put in operation so that a more potent beer can be offered to guests. Women put the final touches on the new dresses they have made from trade cloth. Huge amounts of powdered coca are made, many cigarettes of cured tobacco and banana leaves are assembled, and the large trough used for manioc beer is washed and put to dry in the sun.

Forming a border to the semicircular plaza in front of the longhouse are various fruit trees such as pupunha (*Gulielma gasipaes*), lime, papaya, mango, and breadfruit. Some plants are cultivated near the longhouse, including various medications and preventives, as well as plants for smearing on blowguns and other weapons to attract game. Plants difficult to cultivate, such as tobacco and pepper, are also grown near the longhouse. If a kitchen or side building is no longer in use, these crops are sometimes planted there after the roof has rotted away or been dismantled, because the soil is rich in ash and nutrients.

The front door of the longhouse is usually oriented to the east. River location is irrelevant to longhouse siting, except that the men's door will be facing more toward the river than the women's.

In the earlier times most longhouses had palisades and moats (see Goldman, 1963, p. 32), and "escape routes," consisting of a tree trunk crossing the moat, which could be removed when danger threatened. Paths leading to the longhouse were sometimes boobytrapped with fire-sharpened sticks.

Inside the longhouse

The division of space into male and female, public and private, formal and relaxed, and visitor-oriented and domestic areas is even more pronounced inside the longhouse than it is outside.[3] The area inside along the sides of the building, which is divided into sections by those vertical roof supports closest to the walls, is intended for the use of individual families. Each of these sections forms the sleeping and eating quarters of a single hearth family. Communal activities use the center aisle away from the sides of the longhouse and the compartments positioned off for families. This lateral division cross-cuts the front-to-back distinction already mentioned in reference to the space outside the longhouse. Visitors are entertained and exclusively male activities take place toward the front, whereas casual and spontaneous activities, especially those in which women and children predominate, cluster toward the rear.

The massive posts supporting the roof strike the eye immediately when one enters a longhouse. Reaching up into the darkness, they themselves have been darkened by years of fires. Once, such posts were painted with designs, but now, at least in the Papurí region, they are more likely to be decorated, if at all, with a saint's picture or a calendar. The hammocks strung between the posts are detached at one end, rolled up, and tied to the posts during the day except for one hammock in each compartment left open for lounging.

When visitors arrive, after being greeted they are offered the traditional **quiñapira** (Lingua Geral term for pepperpot sauce), **cazabe** (manioc bread), and a beverage of either **manicuera** (boiled manioc juice) or **fariña** (toasted manioc granules) mixed with water. Male visitors usually stay near the front of the longhouse and sit on the finely made and decorated Tukano stools reserved for men. Some, however, especially younger men, may be invited to lounge in a hammock after a while or may stroll to the rear of the longhouse and join in the activities there. Female visitors either sit on the ground or on much lower and more poorly made stools.

The headman assigns guests a space near the front door for their hammocks. No longhouse is ever so crowded that permanent residents fill all of its eight or ten compartments. I was told that longhouses used to be built with sixteen compartments, but I never saw one with more than ten. The longhouse with the largest number of residents in my census had seven hearths occupied. Figure 3 shows in schematic form the use of space inside a longhouse.

Some hearth family compartments are screened off with mats, but they are not so enclosed as to keep all light from entering, nor of course do the mats appreciably deaden sound. A longhouse is noisy at almost any hour, and everyone can hear what everyone else is saying and doing. Private conversations, most sexual activity, and excretion take place outdoors. The longhouse falls quiet only during the late morning and early afternoon and then only on days when everyone is away at the same time. Tukanoans sleep easily in this noisy environment, and

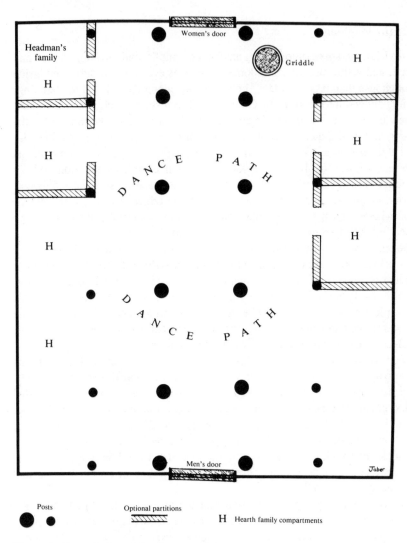

Figure 3. Ground plan of longhouse interior.

most people wake up at least once or twice during the night. At times the residents present a well-orchestrated choral piece, featuring dog barks, baby cries, coughs, farts, laughter, bad dreams, conversation, goings and comings (which involve lifting the heavy door each time), replenishing the fire, and songs. Anyone who feels the urge to sing will do so at any hour, and I never heard a request for quiet. Sometimes women will begin some part of the day's manioc processing at 2:30 or 3:00 in the morning.

The larger the longhouse is, the more comfortable: it is cooler, freer of insects,

34

less smoky, and generally more orderly. Guests, moreover, can be accommodated much more easily. It is ironic that in mission towns the houses that most closely follow missionary architectural specifications also have the most difficulty handling visitors – ironic because missionaries and mission Indians encourage visits, particularly for the fiestas given on saints' days. Houses in such nucleated villages inevitably appear much more disorderly than longhouses: they are smaller, have lower roofs, and their mud walls and solid room divisions cut off a great deal of light and air. Some of the smaller houses in the villages either lack one or more walls, or their walls are flimsily constructed of branches and matting. These houses are much more tolerable in the heat of the day but can literally be a sometime thing in a tropical thunderstorm.

Villages without longhouses cannot hold proper festivals. Two such villages, Yapú on the upper Papurí River and Trinidad on the Tiquié, have built longhouses specifically for ceremonial occasions, and in 1970 a ceremonial longhouse was under construction at Melo Franco on the Papurí. A longhouse has also been built across the river at Mitú, but this one is intended mainly for the tourist trade, to demonstrate indigenous ceremonies and culture to non-Tukanoans. Inasmuch as these nucleated villages are returning to traditional ceremonies and associated activities, the new longhouses advance this renaissance and stand as symbols of it.

Inside the longhouse, individual hearth family compartments contain an assortment of pots and gourds for cooking, baskets of various shapes and function, and three pottery fire cylinders to support cooking pots. Stored food may include some meat smoking on a rack over the fire, plantains, peppers, or corn drying in its husks suspended on the lateral poles over the compartment. The rubber pouch a man takes hunting to hold shot, primer, powder, and tobacco hangs on a nail, and harpoons and similar tools are stuck in the thatch of the roof. Any young men in the family are likely to keep a cheap suitcase holding shirts and trousers on a shelf over the compartment. (Young men seem to care more than young women about neat clothing; some have irons.)

Immediately outside the entrance to the family compartment sits the daily supply of manioc bread (**cazabe**). kept in a basket on a palm wood pedestal. In houses invaded by leaf-eating ants at nighttime, everything must be suspended from the floor. In others, only rats and cockroaches (the latter impressive in both size and number) get at the food. Fires burn all night, not only to warm the longhouse but also to keep away roaches and bats. The latter, particularly the vampires, which are small enough to enter even a tightly sealed longhouse, are real pests. Sometimes they attack children, particularly those sleeping in low-slung hammocks, from which a dangling foot often rests on the floor. Vampire bats do not swoop down on their victims, as is commonly supposed, but hop along the floor, and are too timid to attack except in total or near-total darkness. Tukanoans, knowing this, sometimes place baskets over sleeping dogs and other animals to protect them.

35

An inventory of the many artifacts found in and around the longhouse would require more space than is available, as would a comprehensive description of the technology involved in making them. One impression all visitors take away with them is the skill with which both sexes manufacture any object. The overall picture of Tukanoan artifacts is one of a deceptive simplicity, a restrained elaboration with some high points of flamboyant decoration, and a beauty of function and design remarkable in its ingenuity and understatement. A wide variety of forest products are utilized, their natural qualities well understood and put to the best advantage.

Significance of the longhouse

The longhouse unit is traditionally the most important social grouping in the Vaupés. With very few exceptions the maximal unit of food consumption and production, it (or the more recent nucleated village) is quite isolated and, as a consequence, highly autonomous. The tightly knit group of people forming its membership see each other constantly and others only once in a while, and the children reared in this setting develop far closer ties with one another than with outsiders. Members, however, always include inmarried outsiders, thus representing at least two language groups other than the longhouse's father language. Children spend most of their time with mothers and inmarried aunts, women who speak their own father languages among themselves. This intersection of linguistic and descent group ties found within all longhouses (and all villages) gives considerable saliency to these divisions even at the most local level of regional organization.

The longhouse, as the setting in which children learn the nuances and intricacies of proper behavior, radically shapes childhood socialization. Living within a large, semipartitioned barn with minimal privacy, and observing the large and small dramas of life played out on its stage, children at an early age learn tact and the ability to interpret subtle maneuvers and semihidden meanings. And although Tukanoan parents tend to be permissive, and Tukanoan children occasionally indulge in temper tantrums and provocative behavior, the children, when very young, also learn forms of politeness that North American children often resist adopting until well into their teens.

Longhouse activities and the use of space within the building express in a variety of ways distinctions between the individual, the hearth family, and the community. People eat some meals by themselves (although these are really snacks), some within the hearth family's cubicle, and others publicly in a group. Each type of meal has its own set of rules and takes place in a different part of the longhouse. All these forms for routine meals differ from occasions when guests are being fed.

The longhouse provides multiple metaphors for Tukanoan reality. It symbolizes the human body, proper social interaction, and even the entire cosmos. Many dimensions of existence intersect here, sometimes in opposition to each other – public and private, individual and communal, spontaneous and formal, male and female, secular and sacred, human and nonhuman, and cultural and natural. Later chapters will develop this theme further.

In addition to its role as a symbolic locus of value, the longhouse is the principal unit of social and biological reproduction, the mechanism through which Tukanoan society largely perpetuates itself. Ideally, its male membership is coterminous with the sib, a localized patrilineal exogamous unit, and in many contexts Tukanoans talk of larger units as if they were longhouses. The longhouse, moreover, plays the same role in the natural and supernatural spheres: Each species of animal has its own longhouse and its owner, who is the equivalent of a human headman, and dead Tukanoans go to the longhouse of their ancestors, which have *their* headmen.

Human longhouses, as opposed to those of animals and the dead, stand as the epitome of life and humanity. Babies, who are not quite human, are born outside in the fields, whereas the dead, who were fully human while alive, are buried within its walls. In one dramatic incident I witnessed, a seven-year-old boy bitten on his foot by a fer-de-lance was kept for several days in a hastily constructed hut in the manioc fields, even through a torrential thunderstorm, until he was cured. His isolation, as someone in a dangerous, not-quite-human state, confirms the association between the longhouse and humanness. In order to keep the longhouse safe for its members, marginal beings such as newborns and snakebite victims should not enter or even come near until achieving (or reachieving) fully human status.

In contrast with many other societies, the longhouse does not share its role as the locus of humanity with any other structures or spaces. The men's houses, village centers, and dance grounds found elsewhere in Amazonia disappear in the Vaupés. Although Tukanoans recognize sacred or supernaturally charged places in the large world, such as rapids and the river, their spiritual significance pales before that of the longhouse. During ritual episodes, the essential nature of the building is transformed: It exists in a different time spectrum, and the behavior taking place within it has cosmic meaning. In this respect, Tukanoans differ from many cultures (such as those of Highland Guatemala, Japan, or Ancient Greece) in which sacred places are located away from the home and profane activity, while resembling others (e.g., the Antoni [Cunningham, 1964] or the Tetum [Hicks, 1976] of Indonesia) in which the house itself has extraordinary supernatural value.

Rituals in the longhouse transform the inhabitants as well as the structure. The ceremonies clearly elaborate the theme of endurance through the variety of ways they test the endurance of participants. The entire pace and plan of such festivals seem to have as their purpose the exhaustion of all reserves of physical and mental energy, an outcome that both symbolizes the transformation being sought and provides the direct experience of its reality. The normal demands on stamina typical of everyday life (as on canoe trips or long jungle treks) are exaggerated in the ritual through consumption of large amounts of chemical stimulants – beer, cigars, snuff, coca, and the hallucinogen banisteriopsis – a corresponding absence of food and sleep, and all manner of activities and staged special effects. All of these charge the atmosphere with emotion and a sense of the sacred, helping participants achieve an altered state of consciousness. The unwritten schedule of a festival calls for a long, steady increase in tension, encouraged and regulated by dancing and chanting, until the most sacred time is reached, at midnight.

The longhouse and the people who are successfully transformed by the totality of the ritual are the same building and individuals that continue existing on the everyday plane of secular life. Most of the secular yet essentially human activities, such as transforming crops into food by cooking, share the longhouse with the most sacred rituals (which transform and transport human beings to another plane of existence). In addition, activities such as burning incense when danger threatens and performing curing ceremonies sacralize the longhouse at least partially, without achieving the radical transformation of the festivals. In the Vaupés, the sacred and secular interpenetrate and co-occur in varying proportions rather than exclude each other, and the longhouse provides the most important site for both.

4.

Economic and political life

Daily patterns

With the exception of slothful anthropologists, everyone in the longhouse gets up at least an hour before dawn, blowing fires into life and bathing in the incredibly cold river water. Young men bathe together at this time, pounding the water in unison (which makes a sound similar to kettle drums), on some mornings playing the Yuruparí horns and taking plant purgatives as well. Breakfast, eaten about daybreak, consists of cazabe and quiñapira and occasionally includes leftovers from the previous day's meal. The beverage is **mingão,** a drink made with hot water and tapioca granules. At other times of the day fariña mixed with cold water will do, but a proper breakfast must include a hot drink. In one Bará myth, troubles begin with an angry wife refusing to serve her husband a hot drink in the morning.

Women leave for their fields at about eight o'clock in the morning, taking their small children with them. Older children play near the longhouse or by the river or look for adventure elsewhere. Some men go off to hunt, fish, or clear forest for a new manioc field while others occupy themselves at home with such domestic tasks as longhouse repairs, basketry, or coca preparation.

On a typical day, manioc processing takes up much of the afternoon for most women. The men who left to hunt or fish return in the late afternoon, bringing with them trussed game or gutted fish glistening on a canoe paddle. Hunters sometimes return empty-handed, although fishermen seldom do. A man's wife cooks his catch for the afternoon meal, feeding their hearth family or a larger group, depending on his luck. Later in the afternoon when the heat of the day has diminished, women go out again for firewood, in groups if possible. As the day wears on, the pace of work for both sexes diminishes gradually, and by dusk, clusters of adults are scattered here and there, chatting and playing with children. At sundown everyone goes inside the longhouse, the headman lowers the doors at either end, and until morning no one leaves except to urinate, engage in sexual intercourse, or go hunting. No one eats after dark. The men's circle convenes in the front area of the longhouse, even if only two men are present; it will last anywhere from two to five hours. Beginning and ending their assembly with ritual chanting, they spend the hours in between chewing coca, smoking, and talking. The women hold a similar but much less formal gathering in their area toward the rear of the longhouse. A woman who cannot sit in the public space because of some work that keeps her in her family compartment will nonetheless join in the conversation and laughter.

Tukanoans have a remarkable capacity for talking on and on, despite their isolation from outside people and events and their near-perfect knowledge of each other's lives. Favorite anecdotes return to conversation repeatedly, each time provoking almost as much laughter, surprise, or anger as they did the first time they were told. The minutiae of the day's activities are also picked over in detail. After sitting through such talk for a great many nights, one can only conclude that social ends far outweigh the need for information and that choice of topic has no great importance.

In addition to whatever firelight is available, the longhouse is illuminated at night with a burning lump of resin or a piece of slow-burning wood. Radios may be playing or not, depending on the owner's whim. Several noisy activities often take place simultaneously, an inevitable outcome when many individuals and families live in one building. I witnessed a striking example of this tolerance for noise when attending a festival on the Tiquié River. At the village where it was being held, our longhouse group had been crowded into a single small house with two other groups of visitors, and during the evening one woman suddenly fell seriously ill. She started screaming with the pain (the aspirin I gave her had no visible effect) and continued to scream all night. Throughout, her companions played two different radios at full volume, and all of the men stayed up processing coca, smoking, drinking manioc beer, and laughing. Although at times I felt I had been dropped into an especially nightmarish scene in a Fellini film, their behavior, cacophonous as it was, was probably the best possible response to the situation. The woman was better off screaming than trying to stifle her moans for the benefit of the others. Had the men kept quiet and deprived themselves of their long-anticipated revelry, they would probably not have helped her at all. On the contrary, their resentment at having to be sympathetic and quiet would have been felt by everyone, including the sick woman.

As a rule, people work and relax at their own speed. They seldom seem to have to do anything truly disagreeable, and when they do, they rarely openly complain about it. Both sexes enjoy considerable freedom of choice in planning the day's activities, although inevitably, some tasks demand careful scheduling, hard work, and concentration. To be sure, the effects of years of socialization patterns that stress the value of being good-natured hide behind the apparent ease, with which everyone approaches his or her daily tasks. And freedom in planning the day's schedule does not include the freedom to do nothing day after day. Gossip and ostracism are always standing ready in the wings to appear when needed – for example, when, in the opinion of the women, a young mother plays with her new

40

baby to the neglect of her other tasks. Nonetheless, I acquired a strong impression that Tukanoans find work a largely integrated and rewarding activity. They appear self-motivated, beginning and ending each task without direction or coercion by others. They begin tasks and stay with them until completed with a spontaneity and naturalness of manner both admirable and enviable. Goldman also comments on this self-reliant enthusiasm, noting that "the Cubeo believe that a dispirited fisherman will catch nothing anyway" (1963, p. 54).

Of course, one reason why people are not as conscious of planning and timetables as we is because their life simply is not as hectic as ours and because all tasks are learned from childhood and done by everyone. Another factor is that most work is social. Deeply ingrained expectations of cheerfulness and responsiveness to others present govern all social situations, regardless of purpose or participants. Almost without exception, no one considers a task so difficult as to permit him or her to ignore or remain in a bad mood toward people in the immediate vicinity. Prima donnas and artistic temperaments are not characteristic of Tukanoan communal activities, and it is difficult to imagine how they could be under the conditions of longhouse life.

Productive tasks do not monopolize the whole of every day. Many Tukanoans keep domestic animals and any number of wild birds, such as macaws, parrots, and toucans, as pets. (Some birds are also raised for their feathers.) Fledglings found in the forest are saved and laboriously fed by hand. Although Tukanoans never eat the chickens and ducks found at virtually every settlement (nor the pigs found in a few upper Paca River settlements), they sell them occasionally to missionaries and rubber gatherers. To protect fowl from vampire bats and wild cats, their owners put them in coops at night or train them to sleep on roofs. Domestic cats, though rare, are valued because they feed themselves, often on rats and bats. Dogs are also valued as pets, and some owners lavish attention on their dogs, extracting **níguas** ("chiggers") and killing fleas. Although some dogs look underfed, I never saw any seriously mistreated. I have little sense of how effective they are in hunting, but I did witness two occasions in which a dog trapped a paca, which was subsequently killed by women with machetes.

Personal appearance is even more interesting and time-consuming than pets. Women bathe and comb their hair several times a day, and they often put on **caraiurú** powder (made from the leaves of *Bigonia chica*), especially before leaving for the fields, where it protects them from sunburn. Babies' faces are painted with special "jaguar" dots, and infants are given wrist and ankle bands and beads immediately after birth, practices that confer human status as well as decorate. Tukanoans say this is one way in which they differ from Makú, who have no beads for their babies.

Men are often quite fastidious about their appearance, and some of them, especially young men, will occasionally spend a half hour or more preening and painting their faces. Traditional dress for men consists of beads, earplugs, and loincloth. Boys proudly begin wearing a loincloth at about four years of age,

41

although for a while they must put up with teasing from the men, who try to pull it off at any opportunity. In 1970, the young men who had been to mission school wore swimming trunks or trousers.

Personal appearance is most important on ceremonial occasions, when everyone takes exceptionally great pains with adornment and dress (see Chapter 11). From time to time, however, individuals (men or women) will treat an ordinary day as a special occasion, for no discernible reason taking the time to paint themselves elaborately.

Music also forms part of life's daily round. In the late afternoon, or less often at another time of day, men sometimes play musical instruments such as panpipes (which come in sets of seven) and various small flutes made from bone, reed, snails, pods, and deer heads. Women do not play instruments but do sing impromptu songs to standardized melodies. The late afternoon is also a favorite time for manufacturing household items.

The river

The fluvial environment dominates Tukanoan life, and the Bará in particular see themselves as a riverine people: higher-ranked Bará sibs refer to themselves as Waí mahá, "fish people."

Riverine resources vary from one place to another, as does the social value of different longhouse sites, especially in terms of distance from headwaters and river mouth. At the same time, other factors, especially arrangements with Makú to trade cultivated foods and white-manufactured trade goods for game, influence the nature and intensity of a longhouse's exploitation of the river.

Tukanoans fish with weirs, hook and line, bow and harpoon, basket traps, and poison. Dip nets and harpoons are used when fishing with poison. Fish poisoning expeditions, which take place in the dry season, are festive occasions, initially proposed by the headman and including everyone in the longhouse – the only time the women involve themselves in fishing. The men leave early in the morning to dam up the stream and poison the water. **Timbó** and **barbasco** are generic terms in the ethnological literature for several species of fish poison made from both cultivated and wild plants. The choice of which one to use depends on how toxic an effect is desired and how much river water must be poisoned. The poison, in the form of leaves, woody stems, or vines, is pounded and washed in the water. Although harmless for humans or dogs, it kills or stuns all aquatic life passing through the dammed-up portion of the river, and therefore cannot be used very often.

By late afternoon many baskets and canoe bottoms are filled with fish, and the poison has become much more diluted. Most fish are initially stupefied by the poison rather than killed outright, and catching them in the muddy water when they temporarily rise to the surface resembles an Easter-egg hunt with mobile and greased eggs. Although pregnant women and their husbands cannot enter the

42

water, they help out on the bank, gutting and packing the fish. When the party returns to the longhouse, all the fish are cleaned at the canoe landing, everyone helping to prepare the basketfuls for smoking. Although the expedition involves the whole longhouse, hearth family groups catch and give away fish. There is no anonymity in fish-poison parties, nor does the headman oversee any kind of redistribution. Each family prepares smoking racks, on which it skewers and smokes huge amounts of fish. Another part of the catch is boiled up in large pots for immediate consumption, and a veritable orgy of fish-eating ensues. Neighbors and relatives from other longhouses come and receive gifts of smoked fish, truly one of the delicacies of Tukanoan cuisine. Even after a week of gluttony, their appetite and mine for fish merely declined rather than disappeared.

Fishing technology is well developed. Worms, insects, berries, and small fish are the principal baits. Lines are sometimes tied to branches overhanging the river – one passes a great many on canoe trips – to be pulled in late in the day, although by then animals have gotten at some of the hooked fish. Apart from the flashlights occasionally used in night fishing, the only fishing equipment acquired from whites are fish hooks, nylon line, and the metal used to tip harpoons.

The technology included detailed knowledge of the habits of various species, of daily, seasonal, and microecological variations, and especially of the fishing prospects at different locations. Two sites on the same river can differ substantially in yield. Each man has his favorite fishing spots, and these become familiar to his sons as they grow up. Unlike Goldman (1963, p. 55), I was not told that individuals could lay claim to fishing rights in particular streams or stretches of river. They can, however, install and make exclusive use of weirs, although weir owners are expected to let through enough aquatic life to supply other individuals and longhouses.

Once in a while a group from a longhouse will camp out in the forest for several days to fish, hunt, and smoke their catch. The expeditions of this sort I witnessed all consisted of single hearth families, although I was told that sometimes bigger parties go out.

The most frequently eaten fish are the **waracú** (*Leporinus copelandi* Steind.), **tarira** (*Erythrinus* sp.), and **tucunaré** (*Chichla ocellaris*). The rivers provide other types of food, such as shrimp and caymans. Men often hunt at rivers, in search of edible water fowl and water rodents such as paca and agouti.[1]

Canoes and river travel are a vital part of Tukanoan life. All men are excellent boatmen, and although women are less accomplished at negotiating rapids, they know all of the paddling techniques. Everyone knows a great deal about the rivers of the region, even those far from home. This knowledge involves, it must be remembered, familiarity with each river in several drastically different states at various seasons of the year. A number of men have also become expert at handling outboard motors (although unfortunately not all of them – twice I was involved in serious capsizings while traveling by motorized canoe).

Travel on any Vaupés river is dangerous and requires concentration and

43

familiarity with the territory. Rapids, of course, offer the greatest challenge. The easiest of rapids takes considerable care and skill to negotiate, and the worst ones demand almost superhuman efforts and teamwork. Travelers also expend considerable time and energy carrying cargo overland, portaging canoes around those rapids that are completely impassable, and portaging between rivers. Travel with cargo requires three or more boatmen, and during some parts of my trips, notably at the three-quarter-mile portage between the Vaupés and Papurí drainages, we needed as many as eight.

Between rapids, canoe travel is often pleasant. An outboard motor and a reasonably large canoe increase the pleasure, because paddling soon becomes wearisome, especially when going upstream, and a small canoe requires constant trimming and bailing. Travelers do not stop for bad weather, and ten hours of rain a day can definitely get a bit tedious. Night travel, however, is impossible except on the upper reaches of the Vaupés River itself, because of the hazards of unseen snags and rapids.

Tukanoans enjoy travel. It provides an opportunity to talk and joke with others in the travel party for long stretches of time, to meet people in canoes encountered along the way, and to visit longhouses or villages at each overnight stop. At times irresistible hunting opportunities present themselves en route, and during high water if a canoe party detects signs of monkeys or other game, it will paddle off through the flooded forest in hot pursuit.

As noted in the Preface, I was fortunate to be able to travel often by canoe because it showed me the range of geographical knowledge held by Tukanoans – for most of them it encompasses the entire region – and their feeling that all of it was their territory. In addition to information acquired from spending so much time in canoes, Tukanoans add to their knowledge by showing a keen interest in geographical and ecological topics in their conversations with people at stopover settlements.

Canoe travel provides adventures of all sorts. Some are unpleasant in the extreme, as when a wasp's or hornet's nest is disturbed, or a branch filled with fire ants is unwittingly pushed aside. But even the worst incidents make interesting anecdotes for recounting later on. One such adventure occurred on one of my trips when the only shotgun in the party became jammed, a disappointment because we were paddling and would otherwise have stood a chance of bagging some kind of shore-dwelling game. (The noise from an outboard motor greatly reduces these opportunities.) A large Muscovy duck (*dia katá*) was spotted, flying along ahead of the boat, frustrating the men, who were helpless to do anything. Half an hour went by in which the bird repeatedly settled on a branch ahead, only to fly on as we approached it. As this scene was repeated over and over, the bird eventually became so used to us that it did not fly ahead as we approached. Finally, as the canoe passed under the branch the bird was perched on, the men raised their arms and – as Tukanoans frequently do – yelled "Bam!" giving themselves the pleasure of at least pretending to kill it. The bird, under-

44

standably startled, reacted by covering us all with a foul-smelling, warm white liquid. As it flew off screeching, we threw ourselves in the river, howling with laughter. The bird's well-aimed comments on our intentions toward it were described many times, with accompanying shrieks of laughter from everyone, in the days that followed.

This incident illustrates how Tukanoans handle the discomforts and dangers of river travel and, in fact, most of the discomforts of life. One must laugh if possible and savor the details for future storytelling. Tukanoans have an astonishing ability to turn the most unpleasant happenings (including many far worse than the above incident) into something funny, at times even while it is actually happening.

The river does offer serious danger, particularly at rapids, and drownings do occur, especially of children, although with what frequency I could not even guess. Water animals, however, are generally more frightening than truly dangerous. The anaconda is perhaps the most important figure in Tukanoan mythology and certainly commands a healthy respect from Tukanoans. I never heard of anyone's being killed by either an anaconda or a boa. Piranha are found in most of the rivers, but they are neither so numerous nor nearly so dangerous as they are in other areas of Amazonia, as is illustrated by a tragic accident I witnessed on the Papurí, when a Javerian priest drowned in the rapids. Attempts to raise his body were unsuccessful, and it took forty hours to surface. Yet piranha had barely touched it. The caymans (*Paleosuchus palpebrosus; Caiman schlerops*) in the region are too small to be dangerous.

Tukanoan success in their riverine adaptation depends to a considerable extent on their canoe-building skills. A man and his sons rough out the hull of a dugout canoe in the forest. When it is light enough, they haul it to the river, where everyone in the longhouse joins in the hot and difficult work of finishing it by burning it out and widening it. Some Tukanoans told me that the Bará are specialists in canoe building, but those Bará I spoke with said that expertise in this skill varies from one individual to another and does not follow language divisions.

In general, rivers pervade all aspects of Tukanoan life, social and cosmological as well as technological. As boundary markers, the connecting links between settlements, and the most obvious landmarks in the environment, they are the principal means by which people orient themselves, give directions, and describe themselves. Settlements are usually located near rapids, and when they are not, they often take their name from a characteristic feature of the river (for example, "lagoon"). And when Tukanoans distinguish themselves from Makú, their own association with the river and the Makú separation from it looms large.

Rivers are important to growth in a number of ways. One's humanness, one's self-image as a full-fledged human being and a Tukanoan, involves riverine ritual and symbolism. A newborn infant's first rites take place at the river edge. Sacred trumpets (Yuruparí) are kept in the river, " to maintain their brilliant glow."

45

Young men bathe together before dawn in the river, taking in some of the growth power the river and the ancestors confer to those who maintain their spiritual purity. Sexual intercourse often takes place at the shore, the couple bathing in the river afterward.

Rivers are fundamental in Tukanoan cosmology. The first human beings ascended into the Vaupés by river in an anaconda canoe. The first ancestors emerged at the various rapids sites in the region. The main feature of the underworld (the universe is, strictly speaking, composed of five levels, but the lower two are often spoken of as one) is a river: Opēkó dia ("milk river"). It flows in the opposite direction from rivers of this level; that is, it goes from east to west. Symbolism concerned with rivers is found throughout Tukanoan mythology.

The forest

The forest is conceived of as quite separate and distinct from the world of humans, symbolized by the longhouse and to some degree by the river. Although an extremely important domain in Tukanoan cosmology, in general the forest is more foreign, less connected to human life, and less benign than the river. Nevertheless, although quite separate from the habitat of humans, the forest and its denizens intersect with the human world in a number of ways, of which hunting is the most important.

Tukanoans use a variety of traps and weapons in hunting, including snares, nets, deadfalls, blowguns with poison darts, and bows and arrows. The last are used mainly on birds, often with special arrows tipped with a hard bulb that stuns but does not kill. Tapir and peccary used to be killed with metal-tipped spears. Breech-loading 12- or 16-bore shotguns, however, have supplanted traditional technology to become the dominant hunting weapon. Blowguns seem to be a boy's weapon, used on slow-moving birds like doves and other small game, which are roasted and eaten on the spot. I never saw an adult use a blowgun.

It is difficult to assess to what degree shotguns have affected the overall availability of game, but it is being depleted. A general consensus among informants is that men go out hunting less than they did before the introduction of shotguns. This is at least in part because shot is expensive and difficult to obtain. No one, consequently, will risk a shot unless he has a good chance of bagging the prey. Yet neither does anyone want to return empty-handed after a day of hunting. Therefore, a man will usually stay home or go fishing unless he sees a sign of game in the area.

Men hunt alone, except when chasing white-lipped peccaries, which travel in herds. When they hunt with a companion, imitations of bird calls are used for communication.

Women contribute to hunting by relaying information about game noticed en route to their fields or on trips to abandoned fields and longhouse sites to collect fruit. As noted earlier, women also occasionally kill small rodents such as pacas and **tintíns** (*Dasyprocta* sp.), with the help of dogs.

A few Tukanoans hunt for pelts such as jaguar or otter, but Colombian law has recently and successfully curtailed the pelt trade. The enforcement was rigorous while I was in the country, and on a couple of occasions all luggage leaving Mitú by plane was thoroughly searched.

Game is said to be attracted by certain kinds of face and body paint. The leaves of some of the plants grown near the longhouse are applied to shotguns and blowguns to attract game, especially deer. Dogs are also rubbed with various plants to help them locate game.

Animals most commonly hunted are paca (*Cuniculus paca virgata*), agouti (*Dasyprocta aguti*), tapir (*Tapirus terrestris*), collared peccary (*Tayassu tajacu*), white-lipped peccary (*Tayassu pecari*), deer (*Mazama youzaoubira murelia*), tintín (*Dasyprocta* sp.), and less frequently, armadillo (*Dasypus novemcinctus*). Some animals are killed for purposes other than food. Birds prized for their plumage are currasow (*Crax* sp.), toucan (*Ramphastos sulfuratus*), parrot (*Amazona* spp.), trumpeter, egret, and macaw. Jaguar are not eaten, but their teeth are used for belts and necklaces.

Most small game is trussed after killing and brought back to the settlement. Larger animals may be singed and cut up before returning home, but given how rapidly meat spoils in the tropics, any foreseen delay between killing and cooking necessitates a preliminary smoking in the forest. A man carries his kill to the back door of the longhouse and gives it to the appropriate woman, usually his wife, who takes it to the port for cleaning. Except for the liver, and sometimes the kidney and heart, no viscera are saved.

If there is enough for the entire longhouse, a communal meal of boiled meat ensues. Exchanges between hearth families of game or other food that are not communal meals are neither random nor based on cut-and-dried prescription but rather follow friendship and kinship ties. Thus, normally the closest agnates (including close inmarried women), will share more exchanges, but of course if, for instance, two brothers are not getting along, exchanges will be curtailed.

Although the totemic features found in Vaupés social structure and cosmology do not include a prohibition on eating one's totem (e.g., toucans, armadillos), many animals are tabooed as food. No carnivores are eaten (including the cats, anteaters, snakes, etc.), nor are the herbivorous sloths and many smaller animals such as fruit-eating bats.[2] Tukanoans say that Makú will eat anything, although this is not, in fact, true. The reasons given are either that the Makú cannot feed themselves properly and therefore eat anything because they are starving, or that because Makú are not quite human they cannot be expected to know what is correct human behavior.

A vast amount of symbolism surrounds hunting, in part because hunting is concerned with food and thus shares in the intricate symbolic system relating

47

food and eating to many areas of physical and spiritual growth and well-being. Metaphors, inversions, taboos, and all manner of prescriptions create a link between a particular food and another domain. Another reason is that hunting is tied into the equally large symbolic system concerned with (1) male sexuality and potency, (2) fertility of humans and game animals, (3) warfare and killing in general, and (4) male adolescent growth and transformation into adult men. A third reason is that hunting is related to shamanism, animal–human transformations (i.e., animal spirit familiars), power, and access to the supernatural dimension in order to exchange different kinds of energy and resources. For example, if a certain type of game is scarce, a shaman will go into a trance and visit the home of a "master" of a given species of game animal. This home is in a cave in one of the dome-shaped sandstone hills in the region. There the shaman will bargain with the master, offering to exchange some human souls from a settlement far away if more animals are released from the game owner's pen. A fourth, and final reason is that hunting takes place in the forest, which, although quite separate and distinct from the world of humans, is an extremely important domain in Tukanoan cosmology.

Forest-related (although not exclusively so) dangers include poisonous snakes (especially fer-de-lances [*Bothrops atrox atrox*], and bushmasters [*Lachesis muta muta*]), black widows, vampire bats, scorpions, hornets, and tarantulas. Most of these animals come into direct contact with humans infrequently (with the possible exception of vampire bats), but over time one collects a substantial repertoire of anecdotes about such encounters. Snakebite is a serious threat to life. Everyone has a relative who has been bitten, sometimes fatally or with resulting loss of a limb. The young boy bitten by a fer-de-lance almost certainly would have died without the serum I administered, because snakebite is extremely dangerous to children (due to the higher proportion of venom to blood). The incident was one of the few times I felt able partially to repay the people I lived with for all the kindness and help they showed me. It also demonstrated how helpless Tukanoans are in the face of snakebite. In a certain sense he was already defined as dying, and thus the treatment basically consisted of making him comfortable, although some requirements in fact resulted in increased discomfort, both physical and psychological. For example, he was not allowed to talk with or get close to his mother, and as I noted earlier he had to be kept far from the longhouse, in a hastily built shelter in a manioc field.

Without doubt the true lords of the forest are its insects. Their variety and numbers can make life miserable; at meal times, for instance, sometimes each mouthful a person takes seems to be half food and half gnats. The Tucandira ant has an unbelievable sting, guaranteeing hours of excruciating pain. Tiny fire ants (**magiñá**) deposit formic acid on the skin; if an ant falls in the eye, three days of desperation and agony result. Almost all of the dogs in the region have milky, opaque corneas from repeated contact with magiñá. Sand flies can be extremely irritating, and female sand fleas or chiggers (*Pulex penetrans*) lay eggs under the skin that hatch into formless white grubs. If these are not extracted, they form painful cysts and eventually fall off, leaving a large pit in the flesh. The one saving grace of Vaupés insects is that bees are stingless.

In Bará, game animals are called *waí búhkúra* ("old" or "mature fish"). This category is contrasted with *ñañará* ("bad" or "useless beings"), all nonedible animals. All life forms are part of a universe having a finite quantity of energy (Reichel-Dolmatoff, 1976), which is literally as well as figuratively recycled in various kinds of transformations. This idea is common in many Amazonian societies. Each species of game animal has its own master, who can at times be encountered in the forest. Other spirits are also found in the forests. They are either neutral toward humans (unless provoked into an angry act by broken taboos) or unrelievedly mean and nasty. Any encounters between humans and forest spirits, or any indirect contact with them via the spirits' paraphernalia, symbols, or spirit familiars, are always of great significance. Thus, animal items from the forest brought into the longhouse have power associated with them, regardless of how they are used. Some are worn (e.g., jaguar teeth, monkey hair), and some are used for special occasions (e.g., skin-covered drums, or bird-bone snuff takers).

Also important are areas in the forest known to be especially favorite haunts of a particular spirit. Clearings are examples of these, as are mirití swamps. The origin of all rivers is one such swamp, Ewüra taró, which is relatively near Púmanaka buro. These swamps are important in Tukanoan cosmology, perhaps in part because they are ambiguous: a combination of forest and river rather than one or the other (Douglas, 1966). They are water but not the moving water typical of rivers; although consisting of water, they are filled with trees and other plants, like the forest.

A hunting accident that happened to the headman of a Bará longhouse on the Macucú River illustrates some of these concepts. What follows is a much abbreviated version of an account given me.

About twenty years ago, José of Anüyuhtí longhouse went to hunt white-lipped peccaries. He shot one, which was especially fierce because its mate was about to give birth. The peccary gored José in the knee, but he killed it with his dogs. He limped back to the longhouse, carrying the dead peccary. The wound got very bad. Old Arturo, the most knowledgeable of Bará shamans, started a curing chant, but José was ready to die. His feet were already cold and only his heart moved. Old Arturo went to Ewüra wi, a longhouse near Ewüra taró.[3] He saw José already there, standing outside the door. He was putting on black body paint, festive ornaments, and feathers. His mother and his father were there, and many people awaited him. José had almost finished painting himself and was about to enter the longhouse. If he had entered, he would have died in this world. The people at Anüyuhtí were already crying. Old Arturo came and pushed José away from the doorway. Many peccaries were outside the house waiting, and Old Arturo began to scare them with his power. First he summoned a big wind. The peccaries said that wind had been around since the beginning of the world. Then Old Arturo summoned a tremendous fire, which did scare them. They lined up and began to enter the longhouse. He made them shut all the doors, which he closed with big logs. Old Arturo took away their *aüawüri* (long flutes), taking away their dances, taking away their hearts. When Old Arturo returned to this world, he carried these flutes in his throat, and José recovered. But this is why there are no peccaries in these parts today.

The forest also provides nonhunted foods of many kinds, including grubs, termites, ants, wild fruits and berries, nuts, and palm hearts. The most important plants are the **umarí** fruit (*Poraqueiba sericea*), calaloo (*Phytolacca isconsandra*), similar to spinach, wild Ingá (*Inga* sp.), and assai-palm fruit (*Euterpe oleracea*). Some kinds of fungus in rotting logs are edible. Collecting, except where there are large harvests of wild fruit, is organized along hearth family lines. It is spontaneous, and done mostly by women and children. Honey is a delectable foraged food but is not nearly as abundant as in other areas of lowland South America (e.g., the Aché, see Clastres, 1972; see also Kloos, 1977, on the Akuriyó).[4]

Cultivated foods

Recent debates concerned with geological and ecological variation in the Amazon Basin have focused on issues such as carrying capacity and prehistoric demography (Denevan, 1976; Dobyns, 1966) and the upper limits of horticultural potential, given the region's ecology and the staple crops that are grown.[5] An important outcome of these debates has been the increasing awareness and recognition of extensive microvariation within the basin as well as an accumulation of evidence that South American tropical ecosystems are complex and finely honed systems impossible to understand in a cursory manner (Fosberg, 1973). They most certainly cannot withstand many of the kinds of disturbances currently being undergone as a result of agricultural and other kinds of development programs. These current disturbances, often of a serious and irreversible nature (see Denevan, 1973; Fosberg, 1973; Goodland and Irwin, 1975; Ruddle, 1974; Sternberg, 1969), contrast with the effects of traditional swidden (slash-and-burn) horticulture over the centuries up to the present. The genius of the various types of swidden systems is that they admirably imitate (although only partially; see Hames, 1980a) the natural tropical forest's cycles. This is true only when the ratio of human beings to arable land is sufficiently low (the actual ratio varies, depending on region and horticultural system). Where this is still the case, indigenous utilization of natural tropical resources, including the land used for horticulture and exploitation of wild products from the forests and rivers themselves, generally illustrates ecologically sound practices.

The present ecology of the Amazon Basin is extremely old (in comparison to, for example, the age of the temperate forests of Europe) and is a delicately balanced system. This is belied by the lush appearance of its canopy forests and teeming animal life. We do not know all of the answers to why such good vegetation can exist in such an environment with such a fragile base, but one factor is certainly that it is a closed system within which 70 percent of the total mineral nutrient supply is within the living biomass of the forest (Fosberg, 1973) – a far higher percentage than in Iowa, for example. Decomposition of organic matter is rapid and complete, particularly in the steady high temperatures of the tropics, and the released nutrients are immediately absorbed by surface yet very efficient root structures. One reason why this ecosystem is so easily upset is that almost any shift in the process has far-reaching consequences. For example, when the very thin humus layer is directly exposed to sunlight, several kinds of permanent damage can occur, such as rapid leaching and percolation of nutrients into the lower subsoil, where they are permanently lost. The top layer of soil can literally evaporate. Tropical soils are thin, delicate, and of low fertility. They lack weatherable compounds, such as silicates, and have a high iron content, especially in the older strata of the Guiana and Brazilian shields. The highly destructive effects of tropical rain, wind, and sun can quickly turn these areas into eroded saw-grass savanna with no possibility of reforestation. Or, more drastically, the resulting erosion can produce a landscape looking remarkably like parking-lot pavement and having about the same agricultural potential.

Although these points are somewhat technical, an understanding of the Tukanoan subsistence base or that of any lowland South American society requires a preliminary understanding of rainforest ecology and the biosphere of the Amazon Basin. Furthermore, much of the acculturation undergone by these societies at present ultimately comes from land-development schemes involving agriculture, animal husbandry, or both. The future of these societies is inextricably linked to the outcome of these schemes, and both are in turn linked to the conditions and limitations of their environment.

The ongoing debate over soil fertility and its exhaustion relates to a number of diverse issues. One of these is the cause (or causes) of the periodic shifts in settlement site that are so characteristic of all swidden-based societies in lowland South America. Various authors offer evidence that periodic changes in settlement site cannot be explained in terms of single determinants such as loss of soil fertility.[6] It is obvious that one must take into account such factors as overall diet, the organization of economic activities (e.g., the sexual division of labor), and the integration of these activities with other areas of the society, such as settlement size and warfare. Several authors have suggested that the real limiting factor for many groups is game, both because game and fish resources are exhausted more quickly than cultivable soil[7] and because manioc is poor in several basic nutrients, making it necessary to have reliable sources of protein. Current studies in the nutritional and health status of Amazonian populations will undoubtedly shed further light on the complexity of the situation.

Cultivation in the Vaupés.

Any person who has visited the Vaupés becomes nostalgic when remembering activities relating to the manioc process, for it is one of the primary symbols of

51

the region. Its salience is in part due to the high visibility of the activities in and around the longhouse and because at least several stages, and usually the entire process, occur daily.

A woman leaves the longhouse early in the morning with an old basket, an old machete, a smoldering piece of wood, her very young children, and her dog. In the fields she cuts the manioc plants, burns the tops (helping to return some of the nutrients to the soil), and with the machete digs down to the tubers themselves. She may peel some of the tubers in the field or wait until she is out of the sun. Flimsily built shelters are found in many fields, which are used for relaxing and eating a snack, peeling tubers in the shade, or escaping a sudden thunderstorm.

While in the field the woman will tend other crops as well, including plantains (*Musa paradisiaca*), bananas (*Musa* sp.), ñame (no English equivalent; *Xanthosoma* sp.), sweet potatoes (*Ipomoea batatas*), sugar cane (*Saccharum officinarum*), pineapple (*Ananas comosus*), melons, yams (*Dioscorea trifida*), and such nonfood items as *Bigonia chica* (a bush producing red pigment), bottle gourds (*Lagenaria* sp.), achiote (*Bixa orellana;* a red pigment used by females), and a black dye-producing bush (*Rubiaceae* sp.). Plants tended by men include coca (*Erythroxylon coca*), calabash trees (*Crescentia cujete*), yagé (at least two species: *Banisteriopsis inebrians* and *Banisteriopsis rusbyana*), and tobacco (*Nicotiana tabacum*). Men also plant fruit trees, both in the fields and close to the longhouse, such as jungle grape or cucura (*Pourouma cecropiaefolia;* its leaves are used to wrap fariña or manioc bread and are the preferred ash for mixing with coca), Ingá (*Inga dulcis* – some Ingá also grows wild), pupunha or peach palm (*Guiliema gasipaes*), and more recently introduced trees such as mango (*Mangifera indica*), papaya (*Carica papaya*), lime (*Citrus qurantifolia*), and caimito or star apple (*Chrysophyllum caimito*). The manioc fields show some intercropping (e.g., bananas, pineapple), but corn is usually grown separately because it needs more care, particularly weeding; corn is often planted and tended by men.

Manioc is an admirable crop in many ways, even though deficient in certain important nutrients. It is dependable, is not finicky about soil type or in need of specific combinations of dryness and rain at certain crucial stages of growth (as is true of corn, for example), and needs a relatively small amount of weeding and protection. Compared with a number of other crops high in carbohydrates, it provides an abundant harvest in proportion to the amount of labor required for planting and tending. It is storable while in the ground, and when processed into fariña can keep several months. Several other manioc products will keep for relatively long periods, a very valuable feature because storage of any foodstuff is no mean feat in the tropics. Bitter manioc[8] is used for making manioc beer and cazabe. Thus, bitter manioc is a superior crop to sweet manioc because the variety of products obtained from it and its storability make it a uniquely suitable staple crop. That many Amazonian societies prefer it over sweet varieties is understandable, despite its arduous processing requirements.

After several days of harvesting manioc the woman replants the manioc stems she has accumulated, putting them in the ground at an angle and often mounding the soil around two or three stems to delay erosion caused by heavy rain on the relatively unprotected soil. Coca is also planted by men after a first harvest of manioc (as well as in newly cleared fields). Men plant coca in a very symmetrical fashion, and ordinarily tend it and harvest it by themselves. Still, I have often seen women plucking coca leaves off the stems, although except for older women, women generally chew the final product only at festivals.

Manioc is harvestable after six months, but the tubers are usually dug up after twelve to twenty-four months. Whitten (1976, p. 74) states that toxicity is highest right after flowering, decreasing in the tuber after five or six months.

Goldman (1963, p. 61) is quite correct in describing women as agronomists rather than mere gardeners. Any woman can rattle off a long list of varieties of manioc, describing which ones she prefers to plant and why. Each woman's cazabe and fariña are distinctive in flavor and texture because of her own special blend of manioc varieties.

Later in the day women return from the fields with their tubers, washing them in a small stream or in the river itself and perhaps letting them soak there in an old basket or canoe, which makes peeling easier. Peeling, even with knives, and the subsequent grating are arduous work. Grater boards are obtained from the Curripaco and Baniwa, Arawak speakers living to the north of the Vaupés River. These boards are set with sharp quartz stones. A woman sits on the ground, places a board on her lap, and grates, holding tubers in both hands. She will grate enough mash for at least a day's supply, more if she wants enough for two days or plans on making fariña or beer. The mash is then washed in a tripod-supported basket and squeezed in the **tipití**, a tubular basket woven like a Chinese toy finger trap such that pulling it constricts it. At this point the manioc mash can be sifted and toasted, producing fariña or cazabe, depending on the method of toasting. The liquid from the washing is boiled to make the drink manicuera (extreme heat breaks down the prussic acid in manioc).[9]

Women also make juice from pupunha in the tripod basket strainer; the juice is frequently allowed to ferment. Other fruit drinks are made in this manner as well.

In general, manioc products are not what a Westerner considers gourmet fare, although some are better than others. The blue ribbon for tastelessness goes to a very hard cake made entirely from starch. It resembles cardboard, but is good for trips because it keeps so well. Cazabe is at its best hot off the griddle, but Tukanoans do not eat any manioc product so soon after cooking. Little thin cakes with no fiber content are made from tapioca; these are considered to be an especially pure kind of food.

Although men occasionally help with cooking, they are regularly expected to help only with making manioc beer, which is made with corn, manioc products, and other root crops such as *Xanthosoma* and sweet potatoes. Fermentation is begun by women chewing on baked corn cakes and spitting pieces into a pot. Sugar cane and fruit juices are added to beer made for festivals, resulting in a more potent drink.

All Tukanoans are interested in gardening. Although this is mainly the domain of women, men are also knowledgeable about it. I once brought in packets of seeds: Both men and women became involved, examined their plots daily, and rejoiced when a few plants actually appeared, including melons, tomatoes, and green bell peppers. The bell peppers promised to be a big success but turned out to be the biggest failure, even though they flourished. Everyone had assumed that peppers four times as large as chili peppers would also be four times as hot. Of cultivated foods, only fariña and occasionally fruit are sold to missionaries.

New fields are prepared yearly, at the end of the dry season. Knowing what day to fire and doing it properly is a tricky business. A blazing field is a spectacular sight, and people sometimes gather to watch.

A woman's husband fells and fires a field for her after they have decided where to clear. The field belongs to the woman and is spoken of as hers but only for as long as she uses it. Concepts of ownership are more elaborated with respect to horticultural land than hunting or fishing territories. If someone takes food from a plot without telling the owner, it is considered to be theft.

Paca, agoutis, and deer are the most bothersome pests in the manioc fields. (These animals eat manioc before it is exposed to oxygen and therefore not toxic.) Leaf-cutter ants can also accomplish a great deal of damage when their routes take them through a cultivated area.

The importance of food.

It is difficult to overstate the importance of attitudes and beliefs about food among Tukanoans. Although it is an exaggeration to characterize Tukanoans as "horticulturalists . . . for whom the total food quest constitutes the cultural focus of society," as Ruddle (1974, p. 4) has described incipient tropical forest horticulturalists in general, food is extremely important. It is furthermore symbolically connected to all other important cultural foci in Vaupés society. Food has importance as sustenance, as a form of ceremonial communication, as an expression of emotion (i.e., of affection when given, of anger when withheld), and as a metaphor for such other important symbol domains as the body, society, and the universe.

Foods are categorized into an elaborate system of taboos. This system is so pervasive that it is rare that one or more people in a longhouse are not observing some degree of restriction. When people are in a state of crisis or some sort of precarious condition (either physical or mental), they will be prohibited those foods corresponding to the level of seriousness and danger of their condition. When a person falls sick, certain categories of food are forbidden. Similarly, entering a life crisis such as puberty or pregnancy puts one in jeopardy, and a certain level of food restriction is prescribed. Food restrictions are causally related to illness and curing in a number of ways; for example, people can become sick because they failed to observe a taboo. Many states (e.g., menstruation) and activities (e.g., hunting) require observing a particular level of food restrictions. In cases of illness the shaman (or person substituting for a shaman if one is not present) makes the diagnosis and prescribes the level of food restrictions the patient must observe in order to recover. When the danger is sufficiently past, the shaman will also chant over each type of foodstuff being reintroduced into the diet of the sick person. After this initial blessing, which must be done for each kind of food, the person can safely resume eating it.

The sequence of prohibited foods is an ordinal scale – that is, if a particular level is prohibited, all preceding levels will automatically be prohibited as well. This scheme is a condensed version of the sequencing of foodstuffs that are permitted to children as they grow up. When a child is ready to eat a new item, a sample of that item will be shamanized before the child eats it for the first time. A very abbreviated form of this sequence (C. Hugh-Jones, 1979; Langdon, 1975) is as follows: (1) milk, after being shamanized, along with *kaná* fruits (*Sabicea amazonensis*), in the case of infants (C. Hugh-Jones, 1979, p. 118); (2) "pure" foods (all of which should be cold): pure manioc starch with no fiber, termites, **maniwara** (flying ants) – these animals have "no blood"; (3) most vegetable products, including chili pepper and hot manioc juice; (4) small fish and all manioc products; (5) small game; (6) large herbivorous game. Carnivores are never eaten because not only do they have a lot of blood, but they eat other animals that have blood. Their flesh, consequently, would be far too hot and dangerous. There is a general progression from low to high (the animal's or plant's habitat), from water to land, and from small to large (S. Hugh-Jones, 1979, p. 93).

Different methods of capture and cooking also fit into this scheme of relative amounts of danger. The longer a foodstuff is cooked, the less dangerous it becomes, because cooking removes some of an animal's heat. Thus, boiling is better than roasting.

The correct approach to food and eating is one of moderation. Excess – lavish and ostentatious serving, overly enthusiastic eating behavior, or gluttony – is very much disapproved of. The general apprehensiveness about succulent or hot-off-the-griddle foods underscores this general theme. Self-control and moderation are clearly a part of the food restriction system also.

The emphasis on moderation in eating is revealed most strongly in formal settings. For example, a guest eats a very small amount of food just after arriving at a longhouse. Everyone is supposed to be restrained at communal meals as well. Children, however, are allowed to eat until full and whenever they wish, and under less formal circumstances (for instance, when women snack on bananas in the manioc fields) people are more relaxed and boisterous.

At times people inadvertently reveal more of an interest in food than that

55

prescribed by etiquette. It is not difficult for one who is familiar with eating rules to notice the poorly suppressed impatience right before a communal meal, particularly if meat has recently been scarce. Sometimes people's efforts to maintain appearances while feeling acutely hungry are comic. I have seen women, after a pot of meat has been put in the middle of the floor and the invitation to eat extended to all, "walk" incredibly quickly to their baskets of cazabe. Grabbing a piece, they "walk" back to the pot, feigning nonchalance. (It is very bad manners to go for a piece of cazabe before one is formally invited to a meal, and eating meat without cazabe is unthinkable.)

The requirement of moderation regarding food also means that one should hide one's disappointment or anger when expectations about food giving are not met. Any talking about stinginess or laziness should be strictly in private and certainly not leave the confines of the hearth family group. Still, I heard a great deal of gossip among the women about various kinds of nonsharing of food. It is my impression that women gossip more than men, but men notice slights too and will talk about them with their close kinswomen. Clearly, gossip is the main mechanism of social control regarding food distribution beyond the hearth family.

The amount of formality and moderation in eating behavior directly correlates with the number of people present at a meal and the amount of social distance among them. This is why visitors to a longhouse are never supposed to eat to repletion; the offerings of cazabe and quiñapira that each woman makes to the visitors are token offerings. Tukanoans feel that people should eat a genuine meal only among intimates. A man returning from a long day's hunting is served alone by his wife in his own compartment or immediately outside of it and will eat until he is full. Formal communal meals involving the entire longhouse fall somewhere in between these two extremes. People should never be greedy, but a communal meal is not organized unless there is enough meat to give everyone more than a taste.

Excessive consumption occurs only at festivals, and the overindulgence displayed then involves only those items that C. Hugh-Jones has termed "soul food" (1979, p. 213). These include tobacco, coca, banisteriopsis, and manioc beer. "Real" food is not consumed during a festival; this stricture applies particularly to men.

Visitors to a longhouse should never rely on food offered them by their hosts, regardless of how intimate the relationship is, but should always bring provisions with them. The "Jewish mother" model found in many parts of the world of ostentatious offerings of food and disappointment if it is not eaten would be totally incomprehensible to Tukanoans. Guests share food, having brought enough for themselves. If they stay longer than intended, both women and men help produce and process food. If they stay for a month or more, a section of the manioc fields will be turned over to the women.[10]

A man brings any game he has killed to his wife, mother, or sister, depending on with whom he shares a hearth. Many conversations among women focus on

56

men as providers, on their generosity or lack of it. Such judgments and invidious comparisons about a man's laziness, lack of skill, or stinginess should never take place in the ideal Tukanoan society, but one hears them in the real one.

Although most exchange is carried out in as spontaneous and casual a manner as possible, a lot of rather unspontaneous and calculated account-keeping takes place in everyone's head. The differences between this system and ones reported for peasant patterns of reciprocity, for example, is that among Tukanoans the ledger books are memorized and not a proper subject for public discussion. At times a fairly pronounced egotism and spitefulness can come to the fore, particularly when a given situation is somewhat outside of the traditional system of expectations about sharing. I was caught in a number of upsetting squabbles related to my giving gifts and paying for food, in part because these gifts and payments were outside the traditional system, and people felt less compunction to keep silent.

Doubtless some of the lack of fit between the ideal and practice with respect to generosity has to do with limited resources, particularly regarding certain highly desired foodstuffs. This is especially true during lean times in the yearly cycle. A second factor is that whereas the hearth family is the main unit of consumption, everyone nevertheless lives in the same large room, quite able to observe what other families have to eat (although some attempts to conceal take place). Longhouse-wide sharing would be the ideal under ideal conditions. Who actually gives what to whom and when is governed by elastic conditions and allows for a fair amount of personal inclination. Such power doubtless is an incentive to produce and gather food, since one is rewarded not only by being able to eat well and feed one's family, but to give to others – a supreme pleasure for Tukanoans unless they are temporarily at odds with everyone in the longhouse. Still, along with a flexibility allowing for personal inclination in giving food comes the possibility of having one's feelings hurt. Women in particular give one another such gifts as a pineapple or haunch of meat. These decisions are made entirely by the giver, and a strong component in them is the message they carry about the affect existing between giver and receiver. Thus, if a woman does not receive a bunch of bananas she was hoping for, all she can do is reconsider her assessment of the state of the relationship between the (non-)giver and herself.

The degree to which an individual is considered to be the "owner" of a particular foodstuff depends on the amount of effort he or she has put into acquiring it or converting it into food. This is true regardless of the nature of the item or the age or sex of the individual. A piece of uncleared land is potentially available to anyone in the longhouse. When a woman announces her intention to plant it, it is considered hers as are, particularly, the crops she grows in it. Theft is most often mentioned in connection with stealing food from fields; it is even mentioned in a Bará myth. Similarly, anyone can go out and gather edible insects. If a little boy brings back some flying ants in a pot, they are his. He can eat them, share them, or let them shrivel up in the pot if he so wishes. The way in which food is served and received acknowledges who produced and prepared it. Among Tukanoans, serving is not a sign of inferiority but is the privilege of someone with something to serve – something he or she has made. Men will serve other men manioc beer because they are the hosts of the longhouse that is providing it (and also because they have participated in making it). They serve the hallucinogenic banisteriopsis to their guests for the same reason. The one exception to this general rule is the role of a Makú servant, who fetches and serves beer and lights cigars.

The question of just how limited the food resources in the Vaupés *are* in terms of nutrition must remain unanswered until further studies are carried out. I was impressed with the health and vigor of the people at Pűmanaka buro and did not ever observe a general lack of food. Meat and, less often, fish were sometimes scarce, but Bará told me that if things became really desperate, people would concern themselves more with snares and blowguns to kill various small birds. Goldman (1963, p. 85) concurs that real hunger among the Cubeo is not a problem. Langdon (1975) describes a somewhat different situation, of times of real deprivation, for the Barasana of Caño Colorado in the Pirá-paraná.

The Bará of Pűmanaka buro certainly talked about hunger, especially for meat. Juana, the headman's wife, told of a horrible period in her childhood when a windstorm blew off the roof and two of the walls of the longhouse. Hail destroyed the manioc fields. For a while, people were able to harvest the mature tubers, but after this a long period of severe hunger set in until the new fields had tubers mature enough to harvest.

Ability to feed oneself and family and, to a lesser extent, knowing that the entire longhouse community is adequately fed is an extremely important matter to Tukanoans. They see themselves as usually meeting this responsibility, offering the Makú as a contrast. Makú, they say, actually do starve at times, and some Bará have rather lurid tales to support this assertion.

It would be premature to attempt to draw a tight correlation between general characteristics of the ecosystem, the structure of food production and distribution, and values and attitudes surrounding food. Nevertheless, some speculations might be worthwhile if they can help stimulate further thinking and research on this topic.

The economy, as Goldman (1963, p. 85) has suggested, is relatively inelastic, subsistence oriented, and egalitarian. This is connected to a relative lack of abundance of foraged or cultivated foods – in comparison, for instance, to the northwest coast of North America, some other areas of Amazonia, or the yam cultivating societies of Melanesia. It also has to do with the fact that few comestibles, particularly those of greatest value and scarcity, keep for any length of time. Thus, as is true in many societies with similar levels of technology and subsistence bases, people's resources lie in other people rather than in wealth in the form of stored food or items of value that can be converted to food through exchange. This is also the situation in many African horticultural societies, although control over the productive potential of others is far more evident and hierarchically organized than in lowland South America (O'Laughlin, 1974). The difficulty of storing valued food is demonstrated when Tukanoans try to amass enough smoked meat or fish to make a decent showing at a **dabucurí**, a ceremony involving an exchange of meat or fish (brought by the guests) for beer (supplied by the hosts). Other foods, such as mirití pulp, smoked ants, grubs, and so on, are also given. The scurrying around to acquire enough game or fish, the discussions, the oblique references to someone's not doing his share, are, although by-products of the preparations, reminders to everyone of the reality of their dependence on one another. The ceremony itself beautifully expresses the fact that people are fed and taken care of by their own longhouse community and by relations maintained beyond it, rather than by each person's ability to take care of himself or herself.

The nature of the staple crop, manioc, also produces a certain amount of interdependence. The limiting factors on producing surpluses of manioc are not land or other forms of scarce resources (e.g., water or fertilizer) but other people. The bottlenecks in amassing a surplus are the labor and goodwill of the women who process it. This fact – which is very clear to Tukanoans and expressed in many myths in one form or another – is another illustration of the necessity of investing in other people and their good intentions toward oneself rather than attempting to be independent and rely solely on one's own abilities. Such social factors play a larger role in the inelasticity of the economy than technological factors per se.

Exchange in general

The patterns I have described for exchange of food are applicable to the exchange of nonfood items as well. A generalized type of reciprocity exists within the hearth family. It is important to note that both generalized and balanced reciprocity occurring between hearth families in the same longhouse and between closely associated families in different longhouses are thoroughly embedded in the wider sphere of social relations. It is fruitless to attempt a categorical separation between economically motivated activities and other kinds. For example, a man or woman who becomes lazy is far more likely to be expressing bad feelings of some kind than to be wanting to get away with less work. Similarly, intentional theft (of nonfood objects) is more likely intended as an insult or at least a sign of displeasure at the owner than motivated simply by a desire for the object. The kind of alienation from labor and its products that leads to desiring objects strictly as objects and thus being able secretly to take them is only beginning to happen in the Vaupés.

When an item is spontaneously given, very little comment is made. Certainly no expression of gratitude is offered; the debt will be settled with a return gift at some point in the future. In fact, the need to express any kind of thanks, whether

59

in response to gifts from humans or from supernatural beings is a rather foreign concept. When the more formal types of exchange are accompanied by ritual, the rituals are not concerned with expressions of gratitude.

An example of a more formal exchange ceremony is the dabucurí festival, which involves smoked meat and fish and beer. Another example is the basketry that a prospective bridegroom makes and gives to the women of his intended bride's settlement. A third is the *he-teñü* relationship reported by S. Hugh-Jones (1974) and C. Hugh-Jones (1979) for the Pirá-paraná region. This consists of an agreement made by two men standing in a classificatory cross-cousin relationship to each other (and thus automatically from different settlements) who are about the same age. They exchange ceremonial objects from time to time. Whole language groups can be spoken of as standing in he-teñü relationship to one another (C. Hugh-Jones, personal communication). Exchange in general is an integral part of marriage alliances and indeed of all ongoing relationships.

The mental account-keeping discussed in the section on food also applies to exchanges of nonfood objects or services outside the hearth family. A valued object's previous owners will be scrupulously remembered, but normally this type of ledger-keeping is not openly discussed. An exception to this occurred when a young man at Púmanaka buro, Mariquino, was jilted by a young woman. He talked endlessly about getting back the gifts he had given her, enumerating them and their value at the slightest opportunity. He also talked about his demands to her mother that she return everything and supply fariña to compensate for those gifts that were irreplaceable, such as soap. By publicly tallying up the amount of gifts made, Mariquino was explicitly severing the relationship between himself and the girl and her family. One cannot openly speak of debts in this manner without also implying criticism.

Trade and exchange occur at all levels of Vaupés society and between people sharing various degrees of intimacy. Many items are in constant circulation, and ideally one must give away anything asked for. It is in this area that the introduction of valuable goods to which people have differential access has disrupted traditional patterns of reciprocity. Far more than was true previously, objects have come to take on value in and of themselves. Traditionally the social relations standing behind any exchange – which the exchange both acknowledged and maintained – were of paramount importance. The act of exchange was important both because of the intrinsic value in all social interaction and because the maintenance of proper social relations was the means by which one ensured one's continued economic well-being. This is thoroughly illustrated in myths, which present myriad situations in which for various reasons the proper social relations are disrupted or do not exist. Their lesson is that all types of exchange are unsuccessful until the proper social relationships and expectations are reestablished.

Thus, as is true in all small-scale societies, economic relations in the Vaupés are embedded in the broader social web of relations of kinship and friendship. At least in part, one's resources lie with other people, who are either themselves the valued resource or the mediators necessary for access to other resources. Wealth per se, totally divorced from other people, is a rare entity indeed.

Acculturation has already altered this picture and continues to do so at an ever-increasing rate. The rubber camps alone have made a substantial impact, as have the mission towns and Mitú. Obviously one area of radical transformation is the introduction of money, although it is far from being a universal medium of exchange in the region. Actual cash is in fact rarely seen in the area, by either whites or Tukanoans. Perhaps if it were more abundant. white methods of exchange would hold less mystification for Tukanoans. Traditionally, of course, the value of an item or service could never be calculated in terms of an absolute value in a universal currency. Specificity of value and of spheres of exchange characterizes Tukanoan society, because in societies where most production is oriented toward immediate subsistence, specific articles or activities can be exchanged only for other specific articles or activities (O'Laughlin, 1975, p. 353). To sell baskets or labor in the Colombian market economy is utterly foreign to traditional Tukanoan culture, because, first, all traditional economic activity is embedded in the fabric of social relations. Second, many "economic" activities concerned with production are sacred, which greatly differentiates them from more secular ones. As a consequence, it is impossible to see the results of this labor as equivalent in value to other objects or services undertaken in secular contexts (unless one uses an arbitrary, non-Tukanoan standard of exchange). For example, in order to make sacred artifacts such as feather headdresses, one must be ritually pure, having previously observed food and other types of restrictions. How can one calculate the value of these observances into the worth of the resulting products? Tukanoans are dumbfounded when they discover that such objects can be bought like any other.

The **compadre** (coparenthood) system has also been introduced into the region. In the Vaupés only the asymmetrical variety is found, that is, a white becoming the **padrino** (baptismal godfather) of a Tukanoan infant. Even this form is infrequent (when compared to its development in other parts of Amazonia [cf. Murphy and Murphy, 1974, p. 37, with respect to **compadrazgo** among the Mundurucú]) and at an extremely underdeveloped stage. One reason is that at least at present many whites are desperately poor themselves and cannot afford to purchase the gifts required by the asymmetrical type of campadrazgo. Another is that in general white–Indian relationships are neither formalized nor well-established enough to permit such relationships to become customary.

It will be interesting to see the effects of increasing commercialism on native crafts. I would predict that, first, standards of quality will decrease because they will increasingly be applied by outsiders. This means that fine craftmanship will disappear because it will not raise the price. Second, the inevitable homogeniza-tion of style and pattern typical of all processes of folklorization and commercialization will result in the production of a few standard, recognizable types of baskets or pots. These styles, with size of item taken into consideration, will fetch standardized prices. To some degree this had already happened in 1970 with respect to baskets, pottery, Cubeo bark cloth, and a number of items that are not from traditional Tukanoan material culture – such as miniature canoe paddles, tipitís, and cigar holders.

Traditionally, all Tukanoans had more equitable access to scarce resources than they do today. This is not to say there was ever complete equality; for example, upstream and downstream longhouse locations vary in terms of the resources available. But, in general, in the past if a Tukanoan wanted a particular object, he either made it himself or asked someone to make it for him with an expectation of eventual repayment. Inevitably, disagreements occurred and open quarrels erupted. Some people were doubtless seen as stingy or lazy, and others were envied. If a wife was unhappy, she might quit working in her fields, bringing her husband economic hardship and indebtedness. Difficulties arising from ruptured social relations caused economic problems, whereas today increasingly it is the other way around. Tukanoans report that in the past, quarrels were usually over women rather than possessions, whereas today they are just as likely to be over possessions. Many of the disputes I witnessed arose out of disagreements about objects. The people in a Tuyuka longhouse on the Inambú River were irremediably divided in half over who was the rightful owner of a shotgun.[12] At present, factions and long-term feuds seem to be produced mainly by disagreements over white trade goods. Such goods – machetes, shotguns, clothing – are greatly desired and are now necessities for Tukanoans, yet they are difficult to obtain. Sadly, one is more likely to obtain them by ignoring rather than maintaining established patterns of obligations to kinsmen.

Decisions to take care of one's own needs rather than one's obligations to kinsmen not only can result in open quarrels but, more important, can be the source of ongoing and unresolvable negative feelings toward oneself and others – confusion, frustration, and envy. This is perhaps the saddest part of living in the Vaupés, regardless of whether one is a Tukanoan or an anthropologist feeling angry and guilty at representing a society that is destroying a viable economic system yet offering so little in return.

Property

As in all small-scale societies, it is difficult to speak of property as a single concept, because, like exchange and labor, "property" is thoroughly embedded in various social and ceremonial contexts whose meanings vary tremendously.

With respect to ownership of land, a given local descent group is associated with a given territory. The periodic changes of settlement site occur within these borders. Tukanoans have implicit usufruct rights to resources in these areas, but the concepts of "tribal lands," "inalienable rights," or "title" are foreign ones.

In previous times, when indigenous invaders threatened, they threatened life, limb, and above all women, but not land. Regardless of whether raiding and warfare are in fact the result of a need for land, protein, or a similar basic material necessity, with women being only the proximal cause (M. Harris, 1975; Ross, 1978; Siskind, 1973), this idea would not be acceptable to Tukanoans.

The presence of a government-appointed **corregidor** (magistrate), in 1970 a Tukano, in Acaricuara has introduced Tukanoans to some ideas about group and individual rights to land. But at least in 1970 this individual was very confused himself and furthermore lacked the power he needed to put his policies into action. His pronouncements were little more than food for thought for Tukanoans of the Papurí region. Moreover, much of the dominant Colombian ideology is concerned with individual rights rather than corporate rights. The latter, if properly described, would make much more sense to Tukanoans – as they are currently making sense to many Native American groups in the United States and Canada in disputes over treaties and communally held lands.

Individual property seen as inalienably owned by the individual is confined to items of almost daily use. These are the objects that tend to be buried with the person at death because of the strong identification between object and owner. Items used by several people and sacred items are normally communal property. Examples of individual private property are a man's gun or fishing canoe and a woman's old machete and baskets. All forms of adornment (in particular the ubiquitous trade beads) are personal property, in part because body decoration signals personhood. A naked two-week-old baby will be given beads and straps for ankles and wrists. One of the few nonfood gifts spontaneously given to me was a bead necklace, to make me "a Bará woman."

Examples of secular communal property are the cazabe griddle, the vats for collecting and storing starch, the pot for smoking coca leaves, and the sugar cane press. Examples of sacred communal property are the feather headdresses and the Yuruparí instruments. At times, boundaries can become blurred. When I left Púmanaka buro for the final time, Mario, the headman, gave me a beautiful black wood staff and a cigar holder, which had been made by his paternal grandfather. (The gift was actually made to my father, because women are not supposed to own such things.) It is rare to have an old item that can be given away by an individual. Mario explained that normally such items are buried when their owner dies, but his father had wanted it so much it was bequeathed to him. And Mario in turn, had saved it when his father died.

The most sacred kinds of ritual property are always communally owned. Examples are the sib's set of personal names or the Yuruparí horns (which at times are shared by two sibs; see S. Hugh-Jones, 1979, p. 143); similarly, members of a given language group own their language and mythological tradition (C. Hugh-Jones, n.d., pp. 30–31). It is impossible to divorce the strictly material from the nonmaterial, for this type of intangible property *is* property, just as it is in other small-scale societies (e.g., the Northwest coast groups or

63

Eskimo). Power is contained in ritual chants and Yuruparí music, and only people with a right to do so should engage in activities involving them.

Another type of property right, although not an exclusive one, associated with the language group is the manufacture of certain artifacts, often ceremonial in nature. An example is the bone snuff taker associated with Tatuyos. No association is made between item manufactured and name of group (for instance, Tukanos making something from toucan birds or Tatuyos from armadillos). Although perhaps not so in the past, any adult male Tukanoan today may manufacture or own one of these items; but there is still a clearly symbolic association between specific items and language groups. Another example is the finely crafted Tukano stool. Some informants, as noted earlier, mentioned Bará in connection with canoes. At present, canoes are not ceremonial objects, although they are sometimes used to hold manioc beer during festivals and are used as coffins. In the past, however, the larger canoes owned by the headmen were ceremonial, for they brought people to festivals. Unlike the smaller individually owned fishing canoes, these canoes were carefully finished and painted on the inside.

These different kinds of property rights are often symbolically associated with each language group's founding ancestors and history and are connected to the distinct roles played by each language group in Tukanoan mythology. Thus, they are important in Tukanoan cosmology and also have a more strictly economic role to play – which may have been even greater in the past.

The earlier role of specialization in manufacture of individually owned objects is not certain, but it may have resembled the situation described by Chagnon for the Yąnomamö. He describes a division of labor and craft specialization by village, adding that it is "artificial" and actually functions as "the social catalyst, the 'starting mechanism' through which mutually suspicious allies are repeatedly brought together in direct confrontation" (1968, p. 100).

As already indicated, Vaupés settlements are not mutually hostile, suspicious, or hesitant to visit one another, particularly if ongoing marriage alliances exist between them. But a more strained and mutually suspicious situation may have existed in a past involving active raiding and feuding. In much the same way as basketball games between Cuba and the United States in 1976 smoothed the way to diplomatic and economic interactions of a more delicate and potentially volatile nature, preliminary exchanges of "needed" artifacts may have facilitated marriage making and other sensitive negotiations in the Vaupés. Chagnon states that the Yąnomamö are so suspicious of settlements other than their own that they say they would not visit even those with potential wives if they did not desperately need the artifacts these villages specialize in. Yąnomamö settlements find it easier to accept another settlement's interest in their clay pots, dogs, hallucinogenic drugs, cotton hammocks, and baskets than an interest in their women. Continued intervillage contact is ensured through the obligation to repay with a different kind of item. The exchanges are always between individuals, and

64

are reminiscent of the "ceremonial brother-in-law" relationship found in the Pirá-paraná region.

According to Chagnon, such specialization among the Yąnomamö cannot be explained in terms of the distribution either of natural resources or of the technical knowledge and skills required to make the item. As evidence for this, he cites a case in which a settlement's alliance with a pot-making settlement grew so cool that they could not ask for any more pots. The villagers responded to this by suddenly "remembering" how pots were made and "discovering" that the clay in their neighborhood was suitable after all (1968, p. 100).

Private property is always lent if borrower and lender are on good terms. Thievery is usually an expression of disrupted social relations more than anything else, because it is difficult to conceal the fact that one has stolen something. Nevertheless, Tukanoans are becoming familiar with the idea of stealing and "getting away with it," and they talk about earlier times when one's cargo was safe in a canoe overnight, which is not always the case at present. A quasihuman or subhuman character is frequently imputed to cases of theft. Makú are said to steal, for example. When a danger exists of theft of cargo left overnight in canoes, the thieves are spoken of in somewhat supernatural terms – they are sometimes said to be able to fly, for example. The same is true for whites, who comprise another not-quite-human category. The Bará described to me a kind of forest demon who comes to a longhouse when everyone is gone and steals valuable objects, including any small children who have stayed behind. He always signs his name on pieces of paper and scatters them about so that people will know who has been there, and he dresses in shirt, trousers, and rubber boots.

Leadership

The Vaupés share with other Amazon Basin societies certain characteristics in leadership and political organization. For example, in general, leaders have relatively little power and authority, and although headmen in many societies, including Tukanoan society, inherit their office, they cannot become lazy or despotic with impunity. Most often, leaders must give more than the others in order both to attain and to maintain their positions even though the position of headman is usually inherited (but see Kracke, 1978). This contrasts with some other parts of the world, for example, Melanesia, where the opposite holds, and the ability to accumulate is the path to power and prestige.

Leadership in the Vaupés and other Amazonian societies has an ad hoc quality. Positions are often task-specific and temporary. A contributing factor in the relative lack of importance and permanence attached to leadership positions is the ease with which a disgruntled individual, family, or faction can leave a settlement and live elsewhere. Because one of the main tasks of a headman (and an important diagnostic of his success and source of his higher status) is to hold a community together, the possibility that some of his constituency might leave is a continual and unpleasant consideration. Thus the relationship between leaders and followers is a strongly voluntary one, a fact that undoubtedly plays a role in determining the type of person who can become a successful leader.

In general, the political structures characterizing the Vaupés and other low-land South American societies are relatively acephalous, with legal and juridical procedures informal and largely implicit. Much more research needs to be carried out in this area, and the *meaning* of such concepts as power, authority, or influence in societies of this type needs to be better understood (Arvelo-Jiménez, 1971; Rivière, 1971). These generalizations regarding personal power do not apply as much to Tukanoan war leaders, although like the others these leadership roles were characterized by task specificity and temporality. During hostilities, war chiefs apparently had a fair amount of personal power, at times over a much larger group of people than normally. This seems to be true for the Vaupés (Markham, 1910). It is generally true in the Amazon Basin that any manifestation of personal power by an individual, whether over humans, super-natural beings, or game, is met with ambivalence and suspicion on the part of other members of the society. This undoubtedly lessens the desirability of these kinds of positions and decreases the number of aspirants. Leaders are often little more than older men with certain not-too-remarkable qualities – better judge-ment, diplomatic skills, ability to organize and entertain – or simply well-respected adult men. Many of the traits we tend to associate with political leaders, such as arrogance, cunning, and egotism, are much more likely to be seen as characteristics of misfits or overly ambitious malcontents, who are very seldom chosen as leaders. (See Murphy [1961] for a well-presented discussion of the dif-ferences in leadership qualities found between Brazilians and the Mundurucú.)

Although political structures in these societies are in general acephalous and decentralized, social control mechanisms such as ordeals, duels, feuds, and "voluntary" emigration do maintain a certain degree of order (Dole, 1966). Serious cases of antisocial behavior are most often seen to be spiritual as well as secular crimes – indeed, this dichotomy is meaningless in most instances. Executions and other serious punishments meted out by headmen or shamans are often seen as having been decided and sentenced by higher authorities. For example, in some groups an execution takes place only after a divination has demonstrated supernatural approval of it. The participation of spirits or ancestors is necessary, because all such "criminal" cases involve a disruption of harmonic relations between human and spiritual worlds (Butt, 1965–66; Dole, 1964).

I did not have the opportunity to witness a truly strong headman on a day-to-day basis in the Vaupés. When I arrived at Pûmanaka buro, it consisted of five families, and when I left, only two families were still living in the longhouse under the headman, Mario. A satellite house built alongside the longhouse during my stay started with one hearth family but grew into three following two marriages. One of the three hearth families who left during my stay had a history of moving in and out. They had a small house upstream. The head of this family, Anastasio, was older than Mario, and a certain amount of rivalry existed between them. The two other hearth families moved out over a single issue. The precipitating reason was a young woman, Magdalena, in one family who became pregnant by a young man, Juanico, in the other. As is always the case, these departures were also the result of a number of long-standing frictions. The headman, Mario, played a complex role in all of this, both as the head of one hearth family and as headman.

It is difficult to generalize about the position of headman when only one specific person playing the role is seen on a day-to-day basis. It is my impression that Mario was a typical headman in many respects, despite his failure to resolve the crisis just mentioned. Other information I have about the position comes from myths and anecdotes and hearing news about other settlements and their headmen from time to time.

The headman of a longhouse has some authority and almost no real power (i.e., being able to back up requests made to others with a threat of sanction). Vaupés headmen undoubtedly have less power and authority than those in many other places where villages are larger or where the possibility of warfare still exists. A Tukanoan headman rarely directly tells another individual what to do. He leads by initiating activity himself or by suggesting what should be done to the group as a whole. Tukanoans have learned that whites attribute more power to headmen than they actually have, and when the people talk with whites (particularly if in Spanish) they will often exaggerate the power of the office and of a given headman. If the traditional headman is the same person as the **capitán** (the position of headman recognized by missionaries) – which is not always the case – his power is thereby increased. Sometimes an older man is the traditional headman, and his son, more missionized and able to speak Spanish, is called capitán by the priests, who will refer to that settlement by the younger man's name. Some priests are unaware of the traditional headmen in the settlements they visit.

The term for longhouse headman can be roughly glossed as "owner of the house." A specific longhouse will be referred to by its site name (most also have a saint's name given by the priests) or as "so-and-so's house." Sometimes a headman's Tukanoan name is used (e.g., Pai ya wi; Pai is the traditional personal name for a man in the headman line for the *Bará Yóara* sib at Pũmanaka buro), but his Spanish name is also used: Mario ya wi ("Mario's house").

Although he usually inherits the position, an effective headman must also have certain qualities. These include a level head, good judgement, tact, an ability to contribute more than others, and an ability to initiate and direct activities without being overbearing. An asymmetrical exchange occurs between the other residents of the longhouse and the headman and his wife, for they give more energy to the group as a whole in exchange for higher status. A headman's wife works harder than the other women throughout her life. She invariably helps with communal labor (e.g., sweeping), most often initiating it. She must also produce more manioc beer than the other women.

Any individual who does not want to live under a particular headman will move out. However, when a family moves out it is for complex reasons. Disagreements with the headman can concern him as head of another faction in addition to his role as headman.

Ideally, everyone who "belongs" to a longhouse should live in it (i.e., people should live with their closest agnatic kinsmen). It is the headman's job to see that this happens as much as possible. He should also try to see that the affairs of the longhouse are decided and carried out in as democratic a manner as possible.

Perhaps when the office of headman did involve more decisions and power, refusal to live under the authority of a particular headman *qua* headman was more frequently the reason for a longhouse fissioning. The disputes I heard about all concerned other types of problems. But in the past more hearth families lived under a single roof, and thus a greater need existed for organization and leadership, which when not forthcoming was more visible and intolerable. Headmen who were successful war chiefs undoubtedly had much more power, at least during times of crisis.

At present, no political organization in a formal sense exists in the Vaupés at a level above that of the settlement. There is evidence that in the past, Indians formed federations in the various uprisings against rubber gatherers and other whites (Markham, 1910). And in the future, if the federation plans of some of the corregidores (Tukanoans appointed by the government in each of the mission towns; their tasks are unclear, but they are to represent the town and their language group) are successful, a corporate decision-making body may emerge that involves a substantial number of settlements. At present, political activity that includes Tukanoans from more than one settlement is not organized along any formalized lines and does not involve anything more than the most temporary ad hoc kinds of groups.

5.

Vaupés social structure

The settlement

At 0.2 inhabitants per square kilometer (Instituto Geográfico "Agustín Codazzi," 1969, p. xii), the population density of the Vaupés is comparable to that of many hunter–gatherer groups as well as to the more sparsely populated horticulturalist societies in New Guinea (Glasse and Meggitt, 1965). Thus, although Tukanoan settlements are concentrated on or near rivers and streams, they are still extremely isolated, an isolation compounded by the difficulty of traveling either by river or by land. Longhouses currently hold approximately 20 to 40 people (some of these are children who attend mission school for up to eleven months of the year). Nucleated villages have anywhere from 12 to approximately 60 inhabitants, and some mission towns have more than 100 people.

The census I took in 1968–70 shows approximately 165 settlements for the region south of the Vaupés River, including the Papurí River and its tributaries, the Tiquié above Buena Vista, and the Pirá-paraná above Carurú Rapids. In 1970 this figure included 24 longhouses. The remaining settlements are a variety of arrangements, from one- or two-family groups to large mission towns, so making generalizations about the Vaupés settlements is somewhat tricky. Although the majority of settlements are nucleated villages, these do not necessarily represent a simple changeover from longhouse to several small one-family houses containing the same inhabitants. As has been pointed out, several longhouse groups, or segments of them, may make up one of the larger villages. And household composition in settlements on the Vaupés near Mitú is sometimes based on affinal rather than agnatic ties, usually involving a couple, their daughter and son-in-law, and at times various other relatives.[1]

Tukanoans located on downstream sites, on major rivers, and near mission towns are more acculturated than their upriver counterparts. To some extent this allows generalizations about degree of acculturation for entire language groups. For example, the Desana, Tukano, and Uanano are as a whole more acculturated than the Tuyuka, Bará, and Tatuyo because traditionally the former have been

69

located in the more accessible parts of the region. As has been indicated, the more acculturated Tukanoans feel superior to their "backwater" compatriots.

The overall recent trend has been to abandon longhouses,[2] in part in response to pressure from missionaries, and to build smaller mud-walled houses in nucleated villages or mission towns. The patrilocal rule of residence and settlement exogamy are also breaking down, both because missionaries settle members of different language groups in the same settlement and because Tukanoans now are starting to form households based on affinal ties between males.

In traditional Tukanoan life, people living in a settlement are linked to one another in terms of two profoundly important organizational principles: coresidence and local descent group membership. Obviously all the people living at a settlement are its coresidents, although at times it is difficult to distinguish between those who are residing there and those who are merely visiting. The local descent group is (ideally) composed only of those people who are born there and who are one another's closest agnatic kin. Inmarried women are not adopted into this group but remain members in absentia in their natal local descent groups. Thus these women are in a pivotal position, living in and identifying with their new settlement as residents, creating ties to it through their husband and children in addition to any they may have had prior to marriage. But their ties to their own natal local descent group remain strong, and conflict occurring between the two can produce psychic turmoil in women caught in the middle. This theme is found in a number of myths, which picture these conflicts in the starkest of terms, resulting in betrayal and death of either husband and children on the one hand or of parents and brothers on the other. Where a woman's sympathies *should* lie is a moot point, one of the paradoxes of this type of social structure, and the portrayal of this in myths supports the Lévi-Straussian view that myths fundamentally deal with the unresolvable and unwelcome contradictions of life (Leach, 1970, p. 80).

It is important to note that coresidence is in itself a crucial factor, regardless of how the members of a settlement are otherwise related. Virtually all settlements have people living in them who "do not belong" in terms of the patrilocal residence rule. These people participate fully in the life of the community and, over time, form close bonds with their fellow residents. Still, it would undoubtedly take at least two generations for them and their children to be assimilated into the local descent group as bona fide members, and it might take much longer (I have no actual cases of such assimilation). Further evidence of the strength of the coresidence factor is that settlement exogamy is the norm even when the actual kinship relations between two people would allow them to marry; I recorded no such marriages, with the exception of a few made by Tukanoans living in the same mission town. I asked informants about hypothetical matches, for example, one involving a Bará boy and a Tuyuka girl (whose father was away at a rubber camp) growing up at Púmanaka buro, and was told that they would not want to marry each other.

The levirate (i.e., a widow's being expected to marry her dead husband's brother if at all possible) is further evidence of the strength of ties built up over time by coresidence and of the desirability of having the children born into a community reared in it.

Thus the local descent group is a corporate group – the only descent-based group that invariably is, because both descent and residence are requirements for membership. Although some residents at a particular settlement are not members of its local descent group, for many purposes we can consider them as if they were. Thus, regardless of whatever the actual kinship relations are, the coresidents of a settlement live, work, and communicate with one another as a unit, and form strong bonds on these bases alone. Special ties are forged between pairs or larger groupings of individuals because of their daily interaction and the special emotional flavor and intensity produced by this closeness. The strength of these ties is revealed when a chronic dispute becomes so intolerable that a family or other segment decides to leave. The major rift of this sort that occurred at Púmanaka buro during my stay was precipitated by a case of incest, but many other types of quarrels can leave wounds that do not heal. When a family leaves, the entire settlement is critically wounded, not only because of the blows to its pride and sense of unity but also because its members must sever many personal ties created over a long period of intimate interaction and sharing.

The sib

Vaupés sibs (clans) are named, ranked, exogamous, localized patrilineal descent groups. Sib structure and unilineal descent in general were once thought to be far more common in the Amazon that has turned out to be the case: Many lowland South American societies have been reclassified from unilineal to cognatic, but this is not true of those of the Northwest Amazon. Sibs were correctly identified for this region by Whiffen (1915) and Nimuendajú (1950), with further clarification appearing in accounts by Goldman (1948) and Fulop (1955).[3]

In principle, the local descent group is coterminous with the sib. That in reality it most often is not is the result of many factors, one of which is the inroads of acculturation on traditional social structure. But the lack of fit between idealized structure and reality also derives from the fluidity found in Vaupés social groups even in their most traditional state. Although the sib is a very important social unit for Tukanoans, a concern with sib boundaries as such (or for language group or phratry boundaries), particularly with respect to genealogical reckoning, does not characterize Tukanoan thinking about sibs. An indicator of this is the lack of tightly defined labels for sibs and other social structural units. The expressions used are imprecise (e.g., "children of one parent," referring to the original sibling group ancestral to a present-day sib; or "children of such-and-such anaconda") and are sometimes applied to different levels of inclusion. This lack of precision does not appear only when applied to specific on-the-ground group-

71

ings over time but characterizes some of the idealized statements about sibs as well. At the highest level of abstraction, illustrated by Figure 4, everything is tightly bounded and precise. Of course, assimilation and fission due to demographic fluctuations and acculturation create ambiguity and contradiction; today the system is changing in a very speeded-up fashion. But the fluidity appears at more than an empirical level and is due not only to some sort of "breakdown" but to built-in features of the system that allow it; this point is made by other Vaupés specialists as well (for instance, C. Hugh-Jones, 1979, pp. 22–23). Paradoxically, the clearest picture to be had of the underlying principles of Vaupés social organization appears when a Tukanoan is asked about an unfamiliar group; although concrete information is more scanty, what the individual knows will be described in regularized terms that conform to these principles – a much more difficult task when describing more familiar groups whose aberrations and exceptions to such principles cannot be ignored.

At present, very few local descent groups are exactly coterminous with the sibs to which they belong.[4] A local descent group may be a lineage forming part of a sib, parts of two sibs, or two entire sibs (Jackson, 1972, app. 1). Usually this lack of fit does not matter, and sibs and local groups are spoken of as if they were always the same thing, and in many respects they are. Both are local groups. Membership in both is reckoned primarily through agnatic links – although Tukanoans do not care about lineage formation per se, and genealogical memories are shallow.

Sibs are named, and these names often refer to plants or animals. Sib names can also refer to sib ancestors and their immediate descendants; this is also true for the personal names owned by each sib. These personal names are given to infants in a prescribed order. The eldest son of the headman ideally is the first-born male of his generation and receives the first name on the list. This sib-supplied name fosters growth, for it associates the newborn child with a nurturing group of agnatic kinsmen. The infant becomes more human upon receiving a name, for it is an explicit affirmation of membership in the sib, entitling it to the power and nurturance available from the ancestors.

The sib name is an important component of its definition: C. Hugh-Jones has noted that the "identity of a sib is so intimately bound up with the name that, in a sense, the name is the sib" (1979, p. 26). She also notes that dispute over sib membership revolves around which named sib a person properly belongs to, as opposed to disagreements about genealogical links.

The sibs in a given language group are ranked. The order of ranking is explained as corresponding to the order in which a group of brothers, the ancestors of the various sibs, emerged from the rocks at a particular rapids site. According to Bará informants, the "first people" came from the east in an anaconda canoe[5] piloted by Koá-mahkū, a culture hero. The Bará were the last to leave the canoe, getting off at Yapú Rapids on the upper Papurí. Beyond this point, Diró koá poná (literally, "piece-of-meat-bone-offspring"), two

Level	1						2		3
I	1						2		3
II	Bará			Tukano	Wühaná	etc.	Tuyuka	etc.	etc.
III	Bará Yóara	Waíñakoroa	etc.	(approx. 30 sibs)	etc.				etc.
IV	A (Pümanaka buro, 1979) co-agnates · B · C · etc.	M N O P Y Z		etc.					etc.

Figure 4. Traditional Vaupés social structure. Level I represents the phratry, an unnamed unit composed of various language groups; at level II is the language group, which is commonly referred to as "tribe"; at level III is the sib, a named group that occupies one or more settlements along a stretch of river; and at level IV is the local descent group, which can be coterminous with the sib and is composed of coagnates who are one another's closest agnatic kin and who share the same settlement (traditionally a longhouse). The capital letters in level IV represent current locations of local descent groups, who are known by their settlement name, which, unlike the sib name, changes when the local descent group moves its longhouse site.

culture heroes who are brothers, closed off the land, making it impossible for the canoe to travel any farther. They did this by creating Ewüra taró, a mirití swamp from which all rivers are said to originate.

The ranking of sibs is continued today with the use of elder–younger sibling terms between members of different sibs. However, in some language groups the difference in rank between certain pairs of sibs is so great that generational divisions are brought into play. This results in an unusual and initially surprising usage of coagnatic terminology. A person who belongs to a considerably higher ranked sib than another will address the other as ''uncle'' or ''grandfather.'' This seemingly incongruous state of affairs is explained by Tukanoans as follows: The first ancestors of all the sibs of one language group were brothers to one another. The eldest brother emerged from the rocks at the rapids first, and the youngest last. However, there were many brothers in the beginning, and obviously there were many years between the birth of the eldest and the youngest brother. By the time the youngest brother emerged at the rapids, the eldest was very old, and had great-grandchildren. Thus, although the eldest and youngest brothers called each other ''brother,'' because many years had passed between their births the younger brothers were addressing as ''grandchild'' those individuals in the eldest brother's sib who were close to them in age. This is why, today, when people of about the same age are heard using grandparent and grandchild terms to each other, it is the one who says ''grandfather'' and who is called ''grandson'' who is of higher rank.

Sib rank is signaled in other ways as well. One method of indicating a sib's very low rank is to impugn its origins with the claim that it is a ''new'' member of the language group. It will be implied that this sib was originally a Makú-like group, ''who were our servants, who had to be taught how to build houses and speak our language. Then, taking pity on them, we adopted them as our youngest-brother sib.'' (This is not a verbatim quotation but a composite of a number of conversations.) The *Wamütañará* (named after a fernlike plant, *Selagenella* sp.), a Bará sib, is ascribed this origin by members of higher-ranked sibs.

Another way of indicating a sib's low rank is to imply, during a recital of the origin myths, that the sib's ancestors did not come from the underworld river (Opēkő dia, sometimes identified with the Amazon River), which joins the Vaupés far to the east, but rather were picked up much farther upstream. The Wamütañará sib is spoken of as boarding the canoe at Yapú Rapids on the upper Papurí, rather than farther downstream. The ascent of the ancestors from Opēkő dia concerns the origin of both sibs and language groups. But the origin of sibs is usually depicted as the emergence of each sib's ancestor – siblings to one another – out of the rocks at a specific rapids site, their ''birth'' order determining subsequent sib rank. Speaking of an ancestor of a Bará sib as ascending in the anaconda canoe, in this case the Wamütañará, hints that this sib is seen as rather distant from other, higher ranking Bará sibs. The distinction

74

between the ancestors as parents of sibs and parents of language groups is often murky in regard to specific groups and categories; this will be discussed later.

Another mythical reference to sib rank occurs in the myth of Waí Pinó Mahkó, "Fish Anaconda Daughter." Anacondas are considered to be the progenitors of all fish. The various species of fish are also ranked like sibs, with Fish Anaconda at the head. Fish Anaconda Daughter marries a human, Yebá Mahû who travels with her to her longhouse – where all the fish people (Waí mahã) live. Yebá Mahû sees fish all around him and wants to eat some. His father-in-law, Fish Anaconda, seeing this tells him to eat Tarira fish (*doé, Erythrinus* sp.) because, "although Doé were Fish Anaconda's younger brothers, they were like Wamûtañará are to us" (i.e., they were the lowest-ranking species and therefore the most expendable).

A different way of pointing out low sib rank is to imply that such-and-such sib, in the recent past or now, behaves inappropriately. One Bará man of (according to him) the highest-ranking sib, Bará Yóara, assured me that in the past his sib always wore bark-cloth loincloths (*wedira*), whereas the men of the lower-ranking sibs went totally unclothed.

Linguistic cues can also signal low rank, at least according to members of high-ranked sibs. Members of the Wamûtañará sib were described by other Bará as speaking ungrammatically and with incorrect pronunciation (C. Hugh-Jones, 1979, p.18; also see Chapter 9).

It may be that in the past the most appropriate marriages were seen to be between people from equivalently ranked sibs of affinally related exogamous groups (i.e., language groups). This would follow the ideal Cubeo pattern, although the Cubeo case does not involve different language-affiliated exogamous units. I did not find any evidence of this, however, and S. Hugh-Jones notes that contemporary Barasana deny that this would happen (1977, p. 206).

With so many available indicators of sib rank, one might expect that investigating and drawing conclusions about the names of present-day sibs, their relative ranking, and the meaning and function of sib structure would be an easy task. Such is unfortunately not the case. Although the lists I obtained concerning Bará sibs were in general agreement as to their locations and rank, they never completely tallied with one another. And Bará elsewhere (for instance, in the Pirá-paraná) have rather different classification systems; for example C. Hugh-Jones's data indicate that Inambú Bará belong to the Hamoa sib; I have no mention of such a Bará sib in my notes. In general, therefore, Tukanoans can be seen as notoriously slippery in their evaluation of relative sib rank and understanding of who lives where. All Bará I spoke to did, however, agree that Wamûtañará were the lowest ranked.

The meaning of sib structure, including the question of hierarchy versus equality and its functions in present-day Tukanoan society, is also problematic. We can certainly conclude that sib hierarchy today has almost an exclusively symbolic meaning. One would expect, of course, symbolic statements ultimately to reflect social processes in some fashion; in the Vaupés this association, if existing at all, did so only in the past, and the nonritualistic behavioral correlates have been lost owing to declining population numbers and cultural loss as the result of acculturation. The Hugh-Joneses discovered an extremely interesting system of five-tiered sib ranking differentiated by specialist roles. These are (in descending order): headman, dancer, warrior, shaman, and "cigar lighter." This last category is obviously close to Makú status. (The ranking is in fact more complex; see C. Hugh-Jones, 1977, p. 186; 1979, pp. 27, 65–67.) They also discuss the possibility of this being a pan-Vaupés system. I cannot supply any additional data with respect to this set of specialist roles (which play no significant role in daily life today, and perhaps did not in the past) except to point out bits of confirming evidence in myths, some associations made between Makú and low-ranking Bará sibs (see Chapter 8), and some connections in present-day Bará sib names. For example, Bará Yóara, the sib represented at Púmanaka buro, almost certainly corresponds to the Hugh-Joneses' dancer specialization. Awareness of this as a system seems to have virtually disappeared for the Papurí region (it could also be, of course, that I did not ask enough of the right questions).

Sibs are exogamous, but this is not their function; nor can we find evidence for any economic, political, or other social regulation that might fall under control of the system of ranked sibs. The *only* current economic difference, an indirect and very slight one, is the tendency for higher-ranked sibs to be located more downstream than the lower-ranked ones (see Chapter 4). Thus, at least today, sib rank does not imply any difference in power, wealth, or style of life (S. Hugh-Jones, 1979, p. 2).

Sib organization today seems mainly to make statements about group membership and relative closeness among various units. These statements are almost exclusively symbolic. Ritual property seen as owned by the sib includes a set of Yuruparí instruments and the right to avail oneself of the benefits from their use. Speech differences, as mentioned earlier, also are seen to correlate with sib boundaries (although not nearly so extensively as those that ought to separate exogamous units); minute differences in speech behavior, therefore, are certainly markers and perhaps can be seen as intangible property belonging to a sib (this is discussed further in Chapter 9). Other kinds of customs, for instance, those related to artifact manufacture, sometimes are described in similar fashion, although expectably this is hard to pin down in black-and-white terms (the minute one attempts to do so, one is contradicted by a Tukanoan quite clearly uncomfortable with someone else's making the kinds of invidious comparisons he or she has just finished making).

In general we can say that the closer a given pair of unilineal descent-based units is (closeness loosely conceived of in genealogical and geographical terms) the more similar will be their ritual property and rights to its use. Because such property and rights ultimately relate to ancestral power, "it is quite appropriate that variation in rights to ritual items should mirror descent ties between groups'' (C. Hugh-Jones, 1979, p. 30).

Before leaving localized groups for larger units, it might be helpful to summarize their important characteristics, disregarding for the moment the differences existing between types of unit (e.g., local descent group, sib, settlement). The group of people living at a single place – the settlement – is the most important unit in the Vaupés social system. Residence and kinship, both crucial for building cohesive, long-lasting social groups, operate at this, and only this, level. The settlement's importance is further underscored when we consider its isolation from other settlements and the degree of autonomy it has in many interactional, economic, political, and ritual areas of life. Undoubtedly the more inclusive units of Vaupés social organization are not as cognitively and affectively important to Tukanoans.

The important features of traditional local group organization in the Vaupés include (1) communal multifamily longhouses, one per settlement; (2) named patrilineal, exogamous, localized sibs; (3) patrilocal rule of residence; (4) settlement exogamy; (5) a tendency to classify affines as ''not like us,'' or ''outsiders''; (6) a list of personal names possessed by each sib given at birth in a specified order; (7) sib names that sometimes have a ''totemic'' flavor, that is, an association with a plant or animal.[6] Sometimes this association is made more explicit by attributing similarities in qualities between the members of a sib and its eponym.

This constellation of features is found only in the Central Northwest Amazon area and is the key to understanding many aspects of its social organization. Probably most important are the patrilineal localized sibs, and settlement exogamy.

The language group

Tukanoan settlements exhibit an autonomy in many important respects and an equally fundamental dependence on other settlements in others. Settlements have been structurally interdependent at least since the establishment of the rule of local exogamy; it is perhaps this feature of Tukanoan social organization that has been most influential in producing the degree of regional network organization found at present in the Vaupés. I do not know when the rule of local exogamy came to be observed completely (as it is today, with the exception of some marriages made in mission towns). Earlier documentary evidence (e.g., Koch-Grünberg, 1909–10; Wallace, 1889/1972, p. 346) indicates its existence during their visits. In some respects settlements were more autonomous in the past, simply because longhouses were much larger than now (MacCreagh, 1926; McGovern, 1927) and some settlements may have contained more than one longhouse.

As is true for relationships within the settlement, most intersettlement interac-

77

tion is structured along kinship lines. Every Tukanoan is in some respect a kinsman of every other Tukanoan, or at least potentially so. One important way in which kinship ties, agnatic or affinal, are structured is through the system of more than sixteen exogamous language groups.

In Tukanoan mythology, language groups originated when the anaconda canoe ascended Opēkő dia and the Vaupés River, bringing the ancestors into the region. As they traveled upstream, they became increasingly more human, acquiring skills and knowledge about useful plants and animals. As the canoe passed various rapids and other landmarks, the ancestors of specific groups left the canoe and began settling the surrounding area. According to the Bará they were the last to leave the canoe, and the ranked sibs emerged at Yapú Rapids. In another version of the myth, the "children of one parent" (*hiká poná*, full siblings), who spoke the same language (*maniya waderá*, "our language"), emerged from Yuruparí Rapids on the Vaupés River. This group included the Waí mahā ("fish people"), Dahea (Tukano), Kümará poná ("children of the rainy season," now a Tukano sib), and Wahüná (a group living on the Vaupés River and probably the same as Koch-Grünberg's Uásona, "Pisa-Tapuyo"). Underneath the Yuruparí Rapids is what can be glossed as the "first-people longhouse" (Pamüri Wi), which is also known as the longhouse of the Waí mahā. Thus, whereas Yapú Rapids and in general the upper Papurí refers to the Bará when conceived of as a group of ranked sibs, Yuruparí Rapids refers to the emergence of an exogamous group. As is typical of myths, basic "facts," or truths, are approached from different vantage points and described in different and at times contradictory ways. It should also be noted that the list of four groups emerging at Yuruparí Rapids is undoubtedly one of several versions of this section of the origin myth.

Thus, the basic features of Vaupés social structure dealt with in the Bará origin myth are (1) the arrival of separate groups of Tukanoans and the process of becoming fully human through the acquisition of artifacts and materials, knowledge, and skills; (2) the origin of the system of ranked sibs in the birth order of the original sibling set; (3) the origin of the "children of one parent" who must seek marriage partners from other groups; and (4) the assertion that in the beginning, such "children of one parent" spoke the same language. The emerging of four groups at Yuruparí Rapids implies that they all spoke the same language, even though now two of these groups, Dahea and Kümará poná, are identified with Tukano (this is discussed later in the section on phratries).

Keeping in mind that the actual situation is more complex, we can initially define the language group as it exists today as a named patrilineal descent unit composed of from six to more than thirty sibs, ideally identified with a distinct language. Sixteen or more are found in the region. Their members observe a rule of exogamy and most often terminologically distinguish agnates from other kinsmen at this level. Members of a given language group identify with co-members as "brother people." Distinguishing features that serve as significant symbols of

identity are (1) the language and name themselves; (2) separate founding ancestors and distinct roles in the basic Tukanoan origin myth cycle; (3) the right to
ancestral power through the use of certain linguistic property such as sacred
chants; (4) the right to manufacture and use certain kinds of ritual property such
as the Yuruparí instruments (which may actually belong to the sib); and (5) a
traditional association with certain ceremonial or near-ceremonial objects. The
difference between items 4 and 5 is that the latter type of object may be
manufactured or owned by Tukanoans not of the language group associated with
it. The exceptions to this definition of Vaupés language groups are discussed
later.

Language groups do not occupy an exclusive and continuous territory. Map 2
shows the distribution of some Vaupés settlements according to language group
affiliation. The degree of language group interspersion by settlement varies
subregionally; for example, they are more territorially circumscribed in the
Pirá-paraná region. All language groups *are* confined to specific areas within
the region as a whole, but it is equally true that all language groups have some of
their member settlements interspersed with settlements belonging to other language groups.

I have chosen to emphasize the feature of language affiliation in my choice of
terminology for these units (as opposed to *tribe* or the Hugh-Joneses' *exogamous
group*) for several reasons. The first and most important one is that this is the way
the Tukanoans talked about it. Of course, what people say they do and what they
actually do may not be entirely the same. But the notion of the coincidence of
linguistic and agnatic boundaries is an extremely strong one, and my research has
shown that this ideal coincidence is almost perfectly matched in practice among
Papurí groups. C. Hugh-Jones notes that the number of exceptions to this
"among Pirá-paraná groups probably reflects their marginal position at the
southwestern extreme of the Tukanoan culture area in the same way that the
exceptional language situation among the Cubeo probably reflects their extreme
northerly position" (1979, p. 19). Doubtless in part because the Hugh-Joneses
worked in the Pirá-paraná and therefore the exceptions made a strong impression on them (I was unaware of *any* exceptions until conferring with them), they
have opted for the term *exogamous group*. For the same reasons, although
reversed, I stick to the term *language group*. I do want to make clear that I can
incorporate exceptions into the general model, and in those instances language
obviously will not be an invariant feature; the difference has to do with what we
wish to highlight with our choice of label. And, just as the existence of
exceptions raises problems with my terminology, so does the existence of a
phratric organization at a level more inclusive than "simple exogamous groups"
create difficulties with that label (C. Hugh-Jones, 1979, pp. 15–20). In sum, the
situation is complex and it is not easy to find a term both clear and yet not
oversimplified. *Language group* is a perfectly adequate term if the exceptions are
borne in mind. In general, the language–exogamous unit equation is extremely

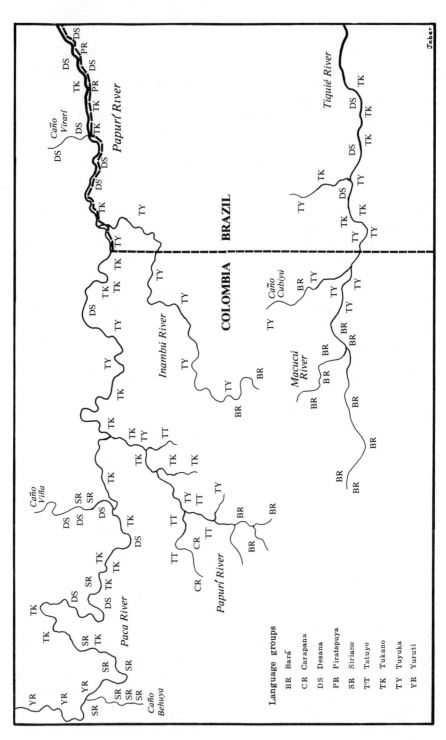

Map 2. Membership of settlements, either longhouses or small villages, by language group of a section of the Vaupés.

pervasive, being found even among the Yukuna, Tanimuka, Letuama, and Matapí groups in the Apaporis region to the south (Jacopin, 1981).

Table 1 lists the language group affiliation of Tukanoans in the marriage sample I collected during fieldwork in 1968–70. Although it is not by any means a complete census of language group membership for the multilingual area, it is a nearly complete census of the living married Tukanoans in the Papurí–upper Tiquié drainage region in 1968–70, including the inmarried women from natal settlements elsewhere and the women born in the area who have married into settlements elsewhere.

Table 1 gives a list of marriages and language group affiliations collected from Tukanoans mainly of the Papurí–upper Tiquié drainage. Thus, the names of the language groups are not to be seen as *the* list of social groups identifying themselves by language and marrying exogamously, a list accepted by all Tukanoans in the entire Vaupés. Although the Tukanoans I talked to agreed completely about people in nearby territory, vague and disputed language group designations appeared when a Tukanoan was discussing groups farther away. It is apparent that the way members of *those* groups describe their social universe is at times quite different from the classifications offered by Papurí Tukanoans. C. Hugh-Jones discusses this issue in general terms by noting that "the problem inherent in all attempts to define social structural units in the Vaupés is that Indians are more concerned with the types of relationship (hierarchy, etc.) outlined in the model above than with the precise definition of social boundaries" (1979, pp. 22–23). In this same paragraph she notes that named groups overlap in membership at times and sometimes the categories are "sliding" – covering a more or less extensive population, depending on context.

These complications stem from several sources, in addition to the one noted of Tukanoans' relative lack of concern about details of boundary maintenance. First of all, a number of Tukanoans (particularly ones in the Papurí–Tiquié region, my principal informants) do not understand, or at least do not admit, that a genuine regional variability exists with respect to the definition of *language group;* these definitional differences are apparently limited to the Pirá-paraná but are important, nonetheless, although there the ideal of a coincidence of language unit and exogamous group (C. Hugh-Jones, 1979, p. 18) does exist. Second, Cubeo do not have to marry out of the Cubeo-speaking unit. Third, all Tukanoans tend to make situations appear neater than they are in fact, with the result that some individuals even in the Pirá-paraná will simplify the situation when talking with an outsider, as was the case with a Carapana informant from Caño Ti from whom I collected some material on social structure. Fourth, some investigators have not fully understood the basic outlines of Vaupés social classification, which has led to contradictory lists and descriptions in the available literature. Fifth, Tukanoans do not have words for "sib," "exogamous group," or "phratry." Sometimes language groups are designated by using the name of one of their high-ranking sibs as well as the language name, but at times this sib name covers some but not

81

Table 1. *Language group affiliation of Tukanoans in sample*

Language	Men	Women	Total
Bará	104	86	190
Tuyuka	160	117	277
Tukano	153	162	315
Desana	65	77	142
Carapana	40	20	60
Tatuyo	28	40	68
Siriano	73	50	123
Yurutí	16	25	41
Piratapuya	8	13	21
Uanano	4	8	12
Cubeo	8	25	33
Barasana	5	25	30
Taiwano	1	6	7
Makuna	3	9	12
Tariano	0	11	11
Curripaco	0	2	2
Carihona	1	1	2
Makú	0	1	1
Wahüná (Pisá–Tapuyo?)	0	2	2
Metuno	2	0	2
Arapaso	2	2	4
Non-Indians	11	2	13
Total	684	684	1,368

Note: The figures in this table are not representative of relative population sizes because this sample was mainly gathered in the Papurí region.

all of the sibs in a given language group. Sixth, the boundaries of the multilingual Central Northwest Amazon are still not clearly defined, and many of the groups living near the boundaries are poorly studied. Seventh, all Tukanoans are undergoing rapid cultural, social, and linguistic change at different rates depending on their location. And, eighth and finally, as noted in Chapter 1, much work remains to be done on the languages of the region themselves. Linguistic surveys have been made (Sorensen, 1967; Waltz and Wheeler, 1970), providing lists of languages with their relative distance from one another. Still, all Tukanoans are multilingual, and establishing the correlation between language differences and cultural differences is problematic in the Vaupés, as pointed out in the discussion of the term *tribe*. In addition, some groups are known to have changed their language (Goldman, 1963, p. 26; C. Hugh-Jones, 1979, p. 19). Thus, the question of dialect versus language is a crucial one, with informants using names somehow associated with speech varieties to designate social units and having strong opinions about language distance as properly correlated with affinal distance. At times, as we shall see, Tukanoan cognitive models of society and language do not coincide with those of the linguists who have worked there, but much more research needs to be carried out on this topic.

The social structure of the Vaupés, at its most abstract so seemingly clear-cut and unambiguous (e.g., as shown in Figure 4), is a dynamic system incorporating a lot of slippage, fluidity, and imprecision. We are not simply dealing with a disparity between an idealized model and on-the-ground reality. Any Tukanoan can, if so inclined, present a clear picture of the social categories in the Vaupés and their articulation with one another. A clear picture of sibs and language groups will emerge, a picture involving common ancestry, geographical location, linguistic indicators, and exogamy; variability emerges, however, in the answers from different individuals (or even from the same individual over a period of time), a variability built into the basic structure of the system. It is foolish to assume that one version is right and one wrong. As we have seen, this variability occurs in names, in definitional criteria, and in the emphasis a group of Tukanoans will place on a given criterion over another. For example, in the Papurí region, language identification is by far, at least at present, the most significant feature of membership in the language group. The most important trait the Bará say they have in common is that they share the Bará language, in a sense "owning" it, and it is the trait that most clearly distinguishes them from members of other language groups. In the Pirá-paraná, although language is an extremely important criterion, Tukanoans are aware and more tolerant of deviations from the ideal of the language-identified unit being identical with the exogamous unit. There the exogamous unit is more clearly distinguishable from the linguistic unit, both empirically and in Pirá-paraná Tukanoans' normative statements about their social structure. Insofar as the Pirá-paraná is less acculturated than the Papurí, it is probably a better representation of an earlier situation existing throughout the Vaupés, although this is extremely hard to document. It is my opinion that the present system of linguistic exogamy in the Vaupés is unstable, the clear-cut association between language and exogamy so strongly expressed in the Papurí region being in part due to the loss resulting from acculturation of certain previously far more important nonlinguistic features that distinguished exogamous groups.[7]

Thus, we must keep in mind that whereas some of the confusion in any discussion of nonlocalized Tukanoan social units will be clarified by further research, a rigid association between actual individuals or groups and the more inclusive social categories that every Tukanoan will accept will never be discovered, because the Vaupés is a dynamic system whose fluid social structure reflects structural and regional variability and past as well as present social processes. Any description from the point of view of more than one local group or more than one point in time will have built-in contradictions.

All observers of Tukanoan life have pointed out the association, in all groups except the Cubeo, between exogamy and language. Exogamy is an important

83

distinguishing feature separating the language groups and very probably a prime factor in bringing the present system into being (this is further discussed later).[8] The sample I gathered in 1968–70 of more than 1,000 marriages (predominantly from the Papurí–Tiquié region), showed that with one exception all Tukanoans had observed the rule of language exogamy. Furthermore, this "exception" was never admitted as being a real marriage by any Tukanoan I discussed it with (this case is discussed in Chapter 7).

Any general discussion of exogamy carried out with Tukanoans invariably involves the topic of language. A Bará is not likely to say, "We are Bará because we do not marry one another" but to say, "We are Bará because we speak the same language; people who speak the same language do not marry one another."[9]

Table 2 shows the most common designation of Vaupés language groups used by Spanish or Portuguese speakers (most of these terms are in Lingua Geral, the Tupian trade language used earlier in the region), followed by their Bará name, and then by an English gloss, when known, of the Bará term. It should be noted that the Bará terms are only those I collected in connection with recording one or more marriages and specified by informants as a language group. Other terms I collected that are used for language groups included Kaiyíara, Mipia (Arawakan speakers to the north of the Vaupés [S. Hugh-Jones, personal communication]), Barea ("food-people," the Baré of Brüzzi Alves da Silva, 1966, p. 89), Kawiria, Wühaná (generally referring to "Makuna" [S. Hugh-Jones, unpublished field notes]), Yawi piria, and Guayavero (Guayabero of San José de Guaviare).[10]

It should be stressed again that this list was obtained from Tukanoans from the Papurí–Tiquié drainage. There are obviously some questions regarding the status of groups on the boundaries of the multilingual area and whether they ought to be included in the linguistic exogamy system. It is also clear that Papurí Tukanoans are not aware of some of the complications in the Pirá-paraná.[11] The basic tendency to associate language with exogamy is clearly found in the Pirá-paraná. Tukanoans of that region are reported as criticizing Makuna who marry other Makuna speakers because "people should not speak like their cross-cousins" (C. Hugh-Jones, n.d.; see also 1979, p. 17). There is also an emphasis on language as an important marker of a social group even among the Cubeo, who do not have an ideal of language exogamy (although many Cubeo do marry outside of the Cubeo unit): Goldman (personal communication) reports that a possible translation of the Cubeo self-name Pamíwa is "people of the language." The Cubeo are clearly a part of the Central Northwest Amazon culture area in the majority of respects. In addition, to the south of the Pirá-paraná, in the Mirití–Paraná region, the traditionally intermarrying Yukuna, Tanimuca, Matapí, and Letuama groups have a rule of linguistic exogamy, although this is no longer the case with the Matapí, because owing to a measles

Table 2. *Names of language groups*

"Spanish" (usually Lingua Geral)	Bará	English gloss of Bará term
Bará "Northern Barasano"[a]	Bará	A sweet-smelling plant placed in a man's G–string over the buttocks during festivals. Sometimes said to be an aphrodisiac. (Goldman translates as "medicine")
Tuyuka	Dohká púara	Mud people or clay people
Tukano	Dahea	Toucan bird
Desana	Winá	Wind
Carapana	Mütea	Mosquito (Goldman translates as "gnat"); Brüzzi Alves da Silva, 1966, p. 99: genera *Stegoniya, Culex*
Tatuyo	Pamoá, Hüná	Armadillo
Siriano	Hütiá	Possibly clothing or masks (Siriano purportedly use masks in mourning rites [S. Hugh-Jones, personal communication])
Yurutí	Waiyíara	Fish people
Piratapuya	Waí mahkara	Fish people
Uanano	Ohkotí mahkara	Water people, medicine people
Cubeo	Kobéua	Bará word similar to Tukano word *kebéwa* meaning "the people who are not" (Goldman, 1963, p. 25)
Barasana "Southern Barasano"[a]	Panefa[b]	Unknown
Taiwano	Eduria, Edulia[b]	Unknown
Makuna	Aüira[b]	Bará gloss: "the people who say 'yes' in this manner"
	Wühaná[b]	Unknown
	Idé mahá	Water people
Tariano	Pavará	Unknown
Curripaco	Behkará	Unknown
Pisá–Tapuyo (?)[c]	Wahüná	Unknown
Metuno	Metuno	Unknown
Arápaso[c,d]	Koneá	Woodpecker

[a]"Northern Barasano" is the designation of language given by Summer Institute of Linguistics (see Waltz and Wheeler, 1970, which also gives *Bará*). "Southern Barasano" is the SIL term for Barasana.
[b]Pirá–paraná grouping in which language and exogamous unit are not coterminous (see Århem, 1981).
[c]Information from Goldman, 1948, pp. 766–67.
[d]Information from Brüzzi Alves da Silva, 1966.

85

epidemic they have given up their language and now speak Yukuna (Jacopin, 1975, p. 41).

The language groups vary greatly in size. The larger ones (e.g., Tukano, Desana) have more than thirty sibs, while others (e.g., Bará, Yurutí) have as few as six. Such unevenness in size of structurally equivalent groups is typical of small-scale societies with no clear mechanism for adjusting group size with demographic fluctuations. Sibs and entire language groups have become extinct, owing to demographic imbalances, migration, and acculturation. Some entire sections on the periphery of the Colombian Vaupés (and probably to a greater extent in Brazilian territory) have experienced so much contact with non-Indians that their indigenous inhabitants have been absorbed into it. This has happened in the Apaporis to the south and to the west in the upper Vaupés River area. Table 3 is a list of population estimates for Vaupés ethnolinguistic groups. I have given all the estimates to show just how approximate they are: The table is useful only as an indication of *relative* numbers.

Although in myths language groups are spoken of as a single group living in one longhouse, it is doubtful that this was ever actually the case, even with longhouse units far larger than they are now. Local groups will behave *as if* they are entire language groups during ceremonial occasions, for they are in fact representing the larger category, but there is no expectation that the language group should be seen as a corporate entity that should periodically convene for group activities. Bará informants were comfortable with the possibility of there being Bará to the south whom they did not know at all.

The phratry

I am defining the phratry (see Figure 4) as an unnamed unit composed of various language groups whose members are not supposed to intermarry, because an agnatic relationship exists among them.[12] The phratry thus is the most inclusive exogamous unit recognized by Tukanoans. Qualification as a phratry includes a consciously stated principle that a given pair or group of language groups are not supposed to intermarry; an observation on our part that they do not in fact do so does not suffice. Certain combinations of language groups probably do not intermarry for reasons having nothing to do with social structure. For example, sometimes a given pair of language groups has its constituent settlements so far from each other that intermarriage is unlikely. Predictably, reasons are not always so easily ascertained in the field, for certain language groups will state that some language groups far away are their "younger brothers" and for this reason they do not intermarry. This is the case for the Bará and Carihona – from the Bará point of view; I do not know if any of the surviving Carihona in the upper Vaupés region have even *heard* of the Bará. In this case, phratric membership is probably epiphenomenal – that is, this pair does not intermarry because of distance factors alone, but people observing that these groups do not intermarry

Table 3. *Estimates of populations of language groups*

Language group	H	SIL	T	DAI	R	S
Bará (Northern Barasano)	300	300	500	—	—	—
Barasana (Southern Barasano)	300	—	500	—	—	—
Carapana (Mütea)	200	150	250–300	500	700	—
Carijona (incl. Hianacoto–Umaua)	100	—	100	60	50	—
Cubeo (Cobewa)	2,000	2,000	750–2,000	1,000	1,000	—
Curripaco (incl. Yavareté–Tapuya)	—	—	1,000	400	2,500	—
Desana	1,000	1,500	750	500	—	—
Guanano (Uanano)	600	800	400	800	1,000	—
Makú	—	—	—	—	1,000	—
Ubde (Tukano Makú)	—	150	175	—	—	200–50
Cacua (Kakwa, Cubeo Makú)	—	100	250	—	—	—
Desana Makú	—	—	200	—	—	—
Makuna (incl. Yauna)	500	400	—	—	—	—
Piratapuya (Uaicama)	500	500	—	600	300	—
Siriano	200	—	—	200	—	—
Taiwano	100	—	—	150	—	—
Tariano	50	—	—	30	50	—
Tatuyo (Süna)	300	300	250	600	—	—
Tukano	2,000	2,000	1,500	1,250	1,500	—
Tuyuka	200	200	200	500	—	—
Yurutí (Yurutí–Tapuyo)	200	—	150	675	—	—

Note: H = Stephen Hugh-Jones; SIL = Summer Institute of Linguistics (figures compiled in 1970); T = Loren Turnage, "Evangelical Work among the Indians of Colombia" (Bogotá), 1969; DAI = government of Colombia, Native Affairs Department (figures compiled 1962–68); R = Reichel-Dolmatoff, 1967; S = Peter Silverwood-Cope. *Source:* Dostal, 1972, pp. 393–96.

group them together in the same set of siblings in an after-the-fact manner. Still, other nonintermarrying pairs quite distant from each other are not spoken of as "younger brothers," whereas pairs of language groups who might easily intermarry in terms of distance do not because they are the "same people," or "brothers." Thus, this highest level of organization must be explained by taking both empirical (i.e., records of actual marriages) and normative data into account.

Two points must be clarified at this juncture. It is fruitless to try to construct exclusive groupings based on phratric principles derived either from known marriage practices or statements by informants. As we shall see, data on actual marriages do show striking patterns, but these do not sort into the categorical groups we might call phratries. Phratric organizing can be done for pairs, and in some cases for larger units, especially in the Pirá-piraná. Very soon, however, other considerations seem to enter the picture, and both the marriage statistics and normative evidence contradict themselves. This is also the conclusion of C. Hugh-Jones, who states that "this is a weak and variable form of organization" that we cannot expect to become stabilized into recognizable groupings (1979, p. 22).

The second point concerns the situation in the Pirá-paraná, where people one should not marry can be classified in terms of links based on an agnatic sibling link, original uterine sibling link (i.e., established in mythical time), or de facto uterine sibling link. Although I obtained many statements about how *individuals* may not marry people they call by the uterine sibling term, no one ever discussed this relationship in terms of an entire language group. Hence, respecting the data I acquired, I have chosen the definition of phratry offered at the beginning of this section.

Some of the difficulties in understanding phratries should be clear by now. A clear-cut congruity does not exist throughout the Vaupés between language affiliation, exogamy, common ancestors, and use of agnatic terminology. Although the language group is often stated to be the maximal exogamic unit, this is by no means always the case, and the elements of Vaupés social structure that play roles in the organization of sibs and language groups – patrilineal descent, language, territory, and exogamy – also play a role, variable at times, in phratric organization. For example, use of agnatic terminology characterizes some pairs of language groups, such as Tukano and Bará, but not others, who nonetheless are said to stand in an agnatic sibling relationship to each other.

It is not clear, historically or functionally, why such a relationship is said to exist in many instances, in particular, why some nonintermarrying pairs are said to be members in the same phratry (e.g., Bará–Carihona) while other pairs are not (e.g., Bará–Siriano). It *is* evidence for the pan-Vaupés organization conceptualized by Tukanoans. At times Tukanoans take pains to present the regional integration of the system in as neat and broadly based terms as possible, and this may account for the tendency to group pairs of language groups from far-flung areas into phratries. Such pairs are also spoken of as "younger-brother" military allies. Several war stories collected from Bará men describe the Wahüná as the younger brothers of the Bará even though the Wahüná are located on the Vaupés River. The Tukano are said to have allies from the Behkará (Curripaco) and Karihona (Carihona – mentioned previously as younger brothers of the Bará), similarly distant groups.

Other pairs of language groups that do not intermarry are said to stand in a "mother's children" (uterine sibling) relationship to each other. This category, which includes all matrilateral parallel cousins who are not agnates, is obviously not equivalent in meaning to an agnatic sibling relationship. (In Bará, "mother's children" are called *pahkó-mahkara* or *pahkó-poná.*) People who address each other by these terms also cannot marry. Although Bará informants never explicitly named a whole language group as standing in a mother's children relationship to another, this is the case in a number of myths. Furthermore, such usage is reported for the Pirá-paraná region.[13]

C. Hugh-Jones (1979, pp. 36–37) describes a complex, tripartite division of intermarrying groups that are mythologically described in terms of people who are associated with either the earth, the sky, or the water, and either the jaguar, the eagle, or the anaconda, respectively. There is some corroboration in the myths I collected, although these are often remnants and were mostly transcribed in Spanish. Many Bará myths deal with "eagle," or "jaguar," or "fish" people. It is clear that Bará belong to the category of fish people and are associated with water symbolism. An old Bará man once described "other" people as "different, not fish people, but *ümürikori mahǎ*" ("day people"). These people were "born with the sun." This classification probably applies to the Desana, who are also reported to be day people (Reichel-Dolmatoff, 1971). Desana are called Winá ("wind") in Bará and several other languages, and the sun and moon are very important elements in their origin myths, whereas the sun and moon, and celestial phenomena in general, are not mentioned at all in connection with Bará origins. The Hüná (one of the Bará names for Tatuyo language group) are also associated with the sky, birds, and the sun and moon (Bidou, 1976). Thus, the origin myths of the region, in addition to setting out the principles of exogamy with respect to single "one parent" language-affiliated groups, also offer a much broader picture of the larger universe with respect to the various equivalent but not identical descent groups inhabiting this level of the universe, revealing differentiation and marriage prescription as well as prohibition.[14] The theme of three (only three are considered at a time) exogamous groups that are clearly differentiated from one another in a number of symbolic ways and are either dependent on or in competition with each other vis à vis the exchange of women is encountered in many areas of Tukanoan culture.[15] The symbolism of differentiation extends into other areas of Vaupés ideation and cosmology. Table 4 shows how these three groups are conceived of at three levels of inclusion.

Despite the closeness of settlements to each other, several pairs of language

Table 4. *Zero generation terminology at three levels of inclusion*

	Ego to alter	Longhouse to longhouse; local descent group to local descent group	Language group to language group
First group (e.g., Inambú Bará)	"my siblings," agnates	"our brothers," "our real brothers," agnates	"our brothers," "brother people," "We speak one language," agnates
Second group (e.g., Inambú Tuyuka)	"my cross-cousins," "my mother's people," father's sisters' children	"our cross-cousins," "our affines,""our brothers-in-law," pairs of longhouses that have exchanged women	"our cross-cousins," "our *mehkó-mahkara*," "father's sister people," "where we exchange women," potential affines
Third group (e.g., Piratapuya of *waíoperi*) [Piracuara]	"my mother's children," uterine (half–) sibling, matrilateral parallel cousin	"longhouses far away," "distant kinsmen," "our mothers are sisters; our fathers are not brothers"	"our mothers are sisters to each other," "mother's children from the waking-up times,"*a* "*pahkó-mahkara*: ["mother's children people"*a*]" affines of affines

Note: " " around statements indicate how Tukanoans talk about relationships.
*a*Information from C. Hugh-Jones.

groups do not intermarry; this is the case for the Bará–Tukano pair, and the Desana–Tuyuka pair have a much lower incidence than would be expected in terms of numbers of potential spouses and proximity.[16] The reasons given were that these pairs are brothers to each other and should not marry their sisters. Sometimes the explanation involves the notion that we used to call each other "brother," and although we do not do this now, we are still too close to marry. Table 5 gives lists of phratry members obtained from three informants.

Living with Bará facilitates the recognition of these unnamed phratries, for not only do Bará and Tukano not intermarry, they also use agnatic terminology between themselves.[17] I do not know whether this is still the case for some of the other pairs. The individuals I talked to did agree that previously all members of a given phratry addressed one another as agnates and spoke the same language. In the section of the Bará origin myth describing Bará and Tukano as "one people," they are "of our [i.e., Bará] language" (maniya waderá). No Bará–Tukano marriages occur in a sample of 190 Bará and 315 Tukano

Table 5. *Phratries listed by three informants*

Language group of informant	Phratry	Language groups included in phratry	
		Spanish	Bará
Bará	1. maní baüra ("our brothers")	Bará	Waí maha ("fish people")
			Kawíria[a]
		Pisá-Tapuyo (?)	Wahüná
		Yurutí	Waiyíara
			Kümará (a Tukano sib)
		Tukano	Dahea
	2. maní teñüa ("our brothers-in-law," "our affines")	Barasana	Panerá[a]
		Taiwano	Edulia[a]
		Makuna	Yebá mahá
		Tariano	Pavará
		Piratapuyo	Waí mahkara
		Tuyuka	Dohká púara
		Desana	Winá
			Bohtea poná (a Desana sib)
		Tatuyo	Hüná
		Carapana	Mütea
	3. ahpērá mahkara ("other people")	Siriano	Hütiá
Tuyuka	1. (no name given)	Tuyuka	Dohká púara
		Yurutí	Waiyíara
		Desana	Winá
			Koroba ("they now speak Cubeo")
			Behkará (Arawak speakers to the north)
	2. (no name given)	Bará	Bará
		Tukano	Dahea
		Barasana[a]	Panerá
		Pisá-Tapuyo?	Wahüná
Tukano	1. hiká poná ("children of one parent")	Tukano	Dahea
		Bará	Bará
			Wagüyara
		Yurutí	Waiyíara
		Carihona	Karihona
			Metuno
			Behkará (Arawak speakers to the north)

marriages. Bará–Tukano exogamy is corroborated by Sorensen: "no Tukano will marry a Barasana [Bará], or a Baré, or a Baniva" (1970, p. x). Although I have no marriages recorded for either Baré or Baniva, I do have instances in which Behkará, an Arawak-speaking group, are spoken of as the younger-brother allies of the Tukano.

Some informants will list language groups as being in a "brother group," "brother-in-law group," and "other-people group." When questioned more closely about the way in which these lists related to the rule of exogamy and language, Bará handled the contradiction thus: "My brothers are those who speak my own language. I call Tukanos 'brothers' because we used to speak the same language. They started to speak differently, and now they speak another language entirely. But we are still close, and I still call them 'brothers.' "[18]

The younger Tukanoans I spoke with did not seem to have a clear concept of phratric groupings as indicated by the lists given by older informants, but when asked specifically about pairs of language groups, such as Tukano–Bará or Desana–Tuyuka, they confirmed that such pairs do not and did not intermarry. They did not accept the suggestion that lack of intermarrying between these pairs was accidental or due to distance factors alone.

An obligatory elder–younger distinction is an important feature of all Tukanoan sibling terminologies. This of course means that in a given phratry, one language group will be of lower rank than another. Bará address Tukanoans as their "elder siblings." Still, Bará say this is not the way it should be, that long ago the ancestors of both groups spoke Bará but that at one point the lower-ranking sibs of this original group began to speak differently. These same sibs also refused to use the elder sibling terms to the others. Finally the people in the higher-ranking sibs gave in and, continuing to speak Bará, consented to call the others by the elder sibling terms. According to the Bará I spoke to, every Bará and Tukano today knows that this is so, but only one Tukano sib, the Bohó (*Dasyprocta* sp.) people, near Paricachivera Mission on the Tiquié, addresses the Bará as elder siblings.

Data collected on actual marriages demonstrate that to some degree these phratric principles operate in marriage making. A quick scanning of Table 6, based on a sample of 534 marriages occurring among eight language groups, illustrates this kind of patterning. Because it is concerned only with eight language groups and marrriage partners predominantly from the Papurí area, the table does not represent the entire Vaupés. Moreover, insofar as these eight language groups have settlements elsewhere in the Vaupés, the picture is not a

Table 5. *(cont.)*

Note: These are lists from single informants and are not to be seen as the only correct list of phratries; glosses of names in Bará are approximate in certain cases.
[a]Cf. C. Hugh-Jones, 1979, Appendix 1. Papurí River informants simplify Pirá-paraná groupings.

complete account of marriages made among these particular eight language groups during the last forty years for the Papurí–upper Tiquié drainage.

Figure 5, based on the data in Table 6, shows the pattern of marriage making in terms of Euclidian space through the use of three-dimensional scaling techniques.[19] The resulting illustration demonstrates quite clearly that the eight groups form four pairs, each of which has a high frequency of intermarriage. The next highest frequency of intermarriage occurs between groups that are adjacent in adjoining pairs.

In sum, it is clear that norms concerning marital preference with respect to language group membership can be elicited from informants. In addition, patterns of preference between certain pairs of language groups can be observed from an examination of actual marriages. Still, much more research and analysis must be done before we have a clear picture of the entire phratry system. In particular, two directions of research suggest themselves. The first is to continue to find out why certain language groups have no or very little intermarriage. It is clear that Tukanoans, or at least the more traditionally oriented ones, have a conceptualization of exogamous phratric groupings of "brother people" and "mother's children people" that are more inclusive than any given language group. More research on Tukanoans throughout the region and their conceptualizations of marriage preferences is obviously indicated. For example, both Sorensen (1967) and Fulop (1955) report a system of five named phratries obtained from conversations with Tukanoan informants. My informants did not talk about a set of five exogamous units, and recent marriage patterns themselves do not support the existence of such a tight organization. Still, various bits of tantalizing evidence continue to emerge (for example, the number five appears in Pirá-paraná Tukanoans' system of ranked sibs [C. Hugh-Jones, 1977]).

The second direction of indicated research is precisely in the area of territory and propinquity, with the goal of a better understanding of the degree to which these considerations do affect ultimate marriage choice. The matter is complicated; given the dispersed nature of the settlements of many language groups and the great variation in size, one must take as the unit of study sections of language groups in circumscribed territories. Doing so will make the measures of propinquity far more meaningful and will make far more noticeable the lack of intermarriage where propinquity would predict its presence. For example, each language group in the following list of pairs has some settlements quite close to settlements belonging to the language group in the pair; yet marriages are either entirely lacking or quite infrequent: Bará–Tukano, Desana–Tuyuka, Desana–Tatuyo, Tatuyo–Siriano, and Tuyuka–Carapana (see Figure 5). Is this in reality a reflection of proximity but proximity of an earlier era, continued through marriage alliance maintenance, before the effects of acculturation brought about the greater territorial dispersion found at present, at least in the Papurí region? The Tiquié and the Pirá-paraná, areas of least acculturation, show a greater association between territory and specific language group. It is also true that the entire

93

Table 6. *Marriage between selected language groups*

Husband's language group		Wife's language group								Total	%
		Bará	Tuyuka	Tukano	Desana	Carapana	Tatuyo	Siriano	Yurutí		
Bará	N	0	55	0	7	2	12	1	0	77	
	%	0.0	71.4	0.0	9.1	2.6	15.6	1.3	0.0	100.0	(14.4)
Tuyuka	N	58	0	71	3	0	6	7	0	145	
	%	40.0	0.0	49.0	2.1	0.0	4.1	4.8	0.0	100.0	(27.2)
Tukano	N	0	47	1	45	4	5	20	5	127	
	%	0.0	37.0	0.8	35.4	3.1	3.9	15.7	3.9	100.0	(27.2)
Desana	N	5	2	36	0	2	0	10	0	55	
	%	9.1	3.6	65.5	0.0	3.6	0.0	18.2	0.0	100.0	(10.3)
Carapana	N	3	0	6	4	0	10	2	2	27	
	%	11.1	0.0	22.2	14.8	0.0	37.0	7.4	7.4	100.0	(5.1)
Tatuyo	N	10	0	5	1	2	0	0	2	20	
	%	50.0	0.0	25.0	5.0	10.0	0.0	0.0	10.0	100.0	(3.7)
Siriano	N	2	8	27	14	5	1	0	14	71	
	%	2.8	11.3	38.0	19.7	7.0	1.4	0.0	19.7	100.0	(13.3)
Yurtí	N	2	0	2	0	1	1	6	0	12	
	%	16.7	0.0	16.7	0.0	8.3	8.3	50.0	0.0	100.0	(2.2)
Total	N	80	112	148	74	16	35	46	23	534	
	%	15.0	21.0	27.7	13.9	3.0	6.6	8.6	4.3	100.0	(100.0)

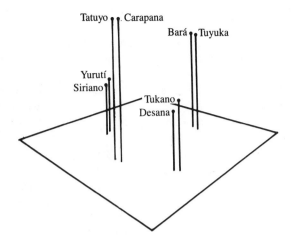

Figure 5. A three-dimensional spatial representation of marriage distance between language groups. Data from Table 6; after Jackson and Romney 1973.

language group is obviously too large a unit of study for some purposes. Although Tukanoans speak of, for example, whom Bará marry, this is most often spoken of relative to a particular Bará settlement. Thus, Bará of one river tend to marry Barasana and Tatuyo, whereas those on another tend to marry Tuyuka and Desana.

Another difficulty with normative statements made by Tukanoans is that the description being made of the "best" type of marriage may in fact operate only under certain conditions (this is discussed further in Chapter 7). For example, a Tukanoan might very well state that people always try to make marriages between bilateral cross-cousins, first cousins if possible, who live in neighboring longhouses. Yet this probably does not apply to all the marriages made by a given generation in a settlement; it may be that once this type of marriage has been made in two or three cases, other individuals are allowed or even encouraged to marry into other settlements, because the new generation has reestablished its ongoing alliances and should seek to set up new ones. This would tend to spread out the available sources of aid and exchange relationships made by affinal ties rather than limiting them to one settlement. Such an arrangement is explicitly stated in the marriage rules among the Yukuna groups (Jacopin, 1975) and the Witoto (Gasché, 1977). The rule states that no man can marry into the same settlement in which his (classificatory) brother obtained a wife, a strategy clearly intended to disperse marriage ties.

Space does not permit a thorough discussion of the literature with respect to phratric organization in the Vaupés. It is scanty and confusing, particularly with respect to earlier patterns and preferences. Sorensen, for example (1967, pp.

95

671–72), states that each language-affiliated tribe consists of several sibs and is aligned with one of five phratries. According to him, phratries are named and exogamous, and all marriages conform to a rule of phratry exogamy. He does not list the names of the phratries, however, nor does he give data on actual marriages.

Reichel-Dolmatoff's (1971, p. 4) use of "phratry" is coterminous with my use of language group. (In his 1975 book he refers to exogamous groups [1975, p. 66].) He does mention that the Piratapuya are considered practically a "second Desana phratry" (1971, p. 7). Waltz and Wheeler, reporting on work done by SIL linguists in the Vaupés, state: "The Barasano . . . intermarry mainly with Taiwanos whose language is almost identical with their own . . . the Guanano are forbidden to marry the Piratapuyo 'because they are brothers'" (1970, pp. 120–25). Fulop (1955) states that the tribe Yepá Majsá consists of five phratries, each of which is aligned with a distinct language: Tukano, Carapana, Barasana,[20] Maniva, and Cubeo. Brüzzi Alves da Silva (1966, pp. 81–123) also lists prescribed and proscribed marriages for his list of twenty-six "tribes."

The Cubeo differ from other Vaupés language-affiliated groups in being able to marry within the Cubeo unit which contains three exogamous phratries (Goldman, 1963, pp. 100–05). Still, the underlying pattern is identical: Several ranked, named sibs make up an exogamous unit intermarrying with equivalent units. Goldman (personal communication) has noted that a Desana once remarked to him that at one time Cubeo and Desana did not intermarry because they were too close. Finally, as has been noted, Appendix I of C. Hugh-Jones, 1979, gives a comprehensive treatment of the Pirá-paraná situation.

Regional integration and interaction between settlements

We have seen some of the ways in which interaction between settlements is vital to Tukanoan life and has brought about a regional orientation in Tukanoans' conceptualization of their social universe. Although much of daily life revolves around intimate relationships within the local group, marriage, visiting, and ceremonies are also essential, for they help in constituting the local group and expanding relationships beyond it. The amount of systemic social and cultural integration beyond the local group is complex and varies in a nontrivial way within the region. This is one reason why the term *tribe* is not powerful enough, for it oversimplifies and obscures the nature of intersettlement relations.

Thus, in some respects, settlements in the Vaupés are not nearly as autonomous as in some other lowland South American societies, despite their very real isolation and autonomy in many other areas of life.[21] For one thing, local groups in the Vaupés are exogamous. Marital interaction, furthermore, is not limited to exchanges between two or three neighboring settlements. Many types of ceremonial occasions require the participation of more than one local group (with the exception of some mission towns, where traditional ceremonial life is very truncated anyway), and the majority of ceremonies includes people from more than one language group. In the past, shamanism also involved interaction of settlements.

In earlier periods an important aspect of such interaction concerned feuding, raiding, and the maintenance of military alliances. Although warfare[22] has ceased, its legacy is still apparent in settlement pattern, choice of settlement site, longhouse architecture, and almost certainly marriage patterns. Raiding and the accompanying military considerations such as defense and inculcation of bravery and other necessary qualities in male children are important elements in present-day ritual, myth, and various communicative events such as greeting behavior. C. Hugh-Jones (1979, pp. 63–64) offers a nice discussion of the interrelationships of warfare, communal rituals, shamanism, and marriage in the past, pulling out common themes of competition and a gradation of hostilities. What little remains of the earlier Vaupés military complex resembles the Yąnomamö of Venezuela and Brazil (Chagnon, 1968).

The dependence of a settlement on other settlements for marriage partners, for ceremonial and military allies, and for economic exchanges has undoubtedly influenced Tukanoan attitudes about the Vaupés as a whole. As already noted, the extensive knowledge many Tukanoans have of the entire region is impressive. It is evident that Tukanoans feel themselves to be much more a part of a pan-Vaupés system than do the peoples of the numerous lowland South American societies, which are characterized by a kind of xenophobia, even toward people living quite nearby. The Tukanoan conceptualization involves an ever-increasing geographical area even beyond the Vaupés region, with no generally recognized natural or artificial boundaries beyond which live people who are categorically enemies or strangers. This is not to say that ''enemies'' or ''other-than-us'' categories do not exist but that the social and cultural differentiation is gradual rather than abrupt.

Differentiation exists, but although the criteria specifying it are explicit they are not based on territorial considerations so much as social ones. The Cubeo on the northern boundary of the region are at times excluded in discussions of ''real people,'' but most of the time the implication is that they are excluded because of their behavior rather than because of innate differences correlated with geographical location. Other times, Cubeo are very much included in categories corresponding to ''us.'' Goldman (personal communication) states that the Cubeo, although conceiving of themselves as a tribal entity, also see themselves as part of a larger entity.

Tukanoans visit other settlements for trade, ceremonies, or courtship. Because the nearest longhouses are separated by anywhere from two hours' to a day's canoe travel, a trip involves much preparation and lasts at least a few days. The Northwest Amazon is famous for its rules of hospitality to overnight guests: One is almost never refused lodging – a place to hang a hammock, a warm fire, and some food – and when possible Tukanoans almost always elect to spend the night in a house rather than make camp in the forest. Furthermore, as indicated in Chapter 4, a visiting family can participate in feeding itself; the man will hunt and fish and the woman process manioc from her hosts' gardens.

Visiting has probably increased in recent times as a result both of more travel to and from mission towns and the end of raiding. The frequency and importance of visiting was forcefully demonstrated to me when I undertook the task of censusing households. Although the patrilocal residence rule states unequivocally that one should live with one's closest agnates, interpreting this in terms of locating people in "their" settlement sometimes involved what were rather arbitrary decisions. Tukanoans travel a great deal and can stay in other settlements for prolonged periods of time, up to several months. Quarrels can result in the permanent dissolution of a residence group, some members of which will go to "visit" other kinsmen but in fact never return. Thus, at any point in time a significant proportion of Tukanoans are not living where they are "supposed" to. Such mobility and fluidity are probably an integral aspect of a system like that of the Vaupés, a point made by Goldman (1963), among others.

A guest's status as a visitor is clearly marked in a number of ways. Greeting and departure rituals mark both the formality of the occasion and the degree of intimacy between hosts and guest. At important ceremonies, greeting rituals are governed by strict protocol and are quite long. Significantly, Makú are never formally greeted. Further evidence of this distinction between guest and host is that members of a longhouse, even though returning from extensive trips, are not formally greeted in this way, because one should not have to go through a formal ritual for close family. Formal behavior is basically a recognition of social distance and/or seriousness of the occasion, neither of which should apply to a fellow-resident's return.

During my stay at Púmanaka buro, the headman's son, Lino, returned with me from Mitú, where he had been for seven years. During this time, only those who had traveled to Mitú (three young men) had seen him. No one approached when we disembarked, despite the sound of the outboard motor. Not only was Lino not formally greeted, he was scarcely greeted at all, so unusual (and tense) was the situation. Everyone tried to appear casual and unexcited; when his mother was overcome by emotion (including, I am sure, anger), she ran to the back field to finish crying.

This example illustrates that greeting forms are based on implications of intimacy contained in social roles rather than the actual amount of intimacy. Lino was a virtual stranger in appearance to everyone and a total stranger to many of the younger children. Yet everyone tried to appear as though he had returned from a few hours' fishing trip, for a member of a settlement does not go off by himself – ideally – for longer periods of time.

As previously indicated, a settlement will normally have the most interaction and the closest affective ties with its neighbors, particularly those on the same stretch of river, regardless of their positions in Vaupés social structure. For example, Pǘmanaka buro has much more contact with the three downstream Tuyuka settlements than with the other Bará settlements in the Macucú–Tiquié region. Goldman (1963) is quite correct in emphasizing the importance of rivers in Tukanoan social organization. They provide natural highways for communication and transportation, and as has already been indicated, are extremely important in Tukanoan conceptualizations of the cosmos.[23]

Another kind of intersettlement dependence, although at present quite attenuated, is the result of a regionally based division of labor in the manufacture of various artifacts of a ceremonial nature. Trade and exchange of these occur in connection with ceremonies and other visits. Some of this division of labor is necessary because of the uneven distribution of certain raw materials (e.g., clay). Other kinds of items are exchanged because of what appears to have been a more artificially created specialization of manufacturing; thus, Tukanos traditionally made a carefully carved stool (cf. A. R. Wallace, 1889/1972, p. 342, who notes stool making by the Tariana as well), Tatuyos made a snuff taker out of the bones of a species of bird, and so forth. The Bará are associated with canoe making as are the Tuyuka, although their name ("mud people") implies that they might have been the first cazabe griddle-making specialists (Brüzzi Alves da Silva, 1966, p. 115). The Desana specialize in making basketsieves, and the Baniva on the Içana make graters (Brüzzi Alves da Silva, 1966, p. 77). As mentioned earlier, at present this is an association between language group and object rather than an exclusive right to manufacture.

This kind of specialization is suggestive of a similar artificially created interdependence described by Chagnon for the Yạnomamö (1968, p. 100), although it is much more elaborate and important among them. Trade between Tukanoans of Makú-manufactured items demonstrates a similar interdependence; only Makú make certain objects (including all manner of highly valued twined baskets), and only some Tukanoans have direct access to Makú groups (this is discussed further in Chapter 8).

It is evident that culturally homogeneous regional systems occur in many areas of lowland South America, involving networks of trade and other forms of exchange such as marriage, feasting, and in the past, military alliances.[24] Still, the Vaupés appears to be culturally integrated into a regionally based network system to a very marked degree. The question of why this is so in this particular area of the Amazon–Orinoco Basin cannot be completely answered, at least at present, but some reasonable hypotheses can be offered.

Population density is undoubtedly a crucial factor in the evolution of the Vaupés system to its present form. It is almost certain that the area has had, in the past, a higher density, more territorially based control over scarce resources, and more stratification among the groups exploiting those resources. Goldman's (1963) description of the Cubeo in 1939–40 certainly indicates this, as do writings from earlier travelers. At that time and earlier, groups with higher rank and more allies – and greater population – occupied the larger rivers, particularly

99

sites on river mouths. Such locations had military advantages and conferred higher status. Control over groups such as Makú and lower-ranking sibs seems to have been a major consideration. The present unimportance of this control strategy is probably due to decline in population and to the disappearance of active raiding and feuding.

The higher population density reported by Goldman for the Cubeo in 1939 probably also lies behind their greater use of the landscape to reflect social arrangements. Cubeo phratric organization and sib rank are expressed quite clearly by the location of settlements. Whether the present situation among other Tukanoans represents a simple breakdown in the system, after falling below a critical minimum population density, or a more creative process of adaptation to the changing demographic situation is an open question. Some of the possible factors producing decline in population density have been mentioned earlier.

It seems evident that changing population density and migration were also important factors in the evolution of the present Tukanoan marriage system. Two kinds of explanation have been offered (Sorensen, 1967) to account for the way in which demographic and spatial factors might give rise to a system involving linguistic exogamy. The first, a fusion model, suggests that a cul-de-sac situation arose owing to pressure from missions, rubber gatherers, and other agents of the national economies of either Brazil or Colombia. The resulting squeeze of territory necessitated more interaction of distinct cultural groups, a necessity increased by declines in population caused by disease. Various mechanisms arose that facilitated interaction of the previously separated or hostile groups. One of these mechanisms was intermarriage; the heretofore truly distinct tribal-like groups assimilated to the point of sharing a common culture, and a rule of exogamy came to be applied to what originally were endogamous units. Language came to be the main marker distinguishing these exogamous units, whereas originally it was but one of many cultural differences separating them. The peoples of the Papurí drainage area seem to have progressed the most in this direction, and those of other areas, especially the Pirá-paraná, probably represent an earlier stage, with more territorially confined language groups and more cultural distinctions separating them. In the more acculturated Papurí, some of the complexity of the traditional system of classification of social units has been lost.

The second type of explanation, a fission model, postulates an original situation characterized by endogamous (again, probably much more tribal-like than at present) units with exogamous moieties within each one. Of the various markers distinguishing one moiety from the other, speech differences came to be the most crucial, until ultimately what was once a single protolanguage spoken by the entire endogamous unit divided into two languages along the lines of the moiety division.[25] The rule of marriage came to be expressed as "We marry people who speak a different language."

These two models perhaps show how different segments of the Vaupés population simultaneously evolved into the present Tukanoan marriage system. While outsider groups were increasingly being incorporated through intermarriage, the idea concerning marriage with a person affiliated with a different language was becoming the most important marriage rule. It diffused into the moiety-based groups, increasing the stress of speech differences in these groups as the most significant marker distinguishing each exogamous unit.

Most of the ethnographers who have written recently on the Vaupés have commented on the degree of homogeneity found throughout the region. They note this to be so despite no or sporadic contact between many of its inhabitants (see Goldman, 1948, pp. 763–64; Reichel-Dolmatoff, 1971, p. 16; Sorensen, 1967, pp. 673–74). The cultural homogeneity is readily apparent even to a nonanthropologist, regardless of how one defines "culture." The similarity of observable phenomena throughout the region is indisputable, and similarities in the cognitive orientation of Vaupés natives can be demonstrated as well. As mentioned earlier, Tukanoans assume that their rules of marriage apply throughout the region, and people who do not observe these rules – whites, Makú, and Cubeo – are criticized and ridiculed for their inappropriate behavior. The origin myths of the various language groups, although occurring in more than sixteen languages, share many basic similarities. They all use the entire region as their setting, and their plots involve representatives of many of the present-day language groups.

Linguistic evidence also shows that the discrete languages of the Vaupés area are by no means indications of similarly discrete cultures. Semantic categories in many of the languages appear to be similar if not identical. This is not surprising, given that Tukanoans everywhere behave very similarly and must deal with the same landscape, physical and social, regardless of formal identification with specific father languages.

The degree to which the differences that are found in the Vaupés – particularly linguistic ones – are cultural differences rather than significant distinctions within a single culture is an important question. Much of the heterogeneity that exists should perhaps be considered an aid in the organization of interaction of the various social units within the region in much the same way as highly visible differences in uniforms aid in the organization and playing of a football game. The fact that it is language that serves as the emblem of distinct units, which must remain distinct for the system to work, has undoubtedly obscured the underlying similarities. Few anthropologists have encountered such widespread multilingualism in either their own society or the anthropological literature. Multilingualism is assumed to be characteristic only of complex societies. Thus, differences separating the language groups of the Vaupés tend to be over-emphasized (exacerbated by calling them tribes), despite the fact that differences in language do not, a priori, indicate deep cultural divisions. The essentially homogeneous and regionally integrated characteristics of the Vaupés have not, in my opinion, been given enough consideration in the ethnographic literature, although recent work has begun to remedy this. As indicated in Chapter 1, this is also one of the major goals of this book.

A fundamental contrast inheres in the situation I have been describing. On the one hand we have a native cognitive model that is theoretically limitless in terms of geography, society, and language. It is a model encompassing a vast area within which all Tukanoans potentially or actually interact but one that permits lack of interaction to the point of total ignorance of a given settlement's existence. On the other hand we must understand the implications of such a system from the point of view of its actors: "Part of the conceptual difficulty in describing Vaupés social structure . . . is the overlap of a comprehensive system based on descent and exogamy with a practical local organisation into longhouse communities, each of which perceives other communities as more-or-less distant outsiders" (C. Hugh-Jones, 1979, p. 32).

This leads us once again to the issue of rigidity versus flexibility. Tukanoans are united by an underlying model of their social organization that involves several dimensions of classification. These dimensions, as we have seen, are concerned with kinship (both present-day terminological classification and ideology about descent group ancestry), mythology, language, geography, and so on. We have seen that these dimensions *cannot* be reduced to a simple model that incorporates both the structure and content of each dimension and still represent Vaupés reality. Even if we are speaking of a unit of analysis much smaller than the Vaupés region, it is impossible to construct a model of Vaupés social structure that provides both structure and a fixed content. A good example of this is the difference in Tatuyo origins as told by adjacent sibs; these differences are profound and cannot be explained away by searching for the one that is "more correct" in terms of some criterion or other, for example, the one that is more traditional (Bidou, 1976; C. Hugh-Jones, 1979, p. 32).

A crucial feature of the model, therefore, is its ability to adopt different content, depending on the context. Flexibility at one level permits the insertion at another of sometimes rigid classificatory principles. Our model must allow argument about and even subversion of surface aspects of the fixed structure, for the Tukanoan model certainly does. In some ways we are reminded of Kurosawa's film *Rashomon* or Durrell's *Alexandria Quartet*. In the Vaupés, as in these examples, there is no final "correct" version of action and intent. What is real and correct is that different points of view produce different content, and yet they nonetheless share an underlying set of common propositions about the nature and meaning of the world. With respect to the raison d'être behind the Vaupés arrangement, as I have indicated, I feel that such flexibility is adaptive. Godelier's (1975) discussion of the way in which a kinship system allows for flexibility in relationships between people and between people and their resources is a persuasive example of the sort of thing I mean. Another way of putting it, if we expand the reference to kinship to include all areas of social structure, is: "Rather than providing a set of rules people must obey, therefore, kinship provides an idiom by which people seek to maintain or transform their relationships to others as the situation demands'' (Bledsoe, 1980, p. 29). Thus, the structure has the capacity to take on different meaning as we move across the Vaupés landscape – seen in physical (geographical) or social terms (e.g., the changes in perspective from one language group to another with respect to roles assumed in myth). As we move vertically the same thing happens, as illustrated by the example of Tatuyo sibs' versions of the origin myth. The issue of hierarchy versus equality is intimately connected to the one of rigidity versus flexibility. Most of the dimensions I have mentioned incorporate some notions of hierarchical order; that is, the distinguishing features of the positions in a given dimension contrast in terms of varying amounts of a particular quality, a quality either positively or negatively evaluated. I have given many examples of what we might call ''differentiated identity'' in the preceding pages, and many more will follow. Hierarchical ordering is the basis for such differentiated identity in many cases, for what is at issue is the possession of greater or lesser amounts of rank, moral superiority, ceremonial purity, and so on. C. Hugh-Jones's point about each exogamous group standing at the center of its own social world – and this is true for each longhouse community as well – is an example of such differentiation, relative though it be: ''From the point of view of each Exogamous Group, the others are not equal – they range from close groups with whom women are exchanged to very distant groups whose members are totally unknown. Only when seen from the point of view of comparable internal structure, or of an artificial 'Vaupés system' seen from the outside, are Exogamous Groups equivalent to one another'' (1979, p. 276). This is a different kind of nonequivalence from, for instance, sib rank, because it is completely relative. Dyadic relations between language groups or other equivalent units exchanging women are based on the principle of equality, as we would expect from a system of direct exchange marriage. Still, a kind of rank ordering occurs here, even though it is completely dependent on the actor's point of view. The ordering is hierarchical in the sense that groups with whom one interacts a lot are differentiated from far-away groups with respect to a number of value-loaded dimensions. This type of ''concentric'' model of social differentiation is discussed further in Chapter 13.

Other types of relationships, such as between sibs in a given language group, between Tukanoans and Makú, or between a headman and his coresidents, are also asymmetrical. In addition we see here the interaction of the underlying system of fixed statuses or ranks and the built-in flexibility in their application to specific people or social units. For example, sib rank relates to the original ancestors' birth order, presumably quite fixed. Still, Tukanoans are notoriously contentious about present-day sib rank, and I have argued that this is a basic component of the system of ranked sibs. In similar fashion, although Tukanoans and Makú are generally conceived of as qualitatively different, sometimes Makú are spoken of as fallen angels who can be reinstated if and when they repent and change their behavior (this is discussed further in Chapter 8). And

103

although a headman's firstborn son ideally inherits his father's position, in reality succession can involve a great deal of argument, schism, and denials of such a right. A headman must initially and continually prove himself worthy of the job.

Such hierarchy does not do much of anything in terms of influencing differential access to scarce resources or even conferring symbolic status of some form or another that is clearly marked in everyday life. Hierarchy is most apparent in classification schemes such as the system of ranked sibs and in ritual.

We might speculate that hierarchy is one more organizing principle to show people where they fit into the system and that it, like many other such principles in the Vaupés, at times seems to be available mainly for the purpose of being manipulated, denied, or inverted. The obligatory hierarchical marking of agnatic sibling terms, for example, tells siblings exactly where they fit, but also affords many opportunities for challenging the implications of the hierarchy. This is illustrated in numerous myths involving elder and younger brothers. On the other hand, people calling each other by the uterine half-sibling term are equivalent in rank. With less of a clear-cut specification of relative position comes more possibility of ambiguity. And, as we shall see, the relationship occurring between ''mother's children'' is ambiguous, a characteristic also illustrated in myth.

The notion of built-in flexibility can take two forms. First, it can operate via what we might call denial mechanisms that challenge a given, clearly specified rigid classification, often hierarchically ordered. And, second, it can emerge in situations that incorporate some form of ambiguity in their very definition. These themes are explored further in the following two chapters.

6.

Kinship

Treating kinship as a separate topic is difficult, for it pervades every aspect of life.[1] Tukanoans spend most of their lives with their family – their hearth family and the extended family making up the longhouse unit – and when this group is temporarily enlarged, it almost always consists of kinsmen. To a much greater extent than in more complex societies, in which people can occupy any number of nonkinship positions (e.g., "working class"; "Brahman caste") and assume any number of nonkinship roles (e.g., doctor–patient; teacher–student), the kinship-based roles a Tukanoan plays throughout life are the primary source of social identity.

Tukanoans address and refer to one another with kin terms most of the time. The name given to each infant at the naming ceremony soon after birth is known by everyone but seldom heard. Naming illustrates temporality and relationality, two themes mentioned in Chapter 1. A Bará receives a name from a very finite list owned by the sib (see C. Hugh-Jones, 1979; Århem, 1980), and the name ideally comes from a FF (father's father) or FFZ (father's father's sister) who has recently died. The deceased's losing his or her name is another stage in the process of dying and joining the relatively undifferentiated mass of ancestor people; the taboo on mentioning the names of the dead accelerates this process.

As noted in Chapter 1, both the naming system (which involves a cycle of only two generations; see S. Hugh-Jones, 1979, p. 106) and the kinship terminology system are less concerned with distinguishing each Tukanoan as a unique individual than their counterparts in the West. Both names and kin terms can be seen to show that a given individual's identity is in part formed by a long line of ancestors (some of whom are namesakes as well as kin) and that the individual as distinct personality, occupying a unique intersection of temporal, spatial, and relational coordinates in his or her social universe, is ephemeral. Specific kin terms are used by any number of people standing as egos and alters, and names are not unique designators of individual Tukanoans in the way they are in the West: thus the kin terms and names are eternal, whereas the individual is not. These features of relationality, nondistinctiveness, and transience are further discussed in Chapter 13.

Nicknames, although more distinct, are more temporary and, as in our own society, purposely less serious than personal names. Spanish and Portuguese names are given more or less spontaneously and have no necessary connection to anyone else (except to a Catholic saint, a connection very imperfectly understood). Although this is changing, in 1970 patronyms were not used systematically. A Tukanoan's use of a patronym is no guarantee that his siblings or father will use the same one, or that it will not be changed on a whim.

In Western society, that John Jacob Jingleheimer Schmidt was at his birth, is, and will continue to be a distinct, individual self is a reasonable and meaningful proposition. Whether or not we believe in life after death, he will survive in numerous records; if he has composed important music or was otherwise famous, he will have a permanent niche in history as an individual. The idea that it is important to survive as a unique personality is not nearly so meaningful to Tukanoans. This is not to deny that ambiguities exist in Western conceptualizations of the ways in which individual personalities maintain themselves as distinct and with recognizable continuity throughout life and after death. But as an issue it is far more salient in Western philosophy and religion, and, I argue, certain features of Tukanoan society and culture can be seen as working against and playing down similar sorts of concerns. The nonuniqueness of Tukanoan names and kin terms and the idea of reincarnation of a person's soul (but not personality) via name transmission is an example of such downplaying.

Thus, whereas in America names are thought of as unique to each individual (and the tag ''Jr.'' serves this purpose when the name does not), they are much less so in Tukanoan society. Furthermore, in the West names are only one of a number of unique tags identifying individuals in terms of their relationship to positions or objects (e.g., social security numbers, driver's licenses, credit card accounts) and, less often, to other people (e.g., marriage licenses). In the Tukanoan system, relationality eclipses such functions performed by Western naming and tagging systems, in part because less need for such identification occurs in Tukanoan society (where everyone knows or knows of everyone else), and in part because our emphasis on individualism greatly exceeds Tukanoan concern with individualism and its analogues.

Kinship terminology

Bará kinship terminology is basically a variant of the Dravidian type.[2] The following distinctions are crucial and pervade the entire Bará system:

1   *Generation.* Five generation levels are distinguished, no skewing is present.
2   *Sex of relative.* Marked in all generations.
3   *Cross versus parallel* (Sex of intervening relative). A distinction made in the 0, +1, and −1 generations. This split can also be referred to as the *agnatic*

versus *affine* distinction, or the "own group" versus "other group" distinction (Buchler and Selby [1968, p. 233]).

The Bará system is different from Iroquois in that it, like all Dravidian systems, "consistently and explicitly distinguishes 'prohibited' women (nonmarriageable categories) from 'lawful' women (genealogically or categorically defined affines). Such systems have positive marriage rules in the sense that Dumont ['The Dravidian Kinship Terminology as an Expression of Marriage,' 1953] . . . uses the term" (Buchler and Selby, 1968, p. 233).

Another important feature mentioned in Chapter 5 is the obligatory marking of elder and younger siblings. Patrilateral parallel cousins are called by the elder or younger term depending on the birth order of their fathers (this is simplified in Table 7).

Sex of speaker is not a general distinction required by the terminology but is marked in the -1 (first descending) generation, and some of the affinal terms of the 0 generation. The basic reason for the differentiation in the -1 generation has to do with the fact that a female's offspring are never her own agnates, whereas a male's offspring are. Thus, although both men and women use the terms *mahkṹ–ó* for their own children, the meaning is different with respect to agnatic ties, and this is clarified by an inspection of other kin types (e.g., a female ego says mahkṹ to her own son, her sister's son, and her husband's brother's son, whereas a male ego says it to his own son, his brothers' sons, and in general all Bará males of the first descending generation).

Patrilateral parallel cousins are separated terminologically from matrilateral parallel cousins. The latter set of terms glosses as "mother's sister's children," and "mother's children" (Table 4). The implication in the latter gloss is that such kinsmen are *not* "father's children" as well. The genealogically closest kinsman called by this term is the uterine half-sibling. Since patrilateral parallel cousins are called by sibling terms, this set of terms designates those same-generation individuals whose mothers are of ego's mother's group but whose fathers are not Bará. This additional set of cousin terms (mother's children) is also found in Tukano and Barasana (C. Hugh-Jones, 1979) and Tatuyo (Bidou, 1976, pp. 117–25, 157). My own incomplete data suggest that Tuyuka can be added to the list. I do not know whether it exists in all Eastern Tukanoan or Arawakan languages in the area, but the fact that it is found in Makú (Silverwood-Cope, 1972), a much more distantly related language, argues for a more widespread distribution than the five languages mentioned above. Goldman (1963, p. 134) gives a term for matrilateral parallel cousins, male and female, among the Cubeo. He notes, however, that these terms are "only those mother's sisters' sons (daughters) who are of the phratry." He does not list another term for those kinsmen outside the phratry who are not classified as cross-cousins.

Two types of cross-cousins are distinguished in Bará: those with Bará mothers (FZS [father's sister's son], FZD [father's sister's daughter]), and those with non-Bará mothers (MBS [mother's brother's son], MBD [mother's brother's daughter]).[3]

Table 7, accompanied by Table 8, outlines the structure of the terminology system. The reader is also referred to Jackson, 1977, for a fuller discussion of the zero-generation terms because virtually none of it is repeated here.

Expectations and behavior

The sociological meaning of a set of kin terms concerns the rights, duties, and privileges existing between kinsmen. Of course one must also look at instances in which these same rights and duties are ignored and challenged (Goodenough, 1965). The relationship of kinship behavior and expectations to the semantic meaning of kin terms is the focus of at times very acrimonious debate.[4] Some authorities, for instance, Wittgenstein (1922; see also Tyler, 1978, pp. 170–72) hold that such "usage" of kin terms is the way the terms ought to be defined.

Any generalized description of behavior among kinsmen will tend to be normative in nature, closer to the official, rule-book version of kinship-related expectations than occurs in reality. In addition, a thorough study of kinship expectations and behavior will reveal some rules that are more hidden than others yet probably at least as important in determining behavior as the more accessible ones. Thus, even when limiting the notion of "rules" of kinship behavior to cognitive rules (as opposed to statistical rules derived from observation), many different kinds of rules operate at different levels of specificity.

As a prologue to discussing the roles kinsmen perform in Tukanoan society, I offer some mythical illustrations of certain basic themes in Tukanoan kinship. The synopses of myths that follow are not intended to address any issues concerning the analysis of these myths and although used as illustrations of kinship themes, no implication is intended that this is the "function" of Tukanoan mythology.[5]

Some myths presented in this section – which emphasizes consanguineal kinship – could just as easily have been included in the following chapter on marriage. The choice is somewhat arbitrary because to some degree all myths deal with agnatic and affinal relationships. The names of the myth synopses are simply for purposes of identification.

Boraro's skin. A man found the skin of a *boraro* (a type of forest spirit) among some logs while the boraro was fishing for shrimps. (The skin was like clothing; the boraro always removed it to swim.) The man put on the skin and it took control, making him eat the boraro, visit the boraro's house, and sleep with his wife. After a while, the man took off the skin and returned to his own house, where two years had passed. His relatives had

Table 7. *Bará kinship terminology*

Term	Address or reference	Kin types	Definition
ñihkü	A,R	FF, MF, FFB, MFB, etc.	all second ascending generation males
ñihkó	A,R	FM, MM, MMZ, FMZ, etc.	all second ascending generation females
pahkü	R	F	own father
pahkó	R	M	own mother
kakü	A	F	own father
kako	A	M	own mother
bügü	A,R	FB, MZH, FFBS, MFZS, etc.	all first ascending generation male agnates (except father)
bügó	A,R	MZ, FBW, FFZD, MMZD, etc.	all first ascending generation female affines (except mother)
mehkü	A,R	MB, FZH, MMZS, MFBS, etc.	all first ascending generation male affines
mehkó	A,R	FZ, MBW, FFBD, MMBD, etc.	all first ascending generation female agnates
hwü	A,R	eB, FeBS, etc.	elder brother; all patrilateral male parallel cousins classified as elder[a]
hō	A,R	eZ, FeBD, etc.	elder sister; all patrilateral female parallel cousins classified as elder[a]
baü	A,R	yB, FyBS, etc.	younger brother; all patrilateral male parallel cousins classified as younger[a]
bayó	A,R	yZ, FyBD, etc.	younger sister; all patrilateral female parallel cousins classified as younger[a]
mehkó-mahkü	A,R	FZS, FFBDS, etc.	all same generation affinal males with agnate (Bará) mother[b]
mehkó-mahkó	A,R	FZD, FFBDD, etc.	all same generation affinal females with agnate (Bará) mother[b]
mehkü-mahkü	A,R	MBS, MFBSS, etc.	all same generation affinal males with nonagnate (Bará) mother[b]
mehkü-mahkó	A,R	MBD, MFBSD, etc.	all same generation affinal females with nonagnate (Bará) mother[b]
pahkó-mahkü	A,R	MZS, MMZSS, etc.	matrilateral parallel male cousins (who are not Bará); uterine half-brother

Table 7. (cont.)

Term	Address or reference	Kin types	Definition
pahkó-mahkó	A,R	MZD, MMZSD, etc.	matrilateral parallel female cousins (who are not Bará); uterine half-sister
mahkü	A,R	S, BS,[c] ZS[d]	all first descending generation male agnates, male speaking; all first descending generation male affines, female speaking
mahkó	A,R	D, BD,[c] ZD[d]	all first descending generation female agnates, male speaking; all first descending generation female affines, female speaking
hõ-mahkü	A,R	eZS[d]	elder sister's son
hõ-mahkó	A,R	eZD[d]	elder sister's daughter
bayó-mahkü	A,R	yZS[d]	younger sister's son
bayó-mahkó	A,R	yZD[d]	younger sister's daughter
hwü-mahkü	A,R	eBS[d]	elder brother's son
hwü-mahkó	A,R	eBD[d]	elder brother's daughter
baü-mahkü	A,R	yBS[d]	younger brother's son
baü-mahkó	A,R	yBD[d]	younger brother's daughter
párami	A,R	SS, DS, SSS, DSS, etc.	second descending generation male
párameo	A,R	SD, DD, SSD, DDD, etc.	second descending generation female
teñü[e]	A,[f] R	WB, ZH, BWB, ZHB, etc.	male cross-cousin; own generation male affine
teñó[e]	R	WZ, BW, BWZ, ZHZ, etc.	female cross-cousin; own generation female affine
numó[e]	R	W	own wife
manü[e]	R	H	own husband
buibahkü[e]	R	ZH,[d] ZHB[d]	same generation male affine, female speaking
buibahkó[e]	R	ZHZ[c]	same generation female affine, male speaking
ühió[e]	R	BW,[d] HZ,[d] BWZ[d]	sister-in-law, female speaking
pehü[e]	R	HW, HBW	co-wife, wife of husband's true brother, female speaking
mohokü[e]	R	ZS,[d] BDH,[d] WBS[d]	all first descending generation male affines, male speaking

110

Table 7. *(cont.)*

Term	Address or reference	Kin types	Definition
mohokó[e]	R	ZD,[d] BSW,[d] WBD[d]	all first descending generation female affines, male speaking
pámokü[e]	A,R	DH,[d] BS,[d] etc.	all first descending generation male agnates, female speaking
pámoko[e]	A,R	SW,[d] BD,[d] etc.	all first descending generation female agnates, female speaking
buí[e]	R	DH[c]	own son-in-law, male speaking
kamí[e]	R	DH[d]	own son-in-law, female speaking

Note: All terms are used by both male and female speakers unless otherwise indicated. Plural forms are not given. See text in this chapter for discussion of sex of speaker distinction in the first descending generation. The endings -ó and -ü are sometimes nasalized, as in mehkü and mehkó. For reasons of diacritic simplicity, none of the terms that have nasalized endings shows this.

Abbreviations and symbols
A = address; R = reference; F = father; M = mother; B = brother; Z = sister; H = husband; W = wife; S = son; D = daughter; e = elder; y = younger.
[a]See Chapter 5 for discussion of use of sibling terminology to denote sib and language group (within the same phratry) rank.
[b]See Jackson, 1977, for discussion of mehkó-mahkü/-ó and mehkü-mahkü/-ó terms.
[c]Male speaking.
[d]Female speaking.
[e]Affinality being stressed.
[f]Used only in address between men.

given him up for dead. He told them what had happened, and one of his relatives wanted to see the boraro's house and fishing territory for himself. They both went back and one of them put on the boraro's skin, and the other put on the boraro's wife's skin while she was fishing. The man wearing her skin then ate her. Finally the two men returned to this world and told their stories, but their relatives did not believe them. They wanted to go and see for themselves, and finally, over the protests of the two men, everyone but one went to the other world. When they arrived, the two original men put on the two boraro skins and ate everyone else. They returned to their settlement, told their story, and all the wives wept. Three men remained, no more.

The most important theme in this sketch is the danger of getting too close to beings who are not "like us." In this case, the man got too close first by venturing

Table 8. *Simplified Bará kinship terminology*

		Agnates				Affines		Affines of affines	
+2	♂					FF/MF	ñihkű		
	♀					FM/MM	ñihkó		
+1	♂	FB	bügű			MB	mehkű		
	♀	FZ	mehkó			MZ	bügó		
0	♂	eB	hwǖ	yB	baü	FZS	mehkó-mahkű	MZS	pahkó-mahkű
	♀	eZ	hō	yZ	bayó	FZD	mehkó-mahkó	MZD	pahkó-mahkó
-1	♂	S	mahkű			ZS	mohokű		
	♀	D	mahkó			ZD	mohokó		
-2	♂					SS/ZSS	párami		
	♀					SD/ZSD	párameo		

Note: Terms for male ego only. No individualizing terms (e.g., F, M) are included. Bará terminology fits a basic Dravidian pattern except for separate "affine of affine" terms and optional MBS/MBD terms when alter is not the child of a female agnate. See Jackson, 1977, for fuller discussion. Cf. C. Hugh-Jones, 1979 and Århem, 1981, for discussion of Barasana and Makuna terminologies.

too near and then by assuming the other's appearance, eating his food, and sleeping with his wife. Tragedy follows, with the protagonist eventually eating virtually all of his own relatives.

Kamaweni. One day the older of two brothers, Kamaweni, was making ceremonial headdresses and other objects. Despite the warning of his younger brother, Kamaweni ate some fish. He then grew very fat and soon was repugnant to his brother. Kamaweni ate everything in sight, and when climbing a log over a river, he vomited up all the fish he had eaten (which turned into a number of present-day fish species). After this, being thin and little, he climbed up on his brother's shoulder and stuck his legs into his brother's chest behind the collarbone (which is why we have holes there today). After some more adventures, his brother became bored with this, and once when a thirsty Kamaweni (after eating too much of a certain fruit) demanded to be taken to some water, his younger brother tricked him into following a kind of toad (which has a voice just like humans) into the forest. When Kamaweni returned, flying, his brother had closed all the doors of the longhouse where they lived. Kamaweni sat on the top of the longhouse, saying, "We are one family, of one father; why don't you love me?" Later, because Kamaweni did not believe what his younger brother said about some jaguars he had summoned, Kamaweni was eaten by them.

A number of points are illustrated in this myth. An older brother is entitled to respect, but only if he behaves properly. Kamaweni does not and begins a process of moral and physical decline that ultimately ends in chaos. He breaks an important food prohibition, eats excessively, becomes ugly, then vomits excessively. Weak and small, he becomes a literal burden on his younger brother, which leads to more excessive eating and drinking, until finally his brother defaults on *his* obligations and lies and plays tricks. Kamaweni's brother refuses to be his brother's keeper when such excessive demands are made and, instead, becomes his slayer. Thus is Kamaweni's brother sucked into Kamaweni's decline. The myth illustrates the need for moderation in one's obligations to kinsmen and the necessity for implicit, unquestioning trust, at least between full brothers.

Kahpéa ōrēro. This myth deals with a family's trip to Ewüra taró (a mirití swamp important in Tukanoan cosmology) to collect thatch. The oldest brother, a shaman, recognized a little creature of the forest, Kahpéa ōrēro ("eye-extractor"), who was eating eyes and making tiny tipitís (manioc-juice extractors) and saying, "these are for taking out the eyes of those people over there." The shaman returned and warned his relatives to hang their hammocks high that night so they would not run the risk of having their eyes stolen. But they did not believe him. That night Kahpéa ōrēro did come, and he took out the eyes of everyone with the little tipití. The shaman woke up and shouted, but his family did not wake up, because they had already lost their eyes. He tried to save the eyes, but it was too late; they had already been cooked. He killed Kahpéa ōrēro. After this, the shaman had to take care of his brothers, leading them with a vine. He finally gave up and deserted them, saying it was their own fault. But then he regretted this action and returned, saying, "These people are my family, how can I throw them away like this?", but it was too late. They had turned into spider monkeys, *mahoká ahké*, living in trees and making noises like these monkeys. The shaman returned to his house alone.

This myth also deals with the theme of relatives becoming overly burdensome, here also because they lacked trust and did not take their brother seriously. The protagonist ends up having literally to lead them because they refused his initial guidance. When he finally gives up on them, they lose their humanness, and he is totally bereft of kinsmen. People must fulfill their kinship obligations if they wish to remain human and continue to have kinsmen.

Live Woman. This myth is about the Tuyuka, Yüküro, a man whose father, who knew many chants and spells, died before having an opportunity to teach them to his son. Yüküro's father's ghost started to harvest coca in Yüküro's manioc field; they met and Yüküro was taken to theTuyuka dead-spirit house on Behuya (weapon) stream. Yüküro's father taught him the proper chants and spells, and Yüküro danced with the dead spirits till dawn and then returned to his house. Although he had been gone only a night, his wife, Live Woman, had become very angry and had burned all the dance costumes and thrown out all his coca and banisteriopsis. Yüküro became angry and then became sick from so much anger and sadness. He realized his death was imminent and told his wife, "When I die, go to such-and-such a path.'' After he was buried, his spirit departed, following the path. He met his wife and told her to follow, keeping her eyes closed, but she saw a little – the dead-spirit house and the stream. His relatives received him, saying "now our elder brother has arrived.'' He was put into a large vat and covered with a cottonlike substance and came out a newborn infant. Live Woman slept outside the house, getting very cold because of the exposure and lack of fire. A number of unpleasant events occurred to her, all because she was a human being in the dead-spirit house: She mistook penises for fire, was disobedient, and, after giving birth to a son, died along with her child.

This myth introduces the idea of the importance of a father teaching his son all the important knowledge; if the father dies before this is finished, difficulties will set in. In Yükúro's case, he deserts his wife (even though only for a night) and she, in retaliation, destroys his ceremonial paraphernalia – symbols of his humanness and membership in Tukanoan society. The story continues with the constant themes of separation, anger between husband and wife, and the wife's jealousy over her husband's loyalty to his own sib-mates. Finally, everything is wrong: Yükúro has died too soon and his wife is in a dead-spirit longhouse without having died. Husband and wife are truly alienated at this point, one dead and one living. They cannot continue as a couple and his descent line cannot continue.

Namakuru. A man died, leaving a wife, two sons, and a little girl. His wife married a wahtí (forest spirit), but her children did not like him because he was not human. The mother had tried to keep her second husband a secret: She would let him in only when the children were asleep, but sometimes they stayed awake and consequently knew everything. The wahtí would bring food, but sometimes it was not human food, such as snakes. The mother would serve the wahtí good things to eat. When the mother became pregnant and gave birth, it was to a deer child, Namakuru. She kept it suspended in a sack high from the ridgepole.

Various versions of the myth differ from here on, but the thrust of the story concerns the mother's deception of her children regarding her newborn child. She makes them spend long hours bathing, even during the night, while she spends time with their stepfather and nurses the deer child. Her children, in turn, deceive her, spying on her and killing their wahtí stepfather by poisoning him with manioc that has not been fully processed. Although in one version the children, particularly the little girl, play with the deer child Namakuru (*ñamá*, "deer") for a while, Namakuru becomes increasingly animal-like, eating only leaves, and finally runs off into the forest. The children fill up the sack he was kept in with ashes, which, when discovered by their mother, enrages her so much she punishes them by smearing hot peppers all over their bodies. They have to "sleep" in the river two nights because of the pain. The myth continues with more and more aberrant behavior, more and more of their world going awry, and after a series of symbolically significant transformations, the myth ends in chaos and disaster for the mother and children.

The story of Namakuru illustrates the jealousy and rivalry that develop between siblings, especially half-siblings. It also demonstrates the inevitable tensions between children and stepparents. Food and sex are the foci of struggle as well as the symbols of estranged affection.

114

Kinship

A number of other myths illustrate the theme of competition between "mother's children" as well. In some myths the characters are uterine half-siblings, as in the Namakuru myth, and in one myth collected by S. Hugh-Jones the plot involves cohusbands of a woman (who would also address one another by the pahkó-mahkǘ ["mother's son"] term). Groups of people (settlements, or entire language groups) who marry women of a third group but do not exchange women between themselves also address one another by this term. The myth about cohusbands of the same wife illustrates this type of relationship between entire groups. The association between wahtí and "mother's children" (pahkó-mahkǘ–ó) appears several times in Tukanoan myths. For example, in several stories the protagonist is on his way to visit his pahkó-mahkara and ends up in a wahtí's house. The ambiguity is clearly intentional.

This myth also deals with good and bad mothers and good and bad children. The mother of Namakuru has made an improper second marriage and lies to her children for her own selfish purposes rather than for their own good. She makes her children do strange, potentially harmful things (such as bathing for long periods of time late at night). When she becomes angry she punishes them far too severely. She demonstrates her "badness" by giving birth to an animal-like infant. Because of her association with her wahtí husband and her rejection of her children, she herself becomes progressively more animal-like, eventually turning into a bird.

For their part, her children also become progressively "bad," unchildlike, and eventually unhuman, turning into birds themselves. They fly into a little hole in a rock, their new home. Their mother, also a bird by now, cannot follow them: She becomes stuck because of her large breast (the one she fed Namakuru with).[6]

Koá-mahkǘ. At the beginning of this myth, the culture hero Koá-mahkǘ is seducing both daughters of Wahóbiro, who gets angry at this sexual greediness and also because Koá-mahkǘ eats excessively and is lazy. Wahóbiro succeeds in abandoning Koá-mahkǘ in a tall tree (a trick that worked partly because Koá-mahkǘ was so greedy), telling him, "You can stay there till you die." Koá-mahkǘ is saved by some birds, *eyoa* (wood ibis) because he helps them get past a huge pillar of fire that reaches from a mountain to the heavens. They take him to the house of their sister, who is the daughter of Nimá Pinó ("Curare Anaconda"). During their visit they keep Koá-mahkǘ hidden, but she discovers him, again because of his greediness. She thinks he has been left by her relatives the Eyoa to be her Makú, that is, her servant. She puts him to work, sending him for water and firewood. He becomes sexually interested in her, and she says, "Make a comb for my hair." Her pubic hair is filled with poisonous snakes, tarantulas, scorpions, and similar stinging creatures. He makes the comb and they begin sleeping together, but he is so greedy that she becomes fed up with his demands. She decides to take him to her father's house, which was exactly what Koá-mahkǘ had hoped would happen. They arrive at her father's house, which is all rock, like a cave, and made entirely of curare. She tells Nimá Pinó, her father, that she has a servant for him, and Nimá Pinó puts Koá-mahkǘ to work. But soon Koá-mahkǘ turns himself into a flea, enters Nimá Pinó's nose and from his heart takes curare, which is the very best kind. Koá-mahkǘ then escapes through a hole he has previously drilled in the rock and

115

uses the poison to kill the hawk Namé, which had been terrorizing and eating all the people.

The myth continues with Koá-mahkũ pretending to be the pahkó-mahkũ of Añá (poisonous snakes) in order to be able to kill them, and he succeeds except for one who escapes to the lower world. He returns to his grandmother's house.

Three kinship-related themes are stressed in this story. The first concerns the inappropriateness of greed for women and sexual intercourse. Koá-mahkũ is pictured as being generally overly lustful, both for the daughters of Wahóbiro and for the daughter of Nimá Pinó. The theme of a man wanting one or, worse, two women, with no indication of a sense of responsibility or reciprocity on his part, occurs in several myths, involving other protagonists as well as Koá-mahkũ. In the areas of sex and marriage, greed and selfishness will lead to unintended and undesirable consequences.

The second theme concerns proper exchange behavior between relatives. Nimá Pinó's daughter is given a gift from her classificatory siblings, the Eyoa: Koá-mahkũ disguised as a Makú-like servant. In turn, she gives the servant to her father.

The third theme is another example of the ambiguity and potential danger inherent in the "mother's children" (pahkó-poná) relationship. Koá-mahkũ pretends that the Añá are his pahkó-poná, which enables him treacherously to kill them.

Some of the general themes expressed in these myth fragments are the following:

1 Relatives are supposed to love one another and look out for one another; when expectations are not met, everything can go haywire, with people eating their own kinsmen, causing their kinsmen to be eaten by jaguars, and punishing their kinsmen too severely or deserting them. But normally one should trust and respect one's kin, for they have one's best interests at heart.

2 Although authority and respect can be initially ascribed by birth order, it must be maintained by behaving appropriately.

3 Ambiguity, potential tension, and even danger inhere in certain relationships, such as between parents-in-law and children-in-law and between pahkó-mahkara ("mother's children").

4 Conflicts of interest frequently occur between the husband and wife and the parent and offspring.

5 Kinsmen who are greedy and irresponsible will upset things in many dire and unpredictable ways. Irresponsible relatives can literally become unbearable burdens, and finally even very close kin will betray and desert the offender. Even the most devoted kin have limits of energy and forgiveness for an erring kinsman.

6 People should associate with their own kind. Because things are seldom what they seem, consorting with beings too different is never successful and

116

inevitably brings many unpleasant surprises. Furthermore, such association is contaminating, and leads to one's becoming like these others, creating disloyalty toward and betrayal of one's other kin.[7]

Specific kinship roles

Before discussing specific kinship dyads, I wish to point out certain factors that affect all Tukanoan kinship-related behavior. One of the most crucial of these is the social structure of the longhouse. The physical structure of the longhouse encourages very close contact among all children and adults in it, although the hearth family is the basic unit of socialization. This creates a primary cleavage between coresident and noncoresident types of kinship relations.

Another consideration is the amount of time men spend at the longhouse: Not only do children constantly interact with many people besides those in their hearth family, but they do so with their uncles and older male cousins to a much greater degree than in most other societies. While growing up, children of both sexes have intimate and long-lasting contact with infants and small children; the amount of preparation for parenting they receive is far greater than occurs – especially for boys – in most other types of domestic arrangements. The contrast in this regard between traditional Vaupés society and our own is particularly striking.[8] The dimensions of age and sex obviously pervade every kind of kinship relationship. The firstborn son or daughter has more responsibility and does not have the experience of being parented by an older sibling. The last child a couple has is said to be the favorite and thus the one most likely to be spoiled. Still, birth order does not matter nearly as much in Tukanoan society as it does in many other traditional societies. As mentioned earlier, the birth of the first child of the new generation in a local descent group is an important event. Ideally it is the son (or grandson) of the headman, because this position implies certain differences in status and expectations.

Parents and offspring.

Both parents nurture very young children, and the sex of the child is irrelevant to the amount of parenting from each. But as they grow up, children spend increasingly more time with their same-sex parent.

From a Western viewpoint, parents are very permissive with young children. Access to parents is almost never denied. For example, no work periods in and around the longhouse require parents' separation from their children. Except for the few genuine dangers, such as fire, very few areas or objects in the longhouse are forbidden. (It is surprising to return to the United States and realize just how lethal a world confronts a toddler in his own home.) If it is impossible to grant very young children what they want, they will be distracted, amused, or simply bought off with a treat; the denial is smooth, soft, and although at times blatantly manipulative, very seldom an outright rejection.

Children should always be in the company of others, but this is true for everyone else as well. The myth of *di wáñako* (described in the following chapter) demonstrates the tragedy that can befall a family if children are punished by being shut out of the longhouse and left alone. Other myths recount a variety of gruesome ends met by children alone in the longhouse or who have strayed into the forest.

Children learn how to behave both by imitation and by gentle suggestions from parents. Past a certain age, they seem far less likely than children in our own society to act out or deliberately to test the limits of patience of their elders. I noticed very little intentional misbehavior in children over three, although this is not to say that children, especially younger ones, do not at times yell with rage or go through phases of seeming to burst into tears at the slightest provocation. When children disobey or otherwise cause displeasure, they are very rarely directly punished, and most often disapproval is not even apparent. The two times I saw a parent hit a child were the opposite of a "rational" technique of socialization, and were obviously unusual behavior on the mothers' parts.

At some point in children's lives (when depends on development, personalities, and birth order position), their parents begin to toughen up and expect them to be more responsible for their actions. None of this is explicitly acknowledged; I heard very little parental philosophy per se discussed. The methods used are not explicitly justified or rationalized and occur rather randomly and unevenly – which in itself is probably an important lesson to be learned about life. Parents apply techniques of social control found in other areas of Tukanoan life: ignoring the behavior, collective ostracism, gentle laughter (at times escalating to ridicule), and similar methods.

Little girls begin to work at an earlier age and for longer periods of time than little boys. In large part this obviously has to do with the nature of women's as opposed to men's work. Nevertheless, little boys take care of younger siblings and run errands for their mothers and aunts. This is partly because the sexes help each other with tasks, even though the tasks themselves are almost invariably designated as either men's or women's. Most often, children are very willing to run errands, and at times they are very proud to be asked. Still, little girls, who sometimes carry water, wash clothes, and gather firewood in quite grown-up fashion, cannot be forced to work, for no one can. This points out a general fact of the parent–offspring relationship: It is founded on an almost natural and spontaneous line of authority based on skill and knowledge, and both parties must voluntarily accept such authority. Parents nurture and give to children far more than the reverse and so have more authority. But the overriding characteristic of this relationship is respect, on both parents' and children's parts; it is also generally true of relations between husband and wife. To a certain degree, parents

118

treat their children like adults, or rather like potential adults, in that they have their own autonomy in many respects. The enthusiasm children at times display in helping out is not abused, because no one can coerce another into doing his or her job. Help may be offered and gratefully accepted, but this never releases a person from working. Even Makú servants do not relieve their masters and mistresses of daily tasks.

Admittedly the above statements are somewhat subjective. Still, it is clear that Tukanoans believe that respect and trust should flow between parents and children. It is a theme in a number of myths (which usually teach by demonstrating the negative consequences when such respect and trust are lacking). Furthermore, a lack of respect (of recognizing that everyone has a right to be one's own person) is an oft-heard complaint when difficulties erupt between parents and their older children. At present, this problem is exacerbated by the younger generation's sometimes being more able to elicit prestige and respect according to the new, intrusive value system as a consequence of their knowledge of Spanish and of mission town culture; a personal acquaintance with missionary personnel; an appointment as the **catequista** of a settlement; and the possession of shirts, shotguns, and other forms of wealth.

The worst fight I witnessed at Púmanaka buro involved a man and his eldest son. Many accusations of lack of respect on everyone's part were hurled. Eventually the entire longhouse became involved when the son picked up a coca-pounding club made of extremely hard wood, and opened a four-inch gash in his father's head.[9]

Uncles, aunts, nephews, and nieces.

Relations between these kinds of relatives depend, first, on whether they are agnatic or not, and second, on whether the individuals are coresidents or not. A child lives with some of his classificatory father's brothers, who are called *bügǘ;* their wives are called *bügó* (classificatory mother's sister). Both terms, especially the bügó term, extend to many more kinsmen; thus the terms can refer to the very close relationship an ego has with coresident father's brothers and their wives (who may be actual mother's sisters, although this seldom happens), whereas in other cases, the terms refer to + 1 generation male agnates, or + 1 generation female nonagnates, respectively.

A child calls his MBs (any + 1 generation male belonging to his mother's language group) *mehkǘ* and their wives *mehkó*. Ideally, only + 1 generation Bará women are supposed to be called mehkó, but the wife of a mehkǘ is addressed with this term, although a mehkǘ's non-Bará wife may be called *mehkǘ-numó* ("mehkǘ's wife"), which usually indicates that she is not Bará. Ego calls all FZs (+ 1 generation Bará females) by the mehkó term. As with the bügǘ/bügó set, expectations of behavior cannot be generalized: The amount of interaction determines these expectations to a greater extent than with

119

the preceding set because these individuals always live in other settlements. Certainly a close mehkǘ or mehkó, if visited frequently (especially if a potential marriage with a daughter is in the offing) is a highly significant individual.

Máñikǘ and *máñiko* are terms that refer specifically to parents-in-law and are never used in address; when used in reference, the affinal relationship is being emphasized. Otherwise mehkǘ/-ó is used.

Siblings.

All older children take care of younger ones to some extent, although girls, if available, will do more. The traditional Tukanoan settlement's isolation undoubtedly plays an important part in producing the close bonds between many sibling pairs. Closeness in age and compatible personalities obviously matter as well in creating particularly strong affective bonds both between real siblings and between coresident parallel cousins.[10] Both brother–sister and same sex sibling pairs can be very close. If an unmarried girl is without a classificatory sister of her age at the settlement, she will probably feel quite deprived. A solution is to try to establish intimacy and confidence with a sister-in-law, but this is more difficult, especially if that woman is struggling with her mother-in-law (who is sometimes the unmarried girl's mother). Close sisters (or a brother–sister pair) face a painful period when one of them marries and moves away.

As siblings grow up, tensions often develop between them. For several reasons this is particularly likely in the case of brothers. First, cultural tradition requires that the bond between brothers be paramount, affectively strong, and permanent. The local descent group's core, ideally if not always in fact, is the set of full male siblings. In fact, a lot does depend on brothers' (particularly full brothers) getting along with one another, and so when difficulties occur, the implications are always serious. Furthermore, brothers often find themselves in situations of real competition and rivalry with one another (e.g., for women or prestige). In addition, because the role of the male adult, more than that of the female, emphasizes face-saving and the need to maintain respect and self-esteem, there is a greater possibility of real or imagined threats to this self-esteem, most often from other men. Finally, whereas sisters eventually leave the sibling group, brothers do not, and thus more difficulties occur between brothers simply because they interact more.

Grandparents and grandchildren.

Relations between grandparents (*ñikǘ/-ó*) and their grandchildren (*párami*) are secure, warm, affectionate, and generally lack threat or anxiety. Few tensions are built into these reciprocal roles in the first place, and the great difference in age limits the manipulation, ambiguity, and accommodation possible. It is also true that this is primarily a relationship between older people and young children, although some grandparents live to see their grandchildren well into their teens: one four-generation family (Pedrina's) resided at Púmanaka buro.

Mehkó-mahkü/-ó: cross-cousins.

Although in part genealogically defined in terms of consanguinity, these relationships are also affinal and are more thoroughly discussed in the chapter on marriage, which follows. Unless a marriage has taken place, because mehkó-mahkara are always living in different settlements, interaction is infrequent and matters less. Moreover, this relationship, both as a potential husband and wife or as one's sibling's husband or wife, is infused with affinal meaning. Of course, while growing up, a Tukanoan child's interactions with mehkó-mahkara are not heavily flavored with marriageability issues. Nonetheless, such interaction ideally sets the stage for later marital negotiations. Thus, while necessary analytically, it is hard to separate the relationship traced through parents from one traced through potential affines.

Pahkó-mahkü/-ó: matrilateral parallel cousins.

I have already briefly discussed this relationship in the form it takes between uterine half-siblings. Otherwise, no specific prescriptions or expectations obtain between *pahkó-poná*.[11] People who are pahkó-mahkü/-ó to each other are matrilateral parallel cousins whose fathers are from different language groups. They cannot intermarry, but neither are they classificatory siblings. The implication is that they compete for women from the language group from which they both obtain women – their respective mothers' language group. Thus the relationship has many affinal aspects implicit in it and is discussed more fully in the following chapter.

Affines.

Kin terms that are affinal as well as consanguineal (but, obviously, never agnatic) are bügó (FBW/FZH), mehkü, mehkó-mahkü/-ó (cross-cousins, mother Bará), mehkü-mahkü/-ó (cross-cousins, mother not Bará), and pahkó-mahkü/-ó (refers to affines of affines; see the reference to the myth about cohusbands of the woman earlier in this chapter). Other terms (see Table 7) refer to specific affinal relations and are not generalizable either from ego or alter to a category of people.[12] These terms have a number of special qualities, connotations, and constraints on usage. In general, they are *not* used if a more polite consanguineal–affinal term can be used (e.g., mehkü [MB] rather than máñikü [WF], or mehkó-mahkó [FZD] rather than *teñó:* the teñó term is so loaded with strictly affinal meaning, especially in cross-sex address, that it is almost never heard). This results in these strictly affinal terms often being used as a default category, having somewhat bare, almost derogatory qualities. (This is because they refer only to affines, which is an awkward and potentially hostile category when no other relationships exist between ego and alter.) These terms are used in discussing affinal relationships, when marriage and its problems and interactions are being dealt with as separate from other kinship relations.

Several terms show, at least in part, some of the strains placed on a basically Dravidian structure when several rather than only two intermarrying groups are actually exchanging women. I have briefly discussed the pahkó-mahkü/-ó set of terms in this regard. This set acknowledges the presence of three intermarrying units in the + 1 generation: ego's group, ego's mother's group, and the group that ego's mother's sister married into – which is obviously not ego's own, because the sibling term is not used for these parallel cousins. The teñó term gives a strong emphasis to the marital relationship itself, because, when· possible, cross-cousin terms are normally used between sisters-in-law and (in particular) between brother and sister-in-law. Teñü, although it also stresses the affinal as opposed to the consanguineal (cross-cousin) relationship, is used more fre-quently between brothers-in-law, because this relationship, even though strictly affinal in meaning, is important in its own right. Another term, *pehü*, when applied to females literally means "co-sister-in-law," "co-wife," and again is used (almost never in practice) when no other term can be substituted. The following myth of women who share the same husband shows the ambivalence and potential conflict of interest between co-sisters-in-law who are bound by no other relationship.[13]

Pehü. A widower takes a second wife. The first wife, now a wahtí, appears to the second in her manioc field, invites her to collect edible ants with her, offers her cazabe and offers to take care of the second wife's baby. Little by little the second wife gets suspicious and discovers the truth when the first wife, while taking a nap, snores and says: "*pehütorono*," acknowledging that she is a wahtí co-wife, the second wife's pehü. After a series of adventures involving some forest creatures described as the pahkó-mahkara of the wahtí, the second wife is saved at daybreak by her husband. They leave the first wife in the forest and are never bothered again.

Virtually all myths deal with affinal relationships. Many of them stress the same themes, one of which is that affines are necessary, can be the source of gifts and benefits, and will make many sacrifices. Still, affines are always different from one's own kind and hence ultimately unknowable. Furthermore, certain built-in risks, conflicts of interest, and competition arise in affinal relationships, for example, the competition with one's same-generation agnates and with one's pahkó-mahkara when acquiring a wife.

The myth of Waí Pinó Mahkó, Fish Anaconda Daughter, portrays affinal relationships in several ways. This woman, who marries Yebá Mahü (a human) is responsible for introducing tobacco and banisteriopsis to humans and illus-trates the help and benefits that can be obtained for establishing good affinal relationships. Still, acquiring these two plants predictably comes about through a series of mistakes and ignored instructions. The next section of the myth is concerned with a trip Yebá Mahū makes to visit his in-laws. This episode was mentioned previously in the discussion of sib rank. Yebá Mahū visits the longhouse of his Waí mahá ("fish people") in-laws, the headman of which is Waí Pinó (Fish Anaconda), the father of Waí Pinó Mahkó, Fish Anaconda Daughter. The Waí mahá eat only "pure" food, such as termites. However, Waí Pinó, seeing that his son-in-law is hungry, offers him his (Waí Pinó's) own relatives to eat, illustrating the sacrifice one must make of one's agnates in favor of one's affines. Waí Pinó offers Yebá Mahū the Doé (Tarira) fish to eat because they are the lowest-ranking species of fish there and are described in the myth as "like the Makú . . . like the Wamūtañará sib is to the Bará."

Another theme in the myth of Waí Pinó Mahkó is the risk and danger inherent in visiting in-laws, because they are by definition dissimilar. At one point, Yebá Mahū is almost suffocated by his father-in-law's anaconda skin, in part because Yebá Mahū disobeyed instructions. Waí Pinó returns in time and strikes the skin, which of course obeys him. This is a graphic demonstration of the very real risk of being suffocated or squeezed to death by one's affines. It also illustrates the fact that all affines are potentially two-faced: generous and friendly when it suits them and when they are obeyed but dangerous when things go contrary to their liking. This last point is also demonstrated when Yebá Mahū is greeted by his affines: They greet him first as anacondas by crawling all over him (their customary greeting!), and he, although full of fear, must withstand it and maintain his equanimity. Following this, he is greeted the way people greet one another.

Fictive and ceremonial kinship.

Some Tukanoans form ritual coparenthood (baptismal godparent) relationships with rubber gatherers during sojourns at rubber camps. My impression is that these are extremely attenuated; for one thing, as in all areas in Latin America where compadrazgo (ritual coparenthood) is found, it requires upkeep and if allowed to lapse is effectively terminated.

S. Hugh-Jones (1979) and C. Hugh-Jones (1979) observed a "ceremonial brother-in-law" (*he teñüa*) relationship in the Pirá-paraná. This involves an agreement between two actual or classificatory brothers-in-law to be friends and to exchange ceremonial artifacts. Pirá-paraná Tukanoans also speak of groups as each others' he teñüa. This is, in other words, an elaboration of and a heightening of the affect implicit in an already existing kinship relationship. Unlike the special bonds that can develop between brother and sister, however, these are necessarily always between individuals from different settlements, which makes a difference in the amount of intimacy that can develop.[14]

7.

Marriage

Marriage in the Vaupés is a kind of movement: People, goods, and intangible commodities such as prestige follow marital paths linking families and settlements. It is thus not surprising that Tukanoans spend a great deal of time and energy negotiating marriages and observing and discussing how similar negotiations progress in other households.

Probably low population density, dispersed settlement pattern, egalitarianism, and a swidden horticultural base with a strong overlay of hunting, fishing, and gathering are the most important reasons why so much extralocal economic interaction is linked to affinal relationships. A strong component of the economic system is that people meet the demand for nonlocal goods and services by depending on their network of ties to other people and settlements through organized marriage exchanges rather than through direct commodity exchanges. This economic system suits an environment and level of technology requiring both extensive lands that must lie fallow for longer than they are cultivated and controls on overexploitation of hunting, fishing, and gathering resources. An evenhanded and flexible economic system involving a strong element of generalized reciprocity and little capital or stored surplus is necessary. A marriage system that allows for continual adjustments to the ecosystem and fosters some economic dependence on social relationships maintained through affinal links in a number of other settlements fits in well with this setting, for it places the most emphasis on exchanges of personnel rather than on exchanges of goods. It thus helps limit the potential for exclusive control of wealth in either goods or scarce sources of energy by any one group. The flexibility of a system preventing such exclusive control permits the most judicious long-term utilization of the ecosystem.

Even the beginning of a marriage (I hesitate to use the term *wedding*) fits this description. Significant contractual agreement, transferral of wealth, or major ritual contact with supernatural powers does not characterize Vaupés marriage making as it does in many societies. Unlike some Gê cultures, Tukanoan initiation ritual is not at all concerned with marriage (Maybury-Lewis, 1979). As C. Hugh-Jones points out, "marriage is solely a redistribution of female repro-

124

ductive powers which makes a new generation socially possible'' (1979, p. 160), noting that the physiological ability to reproduce is established during male and female initiation. Birth and death in Tukanoan culture are also marked by ritual and contact with the ancestors, but marriage is distinctly secular. Sometimes (as when, for instance, a woman is already living at her husband's settlement), nothing pinpoints the beginning of a marriage. Certainly economic exchanges follow the establishment of a marriage, but they depend on availability of resources and how well the social relationships between affinally related families and settlements are going. To the degree that an alliance is established or continued and strengthened, ongoing movement between local descent groups resulting from a successful marriage is a permanent process that outlives all the participants.

Ceremonial bride capture and subsequent negotiations are in a sense wedding rituals, but the ideal marriage lacks such evidence of unfamiliarity and mistrust and is initiated long before a woman moves to her husband's settlement.

I analyzed a marriage sample of 684 marriages, made by 636 men and 664 women. I actually gathered data on many more marriages (more than 1,000), most of them between the parents and grandparents of Tukanoans included in the final sample. The marriages eliminated from the final sample were discarded because of unreliable sources of information or too many missing variables.[1] The marriages accepted for the sample were scored in terms of reliability and were coded for twenty-six variables concerned with information about each partner and about the marriage itself.[2] As mentioned earlier, this sample is not a total census of marriages for the Vaupés, nor is it a systematically selected random sample. It is complete with respect to all marriages made by living individuals in the Papurí–upper Tiquié drainage region: men and their inmarried wives, and women born in this subregion who have married into settlements elsewhere.

Principles of marriage

The following discussion examines some of the underlying principles of marriage in the Vaupés. I am defining ''principle'' loosely to indicate that in Vaupés marital behavior certain patterns are observable to some extent and that Tukanoans verbalize them as norms when discussing marriage making. I do not (and cannot, at this point) imply that marital behavior is determined by these principles. By no means do they predict actual marital behavior all of the time, nor is it clear whether they in fact operate even as norms in all marriages. A future research objective is to discover the degree to which such principles do in fact influence marriage making. Anthropologists tend to be overly juridical in their interpretations of how ''rules'' operate in small-scale societies and too quick to assume that what is stated to be the preferred form of marriage (or any other type of behavior) is the preference under all possible conditions. It was pointed out in Chapter 1

125

that there is a seeming overabundance of rules and categories in Vaupés social structure, particularly as concerns marriage. We cannot rule out the possibility that some of these rules are epiphenomenal: Though stated to be determinants by Tukanoans, they are in fact only after-the-fact rationalizations. Perhaps in actuality such "rules" play much more of a role in ordering the Tukanoan social universe as a conceptual system. Still, it is also possible that some rules are constructed in such a way as to override certain other rules under given conditions. In this case, what we lack is knowledge of the criteria that activate given sets of rules and given them precedence. Silverwood-Cope (1972, p. 176) gives an example of this type of ordering in his discussion of Makú marriage rules: Although Makú are quite aware of the Tukanoan rules that prescribe marriage with a person in the "potential affine" category, Makú have other rules prescribing subregional endogamy that have priority. Tukanoans do not have such stringent territorial rules, and therefore they condemn the higher frequency of improper Makú marriages much more than do the Makú themselves. Undoubtedly, Tukanoans do have rules regulating regional endogamy, but these involve a far vaster territory and thus are not as constraining as those of the Makú. In any case, it is evident that we must avoid overly simplistic conclusions about Tukanoans' obeying or disobeying their marriage rules, whether in thought or action.[3]

Direct exchange and polygamy.

In the ideal Tukanoan marriage, a man obtains a wife by exchanging his real sister for another man's real sister. "Exchanging our daughters for daughters-in-law" also expresses this principle. This phrasing illustrates how, in addition to the one or two pairs of prospective spouses, the two local descent groups perceive their vested interest in any marriage making.

Although an exchange of actual sisters is the ideal, it seldom occurs in practice because of demographic and other factors. In 18.7 percent (79) of a sample of 423 marriages, one or both wives were the actual sisters of each other's husband; in 14.4 percent (61), the wives were the classificatory sisters and of the same settlement as each other's husband; in 24.1 percent (102), exchanges involved two generations (e.g., an FZD for the FZ given in the preceding generation); in 5.7 percent (24), the classificatory sisters were from different settlements from each other's husband; and in 37.1 percent (157), no exchange took place. This last category includes only marriages known to have had no exchange (information on this variable was not available for 249 marriages in the total sample of 684). Several one-couple marriages were described to me as future exchange marriages, but I recorded them as nonexchange marriages. Most involved a sister too young to exchange at the time of the first marriage. Thus, although the ideal type of exchange marriage is rarely realized in actuality, it is evident that marriages where two men exchange classificatory sisters or complete the exchange in the next generation are still very much a fact of Vaupés life.

The Bará terms for marriage describe the exchange. The term *hikaniya* (*hiká*, "one") glosses as "one-couple marriage," and *püaniya* (*püá*, "two") glosses as "two-couple marriage." A married woman will be a *hikaya mahkó* or a *püáya mahkó*, depending on whether or not she was part of an exchange marriage.

That the ideal consists of an exchange of real sisters can be understood by examining the negotiational aspects of marriage and the risk that the second half of an exchange marriage may never come about, despite protestations of good faith (and, in fact, genuinely good intentions) on the part of the local descent group that owes a woman to another group. For example, although an exchange can be completed in the next generation, it is risky to expect people to live up to obligations incurred at a much earlier time, and thus sisters are preferred. It also means that for a considerable amount of time one local group will be indebted to another, which considers itself deprived of a woman. In addition, a man has the most influence over his actual sisters. Classificatory sisters are certainly as acceptable in exchange, but they are likely to be most influenced by *their* father and brothers. Furthermore, a man's real sister will be more likely to consider marrying a particular man if by so doing she can help her brother get a wife. She will be less inclined to do such favors for a less closely related agnate, particularly if he is not of her settlement. In the latter type of marriage, it always seems that the woman would have married the man anyway; the exchange was convenient to all and did not involve any persuasive techniques directed at her. Women always have the final say, at least at present. This is one area in which the Vaupés system differs from certain other direct exchange systems in lowland South America, most notoriously the Yąnomamö.[4] Furthermore, a man can try to persuade his actual sister to return to her natal settlement if his wife leaves him. Because marital quarrels threaten two marriages, more pressure is brought on the couple to patch things up. Thus, Tukanoans say, an exchange of two women guarantees a greater amount of marital stability. An exchange of actual sisters, when possible, has the greatest potential for achieving two stable marriages.

Only women can be exchanged for women. According to alliance theory, "marriage forms may be regarded as partial and incomplete expressions of certain underlying principles of reciprocity" (Buchler and Selby, 1968, p. 103). Marriage in the Vaupés is indeed part of a larger relationship – between families and between pairs of local descent groups. Still, no goods can be given in lieu of a woman, and only another woman given at that time or promised for the future compensates this loss. Goldman says that a headman's prestige and affluence can help him obtain a wife through bride price alone (1963, p. 145), but it is my impression that to some degree he will still be seen as owing a woman to the group that gave him his second wife. If a man, even a headman, receives a woman from a group, he and his own group stand in a position of indebtedness that cannot be erased with bride price.

Tukanoans offer the fact that only a woman given compensates for a woman received as the reason behind a general disapproval of polygyny. A man (almost always a headman) with a second wife is indebted to the local group that she came from – even if she was a widow, divorcée, or without close kinsmen. The unavoidable implications of polygyny, then, are that such men have used two of their close female agnates in exchange for their wives, or that one or two are owed to another local group. Although a headman's wife works very hard and is seen as more deserving of the help of a co-wife (although she herself may not see things this way), his position as a headman does not formally entitle him to make two marriages. A man is entitled to one wife, for general opinion has it that otherwise there would not be enough women to go around. Tukanoans generally feel that all men would get married if they could, and all women could get married if they (only) would.[5]

I did not collect systematic data on age at marriage (an extremely difficult task), but usually women do not marry before or immediately after puberty. This contrasts with some other lowland South American societies (e.g., the Cuiva, Yąnomamö, Guayaki [Aché], Sirionó), in which men are often much older than their wives. In general, in a first marriage husband and wife do not differ markedly in age. Some Tukanoan women do not marry until well into their twenties. That some women live with one or two men prior to settling down with the man who turns out to be their permanent mate complicates obtaining information on age at marriage, for informants giving marriage histories tend not to remember such information easily.

Tukanoans thus see monogamy as the most equitable arrangement for all concerned. In a sample of 672 marriages, only 6 were polygynous, and 4 of these were made by one rather remarkable Tukano man. When a priest discovered the situation, he persuaded this Lothario (my informants giggled at the story) to send three of his wives back to their natal longhouses. It seems reasonable to assume that polygyny was practiced to a greater degree in the past and declined because of Catholic missionary disapproval.

A marriage at Púmanaka buro demonstrates how the principle of exchange operates even in the absence of brother–sister pairs. Estribino, the headman's eldest son, took a Tuyuka wife, Isabel. She came from a family living downstream that consisted of three sisters and no brothers. A week later, Isabel's father, Armando, arrived, saying he wanted Estribino's younger sister, Maximiliana, in exchange. This precipitated a huge quarrel, mainly between Armando and Estribino's father, Mario. Armando maintained that he was owed a woman and, moreover, that he had a right to a second wife because he had no sons and therefore no daughters-in-law to look after him and his wife when they were old. Mario retorted that Armando was too old, that he already had a wife, who could still bear him sons, and that Maximiliana did not want to marry him anyway.

128

Hearing this, Armando took his daughter back home with him, although she did not want to go. Armando was counting on Estribino to pressure his sister Maximiliana into marrying him. His plan was not successful, and Isabel did not return to Pǔmanaka buro. When I left, Estribino was still unmarried.

When Armando and Mario had discussed the upcoming marriage, they had not mentioned an exchange of women: The demographic imbalance (Armando had all daughters) and the fact that he lived alone with his family (a quarrel had resulted in his leaving his natal longhouse farther downstream) meant that the potential bride, Isabel, had no classificatory brothers wanting to use her in their exchange marriages. Armando waited until Isabel was firmly established at Pǔmanaka buro, when his bargaining position was strongest, before coming forward with his demands. Using his daughter as leverage in this fashion with this particular family was perhaps the best possible strategy, for it was common knowledge that Estribino had been trying to get married for several years (he was at least twenty-six). The pressure on him to marry was particularly strong, because a headman's eldest son should be the first to get married.

It is difficult to speculate about the incidence of püaniya in earlier times, although "one-couple" marriages might perhaps occur more frequently today, owing to acculaturation, depopulation, and out-migration. Nevertheless, the principle of sister exchange is still quite strong, and Tukanoans who are quite aware of the changes in marriage patterns due to acculturative influences maintain that püaniya is still the best arrangement. The Catholic missionaries consider it a form of selling women and have prevented exchange marriages from taking place.

I do not have much data on divorce per se. Information on its incidence is difficult to come by because early marriages are often unstable, and a divorce before children are born is obviously far less significant than one that takes place after one or more children. Still, such breakups do happen, and the children tend to move with the mother. Presumably it is difficult for them if she marries a second husband belonging to a language group different from her first husband's, but I have information on only one such case – a Carapana woman who left her Tukano husband for a Tatuyo. That this does not happen often illustrates how much current Vaupés marital patterns differ from those in societies with greater tendencies toward polygyny, brittle marriages, and strong male dominance. In such societies, for example, wives are often "stolen" by other men. Although the wife is often blamed, that men want to take away other men's wives is seen as the natural state of affairs. This is not the case in the Vaupés, although adultery, always a serious matter, does occur – at least accusations are often made. A woman who chooses to leave her husband after having several children by him to run off with another man is seen as unusual. The case mentioned above provoked comments about the first husband's inability to keep his wife, but no coercion was used to bring her back.

I did not record any unquestionable cases of polyandry, although I observed a curious situation involving a woman and two brothers in a downstream longhouse. She was said to be married only to the older one, but the three had been together a long time, she fed them both, and she had given birth to several children. They traveled as a unit. I am suspicious of this case mainly because of informants' surprising reluctance to discuss the younger brother's failure to obtain a wife. I could only conclude that this was a case of polyandry or that he was not interested in women at all.

I did not witness any accusations of adultery at Púmanaka buro itself, but I certainly heard of them at other settlements. Their absence at Púmanaka buro was probably due to the fact that all married people had been married for a long while; in fact each couple had children who were ready to get married. At the time of my arrival, no members of the next generation had married, with the exception of a Bará woman who was staying at Púmanaka buro because her husband was away at a rubber camp. Thus, the most potentially adulterous situations (i.e., involving young couples) did not typify this group. It is likely that sometimes young wives dissatisfied with their situation provoke a quarrel to make their presence felt. Because they have little power, one way of doing this is to flirt with their husband's real or classificatory brother. In any case, women tend to be seen as the instigators of adulterous liaisons. Wives are seen as more likely than husbands to experience difficulties early in a marriage. Women receive more blame and punishment for sexual misbehavior than men, although men are subject to more prohibitions in sexual activities (in connection with hunting or ritual, for instance). Although it was my impression that the young man was equally guilty in the case of incest at Púmanaka buro (see Chapter 5), the young woman was blamed more.

Regardless of who in fact is responsible for beginning a flirtation, the least disruptive view to take is that the outsider women are the troublemakers (see Goldman, 1963). This characterizes a number of patrilineal and patrilocal societies (Collier, 1974; Collier and Rosaldo, 1981). Male solidarity must be maintained, and a rift between brothers is a serious matter, particularly when seen as a result of active seduction rather than the milder crime of passive surrender to overwhelming temptation. Themes of women being sexually provocative, demanding, or even voracious appear and reappear in myths. Other societies' stress on female purity, innocence, and maternal longings does not appear in the Vaupés. An emphasis on chastity, in fact, applies more to men, particularly during special ritual periods. To be seductive, a woman must make an overture; she cannot merely "look" sexually inviting. A picture of a seductively supine woman in an advertisement in my American magazine was only puzzling to Tukanoans, who asked if she were sick.

Kinship relations between spouses.

When specifically asked, Tukanoans will state a preference for marriage to a genealogically close kinsman within the category of cross-cousin (mehkó—

130

mahkǘ–ó). The advantages of such a marriage are several. It is better from the woman's point of view not to move into a totally strange longhouse, and a longhouse where a woman's closest cross-cousins reside will also usually be relatively nearby. Furthermore, not only is this longhouse likely to be inhabited by familiar people and in familiar territory, but most of these people will be related through several well-established connections. This means her link to them will not be merely an affinal one. Should trouble arise, such an inmarried woman will be seen not only as daughter-in-law but also as the close niece of several of the residents. Living with the real or close classificatory siblings of her parents, whether on her father's, mother's, or both sides, probably helps to resolve marital difficulties more easily. She also speaks the language of the longhouse where a real or close classificatory mother's brother is living and is very likely to speak the longhouse language where a real father's sister is living. (She will, of course, be familiar with the language of any longhouse belonging to her mother's language group, and only some of these will contain genealogically close kinsmen.)

In 21.1 percent ($n = 360$) of marriages in which the husband's relationship to the wife's mother ("FZD marriage") was known, the wife's mother belonged at least to the husband's sib or was even more closely related. In 42.8 percent of this sample, the wife's mother belonged to the same language group as the husband.

In a sample of 360 marriages in which the husband's mother's relationship to the wife was known ("MBD marriages"), 20.0 percent involved a woman from the husband's mother's sib or an even closer relationship. Of this sample, 40.8 percent of the marriages involved a woman of the same language group as the husband's mother.

Although a woman remains a member of her local descent group throughout her life, her membership in a residential group shifts at marriage from her natal longhouse to her husband's. As pointed out earlier, this at times places women in a position of conflicting loyalties. A woman's children belong to the local descent group of her husband, and when quarrels arise between the two groups her loyalties to them sometimes conflict with her continuing allegiance to her own local descent group. A pair of local descent groups experiences more pressure to resolve disagreements equitably when they have a long-standing exchange relationship involving more than one married couple, even though it is often these same affinal relationships that sow the seeds of many of the disagreements that occur. A pair of allied local descent groups gains much from continued contact and loses much in a permanent rupture, because so many individual relationships are involved. Therefore, both groups are more likely to keep their promises and work at resolving conflicts when more than one inmarried woman connects them.

In many societies with prescriptive marriage rules, marrying *too* close a relative – a double cross-cousin or a first cross-cousin – is prohibited. In the Vaupés, not only are these close cousins possible spouses, they are stated to be the preferred type. In societies that prohibit such marriages, a moiety system (as

131

opposed to the Vaupés's open-ended system) sometimes operates, or a greater chance exists of local groups forming too exclusive an alliance with only one other local group – because this would most likely always be the preference of the individual parties involved in marriage making. Forming too consolidated an alliance with one other group seems less likely in a situation such as that in the Vaupés, where demographic constraints and the presence of so many exogamous groups mitigate against the likelihood of ending up with all one's affinal eggs in a single basket. In the past, other factors may have served adequately to prevent the formation of too exclusive an alliance between pairs of local descent groups.

In neighboring groups, such as the Yukuna (Jacopin, 1981) and Witoto (Gasché, 1977), a man cannot marry into any longhouse in which his brothers have already married. Tukanoan marriage patterns also show dispersal of group members, although proscriptions of this sort are not explicitly stated.

At present I cannot discern a tendency from the actual marriage data to marry more closely through one of the two patrilines connecting the spouses. Speaking from the perspective of a male ego, Bará informants stated a preference for marriage with an FZD rather than an MBD. Their explanation of this preference concerns a general structural principle rather than presumed advantages to the individuals involved. FZD marriage is preferred to MBD marriage because it is "getting back a woman (FZD) for the one we gave out in the previous generation (FZ)." Marriage with an MBD, on the other hand, creates a double debt to the affinal group because an MBD's local descent group has now given both an M and an MBD.

We cannot combine these two stated preferences into a single composite preference (e.g., "the ideal marriage is with a true FZD"), because informants argue them from different grounds. A woman probably prefers to be both an FZD and a genealogically close kinswoman of her husband, for she would then very probably move into her mother's natal longhouse. This preference for FZD conflicts with ethnographic reports from some societies having prescriptive bilateral marriage in which natives state a preference for MBD as opposed to FZD (Elkin, 1953; Radcliffe-Brown, 1953). Furthermore, some ethnographers working in the Vaupés also report a preference for marriage with MBDs (e.g., Goldman, 1963, p. 138).

I must stress that although Tukanoans may state that marriage to a specific type of relative is preferred, what they actually *do* when arranging marriages is influenced by many other considerations as well.[6] As noted, I tried to see whether any pattern emerged in actual marriages in terms of a greater genealogical closeness between spouses through the wife's father's versus mother's line. But the tests I ran, using a sample of 180 marriages in which the relationship through both lines was known, were statistically inconclusive (see Jackson, n.d. b, for further discussion of this and similar points). A possible consideration is the relative ease with which a father can negotiate for a son's wife through his WB (wife's brother) versus his ZH (sister's husband) (and it certainly is easier for a mother to influence her B than her HZ and HZH). The longhouse in which a WB lives tends to be more of a known and secure place than one in which a man's Z has married (assuming these are different). Although a man's bond with his sister may be strong, he cannot as easily control her affinal relatives, because she, being an inmarried woman, is on less sure footing herself. Still, if a strong marital bond exists between husband and wife, perhaps they can exert considerable pressure on the wife's brother. A man's relationship with his kinsmen at his mother's natal longhouse (where a close MBD would come from) is usually stronger than with people whom an FZ lives with, and therefore we might speculate that whereas from the structural point of view just summarized Tukanoans prefer FZD marriages, from a bargaining point of view they know MBD marriages are generally easier to negotiate. (But I am not saying that we can collapse all the parameters of actual marriage making into this single factor.)

Genealogical closeness does not guarantee familiarity between prospective spouses. For example, during my stay, a marriage was arranged between Nazalio and his first cousin, Fernanda, a Tuyuka girl from the Tiquié. The people at Púmanaka buro knew very little about this girl and her family, because contact had not been maintained after Nazalio's mother, Esmeralda, had moved to her husband's home.

Although Tukanoans agree that marrying a woman from an unknown and far-away longhouse is not the best type of marriage, such arrangements are not automatically "default" marriages. Making new alliances can be advantageous for any number of reasons, many of which are illustrated in myths. Moreover, any thorough analysis of marriage should examine both individual marriages and the total pattern of marriages made during a generation at a given settlement. Where one or two men have obtained wives perhaps has bearing on where their brothers and patrilateral cousins marry. Marriages between distant relatives or between those in settlements previously unknown to either partner increase a settlement's pool of affines, allowing a network with a greater geographical range (discussed later, and in Jackson, 1976). Although such marriages are less likely to be seen as desirable in the abstract, they occur in the real world. Tukanoan men visit, court, and fall in love with little-known women despite the knowledge that the "ideal" marriage is with a neighbor MBD or FZD.

Apparently, mock, or ceremonial, marriage abduction still occurs from time to time, although I did not witness one and was not told of any happening during my stay. Real raids for women no longer occur, and they never characterized marriages gradually arranged by close kin. Wife-capturing raids are still a part of every Tukanoan's heritage, however, in that they figure prominently in stories and myths.

When an "abduction" is planned today, the groom and his close kinsmen arrive during the night in one or two canoes and "kidnap" the bride by sneaking up to the longhouse and entering and escaping through side doors used only for these elopements and by the women during Yuruparí rites (S. Hugh-Jones,

133

1979). The degree to which this is a *real* elopement, that is, secret from the bride's family, undoubtedly varies from case to case. The rest of the longhouse inhabitants wake up in time to fight a mock battle at the canoe landing, involving a lot of yelling but no real damage.

Although not a real abduction, this ritual emphasizes the seriousness of the occasion and the latent antagonism and suspicion on both sides. At times, apparently, the bride's family shows displeasure with the match (see Goldman, 1963, p. 142). This feigned or actual reluctance gives the bride's family leverage in the ensuing negotiations a few days later when they visit the groom's settlement to see if the bride is happy and to arrange for an exchange marriage as soon as possible. The bride must have consented to some degree from the beginning, because at present no woman can be taken from her home completely against her will. She should not, however, give the appearance of happily deserting her home and agnates to live with affines and make their descent line strong, and this ceremony demonstrates, although at times hypocritically, her proper ambivalence and hesitation.[7]

The range of wife-getting procedures, from peaceable exchange to elopement to, in the past, actual capture, illustrates the complexity of the marriage system as a whole. We can assemble an impressive amount of evidence for this range of "proper" marriage and thus eliminate much of the contradiction that first strikes our attention. If we see the range as depending, in part, on the closeness of the potential affines – genealogical, geographical, linguistic, and perhaps other forms of closeness – then we need to know the parameters of each type of marital option rather than assume that one type of marriage is *the* best and the others are by default or due to a breakdown in the system or similar exogenous factor. Despite idealized statements about the benefits of marrying genealogically close, advantages and disadvantages to all types of marital strategies exist, whether one is speaking from a structural or transactional perspective. Contradiction and conflict are inherent both among people with vested interests in specific marriages and among the various goals individual Tukanoans hope to achieve by getting married. The marriage data I collected do not allow for a fine enough breakdown of all the determinant variables to demonstrate which strategies emerge under which conditions, but the various other kinds of evidence we have are compelling.

At one extreme, what we might call a "bilateral first cross-cousin model" says it is preferable to marry this kind of woman, exchanged for another just like her. Each woman will be moving to her mother's natal longhouse, probably nearby, and will also be an FZD. The two marriages will be relatively stable and will join a group of marriages that cement an ongoing alliance between a pair of hyperaffinal settlements, an alliance spanning at least a generation.

What makes these marriages unlikely, in both behavioral and formal terms, is that they depend on ideal conditions – and not only demographic ones. When Tukanoans state that such marriages are the ideal, they are speaking of the way things ought to be: the way marriages ought to be and the way social relations ought to be in general. But reality is not ideal, and Tukanoans are quite pragmatic – in their myths, their anecdotes, and certainly their actual marital negotiations – when operating under less than ideal conditions. Thus, they marry (and talk about marrying) MBDs who are not FZDs (and vice versa), cousins who are only distantly related or who become cousins only after marriage becomes a possibility, or women from a "third" group who are not the traditional affines, either at the settlement or language group level. This "more distant" kind of marital strategy includes a wide range of marriage types, which we can lump together and term a "portfolio strategy model" because it contains the notion that it is best not to have all one's eggs, or assets of any kind, in one basket – at least under less than ideal conditions, which, unfortunately, are the ones under which both we and Tukanoans usually find ourselves.

The fuzziness and ambiguity that emerge – for example, when discussing the meaning of the "mother's children" terms, when discussing affines as generous and yet treacherous, and certainly when trying to understand actual marriages – are intrinsic to the system. Although we cannot conclude that, even when demographic conditions permit, a single type of marriage is the ideal (except under utopian conditions), we can begin to comprehend Tukanoan marriage as a consistent and logical system – albeit a more complex one than conversations with informants about "how we marry" might initially lead us to believe.

Residential exogamy.

Residential exogamy, an automatic result of the rules of language group exogamy and patrilocal residence, can claim to be a principle in its own right, one followed even when nonagnates happen to live together. Feelings about this are especially strong when cross-cousins are raised together (see Goldman, 1963, p. 43). Residential exogamy is a principle found throughout the Northwest Amazon,[8] in contrast to many societies elsewhere in the Amazon–Orinoco Basin in which marriages can be residentially endogamous (for example, in the Xingú Basin, in most of the Panoan and Gê groups, and among the Piaroa and Yạnomamö).

The few exceptions to this rule at present in the Vaupés occur in the mission towns, where members of several language groups have been encouraged to live together – a revolutionary change in Vaupés social and spatial arrangements. Out of a sample of 635 marriages, only 19, all of them in mission towns, were residentially endogamous. In the layout of these towns each language group and sib occupy distinct territories.

Language group exogamy.

The principle of language group exogamy is the one most perplexing to non-Tukanoans – missionaries, local Colombians, and anthropologists alike. Despite the sweeping changes brought about by acculturation, language exogamy is still very much the rule among Tukanoans to the south of Cubeo territory (and many Cubeo do marry into other language groups). Only one exception (and this one questionable) occurred in my sample of more than 1,000 marriages.[9] And, with some exceptions in the Pirá-paraná (see Chapter 5), all Tukanoans affirm that the rule of language group exogamy must be observed.

A two-year union between a Tukano man of the mid-Papurí and a Tukano woman of Yavareté is the one observed exception in my sample. Informants were reluctant to discuss this case, at times saying it was not really a marriage at all and at other times saying that the woman's sib, the low-ranking *ahpŭkeria* ("crab"), was not Tukano and spoke a different language.

Tukanoans see the rule of language group exogamy extending far beyond the Papurí–Vaupés–Tiquié–Pirá-paraná region. They are critical of Cubeo inter-marriages. Bará war stories generally end with the victors going north and killing off all Cubeos except a brother–sister pair, who then *had* to marry each other in order to start the Cubeo people again. This is why Cubeos "marry their sisters" today.

How long the rule of language group exogamy has been in effect is open to speculation; Koch-Grünberg reports it (1909–10), but we do not know whether it was as strongly enforced as it is today. A. R. Wallace (1889/1972) reports marriage with blood relatives, presumably cross-cousins, and Kirchoff states that tribal exogamy is practiced by Tukano groups and blood-relative marriage by Arawak groups. Goldman (1948, p. 780) correctly points out that the two statements are not necessarily contradictory.

As we have seen, certain same-language groups in the Pirá-paraná region intermarry. Other Pirá-paraná Tukanoans state that this should not happen because "people should not speak like their cross-cousins." Some Pirá-paraná Indians also state that these same-language affinal units spoke different languages in the past (C. Hugh-Jones, n.d.). The Yukuna–Tanimuka–Letuama–Matapí groups to the south also have a rule of language exogamy.

The strength of the rule of language group exogamy is more impressive when we consider the degree of acculturation in the Vaupés, particularly in the Papurí drainage. Change agents, especially Catholic missionaries, actively discourage cross-cousin marriage and say the language group exogamy rule is absurd. This part of the marriage system has remained viable, however, despite extensive inroads by such agents into many areas of Vaupés culture.

Sorensen (1967, p. 672) notes that Tukanoans assume that whites also practice language group exogamy. When talking with me, Tukanoans always assumed that my mother and father spoke different languages, and other anthropologists who have worked in the Vaupés report similar experiences.

During my stay, a Tukano man and woman from the mission town of Acaricuara announced that they intended to get married, thereby provoking a huge scandal. Both individuals were highly missionized (for example, both were catequistas),

136

and the priest actively encouraged the marriage. He argued that they had a right to marry each other, but he also supported it because it provided a chance to drive a wedge into the system of language group exogamy. The proposed match would have violated the generally observed rule of residential exogamy as well, but it was the fact that two Tukanos were contemplating getting married that was the most reprehensible to Tukanoans.

Ironically, both the young man and woman had the same Spanish surname; this was pure happenstance, for they came from different sibs. Still, Tukanoans, especially those in Acaricuara, seized on this point to bolster their argument, saying that the marriage would violate Catholic incest prohibitions as well.

I did not find out how the situation was resolved before I left the area. The families of both were horrified, and rumors circulated of violent quarrels and threats made with shotguns.

If, after I departed, the couple was in fact married in the church, then the missionaries had indeed made a significant step in dismantling the traditional marriage system. Such a marriage would have meant that the Tukanoans' many efforts to thwart it were unsuccessful and that the church had triumphed over traditional values. Furthermore, because the marriage involved a man and a woman from respected mission-town families belonging to high-ranking sibs and the young man was the corregidor of Acaricuara, the flaunting of traditional mores perhaps demonstrated to Tukanoans the encroaching power of the Colombian government as well as the church.

Alliance.

"Alliance" simply means that two affinally related local descent groups consider it advantageous to continue to exchange women over time. Alliance is a long-term strategy and as such differs from the more limited, direct exchange strategy, although the two are obviously related. The latter is concerned more with ensuring the replacement of women of the local descent group who are lost through marriage.

Lounsbury (1962, p. 1307) discusses two general types of alliance strategies. The first is concerned with the continuation and reaffirmation of an already established alliance that continues to be seen as advantageous to both sides. As noted previously, some of these advantages in the Vaupés might be geographical proximity, close kinship ties, facilitation of the ceremonial and economic exchanges characterizing most pairs of neighboring longhouses, and increased benefits to the women who have already married into that particular longhouse.

The second type of marital strategy is establishing new alliances that promise economic, political, military, or other advantages. In the Vaupés, alliance with more distant longhouses might be made for such reasons as being assured of hospitality on various river routes or in certain mission towns or having one's close affines dispersed in order to have a wider range of individuals in one's affinal and neighbor relationships. Furthermore, although raiding and feuding have ceased, in the past, military considerations were very much an aspect of marital strategies. Distant marriages being made today may be continuations of alliances formed originally for the purpose of having dispersed military allies.

The influence of geographical distance is a crucial factor in comprehending the way in which principles of alliance actually influence decision making about marriage. For example, if a settlement considers itself owed a woman, its demands will not have much impact if it is located far away from the debtor settlement. This distance is also probably an important contibuting factor in the debtor settlement's continued disregard of the other's claims.

The distance factor also attests to the importance of analyzing the total sample of marriages made by a local descent group over a period of time, such as a generation. For Tukanoans the meaning of distance between marriage partners' settlements is not simply one of a direct correlation between increasing distance and increasing undesirability of a prospective marriage alliance. For example, given that a specific settlement has married several of its women into one or two nearby settlements, it may be less "costly" from its point of view to make the next marriages with settlements relatively far away. This is, however, still probably a less desirable type of marriage from the point of view of the marrying individuals.

It is evident that settlements in the Vaupés do not marry within a tightly constricted geographical field. Looking at the marriages made by any given settlement over two or three generations, we see that some of the longhouse groups exchanging women are quite far apart. Furthermore, many of the "potential affine" settlements (not counting the settlements that cannot be sources of spouses due to prohibitions imposed by the social structure) are closer than some of those that actually have supplied spouses (Figure 6 and Map 3 give an example of this). Yet it is also the case that some marriages are between local descent groups so far away from each other that they are statistically very improbable and are seen as such by Tukanoans.

Measuring geographical distance between marriage partners' settlements at the time of marriage for a sample of 635 marriages gives a mean linear distance of (very roughly) 22 miles, with a standard deviation of 19.8 miles. Some marriages occur between settlements as distant as 90 linear miles. The actual distances are greater, for the river and trail routes used by Tukanoans when traveling between the settlements must be taken into consideration.[10]

Marriage behavior

All Tukanoans possess a remarkable knowledge of the settlements of the region and their inhabitants, even those they do not personally know. Most know a lot about many quite distant settlements, because a favorite topic of conversation is fellow Tukanoans.

Marriage

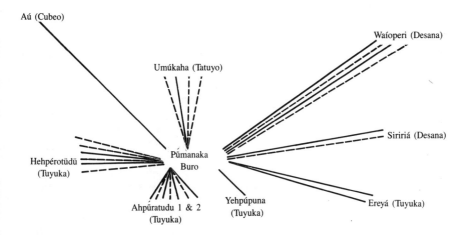

Figure 6. Marriages during three generations at Púmanaka buro. Total marriages: 27 (13 women, 14 men); total number of settlements involved: 8. The solid lines represent men bringing women to Púmanaka buro; broken lines represent women marrying out.

The preferred method of obtaining a spouse is slowly to develop an understanding with a cross-cousin from a familiar settlement. Another courtship pattern is for a group of young men to go traveling together to visit relatives in settlements where there are marriageable women. One such group came to Púmanaka buro during my stay. They remained a week, obviously enjoying themselves, and provided excitement and a change of pace. The group consisted of two Tuyuka and two Siriano men from fairly distant settlements. No one ever mentioned the ostensible reason for their visit. This is understandable, however, because to refer explicitly to a visitor's interest in marrying one of the settlement's women is to impugn his good intentions. These men made baskets for their hostesses, as is the custom in this type of visit. No marriages came of this particular expedition, at least during my stay.

On another occasion a woman, Fernanda, was brought to Púmanaka buro as a prospective wife for the unfortunate-in-love Estribino, the headman's eldest son. She did not take to Estribino but did end up marrying Nazalio, the second son of Manuel. This not only upset Estribino personally but increased the already well-established rift between the two families. It also upset Nazalio's older brother, Mariquino, who ideally should have married before Nazalio but like Estribino had had problems getting a wife. The woman whom Mariquino was most interested in was Gabriela, a Tuyuka from a downstream longhouse. She had gone to mission school and spoke Spanish. For a while she seemed disinclined to live with such backwoods Indians and took up with a **cabuco** near Mitú.[11] But by the time I left, she had finally settled down with Mariquino. The

139

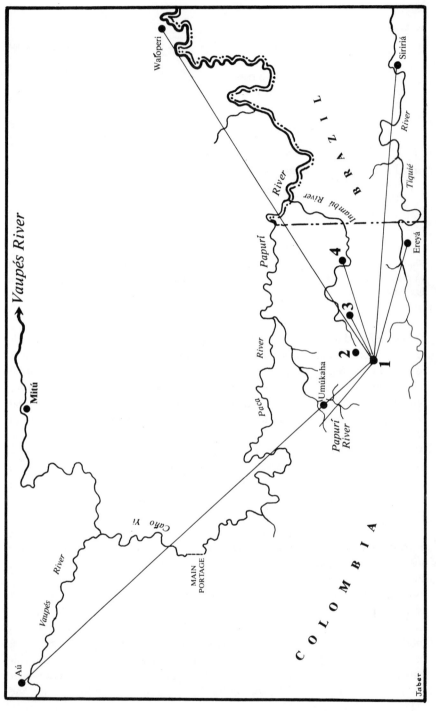

Map 3. Locations of settlements intermarrying with Púmanaka buro. The Bará settlement of Púmanaka buro is located at 1, and Tuyuka

first baby born to the succeeding generation was, in fact, Nazalio and Fernanda's.

Couples in mission towns are expected to marry in the church before the woman changes residence, but this seldom happens. In the past, priests periodically made trips to settlements to baptize and perform marriage ceremonies, but at present they encourage the couples to have the religious rites performed during a trip to a mission town. A substantial number have done so, but the idea of being married in the church before starting to live together is still incomprehensible to Tukanoans. They are not concerned about the virginity of either spouse and know how brittle many marriages are during the first years.

Those marriages at Púmanaka buro that had lasted a number of years seemed very solid. I never saw a serious open quarrel between a husband and wife; quarrels certainly occurred, but, like all other truly private interaction, they took place well away from the longhouse. Couples joke about their quarrels. By the time I left I was aware of one or two long-standing points of friction in each marriage.

One of the closest and most affectionate marriages was between a Bará man and a Cubeo woman. They claimed they had not understood each other's languages at all when they married. This is one of the rare instances when two multilingual Tukanoans do not have a language in common. Being Cubeo, she did not, like almost all other Tukanoans, speak the lingua franca, Tukano (although many Cubeo do speak it). She said it took her two years to learn Bará.

In public, spouses almost never physically show affection, not even touching one another. Physical contact occurs only when joking or during the few public gestures of intimacy, either grooming or administering medication of some sort. A wife will apply body paint to her husband (although he does not reciprocate); she will also delouse him. Men do not delouse each other but women delouse one another and their children. (Both men and women take extraordinarily good care of their dogs, keeping them fairly free of fleas and níguas, "chiggers.") Other intimate public gestures are related to health: picking scabs, removing thorns and níguas, and applying stinging nettle to muscular pain. Otherwise, in public both men and women touch children and members of their own sex far more than members of the opposite sex. The two couples who married during my stay (not counting the week-long union between Estribino and Isabel) were more openly amorous but in a very lighthearted, teasing manner.

The lack of public physical contact between spouses is in keeping with the general pattern of sexual segregation. There is also a general tendency to play down any exclusive or highly charged emotional relationship that might conflict with the interests of the community as a whole. All married partners must stay in good humor and be polite to each other and the rest of the longhouse, regardless of any strains the marriage is temporarily experiencing. A general muting of all displays of sexual attraction when things are going well makes it easier to maintain equilibrium and friendliness when they are not. An indication of the

141

The fish people

soft-pedaling of the emotional closeness between spouses is the lack of publicly used terms of address. One can refer to *yü manü* (''my husband'') or *yü numó* (''my wife''), but direct forms of address consist only of a spouse's Spanish name, or, after the birth of a child, teknonymy. Frequently, the child's Spanish name is used.

This general stricture also helps newlyweds overcome the initial difficulties of adjusting to each other. The couple can ease into deepening love and intimacy rather than having to be demonstrative immediately after marriage. It is difficult for the new wife to adjust to the change of surroundings and associations, the absence of familiar loved ones, and the new longhouse language. Although the husband's life changes very little, it is an awkward time for him as well. Should his wife and his mother disagree over something, and they almost inevitably will, the husband is equally inevitably caught squarely in the middle.

Thus, even when husband and wife have known each other a long time before starting to live together, the period right after marriage is stressful. The wife must not only adjust to her husband and her new surroundings but to her new mother-in-law and sisters-in-law as well, for she will be spending most of her time with them. When young women are contemplating getting married, they consider their future relationships with these women very carefully. Competing claims on loyalty, time, services, and other resources create tension between coresident in-laws as does the fact that affines are always outsiders and agnates are always one's ''own group.''

Still, some of the rivalry, jealousy, and complications found elsewhere – for example, at times in American families – are not so marked in the Vaupés. For one thing, the segregation between the sexes is extensive, which reduces the claim either mother or wife has on a son's/husband's time, attention, or displays of loyalty and affection. It is difficult unwittingly to show favoritism in the Vaupés, whereas in some other societies a man can be more easily manipulated in behind-the-scenes power struggles between his mother and wife or wives. Furthermore, female solidarity is strong in Tukanoan life. Women enjoy one another's company, and members of the same sex enjoy greater ease and familiarity among themselves than with members of the opposite sex. This helps a young wife adjust to her female in-laws.

When problems do surface, the new bride finds herself more powerless than she will ever be again, but not as powerless as she would be in some other strongly patrilineal societies or in some peasant communities. For example, a Vaupés wife can return home knowing she will not be turned away, and this is a threat she can use to her advantage in her new home. She also can make her presence felt by threatening to commit adultery or by engaging in other disruptive behavior. A new bride's mother-in-law does not have as much authority over her as in many other societies (e.g., Northern India), and although a husband is supposed to listen to his mother's advice, everyone is expected to compromise a bit. If a mother has difficulty liking her son's wife even after a substantial amount

142

of time, the general courtesy and good humor demanded of all who live together will prevail in daily life, at least on the surface.

Mythological references to marriage behavior and expectations.

As is apparent from the myths already recounted, affinal relations are a vital part of Tukanoan mythology. As indicated in Chapter 6, a basic theme is the uncertainty and risk inhering in any dealings with affines. But sometimes the message is that one only truly becomes human upon establishing affinal ties. At times the advantages and risks are dealt with at almost the same point in the narrative, producing a counterpoint effect. Frequently given advantages include being able to perpetuate one's own people, reciprocal exchange of services and goods, and sexual activity. For example, Yebá mahũ receives three quintessentially human gifts from Waí Pinó Mahkó (Fish Anaconda Daughter), his wife: manioc, coca, and banisteriopsis. Other benefits are obtained from interactions with in-laws; for example, Waí Pinó offers Yebá Mahũ his hospitality, feeds him Tarira fish (Waí Pinó's own agnates), and protects Yebá Mahũ when he disobeys instructions and is about to be strangled by the anaconda skin.

This myth is a "charter" for the ceremonial food exchange (**dabucurí**) found in the Vaupés. In a part of this myth, recorded by S. Hugh-Jones (personal communication), the prototypical exchange relation between father-in-law and son-in-law is laid out by Waí Pinó giving (via his daughter) manioc and all cultivated crops to Yebá Mahũ in exchange for meat. A present-day dabucurí consists of the hosts offering beer and guests offering fish or meat (see Chapter 4). These exchanges imply (and symbolize) exchanges between men (father-in-law and sons-in-law) for women and exchange between men and women.

It is important to note that although affines are "other people" and potentially treacherous, one receives many benefits from them unavailable from one's "own people," and this dilemma is expressed over and over in myths. The primary benefit, of course, is daughters-in-law in exchange for daughters. Marital exchanges and the mutual ongoing benefits of ceremonial interactions such as dabucurí that accompany them either cannot or in fact generally do not occur between agnates. Another example is the gifts of baskets of various sorts (between brothers-in-law and from a visiting potential husband to his prospective mother-in-law), paralleling the gifts of baskets from husband to wife in exchange for manioc products.

Expectations about proper relationships of exchange between affines in fact are found in most myths. For example, in a myth about "jaguar people" (*yaiwa mahá*), the grandmother of Diró koá poná (literally, "piece-of-meat-bone-offspring") is ashamed and angry when she becomes afraid that her grandsons have not provided enough fish as a gift to her relatives, the jaguar people. But the Diró koá poná actually have acted in good faith, and it is the jaguar people who are treacherous (by nature, is the message) and who are destroyed in the end.

143

The fish people

In the myth of *di wáñako* (a type of long horn), a wahtí shows his gratitude to his human wife's people by supplying them with a huge amount of food, by warning them of an upcoming raid from their affinal enemies and ultimately by sacrificing himself in the war effort. His body is burnt and the plants growing from the ashes are the source of a protective unguent and of powerful horns (di wáñako) that when played render the enemy helpless.

Ambiguity and unpredictability appear often in myths dealing with affinal relations. I have already mentioned the built-in ambiguity of people who stand in an "affine of my affines" relationship with each other – who call each other pahkó-mahkǘ/-ó ("mother's children"). In the Barasana myth recorded by S. Hugh-Jones mentioned previously, two men who are cohusbands of the same woman call each other pahkó-mahkǘ. The potential for competition, jealousy, and suspicion is obvious in the myth. The children in the Namakuru myth are also jealous of their pahkó-mahkǘ but for different reasons; however, the situation is an identical one of competition for affection and favors. The crucial lesson is concerned with the potential jealousy inherent in the relationship, even if it is not always present.

Of course another source of ambiguity in the pahkó-poná relationship arises when we recall the phrase found in many Dravidian systems, that "affines of my affines are (like) my brothers." The pahkó-poná relationship is *truly* ambiguous; denoting neither agnate nor affine, it is a semantic lightning rod for all sorts of interactions and emotions containing ambiguous elements. We can, thus, inter-pret negative statements about pahkó-poná at times as referring to the tensions and antagonisms that crop up between affines (such as cohusbands) but at other times as indirectly characterizing the conflicts that occur between brothers, who at times compete for women, prestige, and other scarce resources but who are not supposed to ever let these tensions become publicly known. Obviously such tensions sometimes do get out of hand and this indeed is expressed in many myths. But pahkó-poná lack the built-in affection, mutual dependence, and solidarity that usually exist between agnates, especially coresident ones, and thus when serving as metonym for brothers the term allows for a stark presentation of competition and jealousy.

A Tukanoan will classify any Indians who live far away as pahkó-mahkara ("mother's children people"), provided they fall within the category of *mahǎ* ("people"). This merely indicates that they are "people like us" who live far away and with whom there is no ongoing interaction. In this context the set of terms expresses relative affective distance with respect to trustworthiness, loyalty, and commitment (or the lack of these). It also expresses relative cultural distance or the notion that the farther away people live, the more likely they are to be different – to do things differently, to speak languages extremely different from the ones one knows, and so on. The terms also express relative social distance, indicating the degree to which one can expect regularized reciprocity, military aid, absence of conflicts of interest, and so forth. Thus, if in a given context a

Tukanoan wants to indicate an ambiguous, if not suspicious, socially distant type of relationship, the terms pahkó-mahkṹ/-ó are selected.

As indicated, many myths illustrate the relatively great social and psychological distance and the ambiguity implied by these terms. An individual's pahkó-mahkṹ is a person rather than a wahtí. Still, almost always in myths one's pahkó-poná play tricks. A man's pahkó-poná are not necessarily his antagonists but rather people who cheat him or do him harm if there are benefits to be gained from such behavior. Reciprocal pahkó-poná are either indifferent to each other's well-being, or when convenient, dangerous. Myths dealing with the relationship between pahkó-poná do not illustrate failure to live up to expectations so much as potential trickery and treachery brought about by opportunism and a lack of obligations. As we have seen in the Namakuru myth and the one about cohusbands of the same wife, however, at times the lack of intimacy and trust between pahkó-poná is not caused merely by indifference and ambivalence but by conflict of interest and open competition.

These themes of jealousy and competition also appear in the pehṹ story: the two co-wives of the same husband are structurally identical to the two men who are cohusbands and call each other pahkó-mahkṹ. Another illustration of this motif of conflict between pahkó-poná is provided in the myth about Koá-mahkṹ, when he pretends to be the pahkó-mahkṹ of Añá (poisonous snakes) in order to slay them more easily.

Although great benefits are gained when expectations are met, ambiguity and risk inhere in all affinal relations. Some of the danger and unpredictability deriving from such relationships are due to the fact that affines are always different, "not-us," "other." The story of Waí Pinó Mahkó, Fish Anaconda Daughter, illustrates this; she is not a human and her father is an anaconda. One danger of associating with people not "like us" is, of course, becoming too much like them. The mother in the Namakuru story is depicted as becoming progressively more like her wahtí husband: One breast becomes excessively large, she learns to speak his language, and she gives birth to an animal. In the myth of *di wáñako,* which involves a little girl locked out of the longhouse by angry parents, a wahtí carries the girl off, adopts and rears her, and eventually takes her as his wife. When she returns to her parents, she is described as having become less human in certain ways, a crucial one is having an enlarged breast.

A similar risk is the possibility of starting to like one's affines more than one's agnates. This is expressed in the Namakuru story when the mother excessively punishes her children and sends them away in order to conceal her attachment to her new husband and baby.

In a sense, women are always suspected of loving the group they marry into too much. The grandmother in the myth about jaguar people is torn between concern for her grandchildren, Diró koá poná, and her agnates, the jaguar people; the idea is that it is *she* who has brought them together, and it is her loyalty that is compromised.

145

Women in the myths are shown at times as not only being pivotal and having divided loyalties but also as betraying either agnates or affines out of selfish reasons. In two myths, women are punished for this by being made unknowingly to eat their lovers' genitals.

In some myths, particularly war stories, women are portrayed as more loyal to their agnatic kin than to their affines. In one, not only are the women loyal but they arm themselves and fight alongside their male agnates. In another war story an inmarried Tuyuka woman overhears her Carihona affines planning to hold a feast and murder their Tuyuka enemies by poisoning the manioc beer, and she warns her agnates of their treachery.

Thus, danger inheres in affinal relations not only because affines are "different from us," but also because real conflicts of interest arise. In this case, it is not so much a question of differences between "us" and "them" as one of similarities: similarities in wanting the same scarce resources, in trying to make a good bargain, and in mutual distrust and suspicion.

The themes of greed and excess frequently appear in myths about affinal relations. In several myths Koá-mahkű is depicted as wanting two women at the same time, with no offer of an exchange for even one of them. In one, this leads to difficulties with Wahóbiro, the women's father, who leaves Koá-mahkű abandoned in a tree.

A frequently encountered progression in a myth's plot begins with a rather innocuous misunderstanding or misdemeanor that sets up a reaction that finally plunges everything into chaos. One war story begins with a man getting angry and beating his wife, who returns to her natal longhouse. Eventually, the two local groups try to kill each other.

Affines are also dangerous because of the risks of sexuality itself. At times this is connected to the dangers of excess and at times to the theme of inherent differences between own group and affines and the consequent danger of all sexual congress with them. Koá-mahkű has to comb out all of the stinging and biting vermin from the pubic hair of Nimá Pinó's (Curare Anaconda) daughter before having intercourse with her, an obvious *vagina dentata* motif.

Excesses, inherent differences, conflicts of interest, and other types of dangers encountered in interactions with affines will lead to total disaster if not corrected. For when affines are killed, chaos and animal-like behavior threaten, because one clearly needs affines to continue being human. Animals have sexual intercourse with anybody, as do Makú or any people who "marry their sisters." Thus, myths demonstrate the necessity of maintaining proper affinal relationships if one wants to continue one's agnatic line. When things go awry and get progressively out of kilter, tragedy is the result. The theme of ever-increasing chaos also occurs in narratives about other kinds of relatives. The protagonists in the story of boraro skin ate their own relatives. Kamaweni is killed by his own brother after a series of excesses. The relatives of the protagonist in the story of kahpéa õrēro turn into monkeys after they lose their eyes and become burdens. Several myths end with such total annihilation that brother must marry sister in order to continue "the people."

Conclusions

Kinship and marriage roles are extremely important components of Tukanoan social categories and groups. Local descent groups and the individuals comprising them care about their reputations as honorable and trustworthy people, and their relations with agnates and affines form a major segment of this reputation.

Unlike other simple marriage systems, such as those found among the Gê or Australian Aborigines, group membership in the Vaupés does not determine affinal relations to the extent of specifying the only group or category one may marry into. This is true despite the basically Dravidian kinship terminology found in many (perhaps all) Tukanoan languages. Adjustments have been made in at least several Tukanoan languages that fit the terminology more closely to the reality – a regionally based system in which more than sixteen exogamous units exchange women. Thus such structural principles as the kinship terminology and the patrilineal language groups and phratries only set constraints on Vaupés marriage making. An acceptable model of marriage for the Vaupés, therefore, is one based on network formation as the outcome of at least three sets of factors: (1) environmental constraints, (2) social structural principles, and (3) shared decision-making rules for choosing among the alternatives offered by the first two sets.[12]

8.

Tukanoans and Makú

It should be apparent by now that the kinds of interaction occurring between Tukanoans and Makú and the categorizations each group makes of the other are very important components of identity. In this chapter, I will deal far more with Tukanoan perceptions of Makú than vice versa, however, because I had very little direct contact with Makú.[1]

Tukanoans stand in a superordinate position to Makú and use the differences between their respective subsistence modes, principles of social structure, and other areas of culture to explain and justify these claims of superiority. Tukanoans are more sedentary than Makú, practice more horticulture, and are more oriented toward the rivers and fishing. These are observable differences; when asked to make comparisons, Tukanoans will also list others, which are more open to question. It should be noted at the outset that although Tukanoans will usually describe differences between themselves and Makú in terms of absolutes, in most of the areas of differentiation (for example, horticultural practices, mobility, property owning, or use of hunted and gathered food), the contrasts are ones of degree rather than category.

The image each group holds of the other embodies key elements of its general conceptualization of the world and humanity. These characteristics at times vary from the flesh-and-blood reality of the other group, and we shall see that they are systematic and meaningful discrepancies.

My own contacts with Makú were infrequent and superficial. Thus, as noted, this chapter is biased: Most of the data on Tukanoans are from my own fieldwork, whereas most of the data on Makú are from published reports and communications with investigators who have had firsthand experience.

Background to the Makú

Simply put, Makú differ from Tukanoans in that they are more sylvan than riverine, they speak non-Tukanoan languages, they can marry within the linguistic unit and have a stronger constraint toward regional endogamy, and they enter into various kinds of "symbiotic" relationships with Tukanoans in which they

148

play a subordinate role. The latter can be relatively temporary, consisting of one- or two-day events in which meat, labor, or various forest products are exchanged for cultivated goods and white trade items. Or they can be long-term servant–master types of relationships occurring between a Makú family or larger group and a specific Tukanoan settlement.

The term *Makú* is generic (Métraux, 1948; Silverwood-Cope, 1972), and like several other terms (e.g., "Guaharibo") can at times designate nothing more precise than the "wild" Indians of a given region – those least contacted, least clothed, and who are alleged to practice no farming, have no houses, and lead a totally nomadic existence. This is the meaning in the Vaupés behind most local Colombians' use of the term and is at times the meaning intended when Tukanoans speak of Makú.

The Makú of the Central Northwest Amazon are divided into three linguistic groups: (1) Cacua, also known as Bará Makú (Silverwood-Cope, 1972); (2) Jupda, also known as Ubde (Giacone, 1955) or Hupdü (Reid, personal communication); and (3) Yohop (Silverwood-Cope, 1972), also known as Yühup (Reid, personal communication).[2]

The origin of the Makú, like the origins of Tukanoans, is problematical. Goldman (1963, p. 14) makes a case for a relatively early Tupian influence in the area with later Carib and Arawak contacts, with no specific mention of Makú origins in either his 1948 or 1963 publications. In the *Handbook of South American Indians,* Métraux (1948, p. 865) gives a scheme in which the Makú and similar groups are "generally considered to be the last representatives of an ancient people who occupied vast areas of the Amazon Basin before they were exterminated or assimilated by the *Carib, Arawak,* and *Tucano,* the carriers of a more advanced culture based on farming."[3]

Still, more recent ethnographic and ethnological work suggests it is a futile exercise to use an extremely rigid and genetic-based classification of lowland South American linguistic and tribal groups for either historical reconstruction or conclusions about present-day interbreeding populations.[4] Many groups that at present substantially depend on foraging may have devolved from earlier, more complex systems. Evidence exists that segments of foraging groups like the Makú are periodically assimilated into a local group of one of their horti-culturalist neighbors. In the case of the Makú, they, as the assimilated segment, take on the status of the lowest-ranked clan of the horticulturalist group (Goldman, 1963, p. 100; Koch-Grünberg, 1906; Silverwood-Cope, 1972). In sum, where the Makú came from is not known, the degree to which they represent a distinguishable breeding population both now and in the past is uncertain (although some ethnographic accounts describe physical differences between Makú and neighboring groups),[5] and it has not been conclusively established whether they have devolved from a previously more complex state or have always been more marginal than their neighbors.

Indeed, a crucial question is to what degree do groups such as Makú maintain

149

their identity and distinctiveness – in language, subsistence mode and other economic activities, or the display of certain stereotypical characteristics that set them apart from their neighbors – in *response* to and for the purpose of maintaining this symbiotic and unequal interaction? It is possible that some of these less complex groups would have been assimilated long ago, were it not for ongoing pressures to maintain distinctiveness. Thus, their current status may not be due to their historically different origins so much as due to the structure of their interaction with other groups.

In contrast to the riverine Tukanoans, Makú inhabit the interfluvial areas of the region. Makú lack the highly developed Tukanoan technology surrounding fishing and river transportation. For example, they make no canoes, whereas Tukanoans excel at this craft. Makú do fish, however, and they practice a fishing technique – for catching eels – unknown to the neighboring Desana (Silverwood-Cope, 1972, p. 86).

Makú practice horticulture at present, and it is not certain whether they ever lived entirely by hunting and gathering. It is questionable whether a strict hunting and gathering life is possible in many areas of lowland South America.[6] Furthermore, no good evidence exists that the Makú were ever totally nomadic. Nevertheless, their houses are far more makeshift than the elaborate traditional Tukanoan longhouse, and the foods that Makú do cultivate apparently do not supply them with all they need and want. In some cases specific crops are not grown at all but are obtained entirely from Tukanoans. In other cases not enough of an item is planted to last through the year. Makú make extended treks into the jungle on hunting expeditions more frequently than Tukanoans. According to Silverwood-Cope (1972, p. 103), Makú actually gather *less* than Tukanoans. Silverwood-Cope's description of the Makú as "professional hunters" who specialize in acquiring game to be used for exchanges with Tukanoans is very much to the point (1972, p. 103).

Makú can marry within the linguistic unit and generally prefer to marry within a circumscribed region, a preference that at times takes precedence over marrying a person in the proper kin category; according to Silverwood-Cope, Makú explained this by saying that Makú in other regions were dangerous sorcerers and jealous with their women (1972, p. 176). These "improper" marriages are usually between individuals in lineages that consider each other agnates.[7] H. Reid (personal communication) notes that marriages do occur between members of different regional groups and that no specific rule proscribes regional exogamy. Tukanoans also occasionally make improper marriages, but the rule of language exogamy is much more stringently observed by them; exceptions are exceedingly rare. Thus, being ignorant of Makú lineage or clan exogamic rules, they are shocked that Makú "marry their sisters" so often. Silverwood-Cope quotes a Uanano who specifically compares Makú marriage to animal marriage, in that both are randomly incestuous (1972, p. 176).

Other elements of Makú social organization include patrilineal exogamous

150

clans, a Dravidian kinship terminology, a preference for classificatory sister exchange, and marriage into a class of relatives including one's bilateral cross-cousin (Silverwood-Cope, 1972, p. 175).

In the areas of ideology and belief system, Makú have an elaborate conceptualization of the cosmos and human beings' place in it. In the area of food restrictions and taboos, Makú appear to have a far less stringent set of requirements, if one compares the information available in Silverwood-Cope (1972) with information on Tukanoans.[8]

Tukanoan attitudes toward the Makú

The Tukanoans who supplied most of the primary information on the Makú (i.e., the Bará and Tuyuka of the Inambú River) considered the Makú to be not entirely "people." Classifications of this sort are common among ethnic groups that do not share the same level of economic and political complexity yet that regularly interact with each other (see Barth, 1969; Lee and DeVore, 1968). The origin of the Makú is not a part of any Bará origin myths I recorded during fieldwork, nor is it in any of the Barasana myths recorded by S. and C. Hugh-Jones (personal communication). Giacone reports that the Tukano, Tariana, and Desana consider the Makú not as people but as "jaguar children" (1949, p. 88). This general subhuman classification frequently appears in reports from travelers as well (Koch-Grünberg, 1906; MacCreagh, 1926; McGovern, 1927; and A. R. Wallace, 1889/1972). Reichel-Dolmatoff (1971), however, states that the Desana do include Makú in their origin myths. Makú definitely *appear* in Bará and other Tukanoan myths; their origin, however, is not that of "true people," that is, emergence from a rapids site or upstream travel in an anaconda canoe. Evidence for Makú inferiority is also indicated in the Tukanoan statements that the Makú do not farm, do not fish or travel by river, and build no houses.

Makú were once described to me as having no *dühpúa kai* (a Bará word glossing as "head-spirit" or perhaps "consciousness"). In this context it probably refers to Makú lack of shame about "improper" behavior. Makú are said to observe no food taboos, eating snakes, sloths, rats, and vultures. Makú are also "shameless" because they "marry their sisters." A disparaging way for Bará to call attention to Makú orientation toward the forest rather than the river is by saying Makú urinate in the river. According to Goldman (1963, p. 91), a Cubeo origin myth that describes a certain sib's arrival at a river via an overland route stigmatizes this sib, because this mode of travel is considered typical of Makú.

In fact, in the Vaupés any comparative statement about the greater forest orientation of a given group with respect to another is most often a statement about relative inferiority of the former to the latter. In this sense, Makú are to be seen as at the end of a continuum. For example, McGovern (1927, p. 227) makes the clearly deprecatory statement that the Desana of the Papurí are more forest-

151

oriented than are neighboring Tukano and Waikana (Piratapuya?). He describes all of the Bará of the upper Tiquié in a similar fashion, contrasting them with their Tukano and Tuyuka neighbors farther downstream. Such a distinction is also made between high- and low-ranking sibs within a particular language group. Low-ranking sibs will occupy headwater locations, resulting in a relatively greater dependence on game than on fish (Goldman, 1963, p. 49). The degree to which a group classifies itself as river-oriented and is disdainful of the forest is probably in part a function of whether it has other groups supplying it with game. For example, Silverwood-Cope describes the Desana as afraid of the forest, particularly of hunting in it at night (1972, p. 44). For the Desana, forest spirits are far more malignant than those of the rivers. In fear of them, Desana lock up their houses at dusk. Silverwood-Cope also notes that at the time of his research, Desana did virtually no hunting, told him they were fishermen, and that hunting in the forest was for Makú (1972, p. 44).[9]

The Bará I lived with certainly hunted, often at night. They also certainly leave the trails when hunting, something the Desana that Silverwood-Cope observed are reluctant to do. It may be said that the Bará, because they are located on upstream tributaries more than Desana, and because they have no Makú to bring them game, stress hunting more. Still, Bará, like Desana, do associate many dangers with hunting, do observe taboos in connection with hunting expeditions and weapons, and certainly know of many dangerous spirits inhabiting the forests.

At times the low-ranking sibs of a given Tukanoan group will be described as being servants to the higher-ranking sibs – hunting for game and carrying out other tasks in a manner parallel to Makú activities. For example, McGovern (1927, pp. 208–09) states that the Waikano consider Makú to be *too* inferior, and had turned their own lowest-ranked sib into Makú-like servants.

Tukanoans will also describe Makú as wearing no clothes. Clothing, body paint, and jewelry all confer human identity; thus, it is to be expected that derogatory descriptions of Makú will include statements that they wear no clothing or body adornment. In general, Makú do decorate their bodies less than Tukanoans (Goldman, 1963, p. 153; Silverwood-Cope, 1972).

The association of cannibalism with Makú is mentioned in the literature (Goldman, 1963; Koch-Grünberg, 1909–10; Reichel-Dolmatoff, 1971, p. 260). This theme, especially one concerned with an organism consuming itself, is recurrent in Makú mythology (Silverwood-Cope, 1972), but otherwise no special cannibalistic practices have actually been reported for them. A Bará informant told me that Makú were people who hunted and ate human beings simply for food. This remark was derogatory not only in its reference to cannibalism but also in its implication that Makú were not able to secure enough food by other means.

In Tukanoan opinion, in addition to their unwillingness to observe basic rules of behavior, Makú are stupid. A country bumpkin flavor comes out in such descriptions. Most frequently the inability of Makú to feed themselves is a theme of a joke. I was told a probably apocryphal tale about some Makú who arrived at a Tukanoan longhouse at night so crazed with hunger that they wolfed down raw manioc mash and subsequently died from the prussic acid it contained. A picture in a magazine I had of starving Biafrans never failed to produce howls of laughter from the Bará I lived with. I was asked if they were "our" (i.e., Americans') Makú, because like Makú, the Biafrans obviously could not adequately feed themselves. That Makú dogs starve to death was given as another piece of evidence that Makú are too stupid to take care of themselves without periodic assistance from Tukanoans.

Occasionally I observed Tukanoans poking fun at Makú who happened to be present, but this was done behind their back. One Makú man who wore an old pair of plastic shoes occasioned much giggling, as did the asymmetry of an old woman's breasts. (In several myths, having only one breast or asymmetrical breasts is a clue that an otherwise normal-appearing woman is really a wahtí.)

A final point made by Bará and other Tukanoans about Makú inferiority is their lack of knowledge about ceremonial lore and behavior. Bará say that Makú adolescents are not initiated (this is not supported by Silverwood-Cope's observations). Nor are they said to have the other ceremonies common to Tukanoan groups of the region. Makú are said neither to sing nor to dance (again, not supported by Silverwood-Cope; however, during festivals held by Tukanoans, any Makú present remain in the background). Makú are also said to have special knowledge about sorcery (Goldman, 1963, p. 107; Reichel-Dolmatoff, 1971, p. 260), which, some authors say, gives Tukanoans an incentive to deal fairly when trading with them.[10] Still, Silverwood-Cope states that Makú are afraid of sorcery practiced by experienced Desana shamans (1972, p. 98). He believes that any current Tukanoan reliance on Makú shamans is probably the result of the relatively less acculturation of Makú than some local groups of Tukanoans, who, as a consequence, have lost their shamans. Koch-Grünberg states that Makú were used as scapegoats; when anything went wrong, Makú sorcery was blamed (1909–10, p. 270). Whiffen concurs, calling them the "proverbial cat" in always taking the blame (1915, p. 70).

Bará informants told me that Makú could make powerful poisons (a Makú specialization is the manufacture of curare) and that some of the older Makú had special knowledge in making trance-producing substances. I was told that the snuff taken by shamans of the various Tukanoan language groups was available only from Makú and was a trade item. This snuff, *Virola* sp. (Schultes, 1972), was said to be more powerful than banisteriopsis, the hallucinogen taken by all initiated men during festivals, and hence only shamans took it.

Interaction between Tukanoans and Makú

Makú and Tukanoan interaction is most often described in the literature (and was described to me by Bará informants) as a servant–master relationship. What this in fact consists of – what it means in terms of expectations and obligations – is complex and variable. At one extreme is a short-term exchange of goods by barter. At the other extreme are long-term (at times described as occurring over several generations) relationships between specific Tukanoans and "their" Makú.

An example of the first type of relationship is given by Silverwood-Cope (1972, p. 97), who reports that some Makú in the Macucú-paraná region, in addition to being the traditional servants of specific Desana, will exchange meat obtained during an extended hunting expedition with Uananos living on tributaries of the Vaupés River. Expectations in terms of either an extended period of contact or "servant" obligations are minimal in these situations; the interaction is fairly straightforwardly economic in nature. Trade objects manufactured by Makú for exchange, in addition to smoked or fresh game, include the highly prized twined baskets of various shapes and sizes, *Virola* snuff, curare for blowguns, and occasionally pelts destined ultimately for trade with whites. At present, in addition to food (e.g., manioc, chili peppers) and other cultigens such as coca and tobacco, it is my impression that Tukanoan items of trade are almost entirely white-manufactured articles such as machetes, beads, and cloth. I observed bartering taking place in longhouses where Makú were visiting. This bartering mostly involved Tukanoan women placing orders for custom-made baskets, and paying with beads, cloth, and similar items.

The question of specialization in manufactured objects in the Vaupés – between Makú and Tukanoans and among Tukanoans – is a complex one. Allen (1947, p. 574), for example, lists blowguns as Makú trade items, stating that Tukanoans had forgotten how to make them. Bará and Tuyuka men of the Papurí drainage still make blowguns, and probably other Tukanoans do so as well, and it is interesting that these people do not have regular contact with Makú, in contrast with some groups of Desana, Uanano, and Cubeo. Silverwood-Cope states that Makú do supply those Tukanoans with blowpipes and hunting poison (1972, p. 97). As we have seen, "forgetting" how to make certain necessary objects that must then be acquired by trade with groups specializing in their manufacture has been reported for the Yąnomamö (Chagnon, 1968). S. Hugh-Jones (personal communication) states that Barasana of the Pirá-paraná say that animal products such as jaguar teeth, bones, and peccary teeth for making ritual gear used to come from Makú. Silverwood-Cope lists additional forest articles for exchange: wild fruits, palm leaves for roofing, tree resins, and reeds for panpipes (1972, p. 97). H. Reid (personal communication) notes that Hupdü Makú supply many objects for use in Tukanoan rituals, such as feathers, nutshells, monkey fur, and teeth.

Straightforward barter often occurs when a group of Makú stays near a Tukanoan settlement. During their visit the Makú exchange their labor for food and the opportunity to participate in a festival. On one occasion I observed a Makú group of about eight adults and several children who were helping with communal work at a Desana settlement on the Papurí River. These Makú helped rethatch a roof, clear away jungle growth near the house and nearby fields, and secure the stairway to the canoe landing. They were paid with a two-day festival during which large amounts of chicha, coca, and tobacco were consumed. Makú were fed during this time, and Makú women helped with the food preparation. Tukanoans from nearby settlements placed orders for Makú baskets.

Another pattern that occurs is the semipermanent attachment of a Makú group to one longhouse. In this situation, the Makú seem to be less independent than those who more regularly maintain their own settlements and cultivations. I observed this type of arrangement when a Makú group stayed for approximately six months at a Tuyuka longhouse downriver from Pūmanaka buro. It was difficult to believe that this particular group could have lived entirely by itself for any appreciable length of time. Their personal possessions were pitifully scant, consisting of a broken and almost useless machete, two hammocks, and some articles of clothing. They had nothing in the way of cooking utensils or hunting equipment, yet they bartered their baskets for nonutilitarian white-manufactured goods such as beads, cloth, and earrings.[11] The one dog with them was obviously starving to death and could barely get to its feet (which it tried to do very infrequently). This group slept in a very flimsy shelter some distance away from the longhouse, although most of their time was spent at the longhouse (with the exception of the dog, who, not being allowed near it, consequently received very little food). After six months, the group departed as a result of a fight between one of the Makú men and a young Tuyuka man. I was told they had gone to the Tiquié in search of another longhouse to which they could attach themselves.

The group consisted of two men, three women, a teenage girl, and four small children. One of the men was absent most of the time, and the other was the personal servant of the longhouse headman. It was this Makú's job to accompany the headman whenever he was wanted, to light his cigars,[12] to light and maintain the resin torch at night, to fetch chicha for the guests during a party, and in general to be at the headman's beck and call. In exchange for these services, there was food for him and his family and occasional drinks of chicha, puffs on the cigar, and spoonfuls of coca.

The women helped in the food-processing chores and in the fields, and the young girl occasionally looked after the children.[13] The women also chopped firewood, tended the fires, fetched water, and deloused other women. I never observed a Makú woman performing the final stages of cooking or serving other people. The Makú waited to be asked to eat and in general were reserved and kept in the background. No Makú woman will perform all or even a substantial amount of the work of another woman. It is my impression that no Tukanoan woman would dream of sitting back idly while another woman, even a Makú, did her work. The nature of Makú servanthood is to help out.

Except when drunk, Tukanoans are not directly cruel to Makú, nor do they openly taunt and jeer at them. Makú status is manifested in more subtle ways. For example, Makú are never formally greeted. Makú are also visibly distinguished by their relatively poorer quality of clothing and relative lack of jewelry. They will eat when asked to and talk when invited to join a conversation, but otherwise they are silent and generally inconspicuous.

During the period when this Makú group stayed at the downriver Tuyuka longhouse, a large party of Tuyuka and Bará, including the Bará I lived with, traveled to the Tiquié River for a large festival. The young Makú girl went along, as did the man who was the headman's personal servant. The girl had been given a new dress for the occasion, but her Makú status was quite apparent during the trip. She was included little by little in conversations held by her Tuyuka and Bará age-mates, but throughout the trip she took care of the headman's youngest child and fetched water and firewood when asked to.

Making generalizations about this type of extended servant–master relationship from observations of a single Makú group is, of course, somewhat risky. However, I was assured by the Tukanoans I lived with that the situation was a typical one.[14] I also received confirmation from informants when they discussed in the abstract norms governing interaction between Tukanoans and Makú. The patterns I have described are also reflected in myths dealing with Makú and Makú-like relationships.

Several authors mentioned Makú women being used as sexual objects by Tukanoans (Goldman, 1963, p. 107; Koch-Grünberg, 1906; McGovern, 1927, p. 259; Reichel-Dolmatoff, 1971, p. 19; Whiffen, 1915, p. 262).[15] Tukanoans denied that such behavior was ever engaged in and condemned the idea, but this does not automatically mean that it does not happen. Ideally, Makú are not considered potential marriage partners.[16] However, some liaisons turn into permanent unions. I knew of one Makú woman married to a Desana in the mission town of Monfort. The information about her tribal identity was very difficult to obtain and cross-check. Goldman reports that according to other more high-ranking clans, the Bahkúkiwa sib he studied was originally a Makú group. The elevation of Makú groups is probably a periodically occurring process: Koch-Grünberg states that three Cubeo clans were probably originally Makú (1909–10, p. 136). Silverwood-Cope thinks that intermarriage between Makú and Tukanoans is probably the crucial factor in the assimilation process. Once intermarriage takes place, steps will be taken by both sides to erase the taint of Makú ancestry (1972, p. 104).

A somewhat different picture emerges from earlier accounts of Makú–Tukanoan interaction. Several reports state that Makú were "slaves," although what was meant by this rather vague term is difficult to ascertain with any precision. At issue is the degree of control a slave's owner had over life and limb, what resources were open to a master should the slave escape, and whether slaves could be lent or sold to other masters.

Some evidence exists of Indians' enslaving other Indians – both Makú and Tukanoans – in previous periods. Such enslavement was connected with the presence of warfare, much stronger headmen, and rapacious white traders and rubber gatherers, all of which are either absent or greatly diminished at present. Both Wallace (1889/1972, pp. 206–07) and Spruce (1908, p. 294) report Tukanoans' preying on each other, sometimes because a headman has been required to turn over a specific number of Indians to a government agent or upriver trader. It should be borne in mind that such reports involve disruptions caused by whites and do not necessarily tell us anything about the aboriginal situation. Furthermore, the two individuals who have firsthand knowledge of Makú seriously question such reports of enslavement. Silverwood-Cope concludes that Makú were less vulnerable to whatever dangers actually existed than were Tukanoans, because at the first opportunity of escape they could more easily disappear into the trackless jungle and survive for a long period, moving constantly. And Reid (personal communication) notes the general tendency of nineteenth-century explorers and travelers to see much more hierarchy than actually existed. Therefore, some of the earlier reports that will be discussed should be taken with a grain of salt. No Tukanoan ever described to me any form of Tukanoan–Makú interaction that could be called "slavery"; and at least at present no Makú can be coerced to stay in a place or work when not willing to.

Several earlier reports state that Makú attached themselves to Tukanoan settlements out of a need for protection against marauding bands of Indians. Koch-Grünberg gives this as the reason why Makú stayed at Paricachivera Mission on the Tiquié River despite their "slave" status (reported by Métraux, 1948, p, 866). He reports that Makú worked for Tukanoans, who treated them like pet animals. According to him, Makú women were at the sexual disposition of the men. Brüzzi Alves da Silva (1962, p. 463) reports that a letter of appointment written by the Franciscan director of Paricachivera Mission in 1885 explicitly prohibits the sale of Makú, and Van Emst (1966b, p. 172) reports the same of a similar document for 1882. Koch-Grünberg states that a Tukano chief on the Tiquié claimed to own several hundred Makú slaves (Silverwood-Cope, 1972, p. 317).

Several authors conclude that greater contact with whites increased the enslavement of Indians. Spruce (1908, p. 294), for example, is quite critical of this practice. A. R. Wallace (1889/1972, p. 236) remarks that he was given a Makú boy for the duration of his travels on the Vaupés River in payment of a debt. Goldman discusses the symbiotic nature of this "slavery" and states that the fact that Makú were traded for ceremonial objects (one Makú male supposedly being equal to one ceremonial staff) does not indicate the absolute power over a person it seems to imply. Makú were fairly easily traded because they had

157

no great attachment to a particular place. Goldman (1963, p. 106) also states that although Makú were valued for their labor, they were mainly wanted to increase the number in a household.

At present, Makú are definitely not "slaves," but otherwise their inferior status has not changed. Van Emst (1966b, p. 191) affirms this for Makú living in mission towns, noting that they live in poorly constructed huts on the periphery of the village and are very subservient to the Tukanoans there. For example, according to Van Emst, if a priest gives a Makú an item, a Tuyuka or other Tukanoan can take it away from him or her then and there, and no one will find it unusual.

In conclusion, although Bará informants denied the potentiality for sexual relations between Tukanoans and Makú and had not heard of a Makú band attaching itself to a longhouse for the purpose of protection from potential enslavers, in general what is reported in the literature on Makú was confirmed during conversations with Bará and other Tukanoans. Informants also mentioned Makú as having been military allies in earlier times. Still, it should be noted that a general tradition exists in which lower-ranking sibs are automatically spoken of as allies, and Makú may have been spoken of in this manner for similar reasons. (When describing a raid that occurred in the past, the excitement is heightened if the narrator comments on the large numbers of people massed on both sides.)

Bará informants never showed any guilt about how Makú were treated and were never reluctant to discuss any aspect of Makú–Tukanoan interaction. They would readily list the services that Makú perform for Tukanoans and would just as readily discuss why they see Makú as inferior.

Makú as symbol to Tukanoans

The range of possible relationships occurring between Makú and Tukanoans clearly shows that interaction between the two groups is a significant part of life for all Makú and for many Tukanoans. Additionally, each group provides the other with illustrations of certain basic premises it holds about the world, human nature, and proper behavior.

Because my encounters with Makú were so infrequent, this section is limited to how Tukanoans use Makú as symbols. For an account of Makú perceptions of Tukanoans, see Silverwood-Cope, 1972, and Reid, n.d.

For Tukanoans, Makú exist not only in everyday life but also in the realities described in and explained by their cosmology. Makú appear time and again in myths and in the Tukanoan variety of just-so stories. When Makú are used as symbols the resulting picture often diverges from what Makú are like in actuality. It is obviously important always to distinguish between the two. In my opinion, Bará and other Tukanoans also distinguish between Makú as flesh-and-blood beings and Makú as symbols. This is not to say that at times Tukanoans are not simply mistaken about real-life Makú, nor do they always clearly make the distinction between symbolism and reality.

Statements from Bará and neighboring Tukanoans about Makú that illustrate the Tukanoan organization of the universe express at least three themes: (1) Makú as examples of what "true people" do not do; (2) Makú as prototypes of the lowest-ranking category in any hierarchy, most typically the ordering of sibs within a given language group; and (3) Makú as examples of the servant–master relationship.

We have already examined the first theme. Tukanoans say Makú are not "true people" because they are animal-like, eat tabooed food, marry their sisters, cannot provide enough food for themselves, live wild in the jungle, and so forth. They thus serve as stern reminders of what can happen when the rules governing proper behavior are ignored. Highly visible negatively evaluated subgroups often play this type of symbiotic role within the dominant culture: Gypsies and lepers are good examples.

To understand the second theme requires examining the similarities between Makú and the lowest-ranked sib in any given language group. A low-ranking sib's origins can always be impugned by suggesting that it was originally a Makú band. Unlike all true Tukanoan sibs, it did not emerge at a rapids site but attached itself to a longhouse and slowly learned the language of its adopted Tukanoan settlement and finally was assimilated. The motives behind the settlement's taking in the Makú group are said to be kindness and pity because of their state of near starvation. As mentioned earlier, just how much this reflects an actual process that occurs periodically is uncertain.

It is important to note, however, that a Tukanoan who is describing a sib origin in this way is not primarily concerned with historical reality. The very next day the same Tukanoan might describe the sib in question as a full-fledged Bará or Tuyuka sib in good standing. Imputed Makú origins are a means by which a sib's present status can be examined and criticized. Such a statement may simply indicate a Tukanoan's quarrel with an individual or settlement belonging to that sib, or a group of Tukanoans may be punishing an individual or group that has transgressed one of the rules by which all "true people" live.

Thus, although members of any low-ranking sibs of any Tukanoan language group are in many ways distinct from Makú, the differences are not as extensive as it at times seems, and Tukanoan evaluations of these differences can vary over time. Some criticisms of Makú – not speaking properly, marrying people who speak the same language, not observing taboos – will sometimes be made about lower-ranked sibs as well. The Bará with whom I lived described the lowest-ranked Bará sibs as having originally been Makú. This was mentioned in conjunction with statements about the inferior dialect of Bará these groups spoke, their sloppiness with regard to proper ritual attitudes, and their supposed previous state of total nakedness. Similar statements are made about Makú.

The fish people

Silverwood-Cope (1972, pp. 195–96), discussing Tukanoan attitudes toward Makú, says that Tukanoans stress those differences that distinguish humanity from the natural world, showing Makú to be far closer to the latter. Human beings do not live in the forest but make large clearings and build large elaborate houses. Human beings do not marry their own kind, and social structure is reflected in the structure of language affiliation and in territorial arrangements (especially in residential exogamy). Animals do not make gardens, plant, make cazabe and beer, nor do they hold rituals. Animals do not wear ornaments. Thus, Makú insofar as they fail to be human in these respects, are much more animal-like.

The third theme concerns the role of Makú as servant. When one is a servant, one is often thought of as qualitatively different from the master. In this sense, the servant–master relationship between Tukanoans and Makú differs from most other relationships existing among Tukanoans – relationships involving trade, services, differential status, or a combination of these. For example, according to C. Hugh-Jones (1979, p. 81), two men can stand in a "ceremonial brother-in-law" relationship with each other. They will belong to different language groups, but the relationship is completely egalitarian: It is between "men who exchange sisters." Asymmetrical relationships involving exchange of goods or services are also found. For example, the headman is entitled to his position partly through inheritance, but he maintains it mainly through providing more of certain services and goods than others, receiving prestige in return. He is not seen as an inherently different human being from his fellows because he is headman. This is also the case for the specialized positions of headman's wife, head dancer, or shaman (although certain shamans become so powerful they are transformed into a different kind of being). Except for the sexual division of labor, none of the occupational specializations is full-time.[17] This is significant, for Makú are always seen as being in the position of servants. (This is, of course, the Tukanoan view of things.)

In short, always to act as a servant is good evidence of one's inherent and permanent lower status, and this is the essence of being Makú. To some degree, other characteristics seen as typifying the Makú (such as a lack of ceremonial knowledge) are thought to be a consequence of the inherent Makú state of servitude. This point can be overstated, however, for at times Tukanoans, when feeling expansive, will give the impression that Makú are not categorically and eternally excluded from the status of true people: When Makú start behaving as they ought to, their penalized status will assuredly also cease. This recalls other ethnographic situations where members of a dominant group claim that when a discriminated-against minority's behavior changes, their status will also change. In all of these cases as well, ambivalence and contradictory statements are found. The ambiguity of the minority's status – one day described as nonhuman and one day described as *potentially* human "if only they would . . ." – is perhaps a general characteristic of dominant–subordinate interaction.

160

The theme of a class of beings who are permanently consigned to a position of being servants to others is revealed in several Bará and other Tukanoan myths. Certain animals are often described as being the "Makú" of other animals. Frequently a symbiotic relationship actually occurs between the two species described (cf. Reichel-Dolmatoff, 1971, p. 211). Many times, for example, a myth's protagonist has as his Makú little birds who keep him company and occasionally take messages or perform other chores. At times these species are spoken of as military allies.

In the myth of Koá-mahkü and Nimá Pinó ("Curare Anaconda") summarized in Chapter 5, Koá-mahkü initially gains entrance into both Nimá Pinó's daughter's house and Nimá Pinó's cave through the ruse of presenting himself as a Makú-like servant. Koá-mahkü's previous stay with Eyoa (wood ibis birds) had also been as a servant, but they finally decided to encourage him to leave, because he had practically eaten them out of house and home. This is a frequently heard complaint about Makú. The daughter of Nimá Pinó also accepts Koá-mahkü as a servant, but he becomes not only a voracious eater but sexually demanding as well; this may express the sexual tensions between Makú and Tukanoans who live in very close contact.

In the myth of Waí Pinó Mahkó ("Fish Anaconda Daughter"), summarized in the preceding chapter, Yebá Mahü visits his wife's father and relatives in their longhouse under the river. All the species of fish are ranked in a fashion similar to the set of sibs of a Tukanoan language group. Fish Anaconda, noticing that Yebá is hungry, tells him to eat tarira fish, the lowest-ranked species. Fish Anaconda says that although all fish are of one family, tarira are "our Makú," and presumably their sacrifice is not horribly serious.

Having Makú or Makú-like servants can definitely indicate prestige and popularity. Goldman states that Makú are most wanted among the Cubeo because they swell the household. An example of this in a Bará myth is in the story of Oá ("oppossum"), a trickster who outsmarts his visitors by claiming to have Makú and therefore to be an important person – which is in fact not the case. At one point Oá wonders out loud where his Makú could be and then "discovers" a termite nest that he says his servants have apparently just brought him (termites are a delicacy).

Conclusions

Relationships between Makú and Tukanoans can be analyzed from economic, political, and symbolic frames of reference. From the economic point of view, these relationships are exchanges of goods for goods or of goods for services. In this they are similar to the servant–master interaction occurring between Pygmies and Bantu Negroes of the Congo (Turnbull, 1965, pp. 293–94). Similar exchange relationships have been reported for several nomadic or seminomadic groups. This type of symbiosis is probably an old pattern of economic specialization, occurring between horticulturalists or pastoralists and hunter–gatherers since the neolithic revolution itself. In many cases it undoubtedly has been affected by a greater perceived need for white-manufactured articles more easily obtained by one of the parties.[18]

Some of the political aspects of Makú–Tukanoan interaction are probably less important than in the past. Makú certainly are not "slaves" at present, but it may be that in earlier times, when Tukanoans were less acculturated and less dominated by missionaries, and when feuding was a much more normal state of affairs (and thus raiding for captives a real danger), groups of Makú were more like the "field slaves" described by Goldman (1963, p. 106). Still, that one investigator with long-term experience with Makú seriously doubts that they were ever slaves (Reid, 1979). Additionally, the right to use Makú women sexually might have been more widespread although never fully sanctioned (McGovern, 1927, p. 249). Finally, Makú might very well have served as military allies, giving their services when needed as warriors in return for protection while attached to a particular settlement.

As a symbol, Makú serve at least two purposes, and in a certain sense this necessarily leads to contradictory statements from Tukanoans about why Makú are what they are. On the one hand, Makú serve as boundary markers and maintainers, reminding Tukanoans of correct behavior. To do this, Makú must be seen as like Tukanoans to some degree – people, or at least potential people, who break the rules and whose fate will be shared by anyone who behaves in similar fashion. On the other hand, Makú are exploited, and it is easier to maintain this type of relationship if Makú are seen as qualitatively and unchangeably different. It is this tension between the purposes to which Makú-as-symbol are put that in part produces the ambivalence and ambiguity of statements elicited from Tukanoans when discussing the Makú.

The literature on ethnic groups and other minorities frequently refers to ways in which members of a stigmatized group are a boundary-maintaining "message" for the dominant group (Barth 1969; Goffman 1963). The outside group's existence affirms each insider's membership and specifies by illustration what the criteria are for membership. Examples abound: the Jews in Nazi Germany and elsewhere, the Ainu in Japan, the Irish in Boston at the turn of the century. Outsiders at times serve as negative examples of what can happen if cultural norms are not adhered to. Although to some degree the outside groups buy the dominant group's view of things,[19] it is also true that frequently each group has a remarkably disparate view of itself and the other group. Both characteristics fit the Makú.

When Tukanoans are discussing human nature in general, the tendency is to include all people – whites and Makú – in the discussion. In this framework Makú are not seen as categorically and eternally excluded from the status of "true people" but potentially as members of the human race in good standing if and when they start to comply with certain rules and regulations. This is apparent

162

when a Tukanoan discusses certain behaviors as right and natural to everyone and disapproves of groups that do not subscribe to the same rules. If Makú were really beyond the pale with regard to their humanity, it would seem that other rules would apply for judging their behavior. In this regard, however, the ambiguity and inconsistency appear to be built in; at times even animals are discussed in terms of human-like characteristics and evaluated accordingly. Thus, when it is useful to use the Makú in a discussion of proper behavior, applicable to all, they are so used.

Still, Tukanoans are also interested in justifying and continuing their exploitation of Makú in the servant–master relationship. This is accomplished in part by emphasizing the differences between Makú and Tukanoans, saying Makú are inferior in these respects and claiming that these are *inherent* differences. These qualitative and unchangeable differences are what necessitates and justifies Tukanoans' treating Makú as second-class citizens. This type of rationalization is almost universally found in situations of social stratification.

In the Vaupés, tendencies toward stratification are not nearly as pronounced as in more complex and densely populated societies. Fixed, hereditary ranking is looser than that found in many other societies because of the ecological setting, demography, and economic organization of Tukanoan society. This is reflected in the actual freedom that Makú have, even though in the past Makú in some instances seem to have been less free than now. The periodic assimilation of Makú by Tukanoan local groups reported by various investigators would not occur so easily in more rigidly stratified societies in which genealogical reckoning is of more importance. Nevertheless, a hierarchy definitely exists in the Vaupés, and expectably, an ideology exists to support and explain it and its correctness. This is what occurs when a dominant group refers to differences between it and a subordinate group as permanent, inborn qualities that make unequal treatment just and inevitable. As we have seen, when it is convenient to describe Makú in these terms, they are so described.

9.

The role of language and speech in Tukanoan identity

It is by now obvious that language and speech are very important areas of Vaupés culture, among other things signaling identity in several social groups and categories. My choice of terminology for the exogamous language groups is based on the overwhelming importance of this factor in Tukanoan conceptualizations of these units. Although everyone is multilingual, individuals identify with and are loyal to only one language, their father language. Linguistic criteria are used as markers for differentiation among other kinds of social units as well – for example, sibs and phratries. In this chapter, I will examine in greater detail the ways in which language and speech are important to Tukanoans and will show how the Tukanoan model of language makes connections between linguistic phenomena and certain features of the nonlinguistic environment in which they occur.[1]

In the Vaupés (as elsewhere), language and speech are used to communicate information in at least two ways. First, languages (and the various genres and registers of any given language) are codes that are used for exchanging referential information. Speakers intentionally use these codes to send messages to each other. Second, language and speech are codes for communicating – sometimes intentionally and sometimes totally unconsciously, social information about the identities of the speaker, interlocutor (the individual to whom the message is directed), and audience.

Tukanoans see language and speech as correlated with a number of features of Vaupés social organization and culture. This process can be one of making links between actual speech forms and nonlinguistic social forms; or the connection between linguistic phenomena and the environment in which they occur can be a more diffuse one not attached to specific speech patterns. For example, Tukanoans in general assume that Vaupés languages are equal to one another – in contrast to many multilingual situations in which the interacting codes are ranked along dimensions such as beauty, logicality, and so on. This linguistic egalitarianism doubtless derives from the social egalitarianism Tukanoans see as existing between the language groups.

The relative emphasis placed on language and speech in a society in general

164

can indicate much about the social environment of the society. The abundant evidence of the importance language has for Tukanoans suggests that a thorough understanding of Tukanoan "ethnolinguistics" (Moerman, 1965) is crucial for a thorough understanding of most areas of Vaupés society and culture.

Vaupés language and speech as badges of identity

People tend to wear badges in situations in which there is a high degree of interaction and in which the differences being signaled by the badges are important for the successful outcome of the interaction. Badges can signal many kinds of social and cultural roles: Examples are sheriff's badges, the crosses worn on the necks of Maronite Christian soldiers in Lebanon, and the name tags people wear at annual conventions. As such, badges are a kind of *message,* a highly specialized kind of message that must meet specific requirements if communication is to be successful.

Badges can signal many kinds of limited or temporary social positions and roles such as "doctor" or "Hell's Angels member." Thus, although one may be a medical doctor all one's life, this part of one's identity is not always signaled – and if it were, it would at times occasion humor. Although being a member of the Hell's Angels may be a total experience, it probably will not last an entire lifetime. In contrast, being a member of a cultural, racial, or ethnic group usually is a permanent identification and frequently an extremely pervasive one.

A number of authors have discussed such badges of identity. Blom discusses multicultural or ethnic situations in which cultural differences separating the interacting groups become *codified* (1969, p. 84). Barth (1964, 1969) refers to these codified differences as "diacritica." In situations characterized by frequent interaction between different categories of people, some of the differences separating these categories become standardized and eventually stereotyped. The more such units interact and the longer the period of interaction, the more these categories of people become structurally similar and differentiated only by a few, clear diacritica. The total inventory of cultural differences is reduced, but the differences that remain, because of their new role as badges or emblems of identification with distinct groups, become more important. Such codified differences function as markers so that interaction can run more smoothly. They are thus quite unlike real cultural differences that are genuine impediments to interaction and communication.[2]

If badges and emblems of identity are a kind of message that must be transmitted, received, and decoded for interaction to take place, they must be reasonably parsimonious and successful most of the time. The reduction of differences satisfies the requirement of parsimony, and those differences that remain undergo transformations to ensure a maximum amount of effectiveness.[3] The particular differences that remain after this reduction have usually changed in directions that increase their *visibility, unambiguity,* and *discreteness,* because these characteristics facilitate the successful transmission of the message that badges and emblems are intended to send. Often the process includes opposition and polarization of the remaining differences, which increase the impact of the message.

Many badges that signal cultural or social identity are literally visible: Hoklo silver hair ornaments worn as "self-conscious marks of differentiation and local pride" are a good example (Ward, 1965, p. 133). Yet badges need not be literally visible to be effective; what is essential is that they be able to be displayed in public, either continually or when needed. For example, Moerman notes that "slight peculiarities of speech may serve as emblems (Fortes, 1945, p. 136; cf. [E.] Sapir, 1949) of a community which has a tribal name . . ." (1965, p. 1218). These slight peculiarities are probably far more important as markers of distinct communities than as linguistic differences per se.[4] Evidence abounds that language is a frequent and highly successful marker of cultural and social differentiation. The Canaanites' inability to pronounce *Shibboleth* is one of numerous cases. Gumperz, one of the scholars who has carried out significant research on language and speech as indicators of social identity, has studied a situation of code-switching between Hindi and Punjabi speakers in which a few linguistic items with a high text frequency "suffice to preserve the necessary minimum of symbols of role specificity" (1964a, p. 1123).

If the message transmitted by a badge of social identity is to be successfully communicated, the sender and receiver must see its content as important enough to warrant their time and energy. It generally seems to be the case that when differences evolve into badges and emblems of identity, they in fact do become very significant in the minds of the individuals involved and become quite charged with emotion. The fact that any outsiders observing this frequently judge the differences separating the groups as quite trivial, superficial, and overemphasized is not accidental. For the participants, the *features* that render each badge distinct from others in the set become highly charged with meaning. Such meaning may have a negative or positive value, for both the badge wearers and the badge observers, but will never produce mere indifference. Similarly, the *dimension* within which all of these distinctive features are contained can also become highly significant to insiders and exaggerated to outsiders. In the Vaupés, the dimension is language or linguistics, and the features are those linguistic elements that are seen by Tukanoans as making Vaupés languages mutually unintelligible. Vocabulary and grammatical differences and the co-occurrence rules that serve to keep Tukanoan languages as discrete category systems are vigorously maintained by Tukanoans. And the dimension of language is of extreme importance to Tukanoans, one that is woven into much of the fabric of their social life.

Although the linguistic picture in the Vaupés is unusual in a number of ways (and unique in a few), language and speech serve as markers of identity throughout the world. Furthermore, the process by which great import becomes attributed to the specific linguistic features marking social differences in class, sex, race, or ethnicity – is the same wherever it occurs. It seems always to be the case that perception becomes selective when specific linguistic features take on this role. The study of the Kannada and Marathi languages made by Gumperz (1964b) is an excellent illustration. In this case, despite high contact frequency, speakers believe linguistic diversity is far greater than it actually is, because of the importance of maintaining the distinction between the social groups identified with each code (Ervin-Tripp, 1969, p. 145). Because these rather trivial differences have a high text frequency, however, they are quite "visible" to the speakers.[5]

In addition to being parsimonious, visible, and significant, badges are also likely to be somewhat arbitrary. The more arbitrary a badge is – the less it is an inherent characteristic of an individual – the more easily it can be manipulated always to apply to just the right group of people even when changing conditions alter the membership of the group. Thus, the form of a badge is most suited to this function when the association between it and the category of people it represents is completely learned as a symbol. A good example of such arbitrariness is the Star of David as an emblem of Jewish identity, literally worn as a badge in Nazi Germany. Yet it is a potent enough association to have led to many consequences – for example, Egypt prohibited the display of any six-pointed stars on imported products after the Six-Day War, regardless of the product's lack of connection to Israel.

Obviously, many badges and emblems of identity are not entirely arbitrary; skin color is a good example. Nevertheless, racism is effective in keeping many people oppressed because of the learned association between various phenotypical traits and socially stigmatized categories of people, and because it serves this purpose so well, it is a well-established institution, despite the sometimes ludicrous expressions that arise.[6]

Language and speech are fairly well adapted to fulfill this requirement of arbitrariness, although not completely so. Shaw's *Pygmalion* dramatizes this theme. Much humor is devoted to chronicling ways in which upwardly mobile individuals betray their origins with their speech, either through slip-ups or hyperforms (Labov, 1966). In the Vaupés one cannot cross boundaries by changing one's speech patterns or identification with a particular father language. This is because one inherits one's father language and cannot change it in any legitimate way, and it is doubtful that any Tukanoan has tried to do it illegitimately. Aside from the fact that there are virtually no motives for *wanting* to switch father-language identity, it would be impossible because everyone knows or knows about everyone else. This is not the case when a Tukanoan is trying to "pass" into the category of "Colombian," particularly if he or she lives in Mitú or San José de Guaviare. An ability to speak Spanish with very little Indian accent is an important factor influencing the degree to which it is possible to carry this off.

167

Languages are also arbitrary in the sense that they can take on the social values associated with the group of people speaking the language. A fair amount of research on this topic has been carried out, showing how languages come to be regarded as superior (or inferior), musical, logical, and so on, mainly by serving as a symbol of the community identified with them, to which these traits are also seen to apply. Speech itself can at times be said to be "high," "thick," or "heavy," because of an association with certain groups (J. D. Sapir, 1975).[7]

Thus, badges and emblems serve their purpose of sending messages best when they are clear-cut, unambiguous, and discrete. This is why the emblematic differences found among interacting social units are standardized, often to the point of caricature. In situations in which dual membership, marginal membership, boundary crossing ("passing"), or secret membership can occur, the orderliness of the interaction and people's assumptions about predictability can become eroded.[8] Although such flexibility may be beneficial to individuals attempting to pass into other social categories (hence the frequency of this theme in fairy tales, Shakespeare, Gilbert and Sullivan, etc.), they do so at the expense of the social system – another reason why this theme is so popular in fiction.

As indicated earlier, identification with a specific language is clear-cut and permanent in the Vaupés. In situations where languages or speech varieties are badges of identity, the criterion of discreteness *may* be met by a relatively few differences, as is the case in an example of Kannada and Marathi, discussed by Gumperz and Wilson (1971), in which two unrelated languages have greatly converged yet are seen as distinct by their respective speakers who identify with only one of the two. Tukanoans see their languages as quite distinct, with clear-cut boundaries. Some Vaupés languages are more different from each other than in some of the situations discussed by Gumperz (1964b, 1969) and Moerman (1965, p. 1218). Yet interesting questions arise in connection with the Vaupés material regarding the nature of dialect versus language and the influence speakers' attitudes and loyalty to only one code has on language change. For example, Sorensen remarks: "It has occurred to me that the exogamic and other cultural institutions . . . may be exerting a force that makes a speaker want to render closely-related languages further apart, even to an artificial extent, but so far I have detected no linguistic innovations to this end" (1967, p. 676).

Much of the sociolinguistic literature deals with the ways in which individuals send and receive information about social identity through the use of language. Most of this work is concerned with speech behavior itself, and some studies have concentrated on the ways speakers themselves understand how speech can indicate social status. Labov's discussions (1966) of stereotype and hypercorrection are good examples.

In some situations in the Vaupés, the public display of language group identity through actual speech occurs. Sorensen gives an example: "Each individual initially speaks in his own father-language during such a conversation in order to assert his tribal affiliation and identification'' (1967, p. 678). A Tukanoan who is publicly acknowledging his language group membership is usually reaffirming this aspect of his social identity rather than announcing a previously unknown fact about himself. Most of the time, Tukanoans interact with other Tukanoans who are well known to them, and hence they know one another's language group identity. Thus, the fact that very few speech events allow one to signal one's language group identity does not indicate that language group identity is not an extremely important aspect of Vaupés life. On the contrary, it is so important that there is little need for Tukanoans continually to remind one another of this aspect of their social identity. In most situations, and in all informal speech events, various other sociolinguistic rules determine which languages will be used in speaking.

That Tukanoans consciously try to maintain linguistic boundaries when speaking is further indication of the role language plays as a badge of identity. Sorensen (1967, p. 675) states that languages appear to be kept fastidiously apart and that when two languages are closely related, Tukanoans will "carefully and even consciously keep them apart." He also states that Tukanoans do not attempt to speak a language being learned until they feel competent to speak it correctly. This suggests that interference in speech from one's father language or another language already in one's verbal repertoire is disapproved of socially. I observed instances of this type of social disapproval when women were scolded for allowing words from other languages to creep into conversations in Bará. Other Tukanoans would comment that such women were not setting a good example for their children, who should learn to speak their father's and mother's languages correctly. Occasionally it was remarked to me that I would shame the longhouse if I learned Bará with Tuyuka words mixed in. I did not try to measure the overall amount of interference from other languages that was allowed to pass or try to estimate the frequency of criticism of such mistakes. It is my impression that attempting to measure such interference objectively would be very hard, because to a large extent what interference *is* in the Vaupés is what is seen as such by the participants at a given point in time. It seems clear that Tukanoans disapprove of using a word from another language in speaking and see it as a mistake. Thus, while convergence may be taking place (and quite probably is, in fact) among Tukanoan languages, at any given point in time strict co-occurrence rules operate to keep the languages separate in a specific individual's or group's repertoire.

The presence of these rules is evidence for the emblematic nature of Vaupés languages. That Tukanoans are aware of speech "mistakes," that they place a high value on correct speech, and that they see Vaupés languages as mutually unintelligible support the hypothesis that the separate languages serve as emblems of structurally similar interacting groups. Otherwise, languages might converge or several languages be dropped, which would certainly be more efficient linguistically. When I directly asked a Tukanoan why they spoke so many languages rather than, for example, relying on Tukano exclusively, because they all knew it anyway, he responded, "If we all were Tukano speakers, where would we get our women?"

Thus, the cognitive model Tukanoans have of linguistic discreteness, especially with regard to mutual unintelligibility. is of great importance in understanding the linguistic situation. For example, I was surprised several times to find that a word that was frequently used in Bará was considered by Bará speakers to be a Tuyuka word. When asked for a translation, they always produced a Bará word and would give a reason for preferring the Tuyuka word. Most important, I would be reassured that "everyone *knows* it is a Tuyuka word." This suggests that Tukanoans are aware of intrusive words in a language's lexicon but that this is accepted as long as the co-occurrence rules separating languages are not seen to be in danger of breaking down.

Messages about social identity can be signaled by language in two ways. The first is through speech itself. Although identifying one's social identity through speech does not constantly occur in the Vaupés, this is due to the fact that Tukanoan language group affiliations are known by almost everyone almost all of the time, reducing the need continually to display this emblem of membership. In other multilingual situations, speech serves this function to a greater degree. For example, in the Xingú Basin, where Indians from various linguistically discrete groups come together for ceremonies, each group continues to speak its own language, even though others present may not understand it (Basso, 1973). The same is reported by Rivero for the Chiricoa-Guahibo and the Achaguas in the Colombian llanos (in Morey and Morey, 1975, p. 9). Such a situation is also found among the Yurok, Karok, and Hupa groups in Northern California. Each community is identified with one tribal language, and within the community only the tribal language is spoken. Separate names exist for many of the same physical landmarks (Bright and Bright, 1965).

The other way in which language can be an emblem of social identity occurs when people have a formal affiliation with one language and limit their loyalty to it, despite any knowledge they might have of other languages. To the degree to which this is public knowledge, it will be a factor in their interactions with others, regardless of their speech behavior itself. Obviously, this second way of having language signal social identity requires that the interacting parties be aware of each other's formal identification with given codes. In situations in which individuals are perfect bilinguals or multilinguals, their formal identification with one language must be known by everyone if it is not overtly displayed in speech. Of course, how one evaluates one's own linguistic affiliation may differ from how others evaluate it: Most Germans probably differ from most Frenchmen regarding the privilege of identifying with German rather than French as one's mother tongue.

Linguistic data on Vaupés languages show the close association between statements about language and statements about language group membership, supporting the assertion that languages serve as badges of such membership. For example, the question *ñe wadegǘ niti mü* in Bará, which glosses roughly as "What [male] language-speaker are you?" invariably elicits a response about the interlocutor's language group membership. This is unambiguous, and a Bará male will answer, *yü ni barayü,* "I am Bará," or *(yü-) ye waderá ni bará,* "My father language is Bará." These inquiries about language group membership are grammatically distinct from inquiries and responses about speech itself, such as *ñe wadegati mü,* "What do you say?" or *nohkõro waderá mahïti mü,* "How many languages do you know [how to speak]?"

Other evidence available from conversations with Bará informants indicates their awareness of the emblematic nature of Tukanoan languages. An example of this is the quotation given earlier regarding the relationship between sibling terminology and marriage rules. The relationship between common ancestry and common language is quite clearly drawn.[9]

How Vaupés languages assume features of the nonlinguistic environment

Phratries: language distance.

As we saw in Chapter 5, the degree to which phratries exist in the Vaupés is problematical, whether one is speaking of Tukanoan conceptualizations of phratries or actual marriage patterns. The Tukanoan model of a phratry probably does not require conceptualizing it as a distinct entity; at least this seems likely in the case of the younger Tukanoans who served as informants. Older Tukanoans, however, give lists of language groups whose members are not supposed to intermarry because of a sibling relationship between them. This may or may not be accompanied by actual use of agnatic terminology. Members of the same phratry are also spoken of as having spoken a single language at some time in the past. This is in keeping with a general tendency to associate an exogamous marriage class with a single language and, conversely, an assumption that intermarrying people are always associated with distinct languages. Thus, agnatic relatedness and linguistic relatedness are indicators of social closeness.

In other words, when confronted with the fact that certain pairs of language groups do not intermarry but nonetheless speak different languages, Tukanoans state that although these languages are mutually unintelligible, they are nonetheless *relatively* close, because the two groups used to speak the same language. Language distance is, thus, still mirrored in social distance, both being based on a (relative) genetic model. Bará say that Tukano is easier to learn than other languages, particularly those languages of the groups with which Bará intermarry. Figure 7 illustrates the lack of fit between Bará statements about relative genetic distance among Vaupés languages and Sorensen's reconstruction of

The fish people

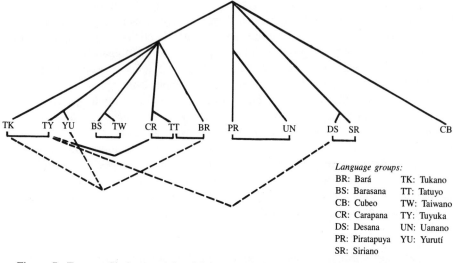

Figure 7. Two conflicting models of language distance. The solid lines represent the Eastern Tukanoan family as reconstructed by Sorensen (1967); the dashed lines represent the Bará model. Groups that intermarry in at least one region of the Vaupés are connected by dotted lines. The geographical locations of the intermarrying language groups shown here are Caño Viña (DS and SR); lower Papurí (PR and UN); middle Papurí (TK and TY); upper Papurí (CR, TT, and BR); Pirá-paraná (BS and TW).

Eastern Tukanoan languages (1967, p. 682), using the comparative method. Sorensen states that "the resulting subgroupings definitely do not correlate with phratric groupings" (1967, p. 674).

Sorensen's reconstruction is generally corroborated by the work on a reconstruction of Proto-Tukanoan carried out by Waltz and Wheeler (1970). Table 9, based on their work, shows the percentage of shared vocabulary for each pair of most closely related languages.

As can be seen in Figure 7, many of the groups most closely related linguistically also intermarry. This is also supported by Sorensen (1967, p. 674) and, with one exception (ignoring the Cubeo, who marry within the tribal unit), by Waltz and Wheeler's information on marriage patterns. Waltz and Wheeler state that Bará marry with Tuyuka, Uanano with Tukano, and Carapana with Tatuyo (they do not give marriage data on all language groups). The exception is the Uanano, who are "forbidden to marry the Piratapuyo 'because they are brothers.'"[10] The Piratapuya and Uanano, then, are the only linguistically valid examples of the Tukanoan model, in which social and linguistic relationships have a close connection.

Bará informants state that there is a close genetic relationship between sibling-related languages and a distant genetic relationship between affinally related languages. Sorensen's and Waltz and Wheeler's work indicate that this is

172

Table 9. *Language distance as measured by cognates*

Languages	% cognates
Piratapuya and Uanano	99.2
Uanano and Tukano	91
Tukano and Pápiwa[a]	93
Pápiwa and Tatuyo	90.2
Tatuyo and Carapana	96.3
Carapana and Bará	91
Bará and Tuyuka	97.2
Tuyuka and Barasana[b]	93
Barasana and Makuna	98.3
Makuna and Siriano	94.5
Siriano and Desana	98.9
Desana and Cubeo	79

[a]Possibly Wahúna; if the same as Sorensen's Yurutí, the two reconstructions shown in Figure 7 differ on which languages are most closely related to Yurutí–Pápiwa.
[b]Identical to Sorensen's Paneroa.
Source: Waltz and Wheeler, 1970; Chart 1.
Note: Tukanoans consider Taiwano and Barasana to be separate languages, and they are listed as distinct in Sorensen, 1967. Waltz and Wheeler (1970) and S. Hugh-Jones (personal communication) consider them the same language.

not true in the majority of cases. Frequently those languages that are genetically the most closely related are those of language groups that do intermarry in one or more subregions of the Vaupés. This suggests that an origin by fission from a protolanguage might be the explanation for such presently separate languages as Siriano and Desana, Carapana and Tatuyo, Bará and Tuyuka, and Uanano and Tukano. This might have involved a previous situation where two moieties speaking the same protolanguage with some differentiation in speech gradually came to be identified with distinct languages. Evidence from the Barasana–Taiwano split (which Tukanoans consider to be separate languages but which Waltz and Wheeler and S. Hugh-Jones [personal communication] do not) supports this assumption. Perhaps, if allowed to evolve, the two intermarrying Makuna groups might eventually separate linguistically as much as some other intermarrying pairs (e.g., Bará and Tuyuka, who share 97.2 percent cognates).[11] Sorensen (1967, p. 670) suggests that the Tuyuka and Yurutí languages (and language groups) are perhaps derived from a common source.

Other evidence exists supporting the case of this type of origin for a number of intermarrying pairs of language groups in the Vaupés. For example, the Piratapuya retain a nonfunctioning moiety system. Goldman (personal communication) has information on an earlier Cubeo marriage system based on moieties with fixed intermarrying ranks. Furthermore, we have seen that a number of

Tukanoan languages have a basically Dravidian type of kinship terminology, which organizes kinsmen into dual structures of agnate–affine and is quite compatible with a moiety structure.

With the exception of Waltz and Wheeler's information about nonmarriage between the Piratapuya and Uanano, Tukanoan assumptions of relatively greater linguistic distance existing between certain other pairs who call themselves "brothers" is not supported by the comparative linguistic data.

Other well-documented instances exist in which social attitudes toward language have led to the disregarding of purely linguistic evidence about relative linguistic distance. Gumperz cites the case of speakers of certain German dialects in Alsace-Lorraine who pay language loyalty to French rather than to German. He also discusses situations where "speakers' claims that they do not understand each other reflect primarily social attitudes rather than linguistic fact" (1968, p. 124). It is evident that attitudes toward language based on social criteria influence popular notions about relative distance between languages, speech boundaries, and the amount of energy invested in keeping two code systems visibly distinct. The Vaupés obviously offers many opportunities for investigating how social attitudes can, over time, affect the "purely linguistic criteria" upon which measures of linguistic diversity are based.

Language groups: linguistic discreteness.

Tukanoan attitudes toward language in the context of the language group per se might be characterized as separate but equal. That they are maintained as separate enough for Tukanoans to state they are mutually unintelligible (which is also the position of the Summer Institute of Linguistics) is doubtless at least in part due to their role as badges of the language groups.

In addition to the feature of mutual unintelligibility is the one of equality. Tukanoans do not agree with suggestions that some Tukanoan languages are superior to others. This corresponds to a similar resistance to suggestions that certain language groups are superior to others. This is expectable in a situation characterized by marriage classes participating in a symmetrical direct exchange system. In contrast to an asymmetrical system (Lévi-Strauss, 1969; Needham, 1962), this type of system does not permit intermarrying classes to have different status. It would therefore be surprising if the emblems symbolizing these classes were seen as having greater or less value vis à vis each other. Status differentiation does exist in the Vaupés, but apart from the use of elder and younger sibling terms among language groups in the same phratry, it is not an aspect of the language group system. (See Zuidema, 1969, on this matter.)

Sorensen (1967, p. 679) states that Tukanos claim a mild prestige as the senior clans of the area. I have heard Tukanos claim (in Spanish) that they were **los primeros** ("foremost") among Vaupés Indians. It is also true that Bará address Tukanos with elder sibling terminology, which generally is an indicator of respect and higher status. Thus, Tukanos may be an exception to the rule of egalitarianism among language groups.

Still, Tukanos are in a somewhat special category, which may account for the mild prestige they claim. They are apparently relative newcomers to the Vaupés, and the distribution of Tukano settlements suggests that they displaced other groups when they entered the region, forcing these groups into headwater areas. This may indicate that in the past Tukanos were accorded respect because of their military strength. Tukanos are also the largest language group and the most acculturated. The fact that there are more Tukanos and that more Tukanos wear Western clothing, are practicing Catholics, and speak Spanish than do members of most other language groups may be sufficiently important to account for their special status. Moreover, the Tukano language is the lingua franca of the region.

In any case, Tukanos do not have more power or authority than other Tukanoans. It is my impression that Tukanos are more likely to claim such prestige in their interactions with whites; open assertion of superiority in the presence of other Tukanoans would surely be met with hostility. In addition, although Bará freely admit that they address Tukanos with elder sibling terms, they also assert that this is not the way it should be, because in fact Bará are the elder siblings of the Tukano.

Vaupés *languages* are in no way ranked. If Tukanos do in fact have a higher prestige, such prestige is not extended to their language. Despite the fact that Tukano is a lingua franca, it is not considered preferable because of its greater clarity or more extensive vocabulary or similar qualities. In fact, Tukanoans resent the fact that change agents such as Catholic priests consider Tukano the only language worth learning. I was told that the Summer Institute of Linguistics has a much better approach than the Catholic missionaries, because its personnel try to learn all the languages. The reluctance of Tukanoans to make invidious comparisons involving language groups or language contrasts with their willingness to do so with respect to different sibs' ability to speak a single language; this is discussed in the following section.

This characteristic of egalitarianism among languages in the Vaupés is an important one because in so many multilingual situations ranking is an integral part of the system (Ferguson, 1959; Lambert, 1967; Labov, 1966). The situation in the Vaupés clearly supports Gumperz's statement that "the common view that multilingualism wherever it occurs also reflects deep social cleavages is clearly in need of revision" (1969, p. 447).

Although unusual, the concept of partial or total language exogamy is not unique to the Vaupés. More research should be done regarding native attitudes to codes, be they dialect differences (Sankoff, 1970, 1974) or mutually unintelligible languages, when these are connected to exogamous marriage classes in some manner. Partial linguistic exogamy apparently occurs in small-scale societies with greater frequency than is usually supposed (Owen, 1965; W. R. Miller, 1970). Total linguistic exogamy has been reported for some Australian groups in

175

which intermarrying moieties speak separate languages: "The members of each moiety are supposed to speak different languages . . . Each class is said to have a language" (Warner, discussing the Murngin, 1937, p. 30; also see Tindale, 1953).

Sibs: linguistic proficiency.

Sibs are named patrilineal descent groups, each one tracing descent from a mythical ancestor. Each language group is composed of a set of ranked sibs, each of which should, and usually does, occupy a continuous territory, although as we have seen, this does not always fit the ideal pattern of one sib per settlement. Sib rank is seen as derived from and equivalent to sibling birth order.

Tukanoans will account for differences in rank in the sibs composing a given language group in a number of ways. One of these is by referring to the relative proficiency with which members of a given sib speak Bará, Tukano, or whatever father language the sib speaks. This criterion was the one most frequently offered by Bará informants when asked why they addressed the members of lower-ranking sibs as "younger brothers." These judgments are most often concerned with lexical criteria, although occasionally pronunciation will be mentioned. Whenever I asked why the Bará Yóara sib addressed the Waiñakoroa or Wamútañará sibs as younger siblings, they responded with statements such as, "They do not speak Bará properly . . . listen to the [inmarried] Bará women of the longhouses downstream . . . they use the wrong words." It is interesting to note that at times a possible hyperform usage enters the picture (Labov, 1966). I was told to use certain words and grammatical constructions I had never heard used by the Bará of Púmanaka buro themselves. When I pointed this out, they would respond, "This is the language of the Bará Yóara . . . this is the correct language, the language of Mario's [the headman's] father and grandfather." It is interesting that my speech was corrected for certain speech forms even though in general there was a hesitance on the part of my informants to correct my speech. For example, I was told to say *bárihke* ("food") rather than *bárihe,* the form I always heard. I was told always to use the /hk/ in words having that suffix, which is a frequently occurring one. Whether this was the common form at an earlier period, whether the /hk/ is used in another, more prestigious dialect of Bará (quite possible, despite the claims of Púmanaka buro to belonging to the highest-ranked sib; such claims should always be taken with a grain of salt), or whether it is an example of the way in which a sound change begins, I cannot say. When I protested, saying that I wanted to speak like the rest, they would say that I had to learn the proper form in order to demonstrate to other Tukanoans that I was being taught the correct speech, the Bará of the Bará Yóara sib. These Bará said that the Summer Institute of Linguistics missionary living with the Wamútañará Bará (the lowest-ranking sib) on Caño Colorado in the Pirá-paraná region would never learn to speak proper Bará, because he had chosen to live with Bará who could not speak it properly themselves. During my stay I collected numerous examples of improper forms spoken by lower-ranked sibs and of "more proper" forms, now "lost," which had been in the language of the ancestors of the higher-ranking sibs.

The importance of language in Tukanoan culture

The discussion of Tukanoan attitudes toward language distance, discreteness, and correct speech gives an idea of the overall importance of language and speech in Tukanoan culture and society. Aspects of language and speech are markers of identity in several kinds of social groups and categories in the Vaupés. In addition, language – as a concept and in the sense of linguistic performance – is extremely important in the Tukanoan model of society and, indeed, the universe, and linguistic criteria symbolize many crucial facts of Vaupés life.

Sorensen points out that "Indians are quite unself-conscious about their multilingualism" (1967, p. 679), and this is true in the sense that a polyglot in a society in which all members are multilingual is not the remarkable individual he or she is in American society. Nonetheless, Tukanoans possess distinct father languages, and the ability to speak, to speak well, and to be able to use power available from linguistic performances are considerable assets for those individuals and groups that have such abilities and can claim such prerogatives.

Tukanoan mythology frequently refers to a connection between power, humanity, or life itself, and the ability to speak (and, by analogy, to make sounds).[12] Shamans speak an esoteric language in ritual, which nonspecialists cannot understand (S. Hugh-Jones, 1979, pp. 58–59). They validate their claims to their special status by their ability to communicate with nonhuman beings in this world and in other levels of the universe. Much of the respect they acquire in their career is due to these special linguistic abilities.

In other areas of Tukanoan life, speech is one of the means of distinguishing among classes of people in terms of status and prestige. A command of ritual lore and knowledge and an ability to speak effectively and beautifully are ways of distinguishing high-ranking sibs from low-ranking ones, men from women, and old men from younger men (Reichel-Dolmatoff, 1971, pp. 249–52). Thus, formal occasions provide opportunities to demonstrate one's grasp of esoteric and ritual knowledge and of etiquette in general. In fact, speech itself plays many important performative roles (Austin, 1962), and in this capacity is crucial in Tukanoan ritual and symbolism (Bidou, 1976; S. Hugh-Jones, 1974; Jacopin, 1972). The ability to perform chants and myth narrations well is important in tapping the power of the ancients.

Language also distinguishes humans from nonhumans, although in some instances this is not signaled simply by the presence or absence of a language. Each species of animal is seen as having its own language, as do the ubiquitous wahtía, forest spirits. All the other denizens of the universe, insofar as they have any humanoid characteristics, have speech. For example, during my fieldwork, at times an uncanny noise would be heard in the sky right before a thunderstorm. I imagined this to be bird cries that were greatly distorted by the unusual acoustics of the very low clouds. My Bará informants told me that this was "sky-people language," which becomes loud enough to be heard when the sky people become excited about something and start yelling and cleaning out their longhouse.

Many other examples can be given. One way Tukanoans distinguish themselves from Makú is by saying the Tukanoans speak a superior, truly human language. Goldman (personal communication) states that a translation of the Cubeo self-name Pamiwa is "people of the language."

This chapter has been limited to a discussion of certain aspects of social structure and the way in which these are incorporated into the Tukanoan model of linguistics. It is evident that much more remains to be studied and analyzed if we are to acquire a comprehensive picture of the importance and function of language and speech in Tukanoan culture.

10.

Male and female identity

It is difficult to discuss Tukanoan sex roles and identity comprehensively in a single chapter. First, an entire book would be required to do justice to the necessary ethnographic material, particularly with respect to the extraordinarily rich ritual and mythological expressions of sex differences. Fortunately, other investigators have discussed some of the symbolism of Tukanoan sex roles.[1] (*Sex roles* refers to all of the ways in which Tukanoan males and females behave differently, see themselves as different, and symbolically express these differences.)

Second, the nature of the subject matter itself requires more extensive treatment than is possible within one chapter. The fledgling state of the field of sex roles as a topic in its own right creates certain difficulties, which have been discussed in many articles and books. Both our own society and lowland South American societies see men and women as fundamentally different (see Jackson, n.d.-a.). Yet what does this mean? Seemingly insoluble problems arise in connection with objectivity and agreement over basic assumptions and correct research design and goals. How do we evaluate the differences existing between the sexes in all Amazonian societies in terms of crucial questions concerning status, power, solidarity, egalitarianism versus hierarchy, among others? What do these differences mean, comparatively speaking, in a society so unlike our own, a society where age and sex are the main criteria of social differentiation? Yet we can hardly accept uncritically the "inside" view – the native interpretation – of sex differences, even supposing there were a single such view. It is a truism that people are often unaware of significant structures and dynamics in their own society and, when convenient, ignore and distort others. Such systematic (i.e., ultimately explainable) distortions occur as much, if not more so, in the area of sex roles as in other areas of social life.

Still, it is impossible to imagine a book on Tukanoan identity without a chapter on at least some of the issues concerning relations between the sexes. This is particularly important when we consider the prominent place that material from horticulturalist societies, with South American societies prominently included, occupies in many of the more theoretical debates on sex differences.

Lowland South America has been the focus of a number of inquiries into

179

male–female relations, particularly with respect to questions of opposition and antagonism between the sexes. One important debate involves whether these are expressions of "real" male oppression or only wishful thinking on the part of men in the face of strong contrary evidence. A related question concerns the actual amount of female "power" in these societies and to what degree it results from female contributions in economic production and distribution, reproduction, and other areas.[2]

Too many discussions of the position of women in horticultural societies are uninformed, simplistic, and naive. Frequently such concepts of high or low "status" are used in cross-cultural comparative studies with shockingly imprecise definitions. As Lamphere points out (1977, p. 613), the same can be said for "asymmetry," "subordination," "equality," or "power." Serious problems arise in selecting and defining equivalent units of comparison, regardless of the type of evidence (e.g.. economic, symbolic) being marshaled. How can the differences between image and reality found in all cultures be adequately translated into an analytic code for comparative purposes? Of course, this is a general problem in description and comparison – and translation – but the difficulties seem especially thorny with respect to the study of sex roles and identity. This is in part because of the general tendency for anthropologists to investigate, record, and publish only the official, idealized version of cultural patterns and mores, or at least to give undue emphasis to them. In all cultures male and female views of reality diverge, at times extensively. Nevertheless, both men and women in a given society tend to give any outsider the official, male-oriented view, and research concerned with discovering differences between the sexes will be grossly inadequate if the investigator does not probe more deeply. The dangers of such inadequacy are increased when the researcher is male, talks only to males, is unaware of his own ethnocentric assumptions about sex differences (which we all have to some degree and are all somewhat unaware of), and is satisfied with a "rule-book" version of culture. To use such information for drawing cross-cultural generalizations about sex roles is obviously unwise; sad to say, at times such reports are the only ones available for a given society or region.

Differences in sex roles and their causes are obviously important aspects of life for all of us, and few fields offer such an abundance of explanatory models and theories, each one predicting horrible yet inevitable consequences should its implications be ignored. Of course, some of the more bizarre or dogmatic explanations have little effect on anthropological research and analysis, but the existence of so many theories argued from such divergent premises poses a serious problem to scholars when conducting research, be it devoted to a single culture or comparative in scope.

These comments are intended not only as warnings with respect to the reliability and validity of ethnographic sources dealing with these topics and the theoretical arguments buttressing them but also as reasons for my hesitancy to draw any sweeping conclusions about sex-role differences and their determinants among Tukanoans.

This chapter looks at some "givens" in social structure, economic production, and reproduction in Tukanoan society and examines some of the cognitive models that Tukanoans have evolved for expressing and making sense out of these givens. Some tentative conclusions about Tukanoan views regarding sex-role differences are proposed: (1) To some extent in Vaupés society, women are seen as "outsiders," or "the other," to use de Beauvoir's (1953) terminology; (2) women are seen to be relatively more "natural" than men (who are more "cultural," although this is not a simple association by any means);[3] (3) women need to be "controlled" in a number of ways, at times because of their superiority, at times because of the danger they pose, and at times simply to avoid an excess of what is in itself not a negatively evaluated quality or trait.

It is important to note that although it is true that Tukanoans recognize differences existing between the sexes in all areas of life – and this recognition is expressed in spatial arrangements segregating the sexes, in economic tasks, in social interaction, in ritual, and in myth – such opposition and, often, antagonism are not the entire picture. The processes of synthesizing and permuting male and female symbolic elements are also very much in evidence. Above all, it is important to bear in mind the virtual absence of absolutes that can be lifted from the structures and contexts in which they occur without great distortion. What is one thing at one level is something quite different – at times the reverse – at another.

Relations between men and women

Probably the most important social structural factors affecting female status in the Vaupés are (1) the organization of female economic contribution (particularly food production); (2) patrilineality and patrilocality; (3) the traditional settlement pattern of communal multifamily longhouses, one per settlement; and (4) the rule of direct exchange at marriage. Other significant features are undoubtedly the prescription for language exogamy, the kinds of relationships formed between affinally related settlements, the low incidence of polygyny, the fact that marriages are fairly stable after an initial period of a few years, and the (current) absence of raiding and feuding.

It cannot be denied that Vaupés society is male-dominated. Male activities are valued more highly than female ones. As was pointed out in Chapter 4, a powerful mystique surrounds hunting, male sexuality, and male-controlled religion, including sacred objects and power forbidden to women. Only men are thought of as true spiritual beings (S. Hugh-Jones, 1977, p. 13). Male-focused ritual dominates Vaupés religion, and men can be seen as ritually controlling female (as well as male) areas of life, such as menarche and birth. Male rituals are needed to make relationships with females safe, ordered, and moderated – keeping women at a proper distance describes much of what these rituals are

181

intended to accomplish. Rituals control women and female symbols in a variety of ways – for instance, by neutralizing potentially destructive female elements, or limiting the force of others. Other rituals can be seen as expropriating female power and creativity for male-oriented uses. An example of the latter is the male initiation ceremony, which for most of the ritual excludes noninitiates, particularly women, yet which on the symbolic level utilizes many potent female images, sources of power, and kinds of creativity. Thus, these rituals are both an acknowledgment of female power and evidence of male dominance, for they utilize female power to promote what are predominantly male interests, such as the continuation of the patrilineal descent group. At times women are symbolically "sent back to where they came from, outside and beyond male society" (S. Hugh-Jones, 1977, p. 210).

Much evidence can be found in myth as well as ritual for expressions and justifications of male supremacy. Females are variously depicted as dangerous, selfish, treacherous, and nonhuman. They are enemies who can never really become friends, destructive to "good" male interests, and threats to male solidarity. Although this is not the only kind of female image contained in Tukanoan myths, nor are negative images the only ones of women to be found in Tukanoan ritual, neither is the picture one of equality, a picture where male and female spheres are separate but complimentary and equally valuable. The real situation lies somewhere in between these two poles and is far more complex.

To understand these images more fully requires a careful examination of everyday relations between the sexes, in particular of the relative amounts of power, autonomy, and options available to each. This allows a better understanding of the symbolic plane, not only to see whether such ritual expressions of male dominance are "accurate" reflections of daily arrangements but also better to understand why male dominance is asserted so vehemently in certain rituals. Native cognitive models, whatever their medium of expression, in part exist as mechanisms of perpetuating, rather than actually explaining, social reality (Lévi-Strauss, 1962). They also have an internal logic that to some degree determines their nature apart from any "function." Thus, it is quite probable that myth and ritual sometimes buttress unsteady male positions, giving expression to anxieties and insecurities about the inevitability and justice of male superiority, serving as just-so stories. This argues for initially separating on-the-ground reality from symbolic reality in any analysis of male and female roles – although at a later stage these two levels must be combined.

Food production.

The food Tukanoan women produce and process is a substantial contribution to the Tukanoan diet, although given our state of knowledge about diet in such horticulturally based societies, it is impossible precisely to compare male and female contributions in terms of actual nutrition. Women prepare almost all food.[4] In addition to processing and cooking, women provide most cultivated foods and many kinds of foraged foods. It is the women who plant, tend, and process almost all the edible cultigens (i.e., excluding coca, banisteriopsis, and tobacco), although men are responsible for some fruit trees, some corn, and pineapple plants. It is mainly women who gather fruits, vegetables, nuts, and small insects.

In general men and women are viewed as complementary with respect to subsistence contributions. Fish and game, which supply protein, are the most highly valued foodstuffs, but manioc is the staff of life and other foods cannot be eaten without it. One can, and does at certain times of the year, go without male-supplied foods for one or more days, but it is unthinkable to get through a single day without manioc products. This, added to the fact that women transform virtually all foodstuffs from a raw to a ready-to-eat stage, means that men are constantly reminded of their dependence on women for food. If a man has no wife, he depends on his mother or unmarried sister for his meals. Lacking these, he must eat at his brother and sister-in-law's hearth. The strict sexual division of labor prohibits men from engaging in those aspects of food production and preparation assigned to women, just as women cannot clear fields, hunt, or fish. When men discuss women, their role as food producers and processors is mentioned time and again.

In sum, sex-specific activities related to subsistence are markedly segregated, both in terms of who performs an activity and the symbolic meanings associated with it.[5] An observer is given the impression of interdependence and complementarity, but this complementarity, although very real in both objective and conceptual terms, is not the whole story.[6]

Tukanoan ritual and symbolism portray male and female roles in subsistence in many ways. For example, although women are excluded from much of the male initiation ceremony, certain women are crucial to it, such as those who prepare the food eaten by men and initiates. Furthermore, throughout the male initiation ceremonial cycle, many symbolic equivalences between women and female-related subsistence activities, especially concerning manioc, are ritually expressed. Another example is found during food exchange ceremonies, when the two communities adopt male and female symbolic stances vis à vis each other. The host community, receiving smoked meat, is likened to a woman (who similarly receives game from a man); the food is brought in through the men's door and the host group provides beer, a female contribution (C. Hugh-Jones, 1977, p. 200). Rituals celebrating the harvest of jungle fruits, in particular the mirití palm fruit, are replete with sexual symbolism. I was present at an attenuated one, which involved canoes laden with mirití fruit arriving at the port accompanied by Yuruparí horns; at the arrival the women left the longhouse for the fields, hearing the horns during the ceremony but not returning to the longhouse until the men and horns had left again. In the past these harvest ceremonies were more developed (Goldman, 1963, p. 192), sometimes expressing more overt antagonism between the sexes.

Apart from symbolism contained in ritual, one finds many kinds of associations made between men and women and food or agriculture. For example, C. Hugh-Jones discusses the agnatic core of a community as the respective recipients or "consumers" of children, just as they are of women's economic productivity: "There is no doubt that manioc is regarded as women's offspring for women are called 'manioc-stick food mothers'. . .in ritual language" (personal communication). She also notes a correlation made between the umbilicus giving nourishment to the foetus and the path from the longhouse to the manioc fields (1976, p. 14).

In subsistence as in other areas, men ritually control women and their products. Mother's milk and all other types of food must be shamanized before they are safe for consumption. Cooked food – associated with female symbolism in a number of ways – is dangerous in itself and must be understood and eaten under the proper circumstances and never to excess. As was noted in Chapter 4, a complicated series of food rituals exists that both restricts and makes safe the various categories of food for people going through various kinds of crises.

Domestic roles.

As in the case of subsistence-related activities, there is a marked distinction between the sexes in domestic activities and an interdependence, although an absolute balance does not exist either in complementarity of tasks or in how Tukanoans conceive of this interdependence. Women make bags of *Mauritia flexuosa* fibers twisted into string, and from *Bromelia* fibers they make the ritual garters worn by men (the latter is a rare example of women manufacturing ceremonial items). They also wash and mend all clothing, sweep, gather firewood, and fetch water. All pottery, including items used exclusively by men, is made by women. Men construct all the basket and wood items used by both sexes, build the houses, and make canoes, fishing gear, and hunting weapons. They manufacture nearly all ritual equipment. True, much of men's time is devoted to masculine activities – such as coca-growing and processing – but because men are supposed to be the spiritual guardians of the longhouse, such activities are seen as necessary to the well-being of the entire community. Women's activities more directly serve their families.

With respect to actual work effort, it was my impression that women worked longer and harder than men. Still, I did not keep work diaries and am very aware that such a statement is subjective, because I spent my time mostly with the women. One must also assess the impact of acculturation on the work loads of each sex. Women, for example, must now produce a surplus of manioc, a truly arduous task, in order to make fariña to sell to missionaries and rubber gatherers. The

Male and female identity

Western-style clothing now worn by Tukanoans means a substantial increase in time spent mending and washing, which sometimes must be done without soap.

In conclusion, regardless of the actual proportion of time spent in "work," it is unquestionable that women's economic contributions, both with respect to food production and other tasks, are considerable, necessary, and seen as such by all Tukanoans. Probably the fact that women produce the only cash crop, fariña, has made men's dependence on them especially apparent in recent times.

Roles of wife and husband.

Tukanoans see marriage as difficult to accomplish from a man's point of view but say that any woman could get married if she wanted to. It is probably true that from the perspective of any individual Tukanoan, arriving at a happily married state is difficult to accomplish regardless of whether one is a man or a woman. Nonetheless, all Tukanoans recognize that women make more sacrifices upon marrying. This fact has implications for any study of Tukanoan sex roles.

A woman's marriage benefits, besides herself, three parties: her husband, her husband's local descent group, and her own local descent group. Aside from gaining the services a wife provides (which her spouse reciprocates), a man also achieves the status of married male and can establish a separate compartment in the longhouse. Furthermore, he is on the way to achieving full adult status, which comes when his wife grows manioc in the fields he has cleared for her and bears children. A woman's status also improves upon becoming a wife and later on a mother; however, in some senses her status as a new wife is the lowest position she will ever have in her life – in terms of the *realpolitik* of a longhouse community. Furthermore, because Tukanoans see marriage as difficult to accomplish for a man, getting married is seen as much more of an achievement for him than for a woman. To congratulate a woman on having caught a man would be nonsense.

Obviously statements that all men would get married if they could and all women could get married if they only would are to some extent cover-ups, that is, rationalizations about marriage and a glossing over of the fact that women frequently do want to get married and clearly see benefits for themselves from doing so. Tukanoans understandably play down the idea that women marry out of self-interest, for this implies that they are willing to forsake their agnatic kinsmen and contribute their companionship and labor to an affinal longhouse, increasing its strength by providing it with the new generation. It is easier to see women as getting married for the sake of their brothers, thus enabling them to obtain wives.

A woman's husband's local descent group benefits from the marriage because she will contribute to it economically and help provide it with sons and daughters. As is true in all patrilineal and patrilocal societies characterized by direct exchange or brideprice, Tukanoans regard the arrival of a daughter-in-law to a longhouse a difficult and highly desirable accomplishment.

Finally, a woman's own local descent group benefits from her marriage because
185

although they are losing a close agnatic kinswoman and the benefits of her economic contributions, her brother is thereby enabled to obtain a wife. This new daughter-in-law will replace the daughter in terms of food production and domestic services. Because only women may be exchanged for women, and sisters cannot provide sexual services nor reproduce the local group, the men must lose their sisters. Furthermore, a woman's marriage helps either to create or to strengthen an exchange relationship between the two local descent groups – an alliance.

In one important respect the Vaupés situation differs from certain other patrilineal or bilateral societies, in which women are reared by their families only to be sent as wives to other groups, frequently involving dowry expenses met only at considerable sacrifice (M. Wolf, 1974; J. Schneider, 1971; Michaelson and Goldschmidt, 1971). The contrast is particularly strong in some peasant communities where the outmarrying women of a local descent group are seen as "rubbish." This difference in attitudes toward the sisters and daughters of a local group is in part due to the system of direct exchange in the Vaupés and the importance of Vaupés women's economic roles.

Nevertheless, although Tukanoan women do derive benefits from marriage – such as full adult status, sexual expression, and parenthood – the costs of this action are far greater for them than for men. No matter how close her husband's longhouse is to her natal longhouse, it is the woman who must leave, permanently. In the Vaupés, the emotional stresses that accompany this move are many and in some cases extreme. Residential groups are isolated, autonomous, and (at least ideally) tightly knit, making it difficult for a daughter to leave or a daughter-in-law to enter. Furthermore, not all affinally related longhouses are near one another, with the result that those women who marry into distant settlements are able to visit their natal longhouses only sporadically if at all. Even if a woman moves into her mother's natal longhouse, she nonetheless moves into a house with people whom she does not know nearly as well as those she has lived with all her life. These new in-laws speak a different language from her father language and are *affines*, regardless of whatever consanguineal relationships she might have with them. The anthropological literature is replete with examples of difficulties existing between in-laws, even those with the best intentions. Such built-in stresses certainly exist in all Tukanoan affinal relationships, as was discussed in Chapter 5, and they are particularly painful to the individual living mainly among affines. A new wife must not only adjust to husband and new surroundings but also spend a large part of her day with her mother-in-law and sisters-in-law, whereas before she was with her own mother and sisters (and sisters-in-law). As is true in many societies (for example, see Collier, 1974), the period immediately following marriage is extremely difficult for the young wife, regardless of her love for her husband, and in terms of personal influence and security is probably the lowest point in a Tukanoan woman's life.

A man, on the other hand, undergoes few changes when he marries, and most of these are, from his point of view, positive or neutral ones – excepting those he experiences because of his wife's difficulties in adjusting. He stays in his own longhouse with people he has known since birth. Even though he must adjust to a new wife, this problem is alleviated by the fact that interaction between newly-weds is kept at a minimum. His position at this time is pivotal, fluctuating between loyalty and concern for his new wife and his continuing loyalty and obligations to his local group, in particular his mother and sisters.

New wives' being "strangers" in their new homes in certain ways throughout their lives is a crucial theme in Tukanoan culture. Symbolically, the idea of a united patrilineal core and separated, female peripheral units is expressed in the longhouse structure itself (C. Hugh-Jones, 1977, p. 197), in ritual, in ethno-geography, in concepts of time, and in many other areas (also see Goldman, 1977). Opposition exists between the core group and the separate, structurally equivalent units represented by the wives, an opposition between insiders and outsiders. This is made more apparent by the fact that in the majority of longhouses several languages are spoken and represented by the inmarried wives. The theme of antagonism between affinally related people is ever-present, and even though raiding for women has ceased, the ideology is still very apparent. This cannot fail to affect a woman's attitude toward becoming and being a wife as well as to influence Tukanoan conceptualizations of women and female elements in general. The effect of marriage practices, therefore, is that men live together in an agnatic core with feelings of solidarity, ownership of the community, and dominance as men, whereas women are seen as individuals, outsiders, on the periphery of the longhouse group, and related to each other via the links they share through the men. (Of course, some women in a longhouse can in fact be classificatory or real sisters, but it is the ideology that is important.)

Although women are always peripheral as wives in the longhouse group, they are necessary for its survival. This means that marriage, and more broadly speaking, women, must be supervised and controlled both practically and ritually by men. There is no doubt that men are the agents arranging marriage and that Tukanoans see things this way, although, as noted earlier, Tukanoan women are not nearly as powerless regarding whom they will marry as the women in groups like the Yąnomamö seem to be. An association exists between continuity of growth of the longhouse community and its destruction by women, because marriage breaks up the sibling groups of an established generation (C. Hugh-Jones, 1979, p. 161). Women, thus, are seen as "potentially creative as sisters and actually creative as wives."[7] The general theme of destruction leading to creation, renewal, and growth permeates Tukanoan thought. Women are seen as both destructive and creative; the essential process of the one evolving into the other occurs by exchanging women, and to be successful it must be regulated by men. These themes, derived from Tukanoan social structure and other areas, are symbolically expressed in many areas of Tukanoan cosmology.

Finally, by leaving one group as sisters and coming into another group as wives, women are the expression of reciprocity between groups. This is so

187

fundamental a symbol in Tukanoan myth and ritual that one encounters its expression constantly; many examples are found, for instance, in the synopses of myths in Chapters 6 and 7.[8]

Roles as parents.

As in all patrilineal descent systems, it is the nonagnatic, outsider women who supply the local group with the new generation. This is why daughters-in-law are ultimately of greater value to the local group than the daughters it gives away, an interesting fact because of its indisputable effects on Tukanoan conceptualizations of women in general. The need for women as procreators, accompanied by their necessarily equivocal position as outsiders, and the ensuing anxiety about their loyalty and devotion as mothers and wives are reflected in several Vaupés myths, most notably the ones surrounding the origin of the Yuruparí instruments.[9] The following is a synopsis of one version collected in Bará:

At one time, after they were made, these horns fell into the hands of the women, who were not as lazy as the men. The women would get up earlier in the morning and go down to the river to bathe before dawn. These women obtained the horns by being clever, for the horns succeeded in hiding themselves from the women for a while. The women kept the horns stored in their bodies, first in the humerus (which is why women's elbows are shaped differently from men's), and then in the vagina. The men could not get the horns back. The women grew very strong, and refused to have sexual relations or bear children. The men, realizing that the people would cease to exist, asked a shaman what to do. He suggested a trick, which worked, and the men recovered the horns. Since then the men have got up and bathed earlier than the women. And also since then women cannot see the horns, for they would fall sick and die.

It is obvious that one theme of this myth is an expression of anxiety about women becoming too powerful or seeing their interests as totally at odds with men's. That it is an anxiety based on fact has already been illustrated in some of the myth synopses given in Chapter 7. Although a woman identifies very closely with her children's descent group, she remains a member of her own throughout life. It is significant that Tukanoans whom I talked to did not know whether a woman goes to her natal spirit longhouse at death or to her husband's (and children's). The facts of social structure mean that although women naturally share an uninterrupted physical relationship with their children from the time of conception (which the couvade in part allows fathers to do), they are never linked socially with their children. Thus, male control of women not only breaks up actually existing female solidarity groups by sending out sisters in exchange for wives, but mothers are never identified with their daughters in terms of patrilineal group membership. This continuity in the male line is expressed ritually in many ways: Men give their children "soul-stuff" (C. Hugh-Jones, 1977, p. 188) by various associations made between soul and semen, bone, and names. It is the men, rather than women, who in their role as parents, create the continuity between generations seen as social units. Thus, the themes of women as outsider, as "destructive" (in that by leaving they break up the longhouse group), and as needing to be ritually controlled also pertain to women as mothers. It will be recalled that all food, even mother's milk, must be made safe by male shamans before being given to babies.[10] Even when female power is seen as neutral or even good, it still must be supervised by men. The fact that men who warm themselves too much at a hearth fire will procreate only daughters is a good example of Tukanoan assumptions that an excess of female power is inimical to male and patrilineal group interests.[11] This is also an example of the overriding theme of moderation and control in general found in Tukanoan thought, which particularly applies to the need for a balance in male and female components and energies.

Male and female sexuality.

Socially sanctioned and openly acknowledged sexual behavior occurs only within marriage. Of course, this requires a narrow definition of "sexual behavior." Men will lie together in hammocks fondling each other's genitals, and women will stroke one another's bodies (including breasts) and play with the genitals of children of both sexes. To speak subjectively, although Tukanoans are not as uninhibited about sex as, say, the Tahitians, in many respects (certainly with regard to touching and joking), they are not pathologically repressed about it.[12]

Sexual relations that are not approved of certainly occur, as attested to by reports from Tukanoans of cases of incest and adultery. Goldman has noted a relationship that can develop between a Cubeo brother and sister in which many kinds of sexual behaviors are permitted with the exception of intromission (I did not obtain data regarding this type of relationship). It is possible that pregnancies occasionally develop in these relationships because the prohibition on intercourse is disregarded. C. Hugh-Jones reports that premarital affairs are common (1979, pp. 160–61) and that these can and do occur between people who do not stand in the relationship of potential marriage partners to each other. The settlement pattern obviously affords little opportunity for a sexual relationship with someone who is neither an agnate nor already married.

It is obviously very difficult to draw conclusions about sexual activity, particularly with regard to frequency and participants, because most serious sexual encounters in the Vaupés (as elsewhere) take place in private. Attempting to describe Tukanoan attitudes toward sexuality is a bit easier than discussing the behavior itself but is still a topic full of pitfalls. Although I am not certain whether women are seen as wanting sexual intercourse as much as or more than men (to say nothing of whether they do in fact), the Victorian stereotype of the sexually unresponsive wife who obliges her husband certainly does not apply. In fact, Tukanoans place more emphasis on the possible damage to men and patrilineal groups in general resulting from excessive or improper sexuality rather than on the possible damage to females.

189

I have already noted taboos on sexual activity during sacred periods and before hunting and raids. Male sexual activity is linked to a general loss of male potency and purity. The themes of women as outsider and polluter are pertinent to this association as is the overall theme of potential danger resulting from excessive contact with women regardless of the activity. Women are, then, definitely not seen as sexually passive – they are accused of being the instigators in many adultery cases (Goldman, 1963, p. 150). It was the woman who was blamed for instigating the case of incest occurring at Púemanaka buró during my stay. Again, the actual behavior of women in initiating illicit sexual relations is difficult to ascertain. On the one hand, in any patrilineal and patrilocal society, one would expect outsider, troublemaker women to be blamed for initiating affairs regardless of the facts because they are the most convenient scapegoats. On the other hand, adultery is one of the strategies available to a newly married woman (or a disgruntled woman of any age) for making her presence felt and her needs known. This can be an effective ploy, despite the fact that it involves reprisals.

The foregoing characterization of Tukanoan women as the opposite of the Victorian ideal of innocent, passive women – in that they are sexually active and will initiate sexual encounters and are therefore potentially disruptive *because of their sexual drives* – is found in many other accounts of horticulturalist groups, particularly in the Amazon Basin and Highland New Guinea.[13]

Male sexuality, although in some senses just as "natural" as female sexuality, is so very much linked to ritual that it is both difficult and probably unwise to try to separate them completely. To some extent both women and female imagery are seen as more natural than male symbols, and this of course applies to male sexuality as well as to other areas. In other words, men in general are seen as more "cultural" ("spiritual," or "social"). Furthermore, many functions associated with the sexuality of *both* men and women (i.e., fertility, conception, gestation, growth, nourishment) are explicitly carried out by men in the ritual sphere far more than by women. Thus, although it is true that, for example, banisteriopsis vines and bone are explicit male sexual symbols,[14] both phallic in shape and inseminating (as are many other symbols, such as the Yuruparí instruments), they also represent other, more female elements, depending on the context. For example, banisteriopsis is associated with breast milk and the umbilical cord in some rituals. A good example of this is the overtly male ritual of Yuruparí, in which the initiates are openly compared to menstruating women, ritually imitating the loss of menstrual blood, dying, and being reborn (S. Hugh-Jones, 1974). Although in one sense menstruation will always be a female symbol, it is not sufficient to state that this rite is an imitation of female menstruation and leave it at that – it may be enough for the anthropologist, but for Tukanoans this is a *male* rite involving *male* menstruation, which accomplishes real tasks for male initiates. The rite does not only imitate, it expropriates female power available through the menstrual process of losing skin (blood) and growing new skin. The skin change as indicative of immortality or a longer and healthier life is one of the most powerful idioms of growth (C. Hugh-Jones, 1977, p. 189).

Another example of this is the male sexual symbol of the tipití (manioc squeezer), which, according to C. Hugh-Jones, is male both because of its phallic shape (termed – in Bará – *pinó-wü,* "anaconda-long, hollow instrument") and because it exudes "urine." In other contexts, however, it is female, for example, in its association with manioc.

The most sacred ritual objects and concepts in Tukanoan culture share a dual sexual imagery (see S. Hugh-Jones, 1979, with respect to *werea* [beeswax], perhaps *the* most sacred substance of all).

One must be careful to avoid oversimplifying the emotional meaning of male and female symbols in either their negative or their positive value for Tukanoans. On one level, menstruating women are dangerous, polluting, and must be controlled and at times avoided. On another level, as we have seen, menstruation has strong positive, creative, life-giving associations. C. Hugh-Jones (1977, p. 189) notes that the destructive quality of menstruation is limited to the "loss" phase and it is at this time that women are to be avoided. This is tied to a general theme of a two-phase, destruction–creation symbolism. Destruction and loss, almost always involving dispersal, is the only means to construction and creation: Loss of sisters means acquisition of wives and mothers of the next generation; loss of vegetation (in cutting and burning the forest) allows for planting fields; and loss of blood must take place before a new lining of menstrual blood and its benefits (longer life, the possibility of conception) can be realized. Obviously, this complexity of symbolic meaning argues against a too-pat association in cross-cultural studies between menstrual contamination beliefs and an assumption that women and menstruation are only seen as polluting and dangerous (see Kelly, 1976, with respect to sexual intercourse).

The same complexity is found in the Yuruparí rituals. These unmistakably symbolize – to Tukanoans as well as ethnographers – male dominance and superiority. But in addition to rejecting women (both actually and symbolically) and demonstrating the dangers of female sexuality, they are also an expropriation of female power – an excellent example of flattery, envy, and nonrejection. Furthermore, the transformation in Yuruparí ritual of these female elements into male power is beneficial not only to the initiates and the community of men (usually, but not always, the core of agnates living in a circumscribed area, for example on a section of a river) but also to the entire community and society as a whole. The same can be said for male sexuality in general. On one plane it is opposed and antagonistic to female sexuality. Some female symbols in the He wi rituals (e.g., the beeswax gourd) are dangerous to real women (S. Hugh-Jones, 1979). Certainly the restrictions on male sexual behavior contain many statements of the danger and destructiveness of female sexuality. But male-centered rituals and restrictions are also the route to the ancestors, to "good" energy, to reciprocity with the cosmos, to growth and continuity – without which all Tukanoan society would certainly die.

Thus, in the final analysis, male and female sexual symbols are not only opposed and seen as mutually hostile. They, as well as all symbols that are seen at some time as male or female, can take on a dual sexual imagery, combining whatever particular aspects of both are appropriate to the specific symbolic task at hand. As C. Hugh-Jones has so eloquently stated, such a coming together "creates a unity of a higher order than the creative elements. Semen and blood make a foetus; male-produced fish and female-produced manioc make a meal, and men and women make a heterosexual community who eat the meal in the center of the house" (1977, p. 203).

Conclusions

In this chapter we have looked at some of the differences between male and female roles in Vaupés society – as they appear to an outsider, as they are conceived of by Tukanoans, and as they are symbolically expressed in ritual and myth. The contributions both sexes make in the subsistence, domestic, and procreative areas show that women are seen as valuable and powerful individuals, both in and out of marriage. Yet strong and unmistakable avowals of male supremacy are found in everyday, ritual, and mythic life. It is clear that at times women are seen as potentially dangerous, as definitely dangerous when contact with them is excessive, and as in need of ritual and practical control.

The disadvantages and disruptions encountered by women when they marry, particularly at first, are beautifully and artfully captured in myths about affinal relations; this transition, never fully accomplished, is one of many factors contributing to a view of women as ambivalent, unpredictable, selfish, and at times treacherous.

Nonetheless, when compared with some other societies in lowland South America, the status of women in the Vaupés seems significantly higher. One suggestion as to why this might be so involves precisely the fact that women more than men face disadvantages at marriage, with the result that marriage is seen as "the problem of getting daughters-in-law" (as opposed to, for instance, the problem of getting a dowry raised for one's own daughter). Yet women are not coerced into marriage or carried off against their will as they are among, for instance, the Yąnomamö. The fact that women have the final word in the process of marriage making, seen as extremely difficult and yet vital, undoubtedly contributes to the overall amount of power and status they have and are perceived of as having. It is also suggested that the very real contributions made by women in the economic sphere plus the marked segregation of the sexes contribute to their relatively high status.[15] Furthermore, the effects of acculturation, notably the need for the cash crop fariña produced by women, and the cessation of warfare at least fifty years ago have had an impact. Another factor is

192

the relative egalitarianism found in the Vaupés. Although not as egalitarian as hunter–gatherer societies – for ranking is present – social differentiation and stratification are not nearly so developed as in more complex societies.[16] Tukanoans display a general dislike of invidious comparison and at present no stratification exists of the kind that implies greatly unequal control of scarce resources, power, and positions of authority. The area in which the differentiation of power and scarce resources is greatest is, in fact, in relations between men and women. Thus, although it is true that traditional Tukanoan society is marked by strong statements and evidence of male superiority and supremacy (e.g., only men are spiritual beings), it is equally true that when the society is compared with more complex societies, the actual differences are seen to be more apparent than real. The relative egalitarianism in the Vaupés greatly curtails the actual power men have over women.

Another factor contributing to women's higher status in the Vaupés is the general emphasis on cooperation and internalization of expectations concerning work and other obligations. One should be self-motivated rather than dependent on an authority figure to give orders. A nuclear family is not greatly stratified; husbands do not tell their wives what to do, and children are rarely told what to do. Women can use sanctions such as gossip and ostracism as much as men. The sexual segregation also obviously lessens the opportunity for men to give women orders. Tukanoan women are not bullied into working hard, nor are they seen as a kind of domestic servant when they do menial tasks or services or serve men food and wait for them to finish before they eat.[17]

The fact that marriage making is seen as difficult and the continuing emphasis on the desirability of sister exchange probably contribute to the low incidence of polygyny. Even if a man is a powerful headman, the stipulation that only women can be exchanged for women means that the man who wants a second wife will be considered greedy. Added to this is the pressure from Catholic priests against plural marriages. All the Tukanoan women I talked with on the subject did not like the idea of polygyny, and its rarity is at least an expression of their autonomy and influence, even if other factors actually determine its low incidence. Only headmen had second wives in my sample of marriages (0.8 percent of 672 marriages). Thus, although the "harem" or "gerontocracy" may have been typical in the past, and still is in many Australian groups and a number of South American lowland groups (see Chagnon, 1968, and Siskind, 1973b), it is not now found in the Vaupés.

Insofar as I can ascertain, no discrepancy exists between the sexes in terms of numbers in the respective pools of potential mates. I found no significant differences in numbers of men and women in my household censuses and genealogies. Furthermore, although approximate, the age differences recorded for husband and wife do not seem significantly biased for one sex, although husbands seem to be on the average three to four years older than their wives. Still, some men have wives who are considerably older than they.

193

The relative stability of marriages in the Vaupés also appears to be related to the higher status of Vaupés women. Such stability is not seen in many classic South American tropical societies, such as the Yąnomamö (Chagnon, 1968; Shapiro. 1972), Sharanahua (Siskind, 1973a), Mehinacu (Gregor, 1974), Sirionó (Holmberg, 1969), Krĩkatí (Lave, 1966), Shavante (Maybury-Lewis, 1967). Although it is difficult clearly to delineate cause and effect, at present women are not moved around as pawns in the displays of male brinkmanship typical of societies like the Yąnomamö.

The cessation of ''warfare'' in the Vaupés, probably more than fifty years ago, is undoubtedly an extremely important factor in female status. Warfare per se does not preclude the possibility of relatively high female status, measured in any of a number of ways; the Iroquois are perhaps the best example of this (Brown, 1970a). Given certain conditions, such as matrilineality, the presence of female groups, and strong feelings of solidarity among females, a highly developed military complex with its concomitant emphasis on masculine warrior roles and values can peacefully coexist with opposed female-connected values and roles. Such coexistence was economically rational for the Iroquois and actually aided the military effort, for it was the women who outfitted the warparties with food-stuffs for long expeditions and maintained homes during the men's absence. Such a situation does not seem to have occurred in the internal warfare of Amazonian societies, however, where a frequent component of warfare ideology includes conceptualizing women as pawns and even as treacherous betrayers in the strug-gle rather than as contributors to the war effort – although reports of ''Amazons'' fighting alongside their men are certainly available as well. Undoubtedly the frequently found expression of affines as ''enemies'' is an important consider-ation here.

In general, although ethnologists disagree on the causes of warfare, which can range from proteins to prestige,[18] it would probably be generally accepted that polygyny and unstable marriages are likely to be correlated with the Amazonian pattern of active raiding and feuding. Thus, at an earlier period in Vaupés history, it is probable that both polygyny and unstable marriages were much more frequent and were directly connected to feuding, because many more marriages were made by coercion. Following from this, it is likely that the position of women was lower. This is, however, speculation, based on similar situations in other areas of lowland South America and evidence from myths and quasi-historical accounts of earlier periods from Tukanoans.

11.

Tukanoans' place in the cosmos

Shamanism

The shaman is an extremely important figure in traditional Tukanoan culture. As is the case with other specialists in Vaupés society, this position does not relieve him of the normal duties and obligations of an adult man. The shaman is the one who "sees" and understands the relations between his community and the world it inhabits. He interprets and explains this relationship to others, and thereby warns and prescribes. He diagnoses and cures and above all protects by knowing how to maintain harmony and balance between his community and the rest of the universe. Part of this task of protecting the individuals under his care may involve bringing illness or misfortune to others, but good shamans never practice sorcery against people of their own community. Protection involves performing necessary rituals, prescribing correct food restrictions, making divinations, and "seeing" by going into trances. His activities help to ensure fertility of food sources and human fertility. He officiates at all transformations. He ushers newborn babies into the world of humans with water and food rituals and establishes their identities as members of particular language groups by giving them names, and through this, the "soul-stuff" which is passed along patrilineal lines (see C. Hugh-Jones, n.d., p. 9). He officiates at initiations for young men when they are first introduced to the Yuruparí, other ritual substances, and sacred knowledge, and at the menarche rituals for young girls. He officiates at rituals intended to transform the community from a disturbed state to one of equilibrium, as, for example, when a member of the community is bitten by a snake, falls ill from sorcery, or dies and needs to be buried properly and sent on his or her journey to the other world. Very important to the well-being of the community are all large ceremonies in which the shaman transforms the longhouse and its occupants in space and time. The rituals to accomplish this, in which all adult men participate, are organized and conducted by the shaman. At the most sacred point in this process, the group enters ancestral time: The longhouse is the universe, and the people in it, along with the sacred horns, are ancestral people (S. Hugh-Jones, 1979).

195

The fish people

Shamans are able to officiate and transform not because they are priests in any sense but because they know and understand myth. Myth forms the foundation of Tukanoan symbolic structure, and through this, Tukanoan society; it describes and explains the world and provides the rules for the proper maintenance of human society within this world. Shamans must understand myth well enough to be able to translate it for the rest of the community in terms of its applicability to current problems. (To some degree, however, everyone understands certain mythical symbols and meanings.) The esoteric language spoken by shamans (S. Hugh-Jones, 1979, pp. 58–59) is based on analogies and synonyms that only a thorough understanding of Tukanoan mythology can render comprehensible. Thus, because shamans not only know and see this world but understand the other worlds of the universe and how these figure in the activities of this one, they understand the importance of balance and moderation in both human and nonhuman life. They know how to regulate, transform, and recycle energy through the cosmos – an extremely important concept in Tukanoan cosmology.

As ushers-in and transformers, shamans are intermediaries and for this reason are frequently seen as ambiguous. In a number of ways they straddle both sides of important divisions. They are human, yet they have contacts with the nonhuman world. Some shamans become evil and use their power for vengeful or other selfish motives. When this happens, these individuals are no longer considered men and come to be identified with the animal world in several ways – with animals, with the forest, and with the spirits inhabiting the forest. "Normal" shamans *are* humans but can perhaps be described as more than human. They speak a number of Tukanoan languages, as does everyone, but they also have their own. They do everything any ordinary man will do, as well as perform many special activities. They see everything ordinary adults see, and more.

To become a shaman takes at least a year of apprenticeship and involves learning to learn from one's dreams, one's trances. It was emphasized that during this time, a young man only "gets advice" from his teacher. To become an effective curer one must travel to all the houses in the other worlds to learn the proper chants. As expected, the apprentice observes many restrictions in food and activities. Whereas apprentice shamans must travel to all the houses in the rest of the universe, a very powerful shaman can persuade the shamans in these houses (who had been shamans when they were alive in this world) to return here. I collected a long story of a very powerful Bará shaman who was able to do this; the two other-world shamans who visited him charmed a section of territory so that people, so long as they stayed in it, did not die.

People are always somewhat wary of a shaman, even those not suspected of having become evil. A certain amount of ambivalence and potential suspicion seems always to adhere to any position involving leadership and specialized knowledge in Amazonian (and other small-scale) societies. Furthermore, in the Vaupés such a role is dangerous because ritual power and knowledge are always dangerous. Thus a renegade shaman can forsake all feelings of responsibility to

196

human society and become destructive; when this happens a shaman actually turns into a predatory spirit animal. In most, if not all, Tukanoan languages the word for shaman is synonymous with the word for a class of predatory animals including the jaguar (*yai*). It is probably also the case that shamans are somewhat mistrusted, at least in the abstract, because of their intermediary position per se, in the same manner that extremely old people, so evidently straddling the border between the living and the dead, are seen as not quite human and are mistrusted.[1]

Shamans are also the intermediaries between balance and imbalance, for they can divine causes and restore equilibrium through ritual. It is they who protect the local group from the fury of an angered spirit-person. It is they who bring ''unbalanced'' people through their personal crises – which also always affect the rest of the community – brought on by birth, first menstruation, illness, or a similar condition. It is they who regulate and balance the nutritional state of the longhouse. In many senses shamans are food intermediaries (Langdon, 1975). They symbolically stand between food and ''soul food'' (C. Hugh-Jones, 1979) – the sacred substances of coca, tobacco, banisteriopsis, and chicha.

According to S. Hugh-Jones (1977, p. 213), shamans are intermediaries in several senses in the male initiation ceremonies: For example, they are members of both the class of elder men and of the initiates. They also symbolically stand between the world of women and that of men.

Because no shamans lived on the Inambú River, my information about them is incomplete. Very few shamans are left in the Vaupés; of those remaining, most are found in the Pirá-paraná region or in a few far upstream locations. During my stay, no real shaman ever came to Pumanaka buro, although I did meet one Bará shaman during a trip to the Tiquié. At Pumanaka buro the headman officiated at whatever ceremonies continued to be performed, and he performed some curing rituals.

What follows are very abbreviated accounts of the kinds of crises in human lives that shamans oversee and restore to normalcy via ritual. These accounts are meant to illustrate certain basic points about shaman roles and are not intended to be comprehensive descriptions.

Birth.

After a child is born (the birth takes place in the manioc fields), the shaman performs a number of rituals to give the child human status and make it a member of its particular language group. In addition to defining its status, these birth rituals serve to protect it (for example, by making safe the foods it eats) and to protect the rest of the community during this period of heightened risk. Many precautions and restrictions during the course of pregnancy, birth, and nursing have this effect. These restrictions apply to certain foods, activities and rituals, and contact with particular objects. The entire community is involved in a birth and participates in the accompanying rituals, but the stages at which the parents

197

The fish people

and offspring pass from one stage to another – that is, are transformed in some manner – are conducted by a shaman.

Neither babies nor mothers are washed for two days following a birth. They are then painted and undergo a ceremony at the port, during which a gourd of mother's milk is made safe (henceforth permitting the child to suckle). Mother and child are then bathed, and the child is given a name. The shaman also cleans the house out with pepper smoke.

Sorcery and disease.

Diseases never "just happen," and usually malice lies behind an individual's illness or accident. Disease can be caused by an unknown person directing sorcery at a particular individual, by a wahtí, or by a shaman who is exchanging human souls from a distant settlement for game animals. It is also true that people can be in a state in which they are particularly likely to succumb to illness. If they have seen a wahtí, for example, and brood about it, or if excessive sadness or grief is not alleviated, they will fall ill. The prayers after a funeral are in part to ensure that the bereaved relatives do not think too much about the dead, lest they too fall sick and die. Ordinary human beings can cause illness in any number of ways, from actually slipping a toxic substance into someone's food to learning a particular spell and practicing sorcery. In fact, it is interesting to note that killing by sorcery can be described with the verb *doaríhe,* which basically means "to cook." A sorcerer might send a cigar made of "other-world tobacco" through the air to bury itself in a distant longhouse's floor. As it travels through the air it resembles a species of fly, but upon divination and discovery it looks like a cigar (which, however, only a shaman can see). The cure is to return it to the sender's longhouse, where it will cause much sickness. A counter-sorcery exists to punish sorcerers. It is a complicated process based on contagious magic using "dirt" from the sick person's body – hair, nails, urine – which is kept in a bottle and prayed over for many days and finally placed near a fire. When the bottle bursts, the sorcerer dies and the sick person usually gets well.

A spell can also be cast on an object, which will then cause harm to anyone who comes in contact with it. I was told that only the Siriano and Desana can cast these spells onto objects, such as machetes, axes, and canoes. Even trees can be sorcerized so that they fall and close off the trail. Contact with these objects can cause cramps or paralysis.

Most often everyone knows what kind of disease a person has from the symptoms. Still, a shaman must diagnose by divination the ultimate cause of a disease (i.e., the agent willfully causing it), and only shamans can cure a serious illness. Shamans go into a trance to divine the evildoer's identity and to locate the sickness-bearing object. The most frequent disease-causing objects are *wahká* – intrusive thorns, hair, pieces of cotton, and similar items that enter the patient's body and must be extracted. Some of these never lose their power; one reason a

198

longhouse is abandoned after a shaman dies is that the particular type of object strong enough to kill a shaman (looking like a tiny canoe paddle) will kill anyone else who remains in the longhouse.

Sorcery can also be practiced on unmarried girls so that they will be barren or lose their children during pregnancy or after birth. Informants gave unrequited love as the motive. Birth defects can be caused by sorcery. A pregnant woman who eats dirt has probably been sorcerized.

A shaman's equipment includes *Virola* sp. snuff, which was obtained from Makú in the past but which, I was told, is no longer available. The few still-practicing shamans left are thus very reluctant to use their supply unless absolutely necessary. A shaman also owns a cylindrical quartz crystal (*yai-ga*); the quartz is found only in the Tiquié region. One of its names means "thunder stone," and the shaman uses it to "see" – to see into the body of the patient and discover who the culprit is. These quartzes also can be used to send illness in the form of cramps and spasms.

Curing mainly consists of extracting the foreign substance from the patient's body. Shamans cure with techniques involving tobacco smoke, massage, and water throwing. Water throwing requires the most advanced training. The most important part of curing, however, are the prayers. Any adult knows remedies for minor illnesses such as muscle ache, fungus infections, swellings, and eye trouble. And many forms of health maintenance and disease preventives can be used by everyone, such as purgatives, emetics, and snakebite preventives. Many plants used to ward off malign influences are grown. Older men and occasionally old women as well will blow tobacco smoke onto children for this purpose. Only shamans can cure serious illnesses, however, because only they know the proper prayers.

Blowing tobacco smoke, praying, and the water cures occur on the patio in front of the longhouse. The shaman massages the patient, which causes the disease-bearing wahká to go to the extremities of the patient's body and enter the shaman's. The wahká then migrate to his mouth and he pulls them out. I was told that while these items look like thorns and so forth, they really are not these things.

The difference between yai and *kumú,* the two words roughly glossing as "shaman," was never made clear to me. I was told that both kumú and yai cure by blowing smoke and throwing water, but only the yai performs sorcery.

Tukanoans state that many white-introduced diseases do not respond to traditional curing techniques but that traditional cures are needed for traditional illnesses. Thus, it is a matter of concern that no more shamans are being trained in the Papurí region.

The fish people

Death.

When someone dies, the corpse is washed and buried inside the longhouse. Prayers are offered to ensure that the spirit leave quickly; chants also help the bereaved. A woman is buried with her small pouch of personal belongings, but her other personal property (e.g., baskets, pots) is broken or burned. A man is buried with whatever ritual paraphernalia is closely identified with him. Destroying or burying such property gives the spirit less to miss and thus hastens its speedy departure. Fires are sometimes made over a fresh grave to lessen the possibility of seeing the spirit leaving.

I was told that "before we had canoes and only fished from the riverbank" people used to be buried in a crouched position in urns; this is the way children and babies are buried today. For an adult, an old canoe (but one without a split), or a new one if an old one is not available, is lined with the person's hammock. The corpse is washed and groomed but not painted. The canoe is sealed with a piece of wood and resin and bound with fiber ropes. After burial, werea is burned and relatives come to chant and mourn. It is not a proper festival, however, because it lacks chicha and dancing. Three days later normal routines are resumed.

After death, spirits normally go to "dead-people spirit" (*mahoká diari wahtí*) houses, where the ancestors live. These houses are found in specific locations, depending on an individual's language group. For example, Tuyukas go to a longhouse on Behuya stream in the upper Paca River, and Bará go to Pamüri wi at Yuruparí Rapids in the Vaupés. The spirits of people who have had certain kinds of difficulties in life either linger around the area where they died or begin the journey but never succeed in actually entering the dead-spirit longhouse. In a sense, the final stage of dying is entry into this house (see the account in Chapter 4 of Old Arturo's saving the headman José from death by preventing his entrance into the dead-spirit longhouse). The spirits of the dead are not intrinsically bad, but they should be kept separate from the world of the living. When this does not happen, something is wrong and the living begin to be in danger. One example of this is when a man prays and buries a special cigar in the house of his enemy. Later, when the man dies, his dead spirit also goes to his enemy's house to bother him and his housemates. This happens even if the man has died in a way totally unconnected with his enemy. His dead spirit is heard pounding on coca and swimming in the environs of his enemy's house. To exorcise this spirit a shaman has to divine the location of the cigar and destroy it, releasing the spirit.

The spirits of people who steal from manioc fields stay around their graves and have to be banished by prayers of a shaman. This is also true of people who commit incest. Adulterers go to the dead-spirit house but continue to be troublemakers there. Murderers, too, tend to remain at their graves rather than setting off on their journey. The victims of bloody murders (e.g., killed by guns or by

200

knives) are doomed to stand forever outside their dead-spirit house, with blood continually flowing from their wounds. Those who meet accidental, yet bloody, deaths continue to "breathe poorly just as they did right before they died,"[2] indicating that they have not quite died. Thus, a connection is made between an improper death and an incomplete process of dying and separation from the world of the living.

Although the dead-spirit houses are sometimes spoken of as far away, the dead spirit, emerging from the grave, sees them as quite close. I was told that some dying people describe the dead-spirit houses they are already seeing.

Reports about the dead-spirit houses are conflicting. One day people will say no one hunts or fishes there, and another day people will say that people "have everything there that we have in this world." Sometimes dead spirits are said to eat regular food, and yet other times they are described as eating only tobacco, chicha, coca, and banisteriopsis. I was once told that old people turn into young adults again. As noted earlier, Tukanoans are vague regarding whether women stay with their husband's group or return to their own patrilineal dead-spirit house.[3]

Usually dead spirits are not powerful enough actually to take the living with them (however, see the myth of Live Woman, Chapter 6, about a wife who follows her husband to the dead-spirit house).[4] The spirit of a powerful shaman may succeed in this, though, by accompanying his widow everywhere. By thus making her cry all the time, she eventually falls sick (although he does not actually send the sickness), and "he can take her with him." No woman could take her living husband with her in this manner, however (see the myth of the co-wives, Chapter 6).

If a *bayá* (a head dancer) were to die without teaching the chants to the next generation, his relatives might decide to wait seven to ten years and send two men to revisit the abandoned longhouse site during a lunar eclipse. They would make a fence with bamboo slats near the grave and move away, saying, "Grandfather, we've come to learn a chant." Eventually the earth would move, and the dead spirit would emerge and teach them everything.

In summary, the ideas associated with death are that dead spirits are potentially harmful only if in some way they do not completely "die" – a process that lasts until they have left the area and entered the dead-spirit longhouses of their ancestors. This happens when something in the world of the living is not right. Whether the dead were brutally murdered or themselves were murderers or whether they missed their spouses too much, something made the separation and mourning period an abnormal process. The effect of this is to throw other things out of balance so that eventually the whole community suffers.

Festivals

In general, festivals are basically concerned either with relationships within a language group (or sections of it) or with relationships between affines. Within these two categories are several more specific types of festivals, some of which are no longer held in the Papurí region. Regardless of specific type, all festivals have the following characteristics. A festival is a special, nonordinary, sacred event. This is reflected in (and in many symbolic ways signaled by) the alterations that occur in time, space, activity, state of consciousness, and, at certain points, *reality* – at the most sacred point of the proceedings, the participants actually become one with the ancestors. Thus, the festival is a time to transcend everyday reality, to reveal and celebrate its underlying truth; in short, to "make sense" of it. All normal activities stop: One neither eats nor sleeps during a festival. Those items that are consumed are explicitly opposed to ordinary food; C. Hugh-Jones has referred to them as "soul food" for this reason. These soul foods – chicha, tobacco, banisteriopsis, and coca – are intoxicants and are seen as nourishment for the soul rather than for the body. They are also sacred (although coca, chicha, and tobacco can be ingested on nonsacred occasions). How long the participants go without sleep varies, depending on the type of festival and how carefully traditions are followed.

The entire festival, including the preparations prior to its official beginning, resembles a piece of music in that every aspect of the event – the chanting, the instruments and their music, the dancing, the intoxication – all lead to a climax late at night. By this point the people, the paraphernalia, the music, and the longhouse itself have all undergone a profound transformation. This is the opportunity for participants (although we are speaking here mainly of initiated men) partially to experience what shamans experience – to "see" beyond everyday reality and observe the underlying meaning, in effect, the underlying reality, of the world and life itself.

As already noted, festivals that are basically making statements about relations between affines, dabucurí, involve an exchange of smoked meat or fish, brought by guests, for beer, supplied by the hosts. Festivals that focus on the patrilineal concerns of the sib and language group are the ceremonies at which the sacred horns are played over recently harvested jungle fruit and the series of ceremonies involved with male initiation. The food exchange rituals are concerned with reciprocity. The fruit and initiation rituals are concerned with growth, fertility, and continuation. In a deeper sense these two types are linked, the one ensuring the continued production of people and food and the other ensuring the proper exchange of these between groups of people.

Currently in the Papurí drainage, festivals are also held simply for the purpose of drinking and dancing. They do not involve a ceremonial exchange of protein or fruit foodstuffs nor the playing of sacred horns. Whether this practice was also true at earlier, less acculturated periods is uncertain; however, both Langdon,

1975, discussing the Pirá-paraná region, and Goldman, 1963, discussing the Cubeo, state that such "simple" festivals take place in these groups.

For festivals the Tukanoans energetically clean up the longhouse and surrounding area (which may include making substantial repairs to the roof, the port, etc.); amass huge amounts of firewood; prepare large quantities of chicha, usually of more than one kind; grind sugar cane; process a great deal of coca; finish work on new dresses and other items of clothing and decoration; and prepare enough cazabe to serve early arriving guests. Technically no cazabe is eaten after the festivities formally begin, but some women surreptitiously eat throughout the festival, and children are not expected to go without food. Before a dabucurí, those who will be guests feel a great deal of pressure to kill and smoke sufficient amounts of game or fish, because they would be embarrassed if not enough were provided. This obligation itself nicely demonstrates the pressures and responsibilities affines feel toward each other.

Early arriving visitors help prepare the wooden percussive staves (made anew each time) that are used in the dabucurí festival, assist in making the banisteriopsis infusion, and help to process coca. At a certain time, the basket suitcase holding the more sacred ritual paraphernalia is lowered from its shelf and the final dressing and painting begin.[5]

The main activity of festivals is dancing and drinking. One word for these occasions is *hinirike* ("drink"). Dances last anywhere from fifteen to thirty minutes and are followed by breaks for consuming chicha and, for the men, banisteriopsis, tobacco (in the form of cigars and snuff), and coca. Men chant while seated at stools or along benches; some of the older men and the shamans do not dance at all. The more formal dances, consisting of rows of men who are joined by women after the dance is begun (each woman placing herself under the outstretched arm of a man), are led by the bayá. Several dances are performed, each named, and each varying in step and the paraphernalia (rattles or staves, etc.) used. It is the younger men who initiate panpipe-playing dances, starting off in a line, playing and dancing to intricate rhythms and harmonies. Much more of an element of challenge and competition is apparent in these dances. Women join the men, either beside them in the row, or, for panpipe dancing, in side-by-side couples, after a dance has begun and leave before it is finished. During some dances, a woman (*yügó*) – usually one married to a headman or a bayá – stands in the middle of a circle of dancers and periodically emits a long, piercing shriek. At the beginning of the festival the host group and the visitors are clearly demarcated according to which group dances and which watches. Later on, however, the groups intermingle, expressing symbolically how settlements, particularly affinally related ones, interact.

The official beginning of a festival is always about 8:00 a.m., although panpipe playing and coca chewing may have kept the men up quite late the previous night. In any case, almost everyone in the longhouse is involved in making chicha the night before a festival, and no one sleeps much. The peak of the ceremony is after midnight the following night. Festivals vary in duration, but a day and a half of dancing is no mean feat, especially considering the time spent in preparations and the added effects of the intoxicants. Always toward the end, tempers are frayed and hangovers monumental. Not every festival I attended ended in quarreling (as was true in Goldman's experiences with the Cubeo), but I did see a number of disagreements erupt and one serious argument. And, of course, both the hosts and the guests griped and gossiped after parting company.

Regardless of the specific type of festival being held, the host group usually invites its closest neighbors, irrespective of their language group affiliation. S. Hugh-Jones (1979) reports this also to be true for festivals held to celebrate male initiation. Sometimes young men from more than one language group are initiated together, although according to tradition this is not supposed to happen.

The Tukanoan world

Tukanoans know that the world is much, much more than what it appears to be to the five senses. The world was different in ancestral times,.which are recreated during sacred ceremonies. The world as perceived space is also more; for example, the sky is not only a sky but the underside of the level of the universe above this one.[6] Furthermore, many of the distinguishable natural features on this level are more than what they appear to be to the naked eye, although usually only shamans can see beyond this visible reality (other men sometimes travel and see the less immediately apparent reality of this level when taking banisteriopsis during ceremonies). At the most sacred point in Tukanoan rituals, vertical, horizontal, and temporal "space" is transformed. The longhouse itself becomes the universe, the participants become the ancestors, and the realities behind the outward appearances of space, time, and matter are revealed. These characteristics of insubstantiality, mutability, and multiple reality are crucial ones in Tukanoan conceptions of the universe. Any descriptions, therefore, that depict the world only in terms of substantive, concrete, and permanent characteristics are misleading.

Levels of the universe.

The universe consists of five levels, but not much is known about the very top and bottom layers. Whereas the levels adjacent to ours are populated with reasonably nice beings and have features similar to ours, the very top and bottom ones are not very interesting, for they have only ugly, dirty, black, and bad inhabitants. The next highest level is associated with air, this level with earth, and the level below with water. Beneath the layer of this world is Opēkó dia ("milk river"), a very important feature of the Tukanoan universe. Its current flows from east to west, unlike all the rivers of our level, which flow west to east. This is one of many examples of inversions found in the levels adjacent to ours. For example, while it is nighttime here, it is daylight in the level below us, because the sun is crossing that sky after it sets on our level. The same inversion is found in the sky level above us. A myth about "star girl" demonstrates many of these. Star girl was bitten by a vampire bat. The wound did not heal and soon became filled with worms. She smelled so bad that her relatives threw her out, and she fell to this layer. A man found her and washed and cleaned her. When her wound healed, he took her as his wife and they returned to the sky. However, everything was backwards for him: When his wife slept he was wide awake. When the couple engaged in sexual intercourse everyone could see what they did, because it was broad daylight. While he was fishing, she would sleep with other men. Finally, disgusted, he returned to this world.

The heavens.

The Bará at Púmanaka buro were not particularly knowledgeable about celestial bodies and phenomena. To what extent this lack is due to more than fifty years of missionary influence and to what extent it is due to their considering themselves "water people" is not known.[7] For example, although various constellations had names and their movements were tied to the seasons of the year, no one knew a name for the Milky Way, which figures prominently in Desana mythology (Reichel-Dolmatoff, 1971). Bará identify Desana, Tatuyo, and "maybe Siriano" with the sky and say that these groups are "the sun's children" and that they know much more about celestial phenomena. Insofar as I could ascertain, the people at Púmanaka buro placed the most importance on the planet Venus, which has two names as morning and evening star. When Venus is near the moon, it is called his "bride" and this portends a marriage.

Rainbows have separate names, depending on whether they are in the sky of the rising sun or setting sun. An association exists between rainbows, thunder and lightning, snakebites, and rotting fingernails and teeth. A rainbow around the sun is a sign that shamans either are creating sickness in some settlement or teaching apprentices how to cast spells.

Thunder and lightning are closely associated with sickness; they can cause an illness or aggravate an already existing case. The thunderstorm that occurred after the snakebite incident at Púmanaka buro (see Chapter 2) was seen as connected to the event: The anger of the other fer-de-lances in the region and of the spirit snakes brought the thunder, which in turn increased the possibility of additional snakebites and the likelihood of the little boy's dying. Pain connected to thunder is described as similar to a bolt of lightning.

Sometimes one can hear the "sky people" running around above the clouds just before a thunderstorm. They are afraid, and so they yell and bang on pots and pans, which is also the proper behavior during a moon eclipse. These people are three feet tall and have no hair.

The headman, Mario, said that in earlier times a screen of tapir hide would be

205

attached to the pillars just inside the men's door during a festival. This would protect the two chanting shamans sitting behind it from sicknesses sent by enemy shamans through thunder, lightning, and winds.

In stark contrast to a general lack of interest in heavenly bodies and events is everyone's fascination with lunar eclipses.[8] In general the moon is seen as a very sinister personage. The shadows on his face were put there by his sister when she smeared a black dye, *weh* (Rublaceae), on him during the night to be able to recognize her mysterious lover, the moon, in the daytime. During the periods when the moon "sickens" or "dies," which include eclipses and evenings when the moon is a dark red (this is corroborated by Goldman, 1963, p. 245), the moon comes down to this level, hides the light he is carrying under a pot, digs into the earth in abandoned longhouse sites, and eats the corpses. People must make every effort to force the moon into the heavens again, for eclipses are prototypes of periods when everything is out of balance and greatly disrupted. Wahtía of many kinds are about, returning to their graves or dancing in the forests. Everyone must hurry to accomplish tasks and in general create a lot of commotion and activity, neither resting nor sleeping. During this period, as in other times of disturbance, chili peppers are burned, the smoke protecting the longhouse and its inhabitants from the dangers that threaten.

Important places and features of the landscape.

Many geographical formations and specific locations have mythical references and are seen as special, if not sacred. Types of terrain likely to be imbued with sacred meaning include rapids, sandstone outcrops, caves, dome-topped hills, clearings in the forest, mirití swamps and lakes, and lagoons in rivers. The origins of most large and unusual rock formations are given in myths. Particular sandstone hills are known as the houses of specific wahtía. Many features are named and described in the section of the origin myth cycle that deals with the upstream journey of the ancestors of the language groups in the anaconda canoe. People should avoid *tatá,* or clearings in the jungle, all of which are shaman houses. Everyone knows anecdotes about those tatá near their own settlement; these anecdotes usually concern people who remained near a *tatá boa* (*boa* refers to the "rotten" quality of the clearing – i.e., that trees do not grow there) and were swallowed up into the ground.

Ewüra taró is an extremely important mirití swamp because it is said to be the source of the rivers in the region (the Inambú, the Tiquié, and Timíya on the Pirá-paraná). Shamans can see a house inside the earth near this site, which is the ancestral home of peccaries. In the center of the swamp is a huge mirití palm (*neño*), which grows to the sky each day. It is the "center of the world"; shamans see it as a huge snake.

Many other localities are known to Tukanoans as the place where such-

and-such happened in a particular myth; furthermore, these sites are associated with various important facts of present-day life, such as the ancestral home of a species of game animal or the original source of medicinal plants, or first-menstruation longhouse, and so forth. Although these places are distinctive, it is only shamans who can "see" the other reality they have.

At a deeper level, however, every part of the world is sacred. The hidden realities of all places can be comprehensively described only by shamans or people who have "seen" them during their travels under the influence of banisteriopsis. Rivers, the forests, cultivated fields, the longhouse – all have great symbolic meaning, all have a reality behind their ordinary appearance, and all are described and explained in Tukanoan mythology.

Wahtía.

In general, wahtía are humanlike creatures but are not ordinarily seen by humans and are not ordinarily found in areas frequented by humans. Although not all wahtía can be seen as representatives of aggressive and asocial sexuality (Reichel-Dolmatoff, 1971) many wahtía do resemble projections of human feelings and drives. Inasmuch as they represent human yet unacceptable emotions, wahtía are caricatures of human nature, and this is reflected in their appearance: humanlike yet wrong in some fashion. Their appearance can be a rather mild departure from that of normal human beings, as when wahtía are described as looking like human beings but lacking nipples or toes or having only one breast, or they can be truly monstrous. Not all wahtía are monstrous, because the ancestors are a kind of wahtía, as are the dead-people spirits (mahoká diari wahtía). Still, all wahtía do seem only to resemble human beings and, in so doing, expressly highlight an essential nonhumanness.

With the exception of ancestors and dead-people wahtía (which are, at a deep level, identical to and in fact are merged with the living during part of the festival proceedings), all wahtía eat people.[9] A particular kind of wahtía (*weorí mahã*) specializes in looking exactly like someone's kinsman, in order to trick the person into accompanying it into the forest, where he is attacked. Another kind (*hügará*) is actually two beings, attached at their buttocks back-to-back such that when one wants to go one way, the other has to follow walking backward. Another kind (*hüobari wahtí*) calls to victims while facing away from them in order to trick them into thinking the danger is far away. This wahtí's arms are so long that it doubles them up and carries them on its shoulders. Many more kinds exist, all having qualities of exaggerations or reversals of human features: Some are huge and black but otherwise humanlike, whereas others are little and "like whites."[10] Any Tukanoan knows many stories about wahtía. Some have actually heard them yell or have heard of nuts or pits being thrown at someone by a wahtí. Face-to-face encounters are rare; I never talked to anyone who had personally had such a meeting, but many Tukanoans talk about others who have and who were scared out of their wits. Encounters with some kinds of wahtía automatically result in death.

Ordinarily, humans and spirits do not encounter each other; contact is a sign that something has disturbed the normal state of affairs. Dead-people spirits haunt an area only during a lunar eclipse or if something was wrong about their life or the way they died. Both wahtía and spirits in general (e.g., waí mahã, who live below this level – "fire women," "snake women," "star people"), including mythical culture heroes, are normally retired and removed from this world. Only when the world itself is radically altered (i.e., during festivals) is there a merging of human and other spirits, but at these times human beings are not ordinary humans either. Otherwise, only shamans who go into a trance and travel and "see" will have contact with dead people and other-level houses.

Conclusions

Despite the brevity of this presentation of Tukanoan cosmology, it is hoped that the reader has gained some knowledge of the richness of Tukanoan ritual, myth, and symbolism. That such richness is still apparent despite more than a half-century of missionary influence in the Papurí region is remarkable. The effects of missionary activities *have* been extensive everywhere in the Vaupés, greatly disrupting the coherence and integrity of its culture.

Several general themes can be seen in the preceding discussion. One is that the dichotomy between sacred and profane is relative rather than absolute: Whether something is considered sacred or not depends on which of several levels is being conceptualized. At a very profound level everything is sacred, because behind what is perceived by humans as everyday reality, including the most prosaic of events or situations, lies an extraordinary reality or realities. Certain items or concepts are more sacred than others (e.g., men–women; initiated–uninitiated). Some things are always sacred, for instance, beeswax or Yuruparí horn music.

Obviously, shamans, and to a lesser degree initiated men who have knowledge and who drink infusions of banisteriopsis on ritual occasions, can perceive more of the behind-the-visible reality than women and children. Still, all Tukanoans experience these extraordinary realities to some extent during their lives, both as spectators at ceremonies and during their own periods of life crises.

Another general theme in Tukanoan cosmology is the conceptualization of the world as in a state of dynamic equilibrium. In a sense, myths provide a code that explains the system and gives instructions for maintaining or reestablishing this equilibrium. Rituals, with shamans acting as guides and intermediaries, allow people to pass safely through periods of danger.

The symbolism pervading all levels of Tukanoan life also explains and makes sense of the universe and Tukanoans' place in it. For example, although Tukanoans are concerned about proper and moral conduct, issues are frequently

208

too complex to be reduced to questions of right versus wrong behavior. Although at times the status quo is thrown out of kilter by a consciously immoral act (e.g., incest or murder), at other times a community enters a period of danger that is simply due to the process of living. One must eat and therefore run risks by hunting. One must acquire a spouse, invariably a risky undertaking. One must go through puberty rites and be concerned with the fertility of crops and humans, and yet these necessarily affect the overall balance of energy in the universe. This concern – maintaining a balance – in part accounts for the complex associations linking hunting, sexuality, spirit owners of species of game animals, and the strict observance of food and other restrictions. To maintain this equilibrium properly while at the same time exploiting the energy reserves in the universe is a tricky business. To run the risks required for living – to face the dangers of falling sick, of dying, of being attacked (openly or by sorcery) by one's enemies – is, thus, a necessary part of the exchange Tukanoans carry out between themselves in their daily and sacred activities and the rest of the world, a world seen as a closed circuit of energy. With each generation of people, a greater amount of game animals and fish are consumed as food. This inevitably means that there is an ever-increasing depletion of the finite and irreplaceable energy reserves in the universe.

The idea that energy is limited and nonrenewable is a conscious aspect of Tukanoan cosmological structure: Living organisms clearly deplete the resources of their environment (an idea rather new to Western society). Yet these resources can be replenished and new energy created through rituals that foster contact with the nourishment and growth-power available from the first people, the ancestors. S. Hugh-Jones (1979) shows how this is accomplished by rituals that produce a collapse of time, in particular the descent model of time: Lineage time, or sib time – history – is dissolved and, again through ritual, rebirth and renewal are achieved. In essence, these rituals contradict the idea that the energy resources of the world are nonrenewable, for by collapsing genealogical time the power and energy in the universe are recycled. The theme of recycling energy is a powerful one, expressed in many symbolic forms. Rituals to obtain power and nourishment from the ancestors, according to S. Hugh-Jones, use metaphors of rebirth (including skin-changing, perhaps the most powerful symbol of rebirth and immortality), because these metaphors, being concerned with cyclical rather than unidirectional time and space, provide a continual opportunity to tap into the energy available at the very beginning of the world. Tukanoan concepts of reincarnation fit into this structure: Although Tukanoans at death are spoken of as being permanently removed to their ancestral homes located in specifiable areas of the Vaupés region, dead-people spirits are also reincarnated as energy – as life – and remain on this level. It is significant that Pamüri wi, the name of the Bará ancestral house, refers to birth. One translation of this name is "the house where our ancestors were born." It also refers to the birth of present-day Bará, or more specifically, rebirth: metamorphosis and reincarnation. In time, dead-people

209

spirits are forgotten and become further and further removed from the affairs of humans and from any specifically human characteristics. But they remain in this world in their transformed state, eventually turning into little birds. Certain birds, such as the oriole, Guacamaya, and egret are closely linked to Tukanoan conceptualizations of life after death. At some final point in time, human spirits become almost totally inanimate, turning into mist and foam on the rivers.

12.

Tukanoans and the outside world

No phrase captures so well what Tukanoans face in their present and future contacts with the outside world as the subtitle of Erving Goffman's book *Stigma: The Management of Spoiled Identity* (1963). Although the degree and nature of change vary greatly from region to region in the Vaupés, it is apparent to all but the most ethnocentric change agents (regardless of the particular type of change being promulgated) that Tukanoans have suffered greatly from disturbances in their traditional culture. Although the situation in the Vaupés may be better than in most of Amazonia, as Corry (1976) maintains, in my opinion Tukanoans face a bleak future.

In the vast majority of cases the results of regular contact between a small-scale society and a powerful colonizing one are massive, far-reaching, and for the most part negative. This has been well documented for hundreds of band and tribal societies (Bodley, 1975); Tukanoan society is no exception.

Some of the changes in the society resulting from contact with outsiders have been mentioned in previous chapters. Diseases introduced by outsiders brought death and out-migration, reducing the size of local groups so drastically that some customs and institutions have disappeared owing to lack of people to fill the required roles.

The effects of an expanding, development-oriented national and international economy on local systems like the one in the Vaupés are, with few exceptions, devastating (Davis, 1977). All of a sudden native economies that had no universal currency, all exchange being embedded in the network of kinship relations, have to adjust to a cash-based market system. Systems like that of the Vaupés have very little centralization and are predominantly subsistence-oriented. Having to adjust, and adjust very rapidly, to radically different systems inevitably creates a great deal of stress – in the native economic systems and in the natives themselves. New materials and objects are introduced, as are ideas about the monetary value of labor. Many assumptions are introduced regarding what motivates people economically. Also new are the sanctions surrounding economic transactions with members of the dominant culture, such as being kept at a rubber camp until a debt is paid. Most important, of course, is the fact that Tukanoans become

211

increasingly powerless and are exploited in the vast majority of their transactions with outsiders.

In the dominant ideology, cost effectiveness and, usually, profit underlie most strictly economic transactions. Most change agents, whether in the Vaupés for personal economic gain or not, see an internal colony in need of development – "development" meaning improvement in the region's ability to supply raw materials and native manufactures to the national economy. I am not concerned here with denying that the Vaupés's economy can improve with development or that Tukanoan attitudes toward money must change. I am concerned with the problems that these processes create and with understanding the "development of underdevelopment" that too often occurs in marginal areas like the Vaupés.

It is evident from the foregoing chapters that traditional Tukanoan social organization has broken down in many areas. For example, Tukanoans have little acquaintance with true social stratification in their traditional political organization (i.e., in terms of limited or exclusive access to and control over scarce resources). Ranking clearly is a crucial concept in the Tukanoan world view, but is rudimentary with respect to linkage with exclusive economic privileges and thus bears little resemblance to the hierarchy introduced by representatives of the national culture. Traditional headmen (except for war chiefs) have largely ceremonial tasks, and although their authority is certainly greater than that of other adult males, their ability to govern rests on the support given them by the local community. Ability to use power not sanctioned by the local group is minimal, because factionalization and "voting with one's feet" are always possible options. Most decisions are consensual, and most social control informal. In general, leaders rise to their position by their ability to give more rather than to accumulate more. Private property exists, but many checks provide effective limits to an individual's ability to accumulate significant amounts of valuable objects and resources. Before the need for trade goods became so well established, private property consisted mainly of goods that were available to everyone: One could either manufacture an item or acquire it through relatives or friends. Otherwise, property is communal, and often it is sacred as well. Furthermore, effective sanctions exist against nonsharing. Most often people who refuse to share are not so much economically motivated as motivated to make statements about ruptured social relations.

Equally different behaviors and concepts are being introduced in the areas of religion, philosophy, and values. Perhaps, at least in the Papurí drainage, it is in this area that the greatest change has occurred, because by far the most influential change agents have been the Monfortian, Javerian, and Salesian missionaries. These missionaries have introduced a myriad of concepts foreign to traditional Tukanoan culture. There is no codified body of traditional Tukanoan knowledge, law, theology, or ethics. Mythology gives meaning to the world, but it is absurd to view myth as equivalent to Western moral, religious, legal, and philosophical systems that are expressed in nonmythical terms. Certainly the individualism that

212

is so celebrated and so much a part of the very foundation of Western philosophy lacks its equivalent in traditional Tukanoan philosophy. The conflict between Tukanoan values and the Western tradition as taught and practiced by Catholic, and more recently Protestant, missionaries is great. It is virtually impossible to translate Western philosophy into traditional Tukanoan culture. This, however, is not really the goal of missionaries, who wish to eliminate and replace far more than translate.

Thus, a general process of deculturation has been occurring in all spheres of traditional Tukanoan life. Most damaging, however, are the messages Tukanoans receive that they are inferior and that they should relinquish control over their lives in a number of areas. Missionaries may state, and some naively believe, that such psychological blows are not their intention; nevertheless, it is undeniable that they are the result of every increment of missionary presence and influence in the region. Part of the reason the effects on Tukanoans are so devastating is that the traditional Tukanoan culture provides very few counterexplanations or mechanisms for coping with their increasing sense of inferiority and powerlessness to determine and control their affairs. Part of the reason is also that the change agents in the region can back up their messages with so much supporting evidence. In a number of respects the Catholic mission town is a microcosm of a feudal fiefdom. Missionary personnel rule with a heavy hand, although not as heavy as in the past. The governmental bureaucracy, on the other hand, even in such an out-of-the-way place as Mitú, carries the unmistakable stamp of routinized, impersonal transaction. On the surface its representatives rigidly follow policy and are organized along strict hierarchical lines. Behind the scenes, of course, much is accomplished by the tried and true tactics of **palanca** (personal influence); but for the uninformed and naive Tukanoan, such niceties are often missed and usually unavailable.

From the very beginning, whites entering the region have shown their superiority in rather convincing ways – with guns, chains, and other demonstrations of an ability to coerce and apply punishments surpassing any Tukanoan counterparts, technological or ideological. It is true that in the beginning missionaries failed more often than they succeeded at mission founding, but the die was cast even in the unsuccessful efforts, for the creation of needs that could be filled only through contact with whites had begun. Unfortunately, Tukanoans are initially exposed to what appear to be the positive aspects of civilization, seeing the negative ones only later on. This is not to say that they look favorably on the ways guns are used to intimidate them, for instance, but when they look at a missionary or government representative they see tools, outboard motors and planes, communication equipment, a seemingly unending supply of food mysteriously arriving in planes, and a startling amount of luxuries – many changes of clothing, radios, combs, and so on. And the unmistakable arrogance and self-confidence of some whites (at times pathetically imitated by Tukanoans) also dramatically bespeaks power. Furthermore, an economy that supports such nonfood-producing specialists as

213

teachers, police, or priests is striking evidence of wealth. These people occupy enviable, high-status positions; accompanying the envy is the desire to emulate, and thus begins a process of deculturation that can produce some of the most miserable and pitiful human beings on earth. It is impossible for Tukanoans to understand the nature of the dominant social system that is affecting them so totally. A rather complete confusion of cause and effect occurs (encouraged by missionaries, rubber gatherers, and general-store owners), and Tukanoans become confident that having the trappings of power will ease the discrimination against them. It is painful to see the enthusiasm (and desperation) with which acculturated Tukanoans seize upon the symbols of being a **civilizado.** Rather arbitrary white customs such as small items of dress, bearing, and speech are meticulously copied. Yet Tukanoans are not stupid; they know what alcohol abuse does. They see what having a mutilated sense of self-worth does to their own and their kinsmen's and friends' characters. They see the items bought at great personal sacrifice rust, break, peel, or otherwise disintegrate far faster than handmade objects, most often without possibility of repair, and their frustration increases.

An important component of this process is the intermittent reinforcement by whites of Tukanoan attempts to mimic them. On the one hand, laughter and ridicule are always waiting in the wings, to step onstage when a Tukanoan fails to get something exactly right. On the other hand, praise and encouragement are often the reward when a Tukanoan does master a specific behavior, such as asking a priest's permission before removing a shirt when paddling a canoe. Frequently the appropriate behavior indicates a willingness to become more dependent on the national economy and culture in general and to become more appreciative and loyal to the individual change agent in particular. I have on several occasions seen priests show approval of Tukanoan men who bought plastic shoes, even though well aware of the impracticality of such items, which split open in two or three weeks. We can laugh at this, because we are affluent enough to have lost the horror of being too poor to afford shoes. But North American change agents in the Vaupés have their own lists of approved and disapproved behaviors. I believe much of the pleasure so apparent in the faces and comments of these change agents derives from two sources.

First, most change agents, like most people, enjoy personal power. They enjoy being influential and imitated. They enjoy always being on top, but one remains on top only when the value system placing one there is shared by all.

Second, attracting Tukanoans to material goods acquirable from a change agent creates a dependency that helps achieve other goals. In this manner, Tukanoan values slowly undergo a profound transformation without a great deal of direct coercion. Respect for the giver declines, and respect for the receiver increases. Group consensus evolves into a reliance upon individualistic decision making. Arguments about social relations change into arguments about objects. Respect and loyalty to the aged and one's kin turn into resentment of the implied obligations, because not everyone has equal access to white trade goods. These

214

obligations are increasingly avoided whenever possible but not without bad feeling on all sides.

Although change agents often have their own axes to grind when they encourage breakdowns in the traditional system, many times negative consequences have little, if any, relation to the official agenda. One of the sadder parts of acculturative processes in areas like the Vaupés is the amount of harm done by a pervasive, yet often unconscious, ethnocentrism. Especially sad to see is the unnecessary havoc wrought by well-intentioned change agents. Some of the ridicule, racism, exaggerated emphasis on outward signs of inner worth, and encouragement to engage in ultimately harmful behaviors *are* parts of consciously planned programs, because they have a goal of creating dependency and new felt needs. But other instances in which deep shame is induced, pride and confidence destroyed, and dignity trampled into the ground are unintentionally brought about by people who believe they have the target population's best interests at heart. It is a sobering lesson, an illustration of the truth of the proposition that a seemingly necessary requirement for a successful social system is that its members define its values as the only ones possible and condemn out of hand any others. Brief discussions follow of the specific types of change-introducing programs in the recent history of the Vaupés region.

Extractive industries

The only natural resource whose exploitation has ever become firmly established in the Vaupés is rubber. This may be changed in the near future, if rumors about the presence of uranium in the area have any basis in fact. Uranium has been discovered in other areas of Northern Amazonia,[1] but all attempts to locate deposits of valuable minerals in the Vaupés have been unsuccessful up to the present.

Sporadic attempts to make lumber extraction a successful enterprise have always met with failure of one kind or another.[2] A major problem of industries involved in the extraction of any natural resource in the Vaupés other than precious minerals is the tremendous cost of transportation. This is a major reason why the Vaupés is considered to be such a backwater area – and, incidentally, why white-Indian contacts have been relatively benign compared with many other areas. The rivers of the Vaupés region all flow east into Brazil, far from any Colombian centers of population. All rivers of any size are filled with rapids and flood much of the landscape yearly, making road construction extremely difficult. Any exports from the region must first be transported by water or overland to Mitú under perilous conditions and then flown out at great cost. This in part accounts for why there have been no national (not to speak of multinational) corporations represented in the region until very recently.

The domestic rubber industry of Colombia has had its ups and downs since the end of the rubber boom during the first quarter of the century, despite protective legislation that requires rubber companies to purchase a certain amount of

215

Colombian rubber. I was told of some rubber companies that buy their quotas of domestic rubber from the Caja Agraria (the rubber cooperative) in Mitú and immediately dump it in the river. This is cheaper than paying air transportation costs for rubber that is often unusable because it has been poorly processed or has been damaged during river transport.

The **cauchero** (rubber gatherer) works a section of the forest he has staked out and bought a license for. Some Tukanoans have begun to work their own rubber territories, which involves getting a license, acquiring a loan from the Caja Agraria for the necessary equipment (including the extremely heavy **laminadora,** the wringer-press), and transporting the equipment to their territory. White caucheros continue to travel by canoe to Tukanoan settlements before the rubber season to sign up one or more men as laborers. Tukanoans who buy trade cloth, machetes, fishhooks (and, more recently, shotguns), ready-made men's clothing, and transistor radios from these men must work off their debt, which, until recently, could involve a number of years. With very few exceptions, caucheros are universally hated by Tukanoans. Although a few compadrazgo relationships between caucheros and Tukanoans have occurred, in general the situation is too oppressive and the cultural cleavages too great for there to exist any more than the minimum understanding and trust. There seems, in fact, to be a large amount of broken promises and abuses of even the minimal mutual expectations that do exist. Many of the most violent incidents I heard about were justified by caucheros as being necessary punitive measures against Tukanoans, who were described as lazy, irresponsible liars who did not learn without such harsh lessons. I was told that revolvers and other means of delivering on-the-spot justice were necessary as deterrents and sometimes for protection. Caucheros often advised me to carry a revolver.

For the most part, Tukanoan reminiscences of the rubber-gathering period's heyday describe an unrelievedly horrible epoch in their history. Everyone has anecdotes to recount, both about the cruelty of a particular cauchero and illustrations of the general abuses of the system. Caucheros were sometimes refugees from the period of **violencia** in Colombia (a period of political and general violence lasting from 1948 to 1958); some were notorious criminals. Violence and cruelty were inevitable with such men coming to a frontier area like the Vaupés, hoping to get rich as quickly as possible and leave. The rudimentary forces of law and order tended to side with the caucheros, helping to round up and punish runaway Tukanoans and terrorize settlements.

Nowadays, rubber gathering is very much in decline, mainly because of the superiority of imported and synthetic rubber products. Few mourn its passing, with the exception of the various "retired" caucheros living in Mitú, almost all of whom are in dire poverty. These men are eager to recount their adventures and are full of stories of betrayals, tragedies, and occasional moments of hilarity. Most are nostalgic about the past, and a rather different picture from the Tukanoan one emerges from their recollections. Their opinions about the

216

younger generation of Tukanoans, Catholic and Protestant missions, and the situation in Mitú and nationally are salty and occasionally illuminating.

In 1970 the Colombian government issued a decree that Tukanoans must be paid in cash for any labor in rubber camps; by 1974, according to Stephen Corry (1976), debt-bondage had virtually ceased. It is not known whether or not buying and selling the labor of Tukanoans by paying off a man's debts has completely ended. The practice has been illegal for some time, but in Mitú several times I was offered a Tukanoan in exchange for payment of his debts. All debts are supposed to be cancelled yearly by government representatives in Mitú. Sometimes a priest will support a Tukanoan against a cauchero in a dispute. The present situation is a far cry from earlier periods when police were used in raids on settlements to help carry off Tukanoan men, who were manacled and threatened with whipping and shooting. Oftentimes Tukanoans had no recourse but to disappear into the forest for months at a time.[3]

Homesteaders

Very few **colonos** (individuals who migrate into the region with the intention of establishing a permanent farm) were in the Vaupés during my stay, and this continued to be the pattern in 1974 (Corry, 1976, p. 20). One has the impression that the few men who have settled permanently in Mitú and its environs have done so in a spirit of resignation and hopelessness; for some of them it would be dangerous to return to areas of Colombia where they previously lived. Most of them have Tukanoan wives. These families barely manage to eke out a living, and many colonos become involved in affinal exchanges with their Tukanoan brothers-in-law. Most of them drink a lot of alcohol and a few chew coca. This picture contrasts greatly with towns farther to the west, such as San José de Guaviare, which are veritable boom towns. These towns are also reported to have a healthier climate than Mitú, although diseases such as tuberculosis and malaria pose serious problems.

The Colombian government

As indicated in Chapter 2, the presence of the Colombian government in the Vaupés has been low-key and, with a few exceptions (i.e., the police during the rubber boom), inoffensive. Doubtless its unobtrusiveness is in part due to the region's being economically stagnant and with little potential. In such a setting, an indigenous population's self-sufficiency is desirable to a government struggling with terrible poverty in many other areas of the country. Consequently, the government has played a minimal part until recently, putting the Catholic church in charge of providing various necessary services, mainly in the areas of education and health. This arrangement is spelled out in the Concordato, an agreement between the church and the government. This arrangement contrasts somewhat with the more direct influence of the Brazilian government in its section of the Vaupés, which is even more distant from the Brazilian centers of population and areas of development. Colombia is a very Catholic country, a fact that undoubtedly has played a major role in its policy in the Vaupés. It is the only Latin American country that takes care of all of its own missionary needs and actually exports missionaries to other countries. In contrast, Brazil imports many of its Catholic missionaries; all the priests at Yavareté (the Brazilian mission town on the border where the Vaupés and Papurí rivers converge) are Italian. The greater number of non-missionary whites in the Brazilian Vaupés has resulted in Brazilian Tukanoans' possessing more white-manufactured luxury articles such as high heels, and distilling and drinking more alcohol.

In contrast, the only government representatives outside of Mitú during my stay in 1968–70 were a DDT-spraying team and the occasional half-hour visits made by the comisario (the equivalent of a governor) to mission towns on the monthly plane. The **promotor,** a civil servant whose job was to promote indigenous affairs, made only occasional trips to Mitú and was never seen to travel in the rest of the region. He was supposed to act as a liaison between the various government agencies and private concerns dealing with Tukanoans. Unfortunately, he was universally and correctly seen as less than intelligent, and the only thing he was seen to promote was free drinks from everyone.

In 1970 a few agronomists on the government payroll were sent into two or three mission towns. They were to instruct Tukanoans about agriculture, particularly cattle raising. I do not know the outcome of this program; it did strike me that Tukanoans knew a good deal more about tropical horticulture than the individual I talked to in Acaricuara.

Because most of the Colombian government's impact has been until recently through the Catholic church or the Summer Institute of Linguistics, what remains to be said regarding the roles of the state will be discussed in the context of missions.

Missions

After many failures in the previous century, the Catholic church succeeded in establishing a permanent base in the Vaupés with the founding of Monfort in 1914 by the Dutch Monfortian order. It is a task of no mean proportions to attempt to evaluate its success – whether "objectively" or using the church's own criteria. A distinction must be made among the various subregions in the Vaupés, for they vary greatly not only in the general level of Tukanoan acculturation but also, and even more so, in their degree of exposure to missions. For example, at the time of my stay the Pirá-paraná had had SIL personnel for only the past ten years and a permanent Catholic mission base only during the last five. No SIL missionaries were on the Macucú or Tiquié rivers, and the nearest

Catholic mission was Paricachivera, in Brazil. Furthermore, the nature of the Catholic missionary endeavor has changed through the years, particularly after Vatican II had made its impact on the Colombian church. Its effect on the Javerian order was apparently a strong one.

In addition, the very visible and well-organized Protestant missionary effort has influenced the church's methods and strategy in many ways. The Vaupés has been exposed to Protestantism for some forty years through the efforts of the near-legendary Sophia Muller, a New Tribes missionary whose evangelical fervor led her single-handedly to convert thousands of Indians to Protestantism in all parts of Colombia (Stoll, 1981). More recently, SIL established missionary teams in the region, leading to a remarkably high proportion of religious change agents to Tukanoans and creating serious conflict between Catholics and Protestants in the region. These two groups differ from each other in a number of fundamental respects, not all having to do with religious doctrine. Each envies the other; each believes that what it has to offer Tukanoans is superior and at times the only possible solution to indigenous problems. Reading the literature published by each provides glimpses into the internal organization of each group, its implicit assumptions, and its justifications for claiming that it deserves full control of the Vaupés region. Despite a fairly successful policy of maintaining on-the-surface cooperation and congeniality the two organizations are in fact archenemies, and when letting their hair down, members of each will discuss their opponents in highly critical terms. The Catholic church points to the Concordato, its contract with the Colombian government, which states that in exchange for the church's agreeing to be responsible for educating the Indians, the government will expressly forbid any proselytizing efforts by non-Catholic religions throughout Colombia. SIL is very aware of the disadvantage it faces; none of the literature published by it for public distribution in Colombia acknowledges the missionary aspects of the organization.[4] Instead, pamphlets and other printed materials stress the goals of SIL in the areas of contributions to linguistics, bilingual education in Colombia, health services, and preparing Tukanoans for their integration into Colombian national society. Furthermore, SIL has its own agreement with the government (via the Indian Affairs Agency), which gives the organization permission to set up bases in specified areas of the country. The Colombian government pays for the gasoline for airplanes and for constructing the airstrips at each site where a team of two linguists are working. In exchange, SIL agrees to provide transportation, for a fee, to the general public (ironically, some of its most regular customers are Catholic mission personnel). It is an expensive but invaluable service. An important result of the arrangement is that airstrips are being built in remote, otherwise inaccessible areas of Colombia. There are at least ten SIL-constructed airstrips in the Vaupés alone.

SIL's practice of relying exclusively on light aircraft for transportation has had some unexpected effects. Many Tukanoan communities wonder if they will be selected to be the recipients of a SIL team – and the money and goods that inevitably accompany such an event. Once when I was in Mitú I was approached by two Cubeo Indians who requested that I radio SIL and relay the message that their settlement had finished clearing an airstrip and was ready for "their" SIL team. When asked why they wanted a team, they said they needed payment for the work and other kinds of merchandise. I could not ascertain whether in fact an airstrip had been built at that village. The SIL people I talked to about this incident said that they were always receiving offers from Tukanoans to construct an airstrip for a missionary team, but they had not heard of an airstrip actually being built without prior arrangement with SIL.

In accordance with the agreement SIL made with the Colombian government, some information on linguistics and certain ethnographic topics has been made available to scholars (e.g., Summer Institute of Linguistics, 1975). SIL is also interested in establishing a hegemony in bilingual education, because the government's interest dovetails with its own evangelical goals. Its successes in winning important government officials and agencies over to its side has put the Catholic church and in particular the two missionary groups concerned with the Vaupés (the Javerians and the Holy Sisters of the Mother Laura) on the defensive. It is ironic that one of the battlefields of the war between Colombian Catholicism and foreign-oriented Protestantism is the Vaupés, because it is in so many respects a forgotten, backwater region of the country. Yet owing to the region's multilingualism, SIL has organized a large campaign in the Vaupés (the resemblance to a military effort – including a vocabulary that speaks of "bases," "furloughs," etc. – is not lost on anyone). Because of the political advantages of doing so, priests and nuns have recently – and ironically – found it worthwhile to speak favorably of bilingual education. In fact, however, the concept that Tukanoan children should be taught to respect their own language and the more radical idea that they should be taught in both the indigenous language and Spanish are anathema to most Catholic missionaries. Their three goals, very lofty and impeccable in their eyes, and not usually kept separate, are to teach Tukanoans a respect for their country, to teach them a respect for the Spanish language, and to make them good Catholics. Thus, many Catholic missionaries still hold the attitude that the sooner Spanish can be made to replace native dialects, the better, and it is not difficult to bring it to the surface. It is my impression that although some missionaries, both SIL and Catholic, make statements about the value of cultural relativity and the spirit of the Declaration of Barbados on freedom of religion and thought, most in fact are cultural imperialists to a pronounced degree. (The Barbados declaration was promulgated by a group of anthropologists in 1971 on the situation of South American Indians.)

Mutual hostility has always existed between missionaries and caucheros. Often the presence of Catholic priests, particularly in the Papurí, has acted as a deterrent to some of the most excessive abuses practiced by rubber gatherers toward Tukanoans' persons and property. This is recognized by Tukanoans in

220

conversations and in a story they tell of a jungle spirit called Kusiró (undoubtedly from cauchero, although informants denied any connection, stating that this name is derived from the call of Kusiró). Kusiró is a cannibalistic, three-foot-high "demon" who is fat, wears modern clothing,[5] and smokes cigarettes. Tukanoans flee into the forest or lock themselves in their longhouses in fear of him. Barricaded in their longhouses, they quickly run out of food and water but are too afraid when they hear his call to go to their fields or the river. This describes how Tukanoans used to behave when they heard that caucheros were in the vicinity. Finally, a priest banished Kusiró, causing him to flee the Papurí region. This event is described at length in terms of a Catholic ritual using prayers, incense, holy water, and tobacco.

Although the presence of both Catholic and Protestant missionary enterprises[6] serves as a mutual check, and the competition for the approval of the relevant Colombian governmental agencies inspires proposals that at least sound as though they are concerned with Tukanoan welfare in a framework broader than a strictly religious one, the Tukanoans themselves are the real losers in the ideological warfare occurring in the Vaupés. The Tukanoans of the mission town of Acaricuara are a good case in point. This town of some thirty households has a SIL team that has been there about ten years and a full-fledged Catholic mission that includes several nuns, a brother, and a priest. Relations are superficially cordial between the two sets of missionaries, but incidents periodically happen, and rumors are constantly being circulated that serve to create misunderstandings and factions among the Tukanoans there. It is quite clear from the SIL literature I have received that SIL members perceive their main task as saving Tukanoan souls – through long-term efforts at translating the Bible and through short-term efforts at living a good, exemplary life and teaching any Tukanoans who show interest about the life of Christ through songs, stories, and the like. This results in a great deal of confusion for Tukanoans, although they are very much aware of the competition existing between the two missions and will play one side against the other when convenient (although not always successfully). In other areas of the region, such as certain stretches of the Vaupés River, so much competition has developed that one must declare one's religious persuasion before Tukanoans will permit an overnight stay in a given settlement.

In 1969 a catechism program was begun by the Javerian mission to provide religious instruction in all the settlements of the Vaupés rather than only in the mission towns. The priests appointed one or two catechists per settlement who were to conduct nightly sessions and give a little instruction in arithmetic and the alphabet. They received a small remuneration for this. It is difficult to evaluate the program, because it was only begun during my stay. I do know many anecdotes about disputes involving catequistas at many settlements. This was only to be expected in a culture in which people are suspicious of situations that give one person authority over others. The fact that these persons are appointed by an outsider rather than agreed upon by consensus only serves to exacerbate the problem. The catequistas tend to be younger Tukanoans rather than the traditional holders of authority, and are the most missionized individuals in each settlement. The particular situation at Púmanaka buro was ludicrous. The catequista was the eldest son of the family that was constantly at odds with the others in the settlement (this family built a satellite house alongside the longhouse during my stay). In addition, this particular young man was a difficult person in many ways and had very ambivalent feelings toward priests and whites in general. Furthermore, despite three years of mission schooling, he could not speak Spanish (an outcome not unusual in the Vaupés). After a while, people stopped coming to his sessions, despite dire warnings from him that they would bring punishment on themselves from the priest in Acaricuara. In other settlements, however, the catequistas commanded much more respect and were popular enough to weather the inevitable disputes and bad feelings that arose from time to time.

It is completely true that Catholic missionaries' treatment of Tukanoans has vastly improved from earlier periods (Corry, 1976, p. 19).[7] Such punishments of schoolchildren as whipping or making an entire class stand out in the noonday sun with their arms raised shoulder-high have been discontinued. Still, great variation exists among the present Javerians, even though as a unit they are less strict than the earlier Monfortians. One priest proudly described to me in detail how he personally had ordered two longhouses on the Inambú River destroyed and had moved the inhabitants to the town of Los Angeles on the Papurí River. It is ironic that this town, created by priests, is now the location of the SIL team working on the Tuyuka language. A few of the clergy are liberal-minded, but most priests are reactionary and narrow-minded. Furthermore, it is difficult for all Colombian (and foreign, for that matter) missionaries to detect the instances in which ethnocentrism rather than received gospel motivates them to alter Tukanoan attitudes and behavior. Priests tell Tukanoans how to ''eat properly,'' ''walk properly,'' and ''sit properly.'' In general they are authoritarian, have an ingrained sense of their own superiority. and at times seem to revel in the sense of sacrifice and martyrdom they feel without acknowledging the pleasures they receive from their personal power and status. They will not let Tukanoans bathe without clothing on, and even on canoe trips a Tukanoan man must ask a priest's permission before taking off his shirt. Priests must give permission before a couple living in a mission town may get married. I was told of one case involving a woman from Acaricuara and a man from Caño Viña to whom permission to marry was never granted. Tukanoans said permission was not granted because the woman, who worked in the mission kitchen, was a favorite of the mother superior, who did not want the woman to leave.

Trouble erupts between missionaries and Tukanoans from time to time, which sometimes is serious and which is never really satisfactorily resolved. One such instance, described earlier, involved a priest who was openly in favor of a marriage taking place between two Tukanos. Another case, which still rankles Tukanoans, involved a mother superior who secretly paid a Tukanoan to obtain a set of Yuruparí horns for shipment to Bogotá. I also heard rumors of sexual advances made by priests to Tukanoan women. It is, of course, difficult to assess the validity of these rumors, because Tukanoans, especially those not living in mission towns, are very confused about the social structure of the missionary enterprise and often will make unwarranted assumptions about it. Incidents do occur, however, and they create a great deal of anger and resentment in Tukanoans.

The fact that Catholic missions have been in the Papurí drainage region for more than fifty years is readily apparent upon examining traditional Tukanoan religious beliefs. Many intrusive elements from Catholic dogma are included in stories people tell of the supernatural – encounters, strange occurrences, magical formulas, and such. Less syncretism occurs in myths; the effect of Catholicism on mythology is more one of simple extinction rather than radical transformation of form or content. But when Tukanoans are telling quasisupernatural anecdotes about themselves or other living people, often very strange mixtures of traditional and new themes and characterizations appear. For example, a fairly acculturated Tukanoan explained to me that a particular kind of wahtía are red "because they are from Russia." One list of directions for acquiring shaman powers begins with the traditional notion of obtaining magical thorns and inserting them right under the skin but also involves using a needle to open the flesh and obtaining powerful splinters from the cross in the cemetery in Mitú. This has to be done on a night of a lunar eclipse and requires engaging in mortal combat with the wahtí who protects the cross.

Mitú

At times Mitú's inhabitants seem to be characters out of a Buñuel film – surrealistic caricatures rather than real human beings. At other times they seem smaller than life, oppressed and belittled by the same system oppressing the Tukanoans. And sometimes they simply seem to be warm, sympathetic, courageous human beings with remarkable capacities for self-satire and humor when life is at its bleakest. Although not all of Mitú's inhabitants deal with Tukanoans, the overall impact of the town on them is extensive, both directly and indirectly.

Mitú's two or three bars sell soft drinks and beer, both exorbitantly expensive due in part to air transport costs. Tukanoans also consume large quantities of **aguardiente** (cheap cane liquor), and alcoholism is a problem in a number of families, although thus far confined to Mitú and its environs. It is at bars that one of the many forms of discrimination is openly practiced: Although the Tukanoans' patronage is welcome, their presence is not, and they usually consume their beverages outside. (On the rare occasions when a Tukanoan pays for a full meal at one of the two **residencias** [lodging houses] he sits at a table like the others.) A familiar nightly scene consists of Colombian whites gathered inside a bar, drinking and playing pool, and a group of Tukanoans standing outside looking through the windows and door, like moths drawn to the light. It is half-jokingly

223

said that the only place where Tukanoans are welcome inside are the whorehouse on the outskirts of town and the jail.

Occasionally one sees open and hostile discrimination in Mitú, particularly if a white is angry or drunk. Although it is true that some of the abuses against Tukanoans such as "buying" Indians (contracting for the labor of an indebted Tukanoan) have been greatly curtailed, the existence of two classes of citizens is apparent to all.

The terms each group uses for the other are ethnic rather than racial classifications.[8] Everyone affirms that most "whites" (**blancos**) in the region have partial, if not total, Indian ancestry. No term in any Tukanoan language classifies whites racially. Colombians of Negro descent are unquestionably blancos to Spanish-speaking Tukanoans. The local term for half-breed, **cabuco,** comes from the Portuguese **caboclo,** meaning "backwoodsman." It almost always refers to a person with a blanco father and a Tukanoan mother. Apart from this term, no labels exist that classify individuals in terms of their supposed racial origin or by physical features. It is my impression that the criteria used to classify people as Indian or white are (at least from the Tukanoan point of view) in the first place his or her father language and in the second the desire to become a blanco. This means that in one or two generations a Tukanoan can make the switch, even if other Tukanoans in the area continue to be seen as Indian. I have heard a Tukanoan woman living in Mitú speaking only Spanish to her children, although she spoke her own language with friends. This is evidence that the way to "become blanco" involves both the desire to switch and identification with Spanish as one's first language. Of course, other factors are at play as well, involving matters of dress, gestures, and other customs, and a repudiation of behavior seen as specifically Indian.

It is my impression that for a Tukanoan to come to be perceived as white by other whites, a generation is needed. A Tukanoan may be very fluent in Spanish, but if his parents are known to be Tukanoans and their language and customs were taught to the individual as a child, he will not be considered a blanco, despite his volition and behavior. Still, his children will probably be considered blancos if their first language is Spanish. Of course this process sometimes involves denial of knowledge of any Tukanoan languages. Once when this happened in my presence in Mitú, it was greeted with giggles from the companions of the young Bará man who was trying to pass as a blanco by speaking only Spanish with me.

Conclusions

Many kinds of change agents are found in the Vaupés – their number and variety is astonishing when one takes into account the small numbers of Tukanoans who form their target population and the economic stagnation of the region itself. It is difficult to predict whether the Catholic church or SIL and other Protestant organizations will have increasing influence in the years to come. Although denunciations of the presence of SIL in Colombia regularly appear in the national press and other interested publications, to date SIL has not been forbidden to work in Colombia. Rumors to the effect that "SIL has been given three years to get out of Colombia" surface periodically, yet SIL is strong enough (counting on important support from other U.S. interests in Colombia) to withstand this criticism.

It is certain that if both SIL and the Catholic church maintain their toeholds in the Vaupés, the major battles will be fought over education. Tukanoans recognize that several years of schooling for their children is absolutely necessary, given the world they will inherit. This does not lessen the seriousness of charges that can be made against education as it now exists in the Vaupés. In some senses, what occurs in the classroom is representative of the entire religious–cultural acculturation process occurring in the Vaupés up to the present: A very sad corollary is the fact that much of the damage is unnecessary, even taking the missionary perspective and its goals into account. Educational content and teaching methods are archaic, and the real lessons taught to Tukanoan children are the subverted ones mentioned at the beginning of this chapter – the lessons that instill in each child an awareness of his or her own unworthiness. Furthermore, much of what Tukanoans learn is inefficiently taught and virtually useless for the life they will lead. Lessons in Colombian geography dealing with terrains of which Tukanoans can have no conception are a good case in point. From an outsider's point of view, this is true for all religious instruction as well, except for the advantage such knowledge provides a Tukanoan in his subsequent dealings with missionary personnel. In addition, the Spanish that children learn in school is minimal, considering the many hours of instruction given. The outdated, inefficient, rigid teaching methods do teach part of the hidden curriculum rather effectively, however, because they encourage passivity, dependence, resignation, and self-deprecation. And, although instruction outside the classroom is more oriented to practical matters such as how to use a sewing machine, these lessons also have the effect of creating a greater dependence on white goods.[9] These are necessary lessons in any effort at turning autonomous, reasonably self-sufficient groups into "good citizens" – Spanish-speaking Colombians who are at least Christian (and, specifically, Protestant or Catholic, depending on one's point of view) and who participate in the national economy. It is certainly true that by now most Tukanoans want to go in this direction, and in a few years almost all will be interested in giving up what is left of their culture and embracing the variety of Colombian culture existing in mission towns and places like Mitú.

The cost of this change is exorbitant, however, and Tukanoans, although they are the ones who will pay the bill, are unaware of most of the items on it. One item is the decreasing control over their lives, both as individuals and collectively, and decreasing pride and feelings of self-worth. Another is the great reduction in security and predictability provided by their knowledge of their environment,

225

including the complex way it is integrated into their systems of mythology and other symbolic forms. Mythology explains, justifies, and elaborates the world and Tukanoans' place in it; the substitutes being provided are surely not as rich, integral, or satisfying.

Tukanoans are embarked on a journey of increasing integration into the national society and culture, and for many it is a journey toward real poverty, alcoholism, disease, malnutrition, alienation, and despair. To some degree, Tukanoans have unwittingly and often unwillingly sold their birthright for a mess of pottage. It is true that this process has been going on for centuries and that even the most traditional of cultures is never wholly autonomous and lacking contact with other, frequently far more powerful cultures. Nevertheless, the situation in the Vaupés is exceptional because this particular mess of pottage is very poor fare indeed and because it is being forced down Tukanoan throats in a very speeded-up process. The reasons why this change is so rapid, so coercive – at times in the extreme – and replaces so rich a traditional culture with one so deficient are very complex. They have to do with the fact that it is really not Colombian national culture Tukanoans are being integrated into but a position on the lowest rung of an economic and cultural ladder whose highest rungs are outside Colombia, insofar as Colombia itself is a client-state of the United States and the many international corporations that fund the development efforts taking place within its borders. The answers to why the future appears so bleak and poverty-stricken for these people lie in analyses of these global economic and political processes, and not in anything exclusively or intrinsically Colombian.[10]

13.
Conclusions: themes in Tukanoan social identity

Types of comparisons

Much of the discussion in this book has followed out of postulating a series of polarized contrasts in Tukanoan classifications of people. Some of these contrasts constitute entire chapters (e.g., Tukanoan–Makú, male–female, Tukanoan–white), whereas others (e.g., coresident–other, own-language group–other) are described in several chapters. Although most contrasts are dichotomies, some are trichotomies, most notably the agnate–affine–mother's child contrast. Accentuating such polarities is a useful tactic for explicating the major differences between various classes of people and nonpeople important in Tukanoan social structure.

Another type of comparison consists of a class of elements ordered along a continuum according to their possession of varying amounts of a particular property. Examples of this are the birth order of siblings and the system of ranked sibs within a language group.

A third type of comparison also involves the notion of continuum, but in this case one end of the continuum is the core or nucleus and the other end is peripheral, whose significance mainly derives from being the opposite of the core. An example of this is the longhouse, the symbol of all that is human, social, and spiritual. Next in order on the scale are the river, the forest, and finally the wild and anomalous features of the landscape, such as *tatá boa* (naturally occurring forest clearings) and the rocky outcrops and caves sporadically looming high above the forest floor. Another example of this type of continuum is the progression from "us" to "not-us," going from own group (maniya waderá, "our-language people" or "brother people") to affines (mehkó-mahkara) to mother's children (pahkó-mahkara) to other people (ahpẽrá mahkara) and, presumably, to classes of people such as whites and Makú. This particular set of contrasts is also a trichotomy; whether it should be seen as three basic contrasts or as a continuum involving the notion of increasing distance (geographical, social, marital, linguistic, emotional, etc.) and differentiation depends on the context and what is being emphasized.

Identity components vary with respect to permanence. Those that are temporary and relative rather than fixed were discussed primarily in the beginning of the book. One is normally both child and parent in the course of a life-time. The roles of host and guest are similarly relative. These temporary roles often contain symbolic elements derived from more permanent identities; for example, hosts can be seen as female, guests as male. And as S. Hugh-Jones (personal communication) notes, at Yuruparí ceremonies hosts can be seen as humans and guests as spirits.

It is by now apparent that Tukanoan classifications concerned with social identity involve distinctive features and symbols in multiple levels of meanings. The ideas expressed in the *agnate–affine–mother's child* contrast can vary, depending on what is being stressed. It can be a simple tripartite division, especially when three actual language groups are being discussed and the earth–air–water trichotomy is involved, or it can be seen as a core–periphery ordinal scale. The merging or elimination of certain features at a higher level of contrast figures prominently in Tukanoan conceptualizations of identity.

Some comparisons are taxonomic in structure, and some are paradigmatic.[1] An example of a taxonomy is the Tukanoan contrast *like-us–not-like-us* made at different levels of inclusion: One would perhaps begin with one of the divisions in the agnatic terminology such as *generation* and end with the opposition *human–nonhuman*. This taxonomy could involve as many as nine levels. A paradigmatic relationship, on the other hand, is not based on levels of inclusion but on the simultaneous occurrence of at least two dimensions, with a minimum of two distinctive features per dimension. The set of personal pronouns in English is a good example of a paradigm (the dimensions are *person* and *number*). An example of a paradigmatic classification in Tukanoan identity conceptualization occurs when the male–female and Tukanoan–Makú contrasts co-occur. Given the association sometimes made between qualities such as spirituality and true humanity and the features *Tukanoan* and *male,* it is not surprising to find an association sometimes made between categories lacking these qualities: *female* and *Makú.* We have seen that at times both women and Makú are associated with each other and with natural symbols. But this association is appropriate only in some contexts, and in others a connection made between women and Makú would be wrong. It is important to resist the temptation to assume that symbolic connections are universally applicable and permanent. Such simplistic and overly rigid treatment ultimately leads to confusion rather than clarification.

Many more examples can be offered of multiple levels of meaning. One already mentioned is that a sacred–profane continuum exists on one level and yet on another level a sacred quality is imparted to everything. This is in part because reality itself consists of many levels, extraordinary time and space lying behind ordinary reality. This characteristic of multiple levels of meaning is clearly an aspect of the interplay between rigidity and fluidity in Tukanoan social structure, both in terms of on-the-ground realizations of the structure and in terms of the structure as cognitive model. The fixed and the variable in Tukanoan social structure are linked, serving as foils for each other. For instance, Bará (fish people) are associated with water, Tuyuka (mud people or clay people) with earth, and Desana (wind people) with the air. In the Inambú region, the classic affinal relationship is seen as occurring between Bará and Tuyuka. Bará also marry Desana, but Tuyuka, according to some informants, are "not supposed" to marry Desana, and very few marriages have taken place between this pair of language groups. Bará are not supposed to marry Tukano; it may be that Tukano (toucan) are seen as sky people as well. On the Pirá-paraná, Barasana and Tatuyo enter the marital picture with Bará, and Tukano, Desana, and Tuyuka leave it. Thus, we see variability in terms of actual groups, and yet the structure – a tripartite one with one pair seen as archetypical affines, one pair as not intermarrying – is preserved. It is important to note that the situation is variable not only with respect to which language groups are involved but also as regards the location of the language groups' member settlements and these settlements' neighbors. This is part of the reason why it is so difficult to arrive at a description of *the* phratric organization of the Vaupés.

Another example involves the category *Makú*. Sometimes *Makú* is clearly opposed to *Tukanoan* and associated concepts such as humanity, morality, and knowledge. Here *Makú* tends to be paired off with *wahtía,* in the sense of "like human but something wrong," with associations of excessiveness, imbalances, and lacks (e.g., wahtía can lack nipples or toes; Makú are said to lack clothing, body paint, and jewelry). Unacceptable behaviors such as improper language, food, and sex partners, cannibalism, and an association with the forest are also common to both categories. Yet at other times Makú are not opposed to Tukanoans but associated with the bottom position in a ranked group; Tukanoans may speak of the lowest-ranked sib of a given language group as being of Makú origin. Both categories share the designation "cigar lighter" and various symbolic associations. The association with the forest is also shared: Lower-ranked sibs are seen as inhabiting relatively upstream sites. Lower-ranked sibs are not, however, associated with wahtía or powerful sorcery as are Makú.

Another example involves the contrast between Tukanoans and wahtía: Usually wahtía are the antithesis of Tukanoans, in appearance, in character, in behavior. Yet as we have seen, sometimes in myths an ambiguous association is made between wahtía and mother's children, pahkó-mahkara. Here what is being stressed are the shared qualities of unpredictability, potential danger, and absence of ongoing social, emotional, and exchange relationships, which do not occur between Tukanoans and wahtía nor, structurally (they may occur in individual cases), between pairs of pahkó-poná or groups that are pahkó-mahkara to each other.

A final example is the contrast male–female. At times this is a simple dichotomy, but at other times a core-periphery connotation is introduced, as when men are spoken of as the only spiritual, cultural beings, and women are simply the category lacking these qualities. At other times there is a merging into a kind of androgynous state: "A unity of a higher order than the elements" (C. Hugh-Jones, 1977, p. 203) is created.

The *longhouse* and the *shaman,* both extremely complex concepts laden with symbolic meaning, admirably illustrate what I mean by multiple and merging meanings. The longhouse is probably the key metaphor for human identity. It is where such quintessentially human activities as cooking, eating, dancing, and singing are carried out. Babies, not yet human, are born outside and brought in; the dead, recently human, are buried beneath it. Curing is done near its front door. The boy mentioned in Chapter 2 who had been bitten by the snake had to recuperate outside until he had sufficiently returned to human status to be allowed back in. But at times this human–nonhuman association disappears, and all beings are spoken of as having their longhouses: animals, wahtía, dead spirits, and the ancestors. Sometimes, rather than being opposed to *nonhuman* and *nature,* the longhouse merges with them, becoming the whole universe. A taxonomic structure consisting of *human body–family–sib–language group–universe* can be constructed, with the longhouse representing each level.

The shaman is a more complicated symbol. Having a similar quality of multiple meanings, he also demonstrates characteristics of ambiguity and boundary straddling not found in the symbolism of the longhouse.

In a sense shamans are both human and more than human. They are at the top of a hierarchy of people possessing wisdom and sacred knowledge (see Reichel-Dolmatoff, 1971, p. 249), at the bottom of which are women and children. They interpret myth, see many levels of the universe, speak several Tukanoan languages plus their own esoteric language, and in general engage in more activities associated with humanness than do ordinary humans. But shamans are also precariously close to the nonhuman side and at times slip over into it, as when they turn into evil sorcerers and practice magic against their own community. This danger always potentially exists because shamans associate with nonhumans, travel to other levels of the universe, and have supernatural powers. As we have seen, there is always the danger of becoming like that with which one associates.

Shamans are also intermediaries: They usher in new states and statuses at rituals and mediate at other events. Thus, again by association, they are at times seen to be "like" women, animals, or the dead. Shamans are thus a prime symbol of the merging that occurs throughout Tukanoan conceptualizations of identity. By confusing some of his own identities and crossing some boundaries, the shaman clarifies what these are and preserves them – by preventing inappropriate merging, divining what has been crossed or confused, and restoring boundaries already transgressed. This is also what happens in the way Tukanoan social identity is structured and played out in other areas of life, an illustration of my suggestion that ambiguity and variation are features intrinsic to the system of social identity, for they help to define and maintain what does not vary by showing what does and the limits to this variability.

Conclusions: themes in Tukanoan social identity

Themes associated with social identity

Crucial to an understanding of Tukanoan social identity are the themes of maintenance, moderation, balance, risk, relationality, permanence versus transience, and regionality. *Maintenance* refers to two related but distinct ideas in Tukanoan thought: (1) the need to maintain one's identity by behaving properly and (2) the need to maintain Tukanoan society by means of proper individual and collective behavior. The idea of maintenance is connected to the notion that identity is process as much as idea (Crocker, 1977). Numerous examples of this can be offered with respect to individual identity. Kamaweni, by not behaving like a good elder brother, forfeited his claim to be one, with grievous consequences: He was indirectly killed by his younger brother. One must maintain one's identity, one's claim to being human, a kinsman, a Tukanoan, or whatever, by marrying, speaking, and living properly. One must also continue to associate with appropriate others. Many myths demonstrate how people can become like the beings they associate with, whether wahtía or animals, as was mentioned in the case of shamans. Shamans and other leaders, particularly headmen, must continue to show the proper qualities of moral restraint, selflessness, wisdom, and so forth, to continue to merit their positions. And all Tukanoans must engage in certain key behaviors, such as speaking, dancing, and singing, to show they continue to deserve to be considered Tukanoans – individuals and settlements – in good standing with their neighbors and Tukanoan society as a whole.

The second idea concerning maintenance – proper individual and collective behavior to maintain the group and, at the broadest level, Tukanoan society itself – has to do with a longhouse group's observation of proper restrictions on food and other behaviors. Such activities are also for the benefit of the individual, but infractions hurt not only the individual at fault but the entire settlement. In addition are the periodic ceremonies that, when carried out correctly, renew the local group by maintaining continuity with the ancestors and the past in general. Food rituals, horn playing and making music in general, myth chanting, periodically burning beeswax, are all ways of ensuring the continuance of Tukanoan society.

Such activities concerned with maintenance and prevention contrast analytically with rites and other behaviors that can be seen as restorative in nature. These concerns introduce the next three themes pervading Tukanoan conceptualizations of social identity: *balance, moderation,* and *risk.* Themes of balance and equilibrium appear time and again in Tukanoan thinking of how to live a good and happy life, and much of the content of restorative ritual has to do with discovering whatever imbalances exist and restoring harmony. Death, birth, taboo breaking, and illness are all instances of imbalance, and everyone must work to restore harmony and balance when such threats disrupt the moral order. The activities connected with lunar eclipses are excellent examples of this concern, the purpose being to get the moon back into the sky and to restore him to his proper place and activity.

231

Risk and danger cannot be completely avoided, however, for they are inherent in the process of life itself. Life means change: Growth, initiation, marriage, birth, and death are all supposed to happen, and yet all are risky. They must be properly ushered in and lived through, usually with the help of a shaman (the exception is marriage, a completely secular event). Processes inherent to living, in both its physical and social aspects, are potentially dangerous. Eating means killing animals and the possibility of breaking a taboo; sexual activity is dangerous in itself and necessitates association with other classes of people. Maintenance of the moral order is thus a kind of tightrope: To live is to risk and to become imbalanced during certain periods such as birth and initiation. Certain rituals reduce the risk of such periods by ensuring maximum equilibrium in the individual and the community. When the balance is upset, certain ceremonies restore it. For example, naming, painting, washing the infant, and making the mother's milk safe for drinking are ways of restoring balance and eliminating the imbalances in the cosmological order brought about by birth.

The necessity of maintaining boundaries is relevant here, for it is tied in with notions about balance and harmony in Tukanoan thinking about the world and its occupants. In part, both shamans and Makú are complex symbols because they cross boundaries. Shamans cross over into the other levels of the universe, and Makú cross the boundary between themselves and Tukanoans. This occurs conceptually when lower-ranked Tukanoan sibs are described as "like Makú" and in actuality when intermarriage occurs or when a Makú group is absorbed by a Tukanoan language group as its lowest-ranked sib. But the boundaries between shamans and supernatural beings and between Makú and Tukanoans should be kept distinct. The same is true of the boundary between the living and dead as the myths of pehū, and Live Woman demonstrate. The best example of boundary maintenance is perhaps that between the language groups. As shown in Chapters 5 and 9, the differences between Tukanoan languages are seen to be as important as they are because of the role language plays in marking the boundaries between these otherwise similar exogamous units in Tukanoan society.

The theme of moderation appears as an important element in many areas of Tukanoan life, particularly in activities concerned with maintenance and restoration of health and balance in the community and the cosmos. Moderation in eating, sleeping, sexual intercourse, and many other activities goes a long way toward keeping everything in balance, particularly for initiated men. Again, many illustrations in myths can be found. Women, Makú, and wahtía are often contrasted with initiated men with reference to excess. Male restraint and moderation are expressions of male morality, male solidarity, and male responsibility for maintaining the community. Many kinds of ceremonies vividly display such concerns, often through the use of inversion: For example, during rituals excessive consumption is the rule but of soul food rather than food (C. Hugh-Jones, 1979).

With respect to the theme of relationality, in the United States and other Western countries, if we choose to pay attention, we can discern many kinds of

232

identity "tags" that remind us of our uniqueness. These tags range from a myriad of account numbers (such as social security, credit card, driver's license) to all manner of legal conventions that highlight individual existence and responsibility, often to the exclusion of any other kind. An example is the increasing acceptance of an individual's right to take his or her own life; this argument is almost always couched in terms of individual rights, as contrasted to arguments concerned with the rights of others (e.g., the stance of the Catholic church). Arguments both for and against abortion are similarly phrased. A look at earlier periods in Western history reveals that such was not always the case; notions of collective identity in terms of privilege or responsibility, have been greatly eroded. Familiar examples are collective blood guilt and other duties between kinsmen. Such a stress on individualism is not characteristic of Tukanoan culture, even though Tukanoans would probably agree that individual identity derives from a unique intersection of social, spatial, and temporal variables. But, I would argue, for them this has meaning only relationally, whereas there is a much stronger element of permanent distinctiveness in Western notions. True, all those classifying numbers and markers of distinct identity are related logically to the other markers in the same category, but their primary function is to separate each individual from all others (even if, as is the case with social security numbers, it is a separation to allow the bureaucracy to treat us all the same). Social security numbers are relational only in the sense of showing our relationship (one of distinction) to all other workers in the United States. And they continue to distinguish us after a change of name, address, or even death.

Thus, while it is true that certain identity components are clear-cut (no ambiguity, no dual memberships or fence-straddling, etc.), ambiguity and contradiction inhere in all Tukanoan social roles. An example is the pivotal position Tukanoan women assume when they marry. They remain agnates (sisters, daughters, loyal supporters, and members in absentia of their natal longhouses) and must reconcile this with their new affinal roles (wives, mothers, loyal supporters of their husbands' and children's longhouses). These potential contradictions are usually handled by stressing one role in a given situation and deemphasizing another. It is only when this is impossible (e.g., in answer to a question of whether women go to their natal descent groups' ancestor longhouses after death or to their husbands' and children's) that the contradiction becomes apparent. What is important to note here is the familiar theme of fluidity and variability – or, put another way, relationality, because who people are in very large part depends on the social context defining the roles they play. Like the Bororo of Central Brazil, the Tukanoan self exists mainly with respect to, in relation to, other selves (Crocker, 1977, p. 144).

Obviously vast differences are found between Tukanoan society and the West or other complex society – in social structure, scale, political centralization, and so forth. I cannot discuss all the implications of these differences here, but it is clear that certain purposes, if I may speak in functionalist terms, are served by the mech-

233

anisms that establish and maintain individual identity in the West that are not served in the Tukanoan case. Tukanoans have no need to distinguish individuals bureaucratically or otherwise in the fashion we are all familiar with; indeed, the reverse is true. For many reasons the more fluid (temporary) and collective (relational) system of marking selves and others in Tukanoan society suits their purposes.

Another example of ways in which putatively unchangeable, ascribed statuses are affected in Tukanoan society by an individual's relationships with others is language group identity. This is a crucial aspect of a Tukanoan's notion of self, and I would argue that it is a central one, following Barnett (1977, p. 277) and D. R. Miller (1961, pp. 282–83) on the notion of centrality of certain identity components. The meaning this has, however, is highly dependent on the location of one's settlement and its relationships with the other settlements in its sphere of interaction (and their language group identity). Although, for instance, once a Bará always a Bará, what this means is extensively shaped and influenced by whether one interacts with Tuyuka, Barasana, or other language group. How one talks about being a Bará, the normative statements one will make, the mythological statements, are influenced by these factors.

Another example of contextuality that obscures an underlying contradiction is the never-ending dispute about relative patrilineal sib rank. Only after careful discussions with various Tukanoans does one realize that no agreed-upon ranking system exists that classifies *all* presently existing sibs, although the top ranking one(s) will usually be acknowledged as such. Even here, however, at times some Tukanoans will aver that in earlier times the reverse was the situation, but "those people refused to call us elder siblings, so we had to address them this way." These seemingly clear-cut features of identity, when being specified, show that their clarity depends on contextualization and reveal an underlying ambiguity and contradiction: A relational quality emerges.

Tukanoan public ritual expresses relationality and collectivity in many respects and downplays individuality. For example, Tukanoans have no wedding ceremony, and the rituals that express and celebrate affinal relationships and ongoing alliances do not say anything about the individuals as individuals presently or previously in such relationships.

Male initiation ritual is another example – as unlike our initiation rituals (e.g., a Bar Mitzvah) with respect to individuality as one can imagine. Tukanoan boys are initiated in a group with little acknowledgment of them as distinct individuals (S. Hugh-Jones, 1979; rituals such as menarche ritual that do mark individual change are smaller and more private). Furthermore, public rituals in general stress collective identity and behavior, in such activities as dancing and chanting. In the few instances in which an individual does perform alone, this person is constrained by a role that suppresses much of his or her individuality. Of course this is true for many rituals in many societies, but it is pronounced in Tukanoan ritual.

It is interesting to note that the shaman who performs more as an individual than other Tukanoan ritual roles allow is seen as more likely than others to misuse his power. We can characterize this process as one of increasing individuation (in terms of power, self-interest, etc.) accompanied by decreasing humanness (this type of shaman eventually turns into, and is called, a jaguar).

In sum, Tukanoans obviously recognize and think of one another as distinct personalities. The differences between the way they acknowledge the individual and our individualism lie in the degree of overt and covert distinguishing of the individual as such. Ambiguity and contradiction certainly inhere in Western conceptualizations of the individual, whether they be religious, legal, or psychological, but we have many institutions that explicitly work at avoiding ambiguity in some spheres of social action and social classification. These types of institutions are lacking in Tukanoan society. The need for all the distinguishing individual identity features and markers (such as birth certificates) fosters a notion of the individual as existing apart from the group for some purposes, and in the West a person's existence is demonstrated, validated, legitimated, and to some degree, I would argue, created by these various mechanisms. Many instances can be found in Western literature of identities changed or even created or eliminated by various documents (just look at several Gilbert and Sullivan plots). Although Tukanoans certainly go through various ceremonies involving the establishment of or change in a given social status, the group does the work, and to a greater extent the individual is always submerged in a group. Tukanoans can be seen to be selves and others through one another, in collectivized and contextualized relationships. In the West, many relationships are mediated by some form of state or municipal machinery that contributes to a definition of that relationship (e.g., marriage or adoption). This finally has a profound influence on how a citizen, parent, worker, or even deceased person comes into being and is conceptualized.[2]

With respect to the theme of permanence versus transience, it would be difficult to make the argument that Tukanoans conceive of an individual as existing as an individual self throughout time. For us, that John Jacob Jingleheimer Schmidt was at his birth, is, and will continue to be a distinct, individual self is a reasonable and meaningful proposition. This idea of survival of individual identity is not, I would argue, nearly so meaningful to Tukanoans, for many of their identity features are not seen as permanent, and many others are played down more than in Western society. This is not to deny that ambiguities exist in Western conceptualizations of the ways in which individual personality maintains itself as distinct and with recognizable continuity throughout life and after death. But such maintenance and survival is a theme in many religious and secular philosophies (in Christian thought, in purgatory, hell, and heaven; in countercultural and occult thinking, in other worlds or planes of reality). Present in many of these is a concern for a continuation of some identity features acquired during a period of life on earth, especially with respect to responsibilities for one's actions. Why this is true is the topic of another book.

Such ideas are not foreign to Tukanoan thought; for example, murderers are seen as suffering different fates, at least immediately after death, from people who have

235

committed no serious crimes. Westerners are hardly free of ambiguity and uncertainty about survival of the personality, but I would maintain it is of greater concern to many in the Judaeo-Christian tradition than it is to Tukanoans. Tukanoans speak of what we might term "spirits" and "souls," but none of this is clearly worked out: "The 'other world' is not a unitary concept in Indian thought: it embraces the distant natural world of the remote forest, the ancestral world and the sinister world of the recently dead" (C. Hugh-Jones, 1979, p. 113). Some aspects of death, especially matters to do with corpses, are unpleasant matters, about which the less said the better (see Moser and Tayler, 1965, pp. 51–54).

The cyclical features of Tukanoan conceptualizations of the individual self can be seen as a denial of anything like permanent individual identity. Naming involves a cycle of only two generations. Thus, in the name and in the idea of reincarnation of a person's soul via name transmission, the notion of a distinct personality's survival is downplayed. Tukanoans say that after death the spirit goes on a journey to ancestral homes under the rivers. But such longhouses are not the subject of elaborate and comprehensive description (unlike other areas of Tukanoan cosmology). There is only one myth in my collection that deals with life after death (this is also true for the corpus collected by the Hugh-Joneses). Another way of speaking of life after death is in connection with animals, where an equivalence is made between game animals and people, especially children. A third way is as a kind of reincarnation (although it should be noted, my data are very skimpy) in which Tukanoans eventually turn into small birds, then into yellow butterflies, and finally into river foam. A process of decreasing individuation is clearly apparent.

It is important to note that "life" does not end at death: The soul lives on in its namesake and other processes take place involving travel to ancestor longhouses or reincarnation. But the idea that individual personality continues is very minimal and vague. In general, the Tukanoan individual comes from an undifferentiated source and returns to one (such as river foam). Certain ancestors are indeed spoken of as distinct personalities, but these are far from humanlike (S. Hugh-Jones, 1979). They can also be seen as inimical to individual identity, because contact without proper precautions is fatal, for the ancestors want to return with such individuals to ancestral time and space.

Naming is a clear example of the principles of temporality and relationality. If one is a Bará or other Tukanoan, one receives a name from a very finite list owned by the sib (C. Hugh-Jones, 1979; Århem, 1980). The name ideally comes from a FF or FFZ who has recently died. An association is thus made that works in two ways: The deceased loses his or her name (confirming a state of affairs in existence since death because people are very reluctant to mention the names of the dead); and a connection is made between the infant's identity and the long line of ancestors who have possessed that name. Relationality, nondistinctiveness, and transience (the name is eternal, but the individual is not) are thus expressed. Nicknames, although more distinct, are more temporary. The other ways of referring to and addressing individuals, such as by personal pronouns and kinship terms, are even more relational and suppressive of individual identity. Spanish and Portuguese names do differ in certain ways from this characterization. A Tukanoan's Spanish name is given more or less spontaneously and has no necessary connection to anyone else (except to a Catholic saint, a connection very imperfectly understood).

Thus, in this book I have tried to show that although we can analyze Tukanoan social identity in terms of features and dimensions (i.e., in terms of gender, genealogy, exogamy, language, territory, etc.), identity is both structure and action. An important difference between Tukanoans and ourselves is our greater tendency to see identity as ''true'' or ''false'' in a rather absolute sense. This tendency is due in part to the greater possibility of being an imposter in the West; in Tukanoan society everyone knows or knows of everyone else. A second difference is a stress on consistency in the presence of legal or other kinds of formal requirements. For example, one cannot be married and single at the same time in the United States, but the situation is often more ambiguous in Tukanoan society. What one is in Tukanoan society – locationally, genealogically, maritally, and so on – is sometimes far from either categorical or necessarily true or false but something socially negotiated and either agreed upon or disputed and, if disputed, may or may not be resolved. My characterization of Tukanoan social identity as action and process is applicable here. Although we do encounter similar situations in our own society (see, for example, Domínguez's discussion of supposedly rigid racial identity [1977]), in general everyone in Western society would say that such problems are ultimately resolvable when all the ''facts'' are known – and that they *should* be resolved. Of course, such ''facts'' can often be negotiated. In Tukanoan society, however, such situations either do not arise (e.g., of being an imposter or, as occurs in Shakespeare's plays, of mistaken identity) or when they do exist they are not resolved. They simply fluctuate and remain in contradiction or fade from consciousness as interest in them diminishes. An example of this is the chronically disputed question of relative sib rank.

Thus, although a person, whether American or Bará, is obviously unique, the focus in the respective societies is quite different. Tukanoans do not focus on the particular individual as a unique intersection of attributes but emphasize one or a set of attributes, often opposing them to others. This opposition is determined by context and is thus transient; in other contexts it is irrelevant. Memberships in groups and categories are stressed or ignored, depending on the situation. At a Bar Mitzvah the individual is ritually passed from one category to another, as in all initiations, and certainly some features of his identity are irrelevant. But he as an individual is the focal point. Tukanoan initiation rites stress the individual participants as individuals far less; at some initiations even the extremely important exogamous group memberships of the initiates are irrelevant (S. Hugh-Jones, 1979). Therefore, the position of an individual Bará or other Tukanoan is not one of a lack of differentiation but is far less one of unique and permanent

237

differentiation than in our own and many other societies. Discussions abound in both scholarly and popular publications of the implications of this view for Western psychological identity, and specifically mental and spiritual health.

My final theme is the importance of regional orientation and awareness in Tukanoan social identity. The sources of this regional perspective are numerous, as we have seen throughout this book. Tukanoan social structure is a contributing factor, in particular its system of named patrilineal exogamous local sibs. This system has obviously helped to create an extension and complexity of interaction and cognitive orientation far beyond the local group. Tukanoan cosmology mirrors this complexity with, among other things, its tripartite symbolism of earth, sky, and river and their connections with specific language groups. Nearly all aspects of Tukanoan society and culture, from cosmology to language and speech to kinship terminology to marriage patterns, show the pervasiveness of this regional orientation. I have mentioned Tukanoans' pan-Vaupés (and beyond) perspective, discussing their interest in and knowledge about geography, showing their social geographical model to be one of an ever-increasing area with ever-increasing and gradual social and cultural differentiation but one which in theory has "no social, geographical, or linguistic limits" (C. Hugh-Jones, n.d.).

The portion of Tukanoan space we have examined is a rather large one, but I hope that I have illustrated some of the advantages in taking a regionally oriented approach. It is obvious that at least a rudimentary grasp of the regional organization of the Vaupés, both in interactional and cognitive terms, is essential for any comprehension of Tukanoan social identity.

An associated factor is the underlying cultural homogeneity that unifies the Vaupés region. On the strength of numerous pieces of evidence presented throughout the book, I have argued that this homogeneity is extensive, much more so than first appears to be the case – when one is initially confronted with the complex linguistic and "tribal" situation. I am calling the tribes by a new term, which (appropriately) places an emphasis not on a real cultural diversity but on a diversity that serves to organize interaction between basically similar social units. A games analogy suggests itself: Football needs easily distinguishable uniforms and Monopoly needs easily distinguishable tokens. Of course, in many respects the game played in the Vaupés is far more complex – life always is. For one thing, a true cultural diversity does exist, as exhibited by the regional variation described. Such diversity is sometimes due to simple geographical variation, sometimes due to differences in local history, and sometimes due to different degrees of acculturation.

But these factors do not completely explain the diversity occurring in language, in associations made in myths between animal and geographical symbolism and specific language groups, nor in the specialization in manufacture of certain artifacts. These differences, unlike diversity produced by underlying differences in cognitive models of the world, spring from underlying agreements about it. The basic patterns that give rise to these differences are shared –

including rules for action, assumptions about peoples' motives for following or not following the rules, symbolic representations of these rules and motives – in short, much of what life is all about. This does not mean that there is total agreement, for the participants in any social system never completely share their perceptions and understandings. The Vaupés is no exception, as the variability is organized into a rather large and complex system, and this is why one cannot talk about *Bará* or *Tukano* society, even though genuine cultural differences can be found between this pair, or any pair, of language groups. We must speak of *Tukanoan* society and culture because most of the differences we can observe (and they are actually far fewer than the similarities) are the result not of cultural barriers separating units but of cultural links uniting them into a single system.

A note on types of evidence

There is no question but that an epistemologically eclectic approach raises serious problems in research and interpretation. Still, to address the topic at hand, that of Tukanoan identity, such an approach is mandatory because many levels of behavior and thoughts – revealed in mythological vignettes, Tukanoans' comments about real-life cases, statistical descriptions of marriage patterns – pertain to the questions being asked. Extremely thorny problems arise, however, when trying to tie together information from such disparate sources, especially when the results from one type of research are not complete and therefore are suggestive rather than conclusive.

Usually, of course, pieces of information resting on each rung of the ladder reaching from "real" on-the-ground behavior to the most abstract, idealized structures somewhere in the stratosphere reinforce and clarify one another. Many examples of this have been offered in the preceding discussion. It is when they do not that problems of data reliability and validity and painful choices about interpretation arise. I have shown that some of the discrepancies in the data gathered so far are due to the extremely complex nature of the system itself and the genuine regional variability contained within it. The final picture of Tukanoan identity, a goal not yet attained, will incorporate and structure this variability, showing how it fits into the overall scheme.

Another source of complication stems from the fact that ideal and "real" are not simple polar opposites but the top and bottom rungs of a many-runged ladder. The "ideal" statements one obtains from informants about how things ought to be are not the only pieces of information from the idealist section of the ladder. Some cognitive rules for behavior, like grammatical rules, are accessible and can easily be verbalized. Others, at least equally determinative of behavior, are deeper and less likely to surface during interviews and similar types of research. Ample evidence of this has emerged in the discussions of Tukanoan–Makú interaction, male–female roles, and choices about marriage. *Makú* is a category in a postulated Tukanoan domain we might gloss as "beings" or perhaps

239

"human and humanlike beings." As members of this category, Makú serve as projections: They marry their sisters, have no shame, are "jaguar children," do not speak properly, and so forth. But really to understand the meaning of this, we obviously need to understand flesh-and-blood Makú. It is fortunate that two investigators, P. Silverwood-Cope and H. Reid, have provided material that takes us a long way toward that goal. We have discovered that Makú really are "professional hunters" and provide some Tukanoan settlements with forest-derived products for manufacturing ritual objects. Thus they merit their association with the forest. In other respects, however, the chasm between ideal and real is a wide one indeed. With this information we are far better equipped to understand the total nature of Tukanoan–Makú interaction. We are better able to understand the degree to which Makú are different because they actively maintain their distinctiveness (rather than its being due merely to the residue of different origins). It also is clear that some Makú are periodically assimilated into Tukanoan groups via a mechanism proscribed by the rules: intermarriage.

Looking at questions of identity from all angles – seeing the view from as many rungs of the ladder as possible – allows us to see more clearly where ideal and real do in fact fit together. For example, in the Papurí region, the marriage sample reveals a number of patterns that reinforce the information obtained about Tukanoan social structure from more idealist types of evidence. There is in fact extremely low settlement endogamy, all of it due to the effects of recent concerted efforts on the part of Catholic missionaries. The marriage sample also reveals virtually no language group endogamy for the Papurí–Tiquié region. Another finding was minimal (0.8 percent) polygyny.

Statistical patterns also support evidence obtained from other sources of data. For example, I have argued that Tukanoans have a regional orientation rather than a tightly constricted one of three or four neighboring longhouses. There is some evidence that Tukanoans maintain both narrow and wide perspectives; Tukanoans do think of neighboring longhouses as much more important than those far away: Close neighbors tend to be guests at festivals, for instance, and Tukanoans characterize the ideal marriage as one occurring between double cross-cousins – with the implication that this partner's natal longhouse is quite near. Still, the marriage sample revealed an average of roughly twenty-two linear miles between spouses' natal settlements, with an actual travel distance of many more miles. The average marriage, then, does not occur between neighboring settlements (of course many actual marriages do; this figure is the mean distance). It is also interesting to see how many marriages are "two-couple" (direct exchange) marriages, which supports the ideal Tukanoan version. Further work needs to be done on questions of kinship relatedness between spouses (what I have termed FZD and MBD marriage) and on phratric organization, but results obtained so far have shown several very promising leads.

Of course the relationship between "real" and "ideal" is complex: For example, interference from ideal conceptualizations of Tukanoan society undoubtedly influences informants' reports about actual marital behavior. More marriages with Makú undoubtedly have occurred than the single one I recorded (H. Reid, personal communication). Difficulty in obtaining information about the Tukano–Tukano marriage discussed in Chapter 7 is also due to interference from Tukanoan notions of proper marriage – this marriage, in fact, was described as not a marriage. Marriages that do not survive for long and are without children tend to be forgotten, a difference between our legalistic concept of what a marriage is and Tukanoans' processual one. This is the main reason I have not offered any quantitative data on divorce: Determining a rate of divorce in such a situation is extremely difficult to do.

The problems of incompleteness and difficulties in reconciling and synthesizing different types of data that do not of their own accord mesh together are not inconsiderable. But neither are they insurmountable. What I have been able to paint here is less than a complete portrait of Tukanoan society and culture, but the basic outline and some of the detail are clear. We have looked at the ecological setting, briefly examined the history of the area, and noted the important demographic, settlement, and economic features of Tukanoan society. With an understanding of these levels of the substratum, itself in part created and molded by the social system it supports, and with an understanding of the main features of Tukanoan social identity, we can begin to understand the entire social order in both behavioral and ideational terms. We can begin to comprehend the role of physical and social features of the landscape in formulating this social order: from rivers and forests all the way to Makú, whites, and wahtía. We understand far better the enormously complex system of languages, seeing them in their roles as communicators of both referential (semantic) and social information from and about their speakers. We begin to understand the logic of Tukanoan concepts of time and space as they pertain to identity, so that, for instance, we see the sense of signaling high status by referring to certain agnates as "grandchild." We understand far better the range and limits of this social order and are well on our way to comprehending the totality of Tukanoan experience. This experience differs for individual Tukanoans, depending on their location in the Vaupés territory, on whether they are Bará, Tukano, Tuyuka, or other, but it is a similar experience in most respects. More important, we can see that these differences are, at a fundamental level, understood and agreed upon by all Tukanoans as meaningful and essential differences that unite them all in an overarching system in a universe with its own multiple identities.

We have looked at slices of time and space in the Vaupés region, concentrating on understanding social identity in traditional Tukanoan society. "Traditional" is not a static concept, for it is obvious that Tukanoan society has always been evolving, during the pre-Columbian and postcontact periods. Still, as pointed out in the preceding chapter, Tukanoans now face unprecedented change at unprecedented rates, with the tragic result that traditional Tukanoan culture is no longer able to adapt and instead is becoming extinct. The final polarity in Tukanoan

241

social identity – the one of Tukanoan–white – is, like the others, couched in terms of absolute and categorical contrasts, but not simply because such contrasts are meaningful in Tukanoan conceptualizations of identity. Unlike the contrasts of Tukanoan–Makú or male–female, for example, this contrast is not so much used by Tukanoans in their own construction of their world view but is one imposed upon them. The contrast is immense and the cultural barriers are all too real. Many of the differences are incomprehensible to Tukanoans, and others are all too comprehensible, for they convey unmistakable messages about unworthiness, ugliness, powerlessness, shame, ignorance, and the advisability of dependency. Soon we will have one more instance of the label ''traditional'' referring to a past time and an extinct culture rather than to a group of people alive and surviving with their understanding of the world and their place in it intact. I hope that these pages give some glimpse into the genius of Tukanoan culture and the tragedy of this loss, both theirs and ours.

Notes

Preface

1 In general, *Vaupés* refers to the region and *Tukanoan* to the sedentary, riverine populations living there. Except in this Preface, Tukanoan personal names are pseudonyms; site names are not, because many of them have changed since 1970.
2 See, for instance, the sensitive and perceptive accounts by Berreman (1972), Briggs (1970), Maybury-Lewis (1965), Powdermaker (1966), and Rabinow (1977).
3 I was granted permission to do fieldwork by the Instituto Colombiano de Antropología on the condition that I supply $10,000 worth of equipment (in the form of a small airplane) for its anthropological projects. This was unacceptable to the National Science Foundation, which was to fund the project, even if the $10,000 were to come from another source. Several of the restrictions on foreign anthropologists carrying out research in Colombia were eased in 1979.

1. Purpose and organization of the book

1 For discussions of hunter–gatherer populations and regional organization, see Leacock, 1955, pp. 31–47, and Lee and DeVore, 1968, especially pp. 150–57.
2 It is also true that *tribe* has been used to characterize Vaupés social units other than the language-affiliated ones; see Jackson, 1972, pp. 8–18; S. Hugh-Jones, 1979, pp. 22–24; and Sorensen, 1967, for discussions of this.
3 Reported during a symposium on ''Amazonian Marriage Practices'' at the 1973 annual meeting of the American Anthropological Association, New Orleans.

2. Introduction to the Central Northwest Amazon

1 Most of the primary data discussed here were gathered in the Colombian half of the Central Northwest Amazon, resulting in the book's having an overall Colombian perspective. Generalizations made about the entire region are to be seen as more provisional when applied to the Brazilian sector, but for reasons of simplicity, *Central Northwest Amazon* and *Vaupés* are used interchangeably.
2 See Goldman, 1963, p. 14; Koch-Grünberg, 1909–10, vol. 2, p. 65.
3 For information on specific Vaupés languages, see Brüzzi Alves da Silva, 1962; Koch-Grünberg, 1909–10; Kok, 1921–22; West and Welch, 1967, 1972; and Waltz

and Wheeler, 1970, on Tukano; Waltz and Waltz, 1972, on Uanano; Smith and Smith, 1971, on Southern Barasano (Barasana); Stolte and Stolte, 1971, on Northern Barasano (Bará); and Salser, 1971, on Cubeo; See Jacopin, 1972, on the status of Yukuna, Matapí, Letuama, and Tanimuca. Wycliffe Bible Translators / Summer Institute of Linguistics, Inc., dedicates itself to translating the Bible into all the languages of the world. Founded by William Cameron Townsend in 1942, its international headquarters is in Santa Ana, California (Wallis and Bennett, 1959; Hvalkof and Aaby, 1981).

4   I am extremely grateful to S. Hugh-Jones for help in thinking these points through.

5   See Reichel-Dolmatoff (1975, pp. 62–63) for a discussion of the history of the region. See also Coudreau, 1887, and Humboldt, 1822, vol. 7, p. 383; vol. 8, p. 145. The history of missions is mentioned in Goldman (1948, 1963); Koch-Grünberg (1909–10, vol. 1); Misiones del Vaupés (1966); and Stradelli (1890, p. 433).

6   Misiones del Vaupés, 1966, p. 13, quoted in Reichel-Dolmatoff, 1971, p. 7.

7   New Tribes Mission (NTM), founded in 1942 by Paul W. Fleming, has its headquarters in Sanford, Florida, and currently over 1,500 missionary members. "According to an NTM leaflet: 'The New Tribes Mission is a fundamental, non-denominational faith missionary society, composed of born-again believers and dedicated to the evangelization of unreached tribal peoples . . .'" (Wright and Swenson, 1981, pp. 3–4). For a discussion of nativistic movements in the region, see Goldman, 1963, p. 16; Van Emst, 1966b; and Wright, 1981.

8   Sources on the Makú include Biocca, 1965; Cathcart, 1973; Koch-Grünberg, 1906; MacCreagh, 1926; MacGovern, 1927; Reid, 1979; Silverwood-Cope, 1972; Tastevin, 1923; Terribilini and Terribilini, 1961; Van Emst, 1966; A. R. Wallace, 1889/1972 ; and Whiffen, 1915.

3. The longhouse

1   This contrasts somewhat with Goldman's description of Cubeo longhouses and surroundings, which, he says, are oriented toward the river such that "Along a well-populated river such as the Cuduiarí the communities resemble rough-shaped beads widely spaced along the thin strand of the sinuously curving river" (1963, p. 28).

2   See Goldman, regarding poorer Cubeo communities, which tend to locate their fields closer to the house. Fields are always more distant in the more "prosperous and prideful communities" (1963, p. 29). In the Pirá-paraná, fields are adjacent to the longhouse clearing (C. Hugh-Jones, 1979, p. 28; S. Hugh-Jones, 1979, pp. 43–44).

3   The longhouse and its environs and the symbolism of architecture and space are discussed more fully in Goldman, 1963, pp. 39–42; C. Hugh-Jones, 1977, 1979; S. Hugh-Jones, 1977, 1979; Moser and Tayler, 1963, pp. 443–45; Reichel-Dolmatoff, 1971, pp. 104–09; and Rodriguez Lamus, 1958.

4. Economic and political life

1   See Silverwood-Cope (1972, pp. 83–86) for a description of an eel-catching technique found only among the Makú. This is noteworthy because they generally have a reputation for being nonriverine people.

2   S. Hugh-Jones (personal communication) states that the Makuna and Taiwano eat snakes.

3   I.e., Old Arturo went into trance. I am not certain whether this longhouse is an animal longhouse in the sense described earlier.

4   Further discussion of forest- and hunting-related topics can be found in Århem, 1976; Dufour and Zarucchi, 1979; Goldman, 1963; C. Hugh-Jones, 1979; S. Hugh-Jones, 1979; Koch-Grünberg, 1909–10; Reichel-Dolmatoff, 1971; Silverwood-Cope, 1972; and Torres Laborde, 1969.

5   See, for example, the debate regarding settlement pattern and cultural evolution occuring in situ or as a result of migration (Carneiro, 1960; Lathrap, 1970; Meggers, 1973). See Johnson, 1974, on the question of carrying capacity.

6   See, for example, discussions in W. L. Allen and Holshouser de Tizón, 1973; Denevan, 1971; and Harris, 1971.

7   Population numbers vs. resource availability has been the topic of much recent debate (cf. Beckerman, 1979; Gross, 1975; Hames, 1980b; Ross, 1978).

8   Bitter manioc is so called because of its high prussic acid content; this acid must be washed and leached out or cooked sufficiently to render it nontoxic. All varieties of manioc are the same species, *Manihot esculenta* (see Rogers, 1963, and Schwerin, 1971).

9   For an excellent and comprehensive discussion of the entire manioc process, see C. Hugh-Jones, 1979, 174 ff.

10 C. Hugh-Jones (personal communication) comments that this does not totally eliminate guests' being a burden on their hosts. She observed a number of cases of visiting freeloading relatives, who were an undeniable drain on the resources of the families putting them up.

11 It should be noted that the military reasons for staying together in a well-fortified longhouse have disappeared, and this is doubtless also a contributing factor in the current widespread disruption of longhouse units.

5. Vaupés social structure

1   Although I have no real data on why this trend has occurred, I find the arguments correlating uxorilocality with periodic absence of the son-in-law (see Helms, 1970; Casselberry and Valavanes, 1976) and with the father-in-law's availing himself of the labor of the son-in-law and trying to have the balance of power in his favor (see Oberg, 1955; T. Turner, 1979) persuasive and probably applicable to the Tukanoan case. Of course, all of this must be related to the general breakdown in traditional norms in the region as well as why agnatic groups of males are no longer as adaptive as they apparently once were.

2   There are no longer any longhouses in Brazil (Howard Reid, personal communication).

3   See Goldman, 1963, pp. 90–113, for a discussion of Cubeo sib ancestors as distinct personalities. Discussions of Vaupés sib structure can also be found in Bidou, 1976, pp. 135–80; Brüzzi Alves da Silva, 1966, pp. 84–123; C. Hugh-Jones, 1979, pp. 22–31; and Reichel-Dolmatoff, 1971, pp. 189–201.

4   C. Hugh-Jones (1979, pp. 28–29) discusses evidence for several sibs being located at a single site in separate longhouses in earlier times. She notes, however, that this may always have been an ideal only and that then, as now, sibs were located along a stretch of river at different settlement sites.

5   *Pinó kumoa,* sometimes described as a submarine-like vessel, looking like an anaconda, with the ancestors inside. See Kumu and Kenhíri (1980) for a drawing of a Desana anaconda canoe.

6   Many of these characteristics apply to the Northwest Amazon as a whole, although data are lacking for a number of societies. The Tukuna are exceptions to items 2 and 4 in this summary.

7 This is similar to the argument presented by Barth (1969) when discussing ethnic groups and boundaries and the processes of polarization and differentiation occurring among increasingly structurally similar social groups.

8 See Sorensen, 1970, p. v: "The exogamy among these tribes, reinforced by the cultural identification of tribe with language, must supply the energy that keeps each language distinct and alive."

9 C. Hugh-Jones (1979, p. 18) also notes the use of language as a way of talking about descent.

10 Cf. C. Hugh-Jones (1979, pp. 283–86) and Århem (1981, p. 345).

11 Space does not permit a full discussion here (cf. Århem, 1976; Bidou, 1976; C. Hugh-Jones, 1979; S. Hugh-Jones, 1979). Briefly, the Hugh-Joneses have classified the Pirá-paraná into seven exogamous phratries. Although language normally correlates with exogamy, there are a few exceptions: (1) some speakers of Makuna belong to the phratry Makuna, whereas others belong to the Barasana phratry; (2) some speakers of the "Barasano del Sur" language (Summer Institute of Linguistics terminology) belong to the Taiwano phratry while others belong to the Barasana phratry; (3) a Tatuyo-speaking sib belongs to the Bará phratry; and (4) an Arawak-speaking sib belongs to the Bará phratry. The following section offers a somewhat different treatment of the concept of exogamous phratry, which also attempts to make sense of the Tukanoan tendency to include speakers of a different language into a single exogamous group.

12 C. Hugh-Jones (1979, p. 21) has a slightly different definition: the phratry "is an association of Exogamous Groups united by the rule of exogamy but not occupying a continuous area." Cf. also S. Hugh-Jones, 1979, pp. 24–25.

13 For a more comprehensive discussion of the pahkó-mahkara set of terms, see Chapter 7 and Jackson, 1977.

14 I fully concur with C. Hugh-Jones's warning that "it is impossible to arrange Exogamous Groups into three neat and mutually exclusive categories on this basis, just as it is impossible to arrange Exogamous Groups into a pan-Vaupés phratric pattern" (1979, p. 36).

15 For a discussion of Bará kinship terminology with respect to this, see Jackson, 1977.

16 Three Tuyuka men out of 145 were married to Desana women; 2 Tuyuka women out of 112 were married to Desana men in the marriage sample I collected. Brüzzi Alves da Silva (1966. p. 90) also notes no Desana–Tuyuka marriages.

17 Brüzzi Alves da Silva (1966, p. 87) states that some Tukano said that the Bará are their *paxkö-ro* (grandparents), and that he could not find the reason for this designation because there is no allusion to this in their legends, but it is certain that intermarriage is proscribed.

18 This is not a translation of an actual quotation, but a condensation of several conversations.

19 See Jackson, 1976; Jackson and Romney, n.d. A. Kimball Romney analyzed the marriage data and derived the model in Figure 5; I gratefully acknowledge his interest and contributions. Figure 5 represents marriage preferences as they appear after removing the effects of the size of the groups involved, using a technique developed by Romney (1971, pp. 191–213).

20 His list of sibs indicates that this group is Bará.

21 For a discussion of differences in outlook and practices in a sample of lowland South American societies illustrating just how varied their inward or outward focus can be, see Shapiro (n.d.).

22 If such a word can be applied to hostilities as traditionally practiced; "raiding" and

"feuding" are perhaps more indicative of the actual situation. Cf. Service, 1968, p. 160, on Y̦anomamö "warfare"; also see Fried, Harris, and Murphy, 1968, p. xvii.

23 However, it is my impression that Bará and Tuyuka, at least those of the Inambú River, are more forest-oriented than the Cubeo as described by Goldman. His statement about the Cubeo that "the forest is undifferentiated terrain" does not apply to the people of Pꞵmanaka buro.

24 See, for example, the discussions of Colson (1973), Coppens (1971), and Thomas (1972) on the Gran Sabana of Venezuela; Harner (1972), Oberem (1974), and Whitten (1978) on the Ecuadorian Montaña; Bodley (1972) on the Campa; Lathrap (1973) on the Shipibo; Morey and Morey (1974) and Leeds (1964) on the Orinoco llanos; and Basso (1973) on the upper Xingú.

25 Speech differences used for marking exogamous unilineal units have been reported for New Guinea (Sankoff, 1968) and Australia (Owen, 1965). See also Hymes, 1968.

6. Kinship

1 *Kinship* in this chapter is to be seen as interchangeable with *relationship* as a label for the set of terms that show consanguineal and affineal relationships. (See Needham, 1966, for a discussion of *alliance systems of social classification*, which purportedly have nothing to do with kinship, genealogically speaking; a good case can be made for Bará as well [see Jackson, 1977].) I use the term *kinship* because the naming and pronominal systems also show kinds of relationships among Tukanoans and because I use the term *relationship* in other contexts. My use of *kinship* does not necessarily imply that Bará "kin terms" are ultimately derived from genealogical relations.

2 The discrepancy between *Bará* kinship terminology and *Tukanoan* society is unavoidable in a kinship system involving marriage between patrilineal descent groups identified with different languages. Also, classic Dravidian terminologies do not distinguish between types of cross-cousins or between matrilateral and patrilateral parallel cousins, as does Bará (Jackson, 1977), but Bará is still to be seen as a variant of the basic Dravidian type.

3 I stress the "± mother Bará" feature because the transcription of the Bará terms with FZS, MBS, etc., although a good literal gloss, can be misleading. When the MBS, MBD terms are used, they really are not referring so much to the fact that a child is the son or daughter of an MB but to the fact that the child's mother is *not* Bará; it is a default category and avoided wherever possible (Jackson, 1977).

4 For a discussion of the long history of both approaches and the debates between the two schools of thought, see Buchler and Selby, 1968; Goodenough, 1970; Leach, 1958; Lounsbury, 1956, 1965; Needham, 1971; Scheffler, 1966, 1973; D. M. Schneider, 1965, 1972.

5 Space does not allow a presentation of all the myth material I collected. My major focus of research was not on mythology, and I make no claim regarding the completeness of the myths collected or the methodological rigor used when eliciting them. Most of the myths were gathered from non-Spanish-speaking Bará men and were written down with the help of Lino, Mario's second son, who lived near Mitú and spoke Spanish.

6 Both mother and children show progressive dehumanization in their speech, an important point in this and a number of other myths. The mother talks to her wahtí husband in his language, thereby showing her accommodation to him and the accompanying loss of human characteristics. In the end, while her children are

accusing her of loving Namakuru too much, their dialogue turns into pure bird talk. The same situation is portrayed in the end of the Kahpéa õrẽro story: The protagonist's relatives turn into monkeys after losing their eyes, and the myth ends with an imitation of their monkey talk.

7 The dilemma of the necessary but risky association with affines, who, by definition, are never one's "own kind," and for this reason alone somewhat dangerous, frequently appears in myths.

8 With perhaps far-reaching consequences (see Chodorow, 1978; Dinnerstein, 1976).

9 Until this happened, the fight was mostly screaming and rather ineffectual fisticuffs (at least compared with the experts in U.S. films and television). Use of any weapon, however, is deadly serious. After the fight, the eldest son left the settlement for some weeks.

10 Goldman (1963, p. 114) finds Cubeo suffixes distinguishing lineage, sib, and phratry siblings. In Bará, true siblings *can* be distinguished from patrilateral parallel cousins, but a more lengthy construction must be used to be more precise about other degrees of sibling closeness.

11 *Poná* glosses as "children of one set of parents." *Mahkara* glosses as "people." Thus, the term *pahkó-poná* is usually used with reference to a single ego's set of matrilateral parallel cousins, whereas *pahkó-mahkara* is a more inclusive term, referring, for instance, to a settlement's position vis à vis another settlement or at times to an entire language group.

12 The one exception is the seldom-used *teñara*, "in-law-people," from *teñū̃/-ó*, "brother-/sister-in-law."

13 The tactic of showing the essence of a relationship by picturing it in its closest terms, even when this is impossible in actual life, occurs frequently in myths. The Namakuru myth is an illustration of the conflicts and dissimilarities in the uterine half-sibling relationship between totally human children and their deer-child half-brother. In another myth, referred to earlier, the pahkó-mahkū̃/-ó set's affine-of-affine meaning is portrayed by showing the relationship between two husbands of the same wife.

14 See Goldman, 1963, on ceremonial friendship and S. Hugh-Jones, 1979, pp. 114–15, on ritual kinship in connection with male initiation.

7. Marriage

1 Several ethnographic and geographic factors place limitations on gathering such data in the Vaupés. One is the difficulty of travel, which placed constraints on my ability to collect and cross-check firsthand information. The multilingualism of the region is another. A third is the absence of names of local descent groups (when not coterminous with sibs), confusing in an area in which residence sites are temporary and a significant proportion of people do not currently reside where they are "supposed" to according to the patrilocal rule of residence. A fourth related factor is the built-in slippage between named social groups, e.g., sibs, and the people who constitute these groups. A fifth limitation is the general taboo on pronouncing personal Tukanoan names, in particular those of the dead.

2 See Jackson, 1972, pp. 127–34. for further discussion of the sample.

3 See C. Hugh-Jones, 1979, p. 104, and Silverwood-Cope, 1972, p. 194, in this regard.

4 I speak of exchanging sisters rather than exchanging brothers because, first, this is the way Tukanoans talk about it, and second, it is the women who change residence at marriage. This usage in no way is meant to imply that women are to be thought of as

pawns or "rubbish" (Fox, 1967, p. 117) as has been suggested for other strongly patrilineal systems. The Ya̧nomamö (Chagnon, 1968; Shapiro, 1972) speak of women in derogatory terms; this and the manipulation and coercion of women and the frequency of polygyny are not nearly as characteristic of Tukanoan society.

5 Out-migration and perhaps other factors have resulted in many unmarried women in mission towns. Nuns told me that these young women could find no men because they did not want to leave the mission towns to marry "pagan" Tukanoans.

6 One of the goals of this book is to illustrate just how complex decision making about marriage usually is. The above comments are not to be seen as for or against either the "structures" or "sentiments" position in the polemics on "proximate" and "final" causes, because both types of argument are far too simplistic when they claim to explain marriage behavior (as opposed to marriage norms). See Homans and Schnieder, 1955; Lévi-Strauss, 1969; Needham, 1962.

7 See Brüzzi Alves da Silva, 1962, p. 414; Giacone, 1949, p. 21; C. Hugh-Jones, 1979, pp. 64, 69, 93ff., for further discussion of mock capture of wives and actual raiding for women.

8 With the exception of the Tikuna (Cardoso de Oliveira, 1961, 1964).

9 See C. Hugh-Jones (1979, p. 58) regarding close agnatic marriage in a Barasana "servant" sib; also see my discussion of Makú marriage in Chapter 8.

10 For further discussion of these and other measurements, see Jackson, 1972, 1976.

11 This is the Spanish version of Portuguese **caboclo,** "backwoodsman," but in the Vaupés it means half-breed.

12 Just how important a role environmental constraints play in the marriage systems of small-scale societies is a topic of current debate. Some authors argue that the ecological and demographic givens *cause* the particular system being examined. In this view, other factors (e.g., rules of marriage prescription or preference) are "epiphenomena" (Gilbert and Hammel, 1966) or "idealizations of the parameters of performance" (Lehman, 1974). No one would disagree that environmental givens set limits on any abstract marriage system structure, as well as forming the substratum to its design (that is, are determinative in a broadly conceived way – e.g., elementary systems are found in societies with certain levels of techno-socio-cultural integration, and complex systems are found in others). Some excellent studies address themselves to correlations existing between environmental features and marriage patterns – for example, between rainfall and section system development in Australia (Birdsell, 1953; Yengoyan, 1968). And certain demographic variables (related to birth rate, or relative age of spouses) seem to set definite limits on the presence and operation of particular marriage patterns (Gilbert and Hammel, 1966). It would be good if more studies of this kind were carried out among tropical forest horticulturalist societies, such as those found in lowland South America and highland New Guinea (see Glasse and Meggitt, 1965, for promising beginnings).

8. Tukanoans and Makú

1 This discussion of the Makú, particularly in the areas of ecology and social structure, has profited greatly from criticisms of an earlier draft from Stephen Hugh-Jones and Howard Reid.

2 Cathcart (1973), a SIL linguist, uses the term *Cacua* ("people") for all Makú. She states that Makú is a single language with two principle dialects (1973, p. 101). Reid (personal communication) states that at least one, and probably as many as four, different languages of the Makú family are spoken on the lower west tributaries of the Rio Negro and north tributaries of the Japurá–Caquetá (personal communica-

tion; see also his doctoral dissertation on the Hupdü Makú [1979]). Mason classifies Makú as an "independent" (1950, p. 257), whereas Greenberg places it within the Macro–Tukanoan subfamily of the Andean–Ecuatorial family (1960). Word lists are available in Biocca, 1965; Giacone, 1955; Koch-Grünberg, 1906; and Rivet and Tastevin, 1920.

3 Summaries of research on the Makú are found in Biocca, 1965, and Silverwood-Cope, 1972, p. 312. Investigators giving firsthand accounts of contact with Makú include Biocca (1965), Giacone (1949, 1955), Goldman (1963, p. 70), Koch-Grünberg (1906), MacCreagh (1926), McGovern (1927), Spruce (1908, p. 344), and Whiffen (1915, p. 59–61). Silverwood-Cope (1972) and Reid (1979) are the only investigators to carry out full-scale investigations of the Makú. Other sources of information on the Makú include Brüzzi Alves da Silva, 1962; Galvão, 1959; Moser and Tayler, 1963; Nimuendajú, 1950; Reichel-Dolmatoff, 1967, 1971; Schultz, 1959; Van Emst, 1966a, 1966b; and Whiffen, 1915.

4 See, for example, Cardoso de Oliveira and de Castro Faria, 1971; Hymes, 1968; Lathrap, 1968; and Martin, 1969.

5 See, for example, Koch-Grünberg, 1906; MacCreagh, 1926; McGovern, 1927, p. 357; Silverwood-Cope, 1972; and Whiffen, 1915, pp. 59–61. I never heard a Tukanoan classify Makú in physical terms.

6 Examples of such a subsistence mode are the Aché (Guayaki) described by Clastres (1972), the Akuriyó (Kloos, 1977), and the Cuiva (Arcand, 1972). Many groups who have been classified as South American hunter–gatherers in fact either practice horticulture, engage in regularized and fairly frequent food exchanges with horticulturalist neighbors, or both. Examples include the Sirionó (Holmberg, 1969), and the Yaruro (Leeds, 1964). See Hames, 1978, on the question of a purely hunting–gathering existence in Amazonia.

7 McGovern (1927, p. 183) reports exogamous units among the Makú.

8 Including my information on the Bará and that in C. Hugh-Jones, 1979; S. Hugh-Jones, 1974; Langdon, 1975; and Reichel-Dolmatoff, 1971.

9 For a different description of Desana orientation toward hunting, see Reichel-Dolmatoff, 1971, p. 17.

10 This is a similar situation to that described by Turnbull (1965) for Pygmy–Bantu relations.

11 H. Reid (personal communication) notes that such seeming "poverty" is a typical trick of the Hupdü, in order to scrounge more items from their Tukanoan hosts.

12 Makú as cigar lighters is a frequently heard description in the Vaupés (see Galvão, 1959, p. 42), and it is interesting to note a parallel classification for the lowest-ranked sib in those Tukanoan language groups that are characterized by a hierarchy of five ranked sibs. In this scheme, each position is labeled with an occupation: headman, head dancer, warrior, shaman, and cigar lighter (C. Hugh-Jones, 1977; S. Hugh-Jones, 1977).

13 See Fock, 1963, p. 153, for a similar account of a girl taking care of children among the Wai Wai.

14 H. Reid (personal communication) is of the opinion that such a personalized servant–master relationship is rare and represents the Tukanoan ideal rather than the norm.

15 Reichel-Dolmatoff discusses the sexual side of Tukanoan–Makú relationships the most thoroughly, noting that "close emotional and sexual relationships" exist between Desana and Makú and that Makú are "not only servants but represent the female element, a sexual object, upon which very ambivalent ideas and emotions are projected" (1971, pp. 19–20). For Reichel-Dolmatoff, the Desana exhibit a very

marked sexual repression, are puritanical, and view sexual relations "with great fear and anxiety." Unfortunately, he does not give any concrete evidence for this, in particular whether Desana sexual impulses toward Makú are always repressed and sublimated or are ever acted upon.

16 This is confirmed in all the literature on the Makú, with the exception of Whiffen, who says "the Makú will intermarry with any . . ." (1915, p. 61). H. Reid (personal communication), however, who knows of about eight Makú women married to Tukanoans, states that ideally Makú do not mind Makú women marrying Tukanoan men (although at times they object in practice), but that the opposite is disapproved of.

17 Perhaps the only division of labor among the Tukanoans that is the result of qualitative differences between the people concerned is the sexual one.

18 See Barth, 1969; Haaland, 1969; Knutsson, 1969; and Seligmann and Seligmann, 1911, for accounts of these types of "symbiotic" relationships. Both Lee (1968, p. 31) and Woodburn (1968, p. 52) report regularized trading between hunter–gatherers (!Kung Bushmen and Hadza, respectively) and agriculturalists. The agriculturalists requested certain foodstuffs either because they were considered a delicacy, such as honey, or because crop failure had brought about widespread famine.

19 A good demonstration of this happening in an unconscious way among French-Canadians is found in Lambert et al., 1960.

9. The role of language and speech in Tukanoan identity

1 "When specific categories of people are identified with specific speech varieties, such varieties will come to symbolize the cultural values associated with certain features of the non-linguistic environment" (Gumperz, 1970, p. 10).

2 Blom notes that "differences in speech between various kinds of groups that are in frequent contact are not in themselves responsible for the establishment and maintenance of social boundaries. These differences rather *reflect* features of social organization through a process of social codification" (1969, p. 83).

3 See G. Miller, 1963, p. 45, regarding the need for efficiency and redundance in messages.

4 E.g., "How do we explain the fact that language conflict between competing intergroup aspirations and interethnic stereotypes is symbolized by what to the linguist are almost trivial linguistic differences?" (Gumperz, 1972, p. 14)

5 See also Leach (1954, p. 51), who discusses the situation in Highland Burma: "In such conditions (*gumlao*), I suggest, where each petty village leader is prepared to assert that he is as good as his neighbor, we may expect to find an obstinately persistent linguistic factionalism even in the fact of nominally centralized political authority."

6 For example, the use of the expression "money whitens" or the recent declaration by South Africa that Japanese were "honorary Caucasians" and thus could sit in the front of the bus.

7 "Matched guise" studies conducted by W. E. Lambert and associates (1960) of attitudes toward groups of people as "revealed" through their language and speech are quite enlightening. Ferguson notes that Arab attitudes toward other Arabs and the non-Islamic world can be derived from investigating their attitudes toward Arabic itself (1959, pp. 75–82; see also Irvine, 1974).

8 Although it is also true that many systems seem to tolerate or actually to exploit such ambiguity: See Leach's example of an individual in Highland Burma whose family had been both Kachin and Shan for some seventy years (1954, p. 2).

9 For a discussion of other topics related to multilingualism research and the Vaupés situation, see Jackson, 1974, pp. 53–59, 63–64.
10 This is also supported by my own rather skimpy data on these groups. In 21 Piratapuya marriages (8 men, 13 women) and 12 Uanano marriages (4 men, 8 women), no intermarriage occurred between Piratapuya and Uanano.
11 Mason (1950) considers Bará and Tuyuka to be the same language, as well as Piratapuya and Uanano.
12 *Yéripuna,* "soul" or "life force," was described to me as the *sound* of the heartbeat; when it is silent the person is dead. In a myth about Tapir, an association is made between the loss of his voice and his ceasing to be a feared predator. Musical instruments give power; in the story of José in Chapter 4, the peccaries become weak and without courage when the shaman Old Arturo takes their horns away. The association between speech and power occurs in many lowland South American societies. For example, Harner (1972, p. 139) notes that an indication that a Jívaro has acquired an *arutam* soul is his changed speech, with the consequence that visits between Jívaro men are characterized by near-shouting. If a man is lacking in forcefulness of speech, it is a sign that his *arutum* soul has been taken away.

10. Male and female identity

1 See Århem, 1981; Goldman, 1940, 1963, 1964, 1976; S. Hugh-Jones, 1979; and Reichel-Dolmatoff, 1971.
2 See, for example, discussions by Murphy (1956); Murphy and Murphy (1974); J. Shapiro (n.d.); and Siskind (1973a; 1973b).
3 See Ortner, 1974, for a discussion of this concept. Also see Lamphere, 1977; MacCormack and Strathern, 1980; and Quinn, 1977, for critiques. C. Hugh-Jones (1979) also makes this distinction, variously distinguishing between "natural" and "social," "spiritual," or "ritual," depending on the context.
4 Men smoke fish obtained during fish poisoning expeditions and the large joints of game. They also help brew chicha before a festival.
5 Very seldom, however, is any activity *completely* thought of in terms of symbols related to only one sex. This dual sexual symbolism is especially true of the most sacred symbols in Tukanoan culture. Concrete phenomena can represent male or female elements, depending on context and on the relationship between them and their surroundings.
6 "However, the economic tasks of the sexes are not balanced in such a way that they are equal and opposite any more than men and women in Pirá-paraná are equal and opposite" (C. Hugh-Jones, personal communication).
7 See, C. Hugh-Jones (1979) for a discussion relating this kind of "social periodicity" brought about by the rules of exogamy to women's natural periodicity with respect to two phases of the menstrual cycle.
8 The reciprocity is direct and does not involve certain language groups being classified as "masculine" or "feminine" because of a greater tendency to hunt or fish (fishing being considered more "feminine"), as Reichel-Dolmatoff states (1971, pp. 17–18).
9 See Bamberger, 1974; Bolens, 1967; S. Hugh-Jones, 1974; Reichel-Dolmatoff, 1971.
10 C. Hugh-Jones (personal communication) has heard of one or two cases of women doing some types of shamanism for infants.
11 This example is from C. Hugh-Jones, 1979, p. 257. Domestic fire is a symbol of women's creativity in childbearing.
12 In particular, Reichel-Dolmatoff's description of the Desana with regard to sex does

252

not fit with my impressions. Desana are characterized by "a very marked sexual repression . . . puritan trend in which all that refers to sexual relations is viewed with great fear and anxiety. Sex is the greatest danger in life . . . The percentage of homosexuals, female as well as male, seems to be quite high, as well as the incidence of sexual assaults" (1971, pp. 19–20). His statement that Tukano women use herbal concoctions which "in varying concentrations, cause temporary sterility" (1976, p. 312), allowing women to space births, is not corroborated by my information. Sexual abstinence is prescribed following birth, and, insofar as this is practiced, probably accounts for most birth spacing. The existence of infanticide (see Chapter 5 and C. Hugh-Jones, 1979, p. 128) also seems to argue against knowledge of effective chemical contraceptives.

13 See Collier and Rosaldo (1981) on this theme; because an important aspect of their analysis depends on uxorilocality, it does not really apply to the Vaupés situation. See also Gregor, 1974; Murphy and Murphy, 1974; and Siskind, 1973a, for comparative material on the Amazon Basin, and Brown and Buchbinder, 1976; Langness, 1967; Lindenbaum, 1972; and Meggitt, 1964, for material on the New Guinea Highlands.

14 C. Hugh-Jones (personal communication) discusses this at length, for example: "Pirá-paraná culture arranges sexual symbols in a nesting system so that each unit upon which we choose to focus has an overall sexual identity, although it contains within it both male and female elements which may be separated out and combined with other elements from other units."

15 Many studies have pointed out that a strict sexual segregation can result in women having substantial power and autonomy, both because men are not around to keep women under surveillance and because the resulting complementarity of tasks means that men are dependent on women as well as vice versa. See, for example, Brown, 1970b; Friedl, 1975; Murphy and Murphy, 1974; Netting, 1969; Quinn, 1977; and Rosaldo, 1974.

16 See Goldman, 1963, 1977, 1981, for discussions of incipient stratification in the Vaupés.

17 Still, this should not be overstated. The relationship between Makú as servant and women as servant is not clear (see Reichel-Dolmatoff, 1971). See also S. Hugh-Jones, 1977, p. 213, with respect to a "servant" sib (the lowest-ranked in a series of five positions) being represented in part by women and children in the *he wi* (male initiation) ritual, and the association of this rank with Makú. A special flute played by the initiates is described as being the "wives" of the other horns. See also Brüzzi Alves da Silva, 1962, p. 307, in this regard.

18 See Chapter 2; also see Chagnon, 1968; Gross, 1975; Harris, 1975, pp. 338–41; Ross, 1978; Siskind, 1973b; and Shapiro, 1972, for a variety of explanations.

11. Tukanoans' place in the cosmos

1 I collected no firsthand evidence of the occasional geronticide reported by C. Hugh-Jones (1979, p. 108).

2 The relationship between the sound of breathing and the heartbeat and death – or, as is indicated here, stages of death – is very important. In many ways, sound serves as a symbol of life, vigor, and growth.

3 See Amorim, 1926/28, which includes a description of a woman influential enough to have her body returned to her natal longhouse group for burial.

4 C. Hugh-Jones (1979) offers a comprehensive discussion of two quite distinct elements of dead-spirit houses: One is connected to the physical death of the person

(and concerned with underground, rotten liquid, and generally unpleasant and sinister features) and the other concerns the places where the spirit goes – the ancestral dead-spirit houses, which might be spoken of as "under" a rapids, for example, but do not ever have an association with yellow earth and under*ground*.

5 Space does not permit a more thorough description of ritual paraphernalia, musical instruments, or other objects associated with festivals. For a very comprehensive description of He wi and *He rika soria wi*, the festivals associated with male initiation, see S. Hugh-Jones, 1979.

6 Two words are used to describe these levels. Bará distinguishes between *yehpá*, "ground," "earth," "flat"; and *tutí*, any layer in the five-tiered universe.

7 Unfortunately, some of the discussion about cosmology took place during the summer of 1970, when the Apollo program landed a man on the moon. The headman's second son was visiting after a long period of living in Mitú. He spoke fairly good Spanish and listened to the radio constantly. I was asked a number of questions about the moon flight, and this probably influenced the willingness of people at Púmanaka buro to talk about how they conceived of the heavens.

8 No one knew anything about solar eclipses. although they had heard that such things do occur.

9 This assertion seems contradicted by one particular type of wahtí (*wahtí-biyo*) that rapes girls going through the menarche if they should enter the forest but, I was explicitly told, does not devour them; however, one translation of its name is "like-a-wahtí."

10 The *ümüaro wahtí*, however, has the body of a howler monkey and the head of a human being.

12. Tukanoans and the outside world

1 See International Work Group for Indigenous Affairs, 1976, and Jackson, 1978, n.d.-c: the presence of uranium in the territory of Roraima, Brazil, has been known since 1954.

2 A sawmill at the *Internado* (Catholic boarding school) above Mitú produces milled lumber for local use and provides a few jobs to Tukanoans.

3 For a more thorough description of the rubber-gathering industry in the Amazon Basin, including descriptions of patron–client relationships as they occur in other areas, see Murphy, 1960; Murphy and Murphy, 1974; and Murphy and Steward, 1956. Documentation of the atrocities committed by rubber barons and their hired goons is found in Hardenberg, 1912, and Casement, 1913. For a discussion of the situation in the Vaupés, see Fulop, 1953.

4 Individual members of SIL, however, make no attempt to hide the fact that they are there to convert Indians to their form of fundamentalist Protestantism. See also Wallis and Bennett, *Two Thousand Tongues to Go*, 1959, regarding the missionary policies of SIL, and Hvalkof and Aaby, 1981.

5 Sometimes described as a black **sultana** – priests wear white sultanas.

6 The program of groups such as New Tribes and Unevangelized Fields (another North American Protestant missionary group) are included with SIL for this discussion, although obviously some important differences exist among them.

7 During my stay a number of priests and nuns discussed previous missionary efforts in the Vaupés with me; although they acknowledged that many measures taken by those missionaries were too harsh, they frequently added that "it was a difficult time then; the Indians were not as tame [**manso**] as they are now."

8 The Bará term for whites is *pehká-mahã*, "fire people," most probably a

reference to firearms. Spanish words for Tukanoans are *indígena,* "indigene," and the far more rarely used derogatory *índio.*

9 Conscious attempts by change agents to create needs in order to have more access to target populations is an old story. See Holmberg's advocating creating an "addiction" to salt among the Sirionó for this purpose (1969, p. 85).

10 Good discussions of the kinds of international economic and political processes that are the ultimate determinants of the future Tukanoans face can be found in Davis, 1977; Davis and Mathews, 1976; Dostal, 1972; Frank, 1967; Ribeiro, 1972; Whitten, 1976; and Wolf and Hansen, 1972.

13. Conclusions: themes in Tukanoan social identity

1 For a discussion of types of classificatory structures, see Kay, 1966.

2 Sudnow, 1967, provides an interesting discussion of the Western conceptualization of a deceased person.

Glossary

This glossary contains words appearing in the text more than once with the exception of kin terms (see Table 7) and names of social units such as sibs and language groups (see Tables 2 and 9). Most scientific identifications of plants and animals are found in Chapter 4. Definitions of Tukanoan social units are given in Figure 4. *Italics* indicate Bará and other Eastern Tukanoan words, and **bold face** indicates Spanish, Portuguese, and Tupian loan words.

ahpērá mahkara	"other people."
almacén	general store.
añá	poisonous snakes.
aru	period of weather in the rainy season consisting of misty rain and cold temperatures.
banisteriopsis	*Banisteriopsis inebrians; Banisteriopsis rusbyana.* A Malpighiaceous genus containing several hallucinogenic species. Known locally as **yahé**.
Bará yóara	Bará sib at Pŭmanaka buro.
barbasco	fish poison.
bayá	head dancer.
Behkará	Arawak-speaking language group to the north of the Vaupés River.
boa	rotten, putrid.
bohó	see **tintín.**
borarǫ	forest demon
bühkü	old, mature.
cabuco	half-breed (almost always of a Colombian or Brazilian father and a Tukanoan mother).
cachivera	rapids.
caja agraria	the state-run rubber cooperative in Mitú.
capitán	headman.
caraiurú	a chalky red powder made from the leaves of *Bigonia chica.*
catequista	catechist.
cauchero	rubber gatherer.
cazabe	manioc bread.
cerros	flat-topped or domed sandstone hills.
coca	*Erythroxylon coca.*
comisaría	a Colombian political unit similar to the national territories of Canada.

256

Glossary

comisariato	government-administered general store.
comisario	director of a *comisaría;* similar to governor.
compadrazgo	co-parent relationship between the parent of a child and its godfather.
compadre	co-parent.
corregidor	magistrate; among Tukanoans, a government-appointed position in each mission town.
dabucurí	ceremony involving an exchange of meat or fish for beer.
Dahea	toucan bird; the Tukano language group.
dia katá	Muscovy duck.
Diró koǎ poná	"piece-of-meat-bone-children," mythical culture heroes.
doé	See **tarira.**
Ewüra taró	a mythical **mirití** swamp, the source of all rivers.
eyoa	wood ibis birds.
fariña	toasted manioc granules.
friagem	see **aru.**
he teñü	ceremonial brother-in-law (Pirá-paraná groups can be *he teñüa* to each other).
hikaniya	"one-couple marriage."
hiká poná	children of the same parents (full siblings).
Inambú	tinamou bird (*Tinamus* and *Crypturellus* spp.).
kaná	*Sabicea amazonensis.*
Karihona	Carihona, Carib speakers to the west of the Vaupés.
Koǎ-mahkü	"Bone son," a mythical culture hero.
kumoá	canoe.
kumú	shaman.
Lingua Geral	Tupian-based lingua franca.
llanos	savanna.
magiñá	fire ants.
mahǎ	people.
mahkü, mahkó	son, daughter.
mahoká ahké	spider monkey.
mahoká diari wahtí	dead-people spirit.
Makú	indigenous inhabitants of the Vaupés who speak a non-Tukanoan language and are more forest than river oriented.
maniya waderá	"our-language people."
mirití	*Mauritia flexuosa,* a palm tree that grows in swamps and provides an important fruit.
Namakuru	a mythical character, "deer child."
níguas	chiggers, *Pulex penetrans.*
nimá	curare.
Opēkǒ dia	mythical river flowing in the underworld in an east-west direction; "milk river."
padrino	baptismal godfather.
pahkó-mahkara	"mother's children people"; affines of affines.
Pamüri wi	"first-people longhouse." Ancestral longhouse of the Bará under Yuruparí Rapids.
pehü	co-wife; wife of husband's true brother.
pinó	anaconda; snake.
püaniya	two-couple marriage.

257

Glossary

Púmanaka buro	location of field study on the Inambú River.
pupunha	peach palm; *Gulielma gasipaes*.
quiñapira	pepperpot sauce.
tarira	fish, *Erythrinus* sp.
tatá	swamp; land that floods annually.
tatá boa	clearings in the forest.
teñara	"in-law people"; affines.
timbó	fish poison.
tintín	small rodent, *Dasyprocta* sp.
tipití	tubular basket for squeezing manioc mash.
ümürikori mahá	"day people."
Virola sp.	a hallucinogenic snuff, made by Makú.
wahtí	a category of nonhuman beings including forest demons, ghosts, and the ancestors.
waí	fish.
Waí mahá	fish people; most of the Bará language group.
Wamütañará	low-ranking Bará sib, (from *wamüta*, a fernlike plant, *Selagenella* sp.).
werea	beeswax.
wi	longhouse; house.
winá	wind; the Desana language group.
yai	class of predatory animals including the jaguar; a shaman who sorcerizes.
Yuruparí	sacred flutes associated with the male initiation rites.

References

Allen, P. H. (1947) Indians of Southeastern Colombia. *Geographical Review* 37, pp. 568–83.

Allen, W. L., and J. Holshouser de Tizón (1973) Land use patterns among the Campa of the Alto Pachitea, Peru. In D. W. Lathrap and J. Douglas, eds., *Variation in Anthropology: Essays in Honor of John C. McGregor,* pp. 137–53. Urbana: Illinois Archaeological Survey.

Amorim, A. B. de (1926/28) Lendas em Nheêngatú e em Portuguez. *Revista do Instituto Histórico Geográfico Brasileiro* (tomo 100) 154, no. 2 (1926).

Arcand, B. (1972) *The Urgent Situation of the Cuiva Indians of Colombia.* International Work Group for Indigenous Affairs, Document 7. Copenhagen.

Århem, K. (1976) Fishing and hunting among the Makuna: Economy, ideology and ecological adaptation in the Northwest Amazon. *Göteborgs Etnografiska Museum Årsstryck,* pp. 27–44. Gothenburg.

 (1980) Observations on life cycle rituals among the Makuna: Birth, initiation, death. *Göteborgs Etnografiska Museum Årsstryck,* pp. 10–47. Gothenburg.

 (1981) *Makuna Social Organization: A Study in Descent, Alliance and the Formation of Corporate Groups in the North-Western Amazon.* Uppsala Studies in Cultural Anthropology 4.

Arvelo-Jiménez, N. (1971) Political relations in a tribal society: A study of the Ye'cuana Indians of Venezuela. Ph.D. diss., Cornell University.

Austin, J. L. (1962) *How to Do Things with Words.* Cambridge, Mass. Harvard University Press.

Bamberger, J. (1974) The myth of matriarchy: Why men rule in primitive society. In M. Z. Rosaldo and L. Lamphere, eds., *Woman, Culture and Society,* pp. 263–80. Stanford University Press.

Barnett, S. (1977) Identity choice and caste ideology in contemporary South India. In J. L. Dolgin, D. S. Kemnitzer, and D. M. Schneider, eds., *Symbolic Anthropology: A Reader in the Study of Symbols and Meanings,* pp. 270–91. New York: Columbia University Press.

Barth, F. (1964) Ethnic processes on the Pathan-Baluch boundary. In G. Redard, ed., *Indo-Iranica.* Wiesbaden.

 (1969) Introduction. In F. Barth, ed., *Ethnic Groups and Boundaries,* pp. 9–38. Boston: Little, Brown.

Basso, E. B. (1973) The use of Portuguese in Kalapalo (Xingu Carib) encounters: Changes in a Central Brazilian communications network. *Language in Society* 2, pp. 1–19.

Bates, H. W. (1864) *The Naturalist on the River Amazons.* London.

259

References

Bates, M. (1965) *The Land and Wildlife of South America*. Amsterdam: Time-Life International.

Beckerman, S. (1979) The abundance of protein in Amazonia: A reply to Gross. *American Anthropologist* 81, pp. 533–60.

Berlin, B., D. E. Breedlove, and P. H. Raven (1968) Covert categories and folk taxonomies. *American Anthropologist* 70, pp. 290–399.

Berreman, G. D. (1972) Prologue: Behind many masks, ethnography and impression management. In *Hindus of the Himalayas, Ethnography and Change*. Berkeley: University of California Press.

Bidou, P. (1972) Représentations de l'espace dans la mythologie Tatuyo (Indiens Tucano). *Journal de la Société des Américanistes* 61, pp. 45–105.

(1976) Les fils de l'anaconda céleste (les Tatuyo): Étude de la structure sociopolitique. Thesis for Troisième Cycle, University of Paris.

(1977) Naître et être Tatuyo. *Actes du XLIIe Congrès International des Américanistes* 2, pp. 105–20.

Biocca, E. (1965) *Viaggi tra gli Indi Alto Río Negro – Alto Orinoco: Appunti di un biologo*, vol. 1: *Tukâno – Tariâna – Baniwa – Makú*. Rome: Consiglio Nazionale delle Ricerche.

Birdsell, J. B. (1953) Some environmental and cultural factors influencing the structuring of Australian Aboriginal populations. *American Naturalist* 87, no. 834, pp. 171–207.

Bledsoe, C. (1980) The manipulation of Kpelle social fatherhood. *Ethnology* 19, pp. 29–46.

Blom, J. P. (1969) Ethnic and cultural differentiation. In F. Barth, ed., *Ethnic Groups and Boundaries*, pp. 74–86. Boston: Little, Brown.

Bodley, J. (1972) *Tribal Survival in the Amazon: The Campa Case*. International Work Group for Indigenous Affairs, Document 5. Copenhagen.

(1975) *Victims of Progress*. Menlo Park, Calif.: Cummings.

Bolens, J. (1967) Mythe de Jurupari: Introduction à une analyse. *L'Homme* 7, no. 1, pp. 50–66.

Briggs, J. (1970) *Never in Anger: Portrait of an Eskimo Family*. Cambridge, Mass.: Harvard University Press.

Bright, J. O., and W. Bright (1965) Semantic structures in Northwestern California and the Sapir-Whorf hypothesis. *American Anthropologist* 67, pp. 249–58.

Brown, J. K. (1970a) Economic organization and the position of women among the Iroquois. *Ethnohistory* 17, no. 3–4, pp. 151–67.

(1970b) A note on the division of labor by sex. *American Anthropologist* 72, pp. 1073–78.

Brown, P., and G. Buchbinder, eds. (1976) *Man and Woman in the New Guinea Highlands*. Special Publication 8. Washington, D.C.: American Anthropological Association.

Brüzzi Alves da Silva, A. (1962) *A civilização indígena do Uaupés*. São Paulo: Centro de Pesquisas Iauareté.

(1966) Estrutura da tribo Tukano. *Anthropos* 61, pp. 191–203.

Buchler, I. R., and H. A. Selby (1968) *Kinship and Social Organization: An Introduction to Theory and Method*. New York: Macmillan.

Burridge, K. (1979) *Someone, No One: An Essay on Individuality*. Princeton, N.J.: Princeton University Press.

Butt, A. J. (1965–66) The shaman's legal role. *Revista Museu Paulista* 16, pp. 151–86.

Cardoso de Oliveira, R. (1961) Aliança interclânica na sociedade Tukúna. *Revista de Antropologia* 9, no. 1, pp. 15–32.

References

(1964) *O índio e o mundo dos brancos: A situação dos Tukúna do Alto Solimões.* Corpo e Alma do Brasil, 12. São Paulo: Difusão Européia do Livro.

Cardoso de Oliveira, R., and L. de Castro Faria (1971) Interethnic contact and the study of populations. In F. Salzano, ed., *The Ongoing Evolution of Latin American Populations,* pp. 41–59. Springfield, Ill.: Thomas.

Carneiro, R. L. (1960) Slash-and-burn agriculture: A closer look at its implications for settlement patterns. In A. F. C. Wallace, ed., *Men and Cultures: Selected Papers of the Fifth International Congress of Anthropological and Ethnological Sciences,* pp. 229–34. Philadelphia: University of Pennsylvania Press.

Casement, R. (1913) *El libro rojo del Putumayo.* London.

Casselberry, S., and N. Valavanes (1976) "Matrilocal" Greek peasants and a reconsideration of residence terminology. *American Ethnologist* 3, pp. 215–26.

Casson, R. W. (1973) Paired polarity relations in the formal analysis of a Turkish kinship terminology. *Ethnology* 12, pp. 275–98.

Cathcart, M. (1973) Cacua. In *Aspectos de la cultura material de grupos étnicos de Colombia.* Lomalinda, Meta, Colombia: Ministerio de Gobierno, República de Colombia.

Chagnon, N. A. (1968) *Yąnomamö: The Fierce People.* New York: Holt, Rinehart and Winston.

Chodorow, N. (1978) *The Reproduction of Mothering: Psychoanalysis and the Sociology of Gender.* Berkeley: University of California Press.

Clastres, P. (1972) *Chronique des Indiens Guayaki: Ce que savent les Aché, chasseurs nomades du Paraguay.* Paris: Plon.

Collier, J. (1974) Women in politics. In M. Z. Rosaldo and L. Lamphere, eds., *Woman, Culture and Society.* Stanford University Press.

Collier, J. F., and M. Z. Rosaldo (1981) Politics and gender in simple societies. In S. B. Ortner and H. Whitehead, eds., *Sexual Meanings: The Cultural Construction of Gender and Sexuality,* pp. 275–329. Cambridge University Press.

Colson, A. B. (1973) Inter-tribal trade in the Guiana Highlands. *Antropológica* 34, pp. 5–69.

Coppens, W. (1971) Las relaciones comerciales de los Yekuana del Caura-Paragua. *Antropológica* 30, pp. 28–59.

Corry, S. (1976) *Towards Indian Self-determination in Colombia.* Survival International Document 2. London.

Coudreau, H. A. (1887) *La France equinoxiale.* Vol. 2: *Voyage à travers les Guayanes et l'Amazone.* Paris.

Crocker, J. C. (1977) The mirrored self: Identity and ritual inversion among the Eastern Bororo. *Ethnology* 16, pp. 129–46.

Cunningham, C. (1964) Order in the Atoni house. *Bijdragen tot de Taal-land en Volkenkunde* 120, pp. 34–68.

Davis, S. H. (1977) *Victims of the Miracle: Development and the Indians of Brazil.* Cambridge University Press.

Davis, S. H., and R. O. Mathews (1976) *The Geological Imperative: Anthropology and Development in the Amazon Basin of South America.* Cambridge, Mass.: Anthropology Resource Center.

De Beauvoir, S. (1953) *The Second Sex.* Translated by H. M. Parshley. New York: Knopf.

Denevan, W. M. (1971) Campa subsistence in the Gran Pajonal, Eastern Peru. *Geographical Review* 61, pp. 496–518.

(1973) Development and the imminent demise of the Amazon rain forest. *Professional Geographer* 25, no. 2, pp. 130–35.

261

References

ed. (1976) *The Native Population of the Americas in 1492.* Madison: University of Wisconsin Press.

Dinnerstein, D. (1976) *The Mermaid and the Minotaur: Sexual Arrangements and Human Malaise.* New York: Harper & Row.

Dobyns, H. F. (1966) Estimating aboriginal American populations. *Current Anthropology* 7, no. 4, pp. 395–416.

Dole, G. (1964) Shamanism and political control among the Kuikuru. In H. Becker, ed., *Beiträge zur Volkerkunde Sud-Amerikas: Festgabe für Herbert Baldus,* pp. 53–62. Hannover.

(1966) Anarchy without chaos: Alternatives to political authority among the Kuikuru. In M. J. Swartz, V. W. Turner, and A. Tuden, eds., *Political Anthropology,* pp. 73–87. Chicago: Aldine.

Domínguez, V. (1977) Social classification in Creole Louisiana. *American Ethnologist* 4, no. 4, pp. 589–603.

Dostal, W., ed. (1972) *The Situation of the Indian in South America.* Geneva: World Council of Churches.

Douglas, M. (1966) *Purity and Danger.* Boston: Routledge & Kegan Paul.

Dufour, D. L., and J. L. Zarucchi (1979) *Monopteryx angustifolia* and *Erisma japura:* Their use by indigenous peoples in the Northwestern Amazon. *Botanical Museum Leaflets,* vol. 27, no. 3–4, pp. 69–91. Harvard University.

Elkin, A. P. (1953) Murgin kinship re-examined and remarks on some generalizations. *American Anthropologist* 55, pp. 412–19.

Erikson, E. (1968) Identity. In D. Sills, ed., *Encyclopedia of the Social Sciences,* vol. 7. New York: Macmillan.

Ervin-Tripp, S. (1969) Sociolinguistics. In L. Berkowitz, ed., *Advances in Experimental Social Psychology,* vol. 4, pp. 91–165. New York: Academic Press.

Ferguson, C. A. (1959) Myths about Arabic. *Languages and Linguistic Monograph Series* 12, pp. 75–82. Georgetown University Press.

Fock, N. (1963) *Waiwai: Religion and Society of an Amazon Tribe.* Ethnographic Series, vol. 8. Copenhagen: National Museum of Denmark.

Fortes, M. (1945) *The Dynamics of Clanship among the Tallensi.* Oxford University Press.

Fosberg, F. R. (1973) Temperate zone influence on tropical forest land use: A plea for sanity. In B. Meggers, E. S. Ayensu, and W. D. Duckworth, eds., *Tropical Forest Ecosystems in Africa and South America: A Comparative Review.* Washington, D.C.: Smithsonian Institution Press.

Fox, R. (1967) *Kinship and Marriage.* London: Penguin Books.

Frank, A. G. (1967) *Capitalism and Underdevelopment in Latin America.* New York: Monthly Review Press.

Fried, M., M. Harris, and R. Murphy, eds. (1968) *War: The Anthropology of Armed Conflict and Aggression.* New York: Doubleday.

Fried, M. H. (1975) *The Notion of Tribe.* Menlo Park, Calif.: Cummings.

Friedl, E. (1975) *Women and Men: An Anthropologist's View.* New York: Holt, Rinehart and Winston.

Fulop, M. (1953) El cauchero en el Vaupés. *Revista Colombiana de Folklore,* 2d ser. 2, pp. 243–55.

(1955) Notas sobre los términos y el sistema de parentesco de los Tukano. *Revista Colombiana de Antropología* 4, pp. 123–64.

(1956) Aspectos de la cultura Tukana. Mitología. *Revista Colombiana de Antropología* 5, pp. 335–373.

References

Galvão, E. (1959) Aculturação indígena no Rio Negro. *Boletim do Museu Paraense Emílio Goeldi* 7, pp. 1–60.

Gasché, J. (1977) Les fondements de l'organisation sociale des Indiens Witoto et l'illusion exogamique. *Actes du XLIIe Congrès International des Américanistes* 2, pp. 141–61.

Giacone, A. (1949) *Os Tucanos e outras tribus do Rio Uaupés*. São Paulo: Impresa Oficial do Estado.

(1955) *Pequena gramática e dicionario Português Ubde-Nehern ou Macú*. Recife.

Gilbert, J. P., and E. A. Hammel (1966) Computer simulation and the analysis of problems in kinship and social structure. *American Anthropologist* 68, pp. 71–93.

Glasse, R. M., and M. J. Meggitt (1965) *Pigs, Pearlshells and Women*. Englewood Cliffs, N.J.: Prentice-Hall.

Godelier, M. (1975) Modes of production, kinship, and demographic structures. In M. Bloch, ed., *Marxist Analyses and Social Anthropology*. London: Malaby.

(1977) The concept of the "tribe": A crisis involving merely a concept or the empirical foundations of anthropology itself? In *Perspectives in Marxist Anthropology*. Cambridge University Press.

Goffman, E. (1963) *Stigma: Notes on the Management of Spoiled Identity*. Englewood Cliffs, N.J.: Prentice-Hall.

Goldman, I. (1940) Cosmological beliefs of the Cubeo Indians. *Journal of American Folklore* 53, pp. 242–47.

(1948) Tribes of the Uaupés-Caquetá region. *Bureau of American Ethnology Bulletin* 143, no. 3, pp. 763–98.

(1963) *The Cubeo: Indians of the Northwest Amazon*. Champaign: University of Illinois Press.

(1964) The structure of ritual in the Northwest Amazon. In R. A. Manners, ed., *Process and Pattern in Culture: Essays in Honor of Julian H. Steward*. Chicago: University of Chicago Press.

(1976) Perceptions of nature and the structure of society: The question of Cubeo descent. *Dialectical Anthropology* 1, pp. 287–92.

(1977) Time, space, and descent: The Cubeo example. *Actes du XLIIe Congrès International des Américanistes* 2, pp. 175–83.

(1981) Foundations of social hierarchy: A Northwest Amazon case. Paper presented at the New York Academy of Sciences, Section of Anthropology, New York, February 23.

Goodenough, W. (1965) Rethinking "status" and "role": Toward a general model of the cultural organization of social relationships. In M. Banton, ed., *The Relevance of Models for Social Anthropology*. London: Tavistock.

(1970) *Description and Comparison in Cultural Anthropology*. Chicago: Aldine.

(1981) *Culture, language, and society*. Menlo Park, Calif.: Cummings.

Goodland, R. J. A., and H. S. Irwin (1975) *Amazon Jungle: Green Hell to Red Desert?* The Hague: Elsevier.

Greenberg, J. H. (1960) The general classification of Central and South American languages. In A. F. C. Wallace, ed., *Selected Papers of the International Congress of Anthropological and Ethnological Sciences*. Philadelphia: University of Pennsylvania Press.

Gregor, T. (1974) Publicity, privacy and Mehinacu marriage. *Ethnology* 13, pp. 333–49.

Gross, D. (1975) Protein capture and cultural development in the Amazon Basin. *American Anthropologist* 77, pp. 526–49.

Gumperz, J. J. (1964a) Hindi-Punjabi code-switching in Delhi. In H. G. Lunt, ed.,

References

Proceedings of the Ninth International Congress of Linguists, pp. 1115–24. The Hague: Mouton.

(1964b) Linguistic and social interaction in two communities. In J. Gumperz and D. Hymes, eds., The ethnography of communication. Part 2. Special Publication. *American Anthropologist* 66, no. 6, pp. 137–54.

(1968) The speech community. In *International Encyclopedia of the Social Sciences*, vol. 9, pp. 381–86. (Reprinted in *Language in Social Groups: Essays by John J. Gumperz*, pp. 114–28. Stanford University Press, 1971.)

(1969) Communication in multilingual societies. In S. Tyler, ed., *Cognitive Anthropology*, pp. 435–48. New York: Holt, Rinehart and Winston.

(1970) Verbal strategies in multilingual communication (Working Paper 36). Language-Behavior Research Laboratory, University of California, Berkeley. Mimeo.

(1972) Introduction. In J. J. Gumperz and D. Hymes, eds., *Directions in Sociolinguistics: The Ethnography of Communication*, pp. 1–25. New York: Holt, Rinehart and Winston.

Gumperz, J. J., and R. Wilson (1971) Convergence and creolization: A case from the Indo-Aryan/Dravidian border. In D. Hymes, ed., *Pidginization and Creolization of Languages*. Proceedings of a Conference Held at the University of the West Indies, Mora, Jamaica, April 1968, pp. 151–68. Cambridge University Press.

Haaland, G. (1969) Economic determinants in ethnic processes. In F. Barth, ed., *Ethnic Groups and Boundaries*, pp. 58–73. Boston: Little, Brown.

Hallowell, A. I. (1955) The self and its behavioral environment. In *Culture and Experience*, pp. 75–111. Philadelphia: University of Pennsylvania Press.

Hames, R. (1978) A behavioral account of the division of labor among the Ye'kwana Indians of Southern Venezuela. Ph.D. diss., University of California, Santa Barbara.

(1980a) Diversity within monoculture: The polyvarietal gardens of the Ye'kwana and Yanomamo. Paper presented at 79th Annual Meeting, American Anthropological Association, Washington, D.C., December 6.

ed. (1980b) *Studies in Hunting and Fishing in the Neotropics* (Working Papers on South American Indians, no. 2). Bennington College.

Hardenburg, W. S. (1912) *The Putumayo: The Devil's Paradise*. London.

Harner, M. J. (1972) *The Jivaro: People of the Sacred Waterfalls*. New York: Doubleday.

Harris, D. R. (1971) The ecology of swidden cultivation in the Upper Orinoco rainforest, Venezuela. *Geographical Review* 61, no. 4, pp. 475–95.

Harris, M. (1975) *Culture, People and Nature*. 2d ed. New York: Crowell.

Helm, J., ed. (1968) *Essays on the Problem of Tribe*. Proceedings of the 1967 Annual Spring Meeting of the American Ethnological Society. Seattle: University of Washington Press.

Helms, M. (1970) Matrilocality, social solidarity, and culture contact: Three case histories. *Southwestern Journal of Anthropology* 26, pp. 197–212.

Hicks, D. (1976) *Tetum Ghosts and Kin: Fieldwork in an Indonesian Community*. Palo Alto, Calif.: Mayfield.

Holmberg, A. (1969) *Nomads of the Long Bow: The Sirionó of Eastern Bolivia*. New York: Doubleday.

Homans, G. C., and D. Schneider (1955) *Marriage, Authority and Final Causes: A Study of Unilateral Cross-cousin Marriage*. Glencoe, Ill.: Free Press.

Hugh-Jones, C. (1977) Skin and soul: The round and the straight. Social time and social space in Pirá-paraná society. *Actes du XLIIe Congrès International des Américanistes* 2, pp. 185–204.

(1978) Food for thought – Patterns of production and consumption in Pirá-paraná society. In J. LaFontaine, ed., *Sex and Age as Principles of Social Differentiation*,

References

pp. 41–66. London: Academic Press.

(1979) *From the Milk River: Spatial and Temporal Processes in Northwest Amazonia.* Cambridge University Press.

(n.d.) Untitled manuscript on Pirá-paraná social structure.

Hugh-Jones, S. (1974) Male initiation and cosmology among the Barasana Indians of the Vaupés area of Colombia. Ph.D. diss., Cambridge University.

(1977) Like the leaves on the forest floor: Ritual and social structure amongst the Barasana. *Actes du XLIIe Congrès International des Américanistes* 2, pp. 205–15.

(1979) *The Palm and the Pleiades: Initiation and Cosmology in Northwest Amazonia.* Cambridge University Press.

(1980) Stars and seasons in Barasana cosmology. Paper presented at the 79th Annual Meeting, American Anthropological Association, Washington, D.C., December 5.

(1982) The Pleiades and Scorpius in Barasana cosmology. In A. F. Aveni and G. Urton, eds., *Ethnoastronomy and Archaeoastronomy in the American Tropics,* pp. 183–201. New York Academy of Sciences.

Humboldt, Alexandre von (1822) *Voyage aux régions équinoxiales du Nouveau Continent.* Paris.

Huntingford, G. W. B. (1955) The economic life of the Dorobo. *Anthropos* 50, pp. 602–34.

Hvalkof, S., and P. Aaby, eds. (1981) *Is God an American? An Anthropological Perspective on the Missionary Work of the Summer Institute of Linguistics.* International Work Group for Indigenous Affairs, Copenhagen, and Survival International, London.

Hymes, D. (1968) Linguistic problems in defining the concept of "tribe." In J. Helm, ed., *Essays on the Problem of Tribe,* pp. 23–48. Seattle: University of Washington Press.

Instituto Geográfico "Agustín Codazzi" (1969) *Atlas de Colombia.* Bogotá.

International Work Group for Indigenous Affairs (1976) *Newsletter* (December). Copenhagen.

Irvine, J. T. (1974) Strategies of status manipulation in the Wolof greeting. In R. Bauman and J. Sherzer, eds., *Explorations in the Ethnography of Speaking,* pp. 167–91. Cambridge University Press.

Jackson, J. E. (1972) Marriage and linguistic identity among the Bará Indians of the Vaupés, Colombia. Ph.D. diss., Stanford University.

(1974) Language identity of the Colombian Vaupés Indians. In R. Bauman and J. Sherzer, eds., *Explorations in the Ethnography of Speaking,* pp. 50–64. Cambridge University Press.

(1976) Vaupés marriage: A network system in the Northwest Amazon. In C. A. Smith, ed., *Regional Analysis.* Vol. 2: *Social Systems,* pp. 65–93. New York: Academic Press.

(1977) Bará zero generation terminology and marriage. *Ethnology* 16, no. 1, pp. 83–104.

(1978) Instant underdevelopment for Colombia's Indians. Anthropology Resource Center *Newsletter* (December), p. 4. Cambridge, Mass.

(n.d.-a) On trying to be an Amazon. In T. Whitehead, M. E. Conaway, and M. Clark, eds., Sex and Gender in Fieldwork: Exploring Problems and Prospects for Crosscultural Research and Communication. Manuscript.

(n.d.-b) Vaupés marriage practices. In K. Kensinger, ed., *Marriage Practices in Lowland South America.* Champaign: University of Illinois Press. In press.

(n.d.-c) The impact of the state on small-scale societies. *Studies in Comparative International Development.* In press.

Jackson, J. E., and A. K. Romney (n.d.) A note on Bará exogamy. Manuscript.

265

References

Jacopin, P. (1972) Habitat et territoire Yukuna. *Journal de la Société des Américanistes* 61, pp. 107–139.

(1975) Mission Pierre-Yves Jacopin (1969–71). In J. Gabus, ed., *Amazonie Nord-ouest*. Musée d'Ethnographie de Neuchâtel.

(1981) *La parole générative: de la mythologie des Indiens Yukuna*. Ph.D. diss., University of Neuchâtel.

Johnson, A. (1974) Carrying-capacity in Amazonia: Problems in theory and method. Paper presented at 73d Annual Meeting, American Anthropological Association, Mexico, November 24.

Kaplan, B. (1961) Personality Study and Culture. In B. Kaplan, ed., *Studying Personality Cross-culturally*, pp. 301–11. Evanston, Ill.: Row, Peterson.

Kay, P. (1966) Comment on "Ethnographic semantics: A preliminary survey," by B. N. Colby. *Current Anthropology* 7, no. 1, pp. 20–23.

Kelly, R. (1976) Witchcraft and sexual relations: An exploration in the social and semantic implications of the structure of belief. In P. Brown and G. Buchbinder, eds., *Man and Woman in the New Guinea Highlands*. Washington, D.C.: American Anthropological Association.

Kloos, P. (1977) *The Akuriyo of Surinam: A case of emergence from isolation*. International Work Group for Indigenous Affairs, Document 27, Copenhagen.

Knutsson, K. E. (1969) Dichotomization and integration. In F. Barth, ed., *Ethnic Groups and Boundaries*, pp. 86–100. Boston: Little, Brown.

Koch-Grünberg, T. (1906) Die Makú. *Anthropos* 1, pp. 877–906.

(1909–10) *Zwei Jahre unter den Indianern; Reisen in Nordwest-Brasilien*. 2 vols. Berlin: Ernst Wasmuth.

Kok, P. P. (1921–22) Ensayo de gramática Dagseye o Tokano. *Anthropos* 16–17, pp. 838–65.

(1925–26) Quelques notices ethnographiques sur les Indiens du Río Papurí. *Anthropos* 20–21, pp. 624–37, 921–37.

Kracke, W. (1978) *Force and Persuasion: Leadership in an Amazonian Society*. Chicago: University of Chicago Press.

Kumu, U. P., and T. Kenhíri (1980) *Antes o Mundo Não Existia*. São Paulo: Livraria Cultura Editora.

Labov, W. (1966) Hypercorrection by the lower middle class as a factor in linguistic change. In W. Bright, ed., *Sociolinguistics*, pp. 84–113. The Hague: Mouton.

Lambert, W. E. (1967) A psychology of bilingualism. In J. Macnamara, ed., Problems of Bilingualism. *Journal of Social Issues* 23, no. 2, pp. 91–109.

Lambert, W. E., R. C. Hodgson, R. C. Gardner, and S. Fillenbaum (1960) Evaluational reactions to spoken languages. *Journal of Abnormal and Social Psychology* 60, pp. 144–51.

Lamphere, L. (1977) Anthropology. *Signs: Journal of Women in Culture and Society* 2, pp. 612–27.

Langdon, T. (1975) Food restrictions in the medical system of the Barasana and Taiwano Indians of the Colombian Northwest Amazon. Ph.D. diss., Tulane University.

Langness, L. L. (1967) Sexual antagonism in the New Guinea Highlands: A Bena Bena example. *Oceania* 37, pp. 161–77.

Lathrap, D. W. (1968) The "hunting" economies of the tropical forest zone of South America: An attempt at historical perspective. In R. Lee and I. DeVore, eds., *Man the Hunter*, pp. 23–29. Chicago: Aldine.

(1970) *The Upper Amazon*. New York: Praeger.

(1973) The antiquity and importance of long distance trade relationships in the moist tropics of pre-Columbian South America. *World Archaeology* 5, pp. 170–86.

266

References

Lave, J. C. (1966) A formal analysis of preferential marriage with the sister's daughter. *Man* 1, pp. 185–200.

Leach, E. R. (1954) *Political Systems of Highland Burma: A Study of Kachin Social Structure*. London School of Economics.

(1958) Concerning Trobriand clans and the kinship category "tabu." In J. Goody, ed., *The Developmental Cycle in Domestic Groups*. Cambridge University Press.

(1970) *Lévi-Strauss*. London: Fontana/Collins.

Leacock, E. B. (1955) Matrilocality in a simple hunting economy (Montagnais-Naskapi). *Southwestern Journal of Anthropology* 11, pp. 31–47.

Lee, R. B. (1968) What hunters do for a living, or how to make out on scarce resources. In R. Lee and I. DeVore, eds., *Man the Hunter*, pp. 30–48. Chicago: Aldine.

Lee, R. B., and I. DeVore, eds. (1968) *Man the Hunter*. Chicago: Aldine.

Leeds, A. (1964) Some problems of Yaruro ethnohistory. *Proceedings of the 35th International Congress of Americanists* 2, pp. 157–75.

Lehman, F. K. (1974) Foreword. In P. A. Ballonoff, ed., *Mathematical Models of Social and Cognitive Structures: Contributions to the Mathematical Development of Anthropology*, pp. vii–xviii. Champaign: University of Illinois Press.

Lévi-Strauss, C. (1962) Social structure. In S. Tax, ed., *Anthropology*, pp. 321–50. Chicago: University of Chicago Press.

(1969) *The Elementary Structures of Kinship*. 2d ed. London: Eyre and Spottiswoode.

Lindenbaum, S. (1972) Sorcerers, ghosts, and polluting women: An analysis of religious belief and population control. *Ethnology* 11, pp. 241–53.

Lounsbury, F. G. (1956) A semantic analysis of the Pawnee kinship usage. *Language* 32, pp. 158–94.

(1962) Review of *Structure and Sentiment,* by R. Needham. *American Anthropologist* 64, pp. 1302–10.

(1965) Another view of Trobriand kinship categories. In E. A. Hammel, ed., *Formal Semantic Analysis*. Special Publication. *American Anthropologist* 67, no. 5, pt. 2, pp. 142–185.

MacCormack, C., and M. Strathern, eds. (1980) *Nature, Culture and Gender.* Cambridge University Press.

MacCreagh, G. (1926) *White Waters and Black*. New York: Century.

Macfarlane, Alan (1978) *The Origins of English Individualism: The Family, Property, and Social Transition*. Cambridge University Press.

McGovern, M. W. (1927) *Jungle Paths and Inca Ruins*. London: Hutchinson.

Markham, C. R. (1910) A list of the tribes of the valley of the Amazons. *Journal of the Anthropological Institute* 40, pp. 73–140.

Martin, M. K. (1969) South American foragers: A case study in cultural devolution. *American Anthropologist* 71, pp. 243–60.

Mason, J. A. (1950) The languages of South American Indians. *Handbook of South American Indians*, vol. 6, pp. 257–58. Washington, D.C.: Bureau of American Ethnology.

Maybury-Lewis, D. H. P. (1965) *The Savage and the Innocent*. London: Evans Brothers.

(1967) *Akwē Shavante Society*. New York: Oxford University Press.

ed. (1979) *Dialectical Societies: The Gê and Bororo of Central Brazil*. Cambridge, Mass.: Harvard University Press.

Meggers, B. J. (1973) Some problems of cultural adaptation in Amazonia, with emphasis on the pre-European period. In B. Meggers, E. S. Ayensu, and W. D. Duckworth, eds., *Tropical Forest Ecosystems in Africa and South America: A Comparative Review*. Washington, D.C.: Smithsonian Institution Press.

Meggitt, M. J. (1964) Male-female relationships in the Highlands of Australian New

References

Guinea. In J. B. Watson, ed., *New Guinea: The Central Highlands*. Special Publication. *American Anthropologist* 66, no. 4, pp. 204–24.

Métraux, A. (1948) The hunting and gathering tribes of the Rio Negro Basin. *Handbook of South American Indians,* vol. 3, pp. 861–67. Washington, D.C.: Bureau of American Ethnology.

Michaelson, E. J., and W. Goldschmidt (1971) Female roles and male dominance among peasants. *Southwestern Journal of Anthropology* 27, pp. 330–52.

Miller, D. R. (1961) Personality and social interaction. In B. Kaplan, ed., *Studying Personality Cross-culturally,* pp. 271–300. Evanston, Ill.: Row, Peterson.

Miller, G. (1963) *Language and Communication*. 2d ed. New York: McGraw-Hill.

Miller, W. R. (1970) Western Shoshoni dialects. In E. H. Swanson, ed., *Languages and Cultures of Western North America: Essays in Honor of Sven S. Liljeblad,* pp. 17–36. Pocatello: Idaho State University Press.

Misiones del Vaupés (1966) 1914–1964: Los misioneros del Vaupés a sus amigos y colaboradores. Medellín: Misiones del Vaupés.

Moerman, M. (1965) Who are the Lue? Ethnic identification in a complex civilization. *American Anthropologist* 67, pp. 1215–30.

Morey, R. V., and N. C. Morey (1974) The early trade system of the Orinoco llanos. Paper presented at the 41st International Congress of Americanists, Mexico City, Sept. 3.

(1975) *Relaciones comerciales en el pasado en los llanos de Colombia y Venezuela.* Universidad Católica "Andrés Bello," Institututo de Investigaciones Históricas, Caracas.

Moser, B., and D. Tayler (1963) Tribes of the Piraparaná. *Geographical Journal* 129, no. 4, pp. 437–49.

(1965) *The Cocaine Eaters*. London.

Murphy, R. F. (1956) Matrilocality and patrilineality in Mundurucú society. *American Anthropologist* 56, pp. 414–34.

(1960) *Headhunter's Heritage: Social and Economic Change among the Mundurucú Indians*. Berkeley: University of California Press.

(1961) Deviance and social control I: What makes Warú run? *Kroeber Anthropological Society Papers* 24, pp. 55–61.

Murphy, R., and J. Steward (1956) Tappers and trappers: Parallel process in acculturation. *Economic Development and Cultural Change* 4, pp. 335–53.

Murphy, Y., and R. Murphy (1974) *Women of the Forest*. New York: Columbia University Press.

Needham, R. (1962) *Structure and Sentiment: A Test Case in Social Anthropology.* Chicago: University of Chicago Press.

(1966) Age, category and descent. *Bijdragen tot de Taal-land en Volkenkunde* 122, pp. 1–35.

(1971) Introduction. In R. Needham, ed., *Rethinking Kinship and Marriage,* pp. xiii–cxvii. London: Tavistock.

Netting, R. M. (1969) Women's weapons: The politics of domesticity among the Kofyar. *American Anthropologist* 71, pp. 1037–46.

Nimuendajú, C. (1950) Reconhecimento dos Rios Içana, Ayarie, Uaupés. *Journal de la Société des Américanistes* 39, pp. 125–82.

Oberem, U. (1974) Trade and trade goods in the Ecuadorian Montaña. In P. Lyon, ed., *Native South Americans: Ethnology of the Least Known Continent,* pp. 346–57. Boston: Little, Brown.

Oberg, K. (1955) Types of social structure among the lowland tribes of South and Central America. *American Anthropologist* 57, pp. 472–87.

268

References

O'Laughlin, B. (1974) Mediation of contradiction: Why Mbum women do not eat chicken. In M. Rosaldo and L. Lamphere, eds., *Woman, Culture and Society,* pp. 301–20. Stanford University Press.

(1975) Marxist approaches in anthropology. In B. Siegel, ed., *Annual Review of Anthropology,* pp. 341–70. Palo Alto, Calif.: Annual Reviews.

Ortner, S. B. (1974) Is female to male as nature is to culture? In M. Rosaldo and L. Lamphere, eds., *Woman, Culture and Society,* pp. 67–88. Stanford University Press.

Owen, Roger (1965) Patrilocal band: A linguistic and cultural heterogeneous unit. *American Anthropologist* 67, pp. 675–90.

Powdermaker, H. (1966) *Stranger and friend: The Way of an Anthropologist.* New York: Norton.

Quinn, N. (1977) Anthropological studies on women's status. In B. Siegel, ed., *Annual Review of Anthropology,* pp. 181–226. Palo Alto, Calif.: Annual Reviews.

Rabinow, P. (1977) *Reflections on Fieldwork in Morocco.* Berkeley: University of California Press.

Radcliffe-Brown, A. R. (1953) Dravidian kinship terminology. *Man* 53, p. 112.

Reichel-Dolmatoff, G. (1967) A brief field report on urgent ethnological research in the Vaupés area, Colombia, South America. *Bulletin of the International Committee on Urgent Anthropological and Ethnological Research,* no. 9, pp. 53–62.

(1971) *Amazonian Cosmos: The Sexual and Religious Symbolism of the Tukano Indians.* Chicago: University of Chicago Press.

(1975) *The Shaman and the Jaguar: A Study of Narcotic Drugs among the Indians of Colombia.* Philadelphia; Temple University Press.

(1976) Cosmology as ecological analysis: The view from the rainforest. *Man* 11, pp. 307–18.

Reid, H. (1976) Health and nutrition in the Eastern Vaupés. In S. Corry, ed., *Towards Indian Self-determination in Colombia.* Survival International Document 2, pp. 20–21. London.

(1977) Comparative discussion of Makú and Tukanoan social structure. Cambridge University.

(1979) Some aspects of movement, growth, and change among the Hupdü Makú Indians of Brazil. Ph.D. diss. Cambridge University.

Ribeiro, D. (1972) *The Americas and Civilization.* New York: Dutton.

Rice, H. (1910) The River Vaupés. *Geographical Journal* 25, pt. 5, pp. 682–700.

(1914) Further explorations in the North-West Amazon Basin, *Geographical Journal* 44, pp. 137–68.

Rivet, P., and C. Tastevin (1920) Affinités du Makú et du Puinave. *Journal de la Société des Américanistes* 12, pp. 69–82.

Rivière, P. G. (1971) The political structure of the Trio Indians as manifested in a system of ceremonial dialogue. In T. O. Beidelman, ed., *The Translation of Culture: Essays to E. E. Evans-Pritchard,* pp. 293–311. London: Tavistock.

Rodriguez Lamus, L. R. (1958) La arquitectura de los Tukano. *Revista Colombiana de Antropología* 7, pp. 251–70.

Rogers, D. J. (1963) Studies of *Manihot esculenta Crantz* and related species. *Bulletin of the Torrey Botanical Club* 90, pp. 43–54.

Romney, A. K. (1965) Kalmuk Mongol and the classification of lineal kinship terminologies. In E. Hammel, ed., *Formal semantic analysis.* Special Publication. *American Anthropologist* 67, no. 5, p. 2, pp. 127–41.

(1971) Measuring endogamy. In P. Kay, ed., *Explorations in Mathematical Anthropology,* pp. 191–213. Cambridge. Mass.: MIT Press.

269

References

Romney, A. K., and R. G. D'Andrade (1964) Cognitive aspects of English kin terms. *American Anthropologist* 66, no. 3, pt. 2, pp. 146–70.

Rosaldo, M. (1974) Woman, culture and society: A theoretical overview. In M. Rosaldo and L. Lamphere, eds., *Woman, Culture and Society*, pp. 17–42, Stanford University Press.

Ross, E. B. (1978) Food taboos, diet and hunting strategy: The adaptation to animals in Amazon cultural ecology. *Current Anthropology* 19, pp. 1–36.

Ruddle, K. (1974) *The Yukpa Cultivation System*. Berkeley: University of California Press.

Salser, J. K. (1971) Cubeo phonemics. *Linguistics* 75, pp. 74–79.

Sankoff, G. (1968) Social aspects of multilingualism in New Guinea. Ph.D. diss., McGill University.

   (1970) Mutual intelligibility, bilingualism, and linguistic boundaries. In *International Days of Sociolinguistics*, pp. 839–48, Rome: Instituto Luigi Sturzo.

   (1974) A quantitative paradigm for the study of communicative competence. In R. Bauman and J. Sherzer, eds., *Explorations in the Ethnography of Speaking*, pp. 18–49. Cambridge University Press.

Sapir, E. (1949) The nature of language. In D. G. Mandelbaum, ed., *Selected Writings of Edward Sapir in Language, Culture, and Personality*. Berkeley: University of California Press.

Sapir, J. D. (1975) Big and thin: Two Diola metalinguistic terms. *Language in Society* 4, pp. 1–16.

Scheffler, H. (1966) Ancestor worship in anthropology: Or observations on descent and descent groups. *Current Anthropology* 7, pp. 541–51.

   (1973) Kinship, descent and alliance. In J. J. Honigman. ed., *Handbook of Social and Cultural Anthropology*, pp. 747–93. Chicago: Rand McNally.

Schneider, D. M. (1965) Some muddles in the models: Or, how the system really works. In M. Banton, ed., *The Relevance of Models for Social Anthropology*, pp. 25–86. London: Tavistock.

   (1972) *American Kinship: A Cultural Account*. 2d ed. Englewood Cliffs, N.J.: Prentice-Hall.

Schneider, J. (1971) Of vigilance and virgins: Honor, shame and access to resources in Mediterranean society. *Ethnology* 10, pp. 1–24.

Schultes, R. E. (1972) An overview of hallucinogens in the Western Hemisphere. In P. T. Furst, ed., *Flesh of the Gods: The Ritual Use of Hallucinogens*, pp. 3–54. New York: Praeger.

Schultz, H. (1959) Ligeiras notas sobre os Makú do Paraná-Boa-Boa. *Revista do Museu Paulista*, 11, pp. 110–32.

Schwerin, K. (1971) The bitter and the sweet: Some implications of techniques for preparing manioc. Paper presented at the 70th Annual Meeting, American Anthropological Association, New York, November 30.

Seligmann, C. G., and B. Z. Seligmann (1911) *The Veddas*. Cambridge Univeristy Press.

Service, E. R. (1968) War and our contemporary ancestors. In M. Fried, M. Harris, and R. Murphy, eds., *War: The Anthropology of Armed Conflict and Aggression*, pp. 160–67. New York: Doubleday.

Shapiro, J. R. (1972) Sex roles and social structure among the Yanomama Indians of Northern Brazil. Ph.D. diss., Columbia University.

   (n.d.) Marriage rules, marriage exchange, and the definition of marriage in lowland South American societies. In K. Kensinger, ed., *Marriage Practices in Lowland South America*. Champaign: University of Illinois Press. In press.

SIL. See Summer Institute of Linguistics.

References

Silverwood-Cope, P. (1972) A contribution to the ethnography of the Colombian Makú. Ph.D. diss., Cambridge University.

Singer, M. (1980) Signs of the self: An exploration in semiotic anthropology. *American Anthropologist* 82, no. 3, pp. 485–507.

Siskind, J. (1973a) *To Hunt in the Morning*. New York: Oxford University Press.

(1973b) Tropical forest hunters and the economy of sex. In D. Gross, ed., *Peoples and Cultures of Native South America*, pp. 226–41. New York: Doubleday.

Smith, R., and C. Smith (1971) Southern Barasano phonemics. *Linguistics*, no. 75, pp. 80–85.

Sorensen, A. P., Jr. (1967) Multilingualism in the Northwest Amazon. *American Anthropologist* 69, pp. 670–84.

(1970) The morphology of Tukano. Ph.D. diss., Columbia University.

Soto Holguín, A. (1972) Mitos de los Cubeo. *Acts of the 39th International Congress of Americanists* 6, pp. 59–65.

Spruce, R. (1908) *Notes of a Botanist on the Amazon and Andes*. 2 vols. London.

Sternberg, H. O. (1969) Man and environmental change in South America. In E. J. Fittkau, ed., *Biogeography and Ecology of South America*, pp. 413–41. The Hague: Junk.

Stoll, D. (1981) The adventures of Sophia Muller. *ARC Bulletin* 9, pp. 5–7. Boston: Anthropology Resource Center.

Stolte, J., and N. Stolte (1971) A description of Northern Barasano phonology. *Linguistics* 75, pp. 86–92.

Stradelli, E. (1890) Leggenda dell'Jurupary. *Bolletino della Società Geografica Italiana*, 3d. ser. 3, pp. 659–89, 798–835.

Sudnow, D. (1967) *Passing On: The Social Organization of Dying*. Englewood Cliffs, N.J.: Prentice-Hall.

Summer Institute of Linguistics (SIL) (1975) *Aspectos de la cultura material de grupos étnicos de Colombia*. Bogotá: Summer Institute of Linguistics.

Tastevin, P. C. (1923) Les Makú du Japura. *Journal de la Société des Américanistes* 15, pp. 99–108.

Terriblini, M., and M. Terriblini (1961) Enquête chez des Indiens Makú (Brésil). *Bulletin de la Société Suisse des Américanistes* 21, pp. 2–10.

Thomas, D. J. (1972) The indigenous trade system of Southeast Estado Bolívar, Venezuela. *Antropológica* 33, pp. 3–37.

Tindale, N. B. (1953) Tribal and inter-tribal marriage among the Australian aborigines. *Human Biology* 25, pp. 169–90.

Torres Laborde, A. (1969) *Mito y cultura entre los Barasana: Un grupo indígena Tukano del Vaupés*. Bogotá.

Turnbull, C. (1965) The Mbuti Pygmies of the Congo. In J. Gibbs, ed., *Peoples of Africa*, pp. 281–317. New York: Holt, Rinehart and Winston.

Turner, T. (1979) Kinship, household, and community structure among the Kayapó. In D. H. P. Maybury-Lewis, ed., *Dialectical Societies: The Gê and Bororo of Central Brazil*, pp. 179–217. Cambridge, Mass.: Harvard University Press.

Tyler, S. A. (1978) *The Said and the Unsaid: Mind, Meaning, and Culture*. New York: Academic Press.

Van Emst, P. (1966a) Vrijwillige onvrijheid: De Makú in West-Amazonas. *Bijdragen Tot der Taal-land en Volkenkunde* 122, pp. 110–28.

(1966b) Indians and missionaries on the River Tiquié, Brazil-Colombia. *Institute Archives of Ethnography* 50, pt. 2, pp. 145–97.

Wallace, A. F. C. (1961) On being just complicated enough. *Proceedings of the National Academy of Sciences* 47, pp. 458–64.

271

References

Wallace, A. R. (1889/1972) *A Narrative of Travels on the Amazon and Rio Negro*. 2d. ed. (1st ed., 1853) London. (Reprint. New York: Dover ed.)

Wallis, E. E., and Bennett, M. A. (1959) *Two Thousand Tongues to Go*. New York: Harper & Row.

Waltz, N., and C. Waltz (1972) Fonología del Guanano. In B. Elson, ed., *Sistemas fonológicos de idiomas Colombianos*. Vol. 1, pp. 29–40, Lomalinda, Meta, Colombia.

Waltz, N. E., and A. Wheeler (1970) Proto Tucanoan. In E. Matteson, ed., *Comparative Studies in Amerindian Languages*, pp. 120–49. The Hague: Mouton.

Ward, B. (1965) Varieties of the conscious model: The fishermen of South China. In M. Banton, ed., *The Relevance of Models for Social Anthropology*, pp. 113–37. London: Tavistock.

Warner, W. L. (1937) *A Black Civilization: A Social Study of an Australian Tribe*. New York: Harper & Brothers.

West, B., and B. Welch (1967) Phonemic system of Tucano. In V. Waterhouse, ed., *Phonemic systems of Colombian Languages*. Norman, Okla.: Summer Institute of Linguistics Publications in Linguistics and Related Fields.

(1972) Sistema fonológico del Tucano. In B. Elson, ed., *Sistemas fonológicos de idiomas Colombianos*. Vol. 1, pp. 13–28. Lomalinda, Meta, Colombia.

Whiffen, T. (1915) *The Northwest Amazons: Notes on Some Months Spent among Cannibal Tribes*. London: Constable.

Whitten, N. E., Jr. (1976) *Sacha Runa: Ethnicity and Adaptation of Ecuadorian Jungle Quichua*. Champaign: University of Illinois Press.

(1978) Ecological imagery and cultural adaptability: The Canelos Quichua of Eastern Ecuador. *American Anthropologist* 80, pp. 836–59.

Wittgenstein, Ludwig (1922) *Tractatus Logico-philosophicus*. London: Routledge & Kegan Paul.

Wolf, E., and E. Hansen (1972) *The Human Condition in Latin America*. New York: Oxford University Press.

Wolf, M. (1974) Chinese women: Old skills in a new context. In M. Rosaldo and L. Lamphere, eds., *Woman, Culture and Society*. Stanford University Press.

Woodburn, J. (1968) An introduction to Hadza ecology. In R. Lee and I. DeVore, eds., *Man the Hunter*, pp. 49–55. Chicago: Aldine.

Wright, R. (1981) The history and religion of the Baniwa peoples of the Upper Rio Negro valley. Ph.D. diss., Stanford University.

Wright, R., and S. Swenson, eds. (1981) *ARC Bulletin 9*. Boston, Mass.: Anthropology Resource Center.

Yengoyan, A. (1968) Demographic and ecological influences on aboriginal Australian marriage sections. In R. Lee and I. DeVore, eds., *Man the Hunter*, pp. 185–99. Chicago: Aldine.

Zuidema, R. T. (1969) Hierarchy in symmetric alliance systems. *Bijdragen tot de Taal-land en Volkenkunde* 125, pp. 134–39.

Index

acculturation, 24–5; *see also* change, decul-
    turation
  and cultivated foods, 51
  impact on women's work of, 184–5
  and language group exogamy, 136
  and language groups, 69–70
  and patterns of exchange, 61–2
  and regional variation, 238
  and territorial dispersion, 93, 95
  and traditional social structure, 71
adultery, 129, 130, 189, 190, 200
affines
  in kinship system, 121
  and marital patterns, 186
  in mythology, 143
age
  at marriage, 128
  of spouses, 193
agricultural cooperatives, government-run,
    25, 216
airstrips, SIL constructed, 219–20
alcoholism, 223
Allen, P. H., 154
alliance, marital strategy in, 137–8
Amazon, Central Northwest:
  ecological setting of, 13–17
  population of, 17–19
  see also Vaupés region
Arawakan languages, 19
Arawakans, 21
Århem, K., 6, 7, 11, 24, 105, 236
artifacts, 36
  and gender differences, 184
  in settlement interaction, 99
  see also craftsmanship
aru, 16
Arvelo-Jiménez, N., 66
attitudes
  toward money, 212
  toward sexuality, 189
  toward sick, 37, 40

toward work, 40–1
aunts, kinship role of, 119–20
Austin, J. L., 177
Australian Aborigines, 147
authority
  of headmen, 65, 67, 212
  in parent–offspring relationship, 118–19

balance, in social identity, 231, 232
banisteriopsis, 58, 153, 197
  at festivals, 203
  ritual drinking of, 204, 208
  symbolism of, 190
Bantu Negroes (African society), 161
Bará (fish people), 229
  kinship terminology of, 109–11
  language group of, 83
Barnett, S., 234
Barth, F., 151, 162, 165
Basso, E. B., 170
Bates, H. W., 22, 23
Bates, M., 16
beeswax, 191, 208
behavior
  kinship expectations and, 108
  kinship-related, 116–17
  marriage, 138–47
  see also daily life
belief systems; *see* cosmology, Tukanoan,
    mythology
Bennett, M. A., 20
Berlin, B., 28
beverages
  mingão, 39
  manicuera, 53
  manioc beer, 52, 53–54
  offered to visitors, 33
  see also banisteriopsis
Bidou, P., 7, 11, 24, 102, 107, 177
bilingual education, 220
Biocca, E., 24

273

Index

Bledsoe, C., 103
Blom, J. P., 165
blowguns, 46, 154
Bodley, J., 211
border, Brazilian–Colombian, 17
Bororo (South American society), 4, 233
boundary maintenance, 232
Breedlove, D. E., 28
bride
  adaptation of, 142
  role of, 134
bride capture, ceremonial, 125
bride price, 127–8
Bright, J. O., 170
Bright, W., 170
"brother-in-law" relationship, ceremonial,
  65
brothers, in kinship system, 120
brothers-in-law, 122
Brown, J. K., 194
Brüzzi Alves da Silva, A., 5, 24, 84, 99, 157
Buchler, I. R., 107, 127
Burridge, K., 3
Butt, A. J., 66

cachiveras, 16; see also rapids
Caja Agraria, 25, 216
cannibalism, 152
Carib languages, 19
cataracts, 16; see also rivers
category systems, languages as, 166; see also
  classification system, Tukanoan
Cathcart, M., 24
Catholic church, and Colombian government,
  217–18
Catholic missionaries
  influence of, 224–5
  and marriage, 129
  and Tukanoan language, 175
  see also Javerians, missionaries
caucheros
  in debt-bondage system, 217
  Tukanoan view of, 216
cazabe, 33, 35; see also manioc process
census, Tukanoan, 1968–70, 69
ceremonies
  food exchange, 183–4
  greeting rituals at, 98
  intersettlement relations and, 96
  naming, 105
  see also festivals, ritual
cerros, 13
Chagnon, N. A., 9, 64, 65, 97, 99, 154,
  193, 194
change
  concept of, 11
  costs of, 225–6

results of, 241
  see also acculturation, deculturation
change agents, 212
  and deculturation, 213–14
  powers of, 214
chicha, 197, 203
childbirth, role of shaman in, 197–8
children
  grandchildren, 120–1
  in longhouse, 36
  raising, 117–19
"cigar lighter," 229
classification system, Tukanoan
  comparisons in, 228
  continuum in, 227–8
  longhouse in, 230
  Makú in, 229
  multiple meaning in, 228–9
  "other world" in, 236
  polarized contracts in, 227
  shaman in, 230
  wahtía in, 229
climate of Vaupés region, 16
coca, 197, 203
collectivity, in Tukanoan public ritual, 234
Collier, J., 130, 186
Colombia
  as client-state of U.S., 226
  interaction with Tukanoans, 217–18
colonialism, results of, 211
Comisaría del Vaupés, 23
comisariato, 25
comisario, 25
commercialism, effects of increasing, 61;
  see also world, outside
communication
  regional perspective on, 6
  while hunting, 46
  see also language, language groups
compadrazgo, 123
compadre (coparenthood) system, 61
comparisons, taxonomic vs. paradigmatic,
  228
competition, as mythological theme, 145
concordato, 217, 219
conjunctivitis, 19
cooking
  and sexual division of labor, 53
  taboo associated with, 55
coresidence, 70
corn, as crop, 52
corregidor (magistrate), government-appointed,
  63, 137
Corry, S., 211, 217, 222
cosmology, Tukanoan
  heavens in, 205–6
  important features of landscape in, 206–7

levels of universe in, 204–5
Makú in, 158
property in, 64
rivers in, 46
shamanism in, 195–202
swamps in, 49
symbolism of differentiation in, 89, 90
wahtía in, 207
cosmopolitanism, 21
Coudreau, H. A., 22, 23
courtship, patterns of, 139
cousins
cross, 121
marriage of, 131
matrilateral parallel, 121
matrilateral vs. patrilateral parallel, 107
couvade, 188
co-wife, 122
craftsmanship
effects of increasing commercialism on, 61
and sex roles, 184
Crocker, J. S., 4, 231, 233
crops, variety of, 52
Cubeo (language group)
exogamous phratries of, 96
festivals of, 203
regional integration of, 97
Cuiva (South American society), 128
Cunningham, C., 37
curing
and food taboos, 55
by shamans, 199

dabucurí festival, 59, 60
daily life
activities of, 39–42
exchange in, 59–62
forest in, 46–50
impact of river on, 42–6
leadership in, 65–8
manioc process in, 51–4
property in, 62–5
dancing
at festivals, 202
symbolism of, 203
daughter-in-law, role of, 185–6
Davis, S. H., 211
dead-spirit houses, 201
death, ritual associated with, 200–1
de Beauvoir, S., 181
deculturation
process of, 213, 214
role of extractive industries in, 215–17
see also world, outside
Denevan, D. M., 50
Desana (wind people), 229
DeVore, I., 151

dialect
vs. language, 82
as linguistic variety, 19
diet, in horticulturally based societies,
182–3
discrimination against Tukanoans, 223–4;
see also world, outside
disease
diagnosis of, 198–9
epidemic, 18
impact on Tukanoan society of, 211
see also curing
divorce, 129, 241
Dobyns, H. F., 50
Dole, G., 66
Domínguez, V., 237
Douglas, M., 49
dreams, and shamanism, 196
drinking, at festivals, 202; *see also* beverages
Dumont, L., 107

eagle people, 89
economy, Tukanoan, 61
characteristics of, 58
inelasticity of, 59
and introduction of money, 61
see also exchange
ecosystem
and food production, 58–9
South American tropical, 50–1
education
bilingual, 220
and religion, 225
Elkin, A. P., 132
emblems of identity, 165
energy, concept of, 209
environment; *see* Vaupés region
epidemics, 18
Erikson, E., 3
Ervin-Tripp, S., 167
ethnic history, 21–2
ethnocentrism, 215, 222
ethnographic descriptions, 23–4
ethnolinguistics, 165
excess, as mythological theme, 146
exchange
at festivals, 202
impact of acculturation on, 61–2
and intersettlement dependence, 99
marriage as, 124, 129
patterns of, 59–62
and property rights, 64–5
and social structure, 60–1
exogamous group, 79
exogamy
Bará–Tukano, 90, 92
language, 7–8, 83–4, 135–7, 175–6

Index

exogamy (*cont.*)
  linguistic, 20, 21
  residential, 135
  settlement, 70
  sib, 76
expectations, kinship-related, 116–17
explorers, early, 22

fariña, 33, 184
Ferguson, C. A., 175
festivals
  dabucurí, 59, 60
  food consumption during, 56
  main activity of, 203
  preparation for, 203
  purpose of, 202
  "soul food" at, 202
feuding, and control strategies, 100
fish, kinds of, 43
Fish Anaconda Daughter myth, 75, 122–3,
  143, 161
fishing, 42–3
fish people, 42, 89; *see also* Bará
fluidity, concept of, 8–9, 228
folklorization, 61
food
  cooked, 184
  cultivated, 50–9
  distribution of, 47, 56
  importance of, 54–9
  nonhunted forest, 50
  ownership of, 57–8
  "real" vs. "soul," 56
  "soul," 197, 202
  taboos, 47, 54–5
  see also beverages
food exchange ceremonies, 143, 183–4
food production
  sex roles in, 182–4
  and social structure, 58–9
  see also manioc process
forest
  animals of, 47
  dangers of, 48
  hunting in, 46
  insects of, 48–9
  nonhunted foods of, 50
  spirits of, 49
  in Tukanoan classification, 227
Fortes, M., 166
Fosberg, F. R., 50
friagem, 16
Fried, M. H., 7
Fulop, Marcos, 5, 24, 71, 93
Fundação Nacional do Indio (FUNAI),
  Brazilian, 25
fungal infections, 19

gardening, 54
Gasché, J., 95, 132
gender, in social identity, 2; *see also* men,
  sex roles, women
general stores, 25
generation, in kinship system, 107
Giacone, A., 24, 149
gift giving, gossip about, 57
Glasse, R. M., 69
Godelier, M., 7, 102
Goffman, E., 162, 211
Goldman, I., 5, 11, 16, 18, 19, 21, 23, 26,
  32, 43, 53, 58, 71, 82, 84, 96, 97,
  98, 99, 100, 101, 107, 127, 130, 132,
  134, 135, 136, 149, 151, 152, 153,
  156, 157, 158, 161, 162, 173, 178, 184,
  187, 189, 190, 203, 204, 206
Goldschmidt, W., 186
Goodenough, W., 6, 108
Goodland, R. J. A., 50
gossip, 40, 57, 193
government, Colombian, 217–18, 226
governmental bureaucracy, 213
grandchildren, role of, 120–1
grandparents, role of, 120–1
greed, as mythological theme, 146
Greenberg, J. H., 24
greeting ritual, 98
Gregor, T., 194
Guayaki [Aché] (South American society), 128
Gumperz, J. J., 166, 167, 168, 174, 175
Guzmán, Antonio, 24

Hallowell, A. I., 2
Hames, R., 50
Harris, M., 63
harvesting, of manioc, 52
headmen
  qualities of, 67
  and succession, 104
  support for, 212
  tasks of, 65
  typical, 67
  wives of, 67–8
hearth family, 28, 105
Helm, J., 7
Hicks, D., 37
hierarchial ordering, 103–4
Holmberg, A., 194
Holy Sisters of Mother Laura, 220
hospitality, rules of, 97–8
Hugh-Jones, C., 6, 7, 11, 14, 24, 55, 56, 60,
  63, 72, 75, 76, 77, 79, 81, 82, 84,
  88, 89, 93, 96, 97, 102, 103, 105, 107,
  123, 124, 136, 151, 160, 183, 184,
  187, 188, 189, 191, 192, 195, 197, 202,
  230, 232, 236, 238

Index

Hugh-Jones, S., 6, 11, 16, 19, 20, 21, 24, 60, 63, 75, 76. 79, 84, 87, 102, 105, 115, 123, 133, 151, 154, 173, 177, 181, 182, 190, 192, 195, 196, 197, 204, 209, 228, 234, 236, 237
Humboldt, Alexandre von, 23
hunter-gatherers, regional systems among, 6
hunting, 43, 46
  animals hunted, 47
  symbolism surrounding, 47–8, 49
  in Tukanoan world, 209
husband, role of, 185–8; *see also* spouses
Hymes, D., 7

ideal, concept of, 9–11
identification, with specific language, 168
identity, badges of, language and speech as, 165–71; *see also* social identity
illness, and food taboos, 55
incest, 130, 189, 200
individualism
  and names, 106
  of shaman, 234–5
  in Tukanoan social identity, 233
  Tukanoan vs. Western concepts of, 212, 235
initiation ritual, male, 204, 234, 237
insects, variety of, 48–9
intermarriage, Tukanoan–Makú, 156, 240
intimacy
  and exchange, 60
  and fictive kinship, 123
  and greeting forms, 98
Iroquois (North American society), 194
Irwin, H. S., 50

Jackson, J. E., 6, 72, 108, 132, 179
Jacopin, P., 95, 132, 177
jaguar people, 89
Javerians (missionaries), 17, 23, 219, 220, 222
jealousy, as mythological theme, 145

Kaplan, B., 3
Kelly, R., 191
kinship
  and expectations and behavior, 108–17
  and language groups, 78
  mythical illustrations of, 108, 111, 112–16
  names and, 105–6
  and settlements, 77
  in social structure, 102–3
  specific roles, 117
  terminology, 106–8, 109–11
kinship roles
  affines, 121–3
  cousins, 121

fictive and ceremonial kinship, 123
  grandparent and grandchild, 120–1
  nephews and nieces, 119–20
  parents and offspring, 117–19
  siblings, 120
  uncles and aunts, 119–20
knowledge, ritual, 196
Koch-Grünberg, T., 21, 23, 77, 136, 149, 151, 152, 156, 157
Kok, P. P., 24
Kracke, W., 65
Krĩkatí (South American society), 194

labor, sexual division of, 183, 184
Labov, W., 167, 168, 175, 176
Lambert, W. E., 175
Lamphere, L., 180
Langdon, T., 11, 24, 55, 58, 197, 202
language
  as badge of identity, 165–71
  changing, 82
  and exogamy, 83–4
  families represented, 19
  importance in Tukanoan culture, 177–8
  and nonlinguistic environment, 171–7
  and passing as white, 224
  Spanish, 167, 220, 224
language distance
  measured by shared vocabulary, 173
  models of, 172
language groups, 7
  and acculturation, 69–70
  adequacy of term, 79, 81
  boundary maintenance between, 232
  definition for, 78
  dyadic relations between, 103
  egalitarianism among, 164, 175
  exogamy of, 7–8, 135–7
  genetically related, 173
  geographic distribution of, 79
  and kinship lines, 78
  and linguistic discreteness, 174–5
  of Makú, 149
  and marriage, 81, 82, 100
  marriage between selected, 94, 95
  names of, 85
  population estimates for, 87
  and settlements, 80
  and social boundaries, 81
  in social identity, 234
  Tukanoan, 82
Lave, J. C., 194
Leach, E. R., 70
leadership
  headmen, 65, 67, 104, 212
  nature of, 212
  voluntary nature of, 66

Index

leadership (*cont.*)
  war chiefs, 66
Lee, R. B., 151
levirate, 71
Lévi-Strauss, C., 9, 10, 70, 174, 182
Lingua Geral, 19
linguistics
  and descent group ties, 36
  in ethnographic descriptions, 23
  language distance, 171–4
  and social attitudes, 174
  variations, 19–20
llanos, 22
local descent groups, 70
  alliance of, 137–8
  and kinship relations between spouses, 131
  and marriage, 185–6
  in traditional social structure, 73
longhouse, 1
  abandonment of, 70
  ceremonial, 35
  choosing site for, 18, 31
  ground plan of interior, 34
  hearth family of, 28, 105
  inside, 33–6
  outside of, 31–2
  protection for, 32
  setting for, 26, 27
  significance of, 36–8
  structure of, 30–1
  in Tukanoan classification system, 227, 230
Lounsbury, F. G., 137
lumber extraction, 215
lunar eclipses, 205, 206, 208, 223, 231

MacCreagh, G., 23, 77, 151
McGovern, M. W., 23, 77, 151, 152, 156, 162
maintenance, in social identity, 231
Makú (South American society), 21
  attached to longhouse, 155–6
  background to, 148–51
  characteristics of, 149
  ethnographic description of, 24
  interaction between Tukanoans and, 154–8
  intermarriage of, 156, 240
  linguistic groups of, 149
  marriage rules of, 126, 150
  origin of, 149
  poison manufactured by, 153
  role as servants of, 160
  as slaves, 162
  social organization of, 150–1
  as symbol to Tukanoans, 158–61
  status of, 156
  Tukanoan attitudes toward, 103, 151–3
  in Tukanoan classification system, 229

  Tukanoan interaction with, 240
  Tukanoan view of, 178
malaria, 18
manicuera, 33
manioc beer, 53
manioc bread, 33, 35
manioc process, 39, 51–2
  harvesting in, 52
  peeling and grating in, 53
  in ritual, 183, 184
manioc products, 52, 53, 183
Markham, C. R., 66, 68
marriage
  "abduction," 133
  acceptable model of, 147
  adjustment of newlyweds in, 141–2
  age at, 128
  and alliance, 137–8
  and divorce, 129, 241
  exchange associated with, 60, 126
  function of, 185
  ideal, 240
  impact of missionaries on, 136–7
  importance of, 124
  incidence of, 139
  initiation of, 125
  and kinship relations between spouses, 130–5
  and language group exogamy, 135–7
  and language groups, 81, 82, 100
  myths concerning, 115–16
  polygamous, 128, 193
  principles of, 125–6
  real vs. ideal forms, 134–5
  and residential exogamy, 135
  stability of, 194
  in Tukanoan cosmology, 209
Marriage making, phratric principles in, 92–3, 94
Maybury-Lewis, D. H. P., 124, 194
Mead, G. H., 2
meals
  breakfast, 39
  formal communal, 56
  restrictions during, 55–6
  see also food
meaning, multiple levels of, 228; *see also* symbolism
Meggitt, M. J., 69
Mehinacu (South American society), 194
men
  crops tended by, 52
  and gardening, 54
  in male–female dichotomy, 229
  personal appearance of, 41–2
  as providers, 56–7
  supremacy of, 192

see also sex roles
menstruation, symbolism of, 190–1
metamorphosis, in Tukanoan cosmology, 209
methodology
  fluidity in, 8–9
  ideal–real dichotomy in, 9–11
  regional perspective in, 5–8
  social identity, 2–5
Métraux, A., 149, 157
Michaelson, E. J., 186
migration, and marriage system, 100
"Milk river," 204
Miller, D. R., 234
Miller, W. R., 175
mingão, 39
miriti palm, 13
miriti swamp, in Tukanoan cosmology, 206
missionaries
  arrival of, 218–19
  as change agents, 212
  and deculturation, 213
  ethnographic descriptions of, 24
  first, 23
  ideological warfare of, 220–1
  impact on Tukanoan social structure of, 17
  and marriage customs, 136–7
  rivalry among, 219, 221
  trouble with, 222–3
mission towns
  houses of, 35
  and land shortages, 18
  marriages in, 141
  population of, 69
Mitú (town), 25, 218
  and government representation, 218
  homesteaders in, 217
  inhabitants of, 223–4
moderation, in social identity, 231, 232
Moerman, M., 165, 166, 168
money, introduction of, 61
Monfortians, 218, 222
monogamy, view of, 128
moon eclipse, 205, 206, 208, 223, 231
moral conduct, attitude toward, 208–9
Morey, N. C., 170
Morey, R. V., 170
Moser, B., 13, 16, 24, 236
Muller, Sophia, 23, 219
multilingualism, 20, 21
  Indian attitudes toward, 177
  and social cleavages, 175
  widespread, 101
  see also language groups
murder, 200–1
Murphy, R., 61, 66
Murphy, Y., 61
music

in daily life, 42
at festivals, 203
see also Yuruparí instruments
mythology, 212, 226
  affinal relationships in, 122
  cannibalism in, 152
  exchange in, 60
  language groups in, 78, 86
  marriage behavior and expectations in, 143–7
  male supremacy in, 182
myths
  "Fish Anaconda Daughter," 75, 122–3, 143, 161
  about "first people," 72
  function of, 208
  with kinship-related themes, 108, 111, 112–16
  of life after death, 236
  Makú in, 158
  origin, 72, 89, 101
  and shamanism, 196
  star girl, 205
  about women's position, 70
  Yuruparí instruments in, 188

names
  of language groups, 85
  patronyms, 106
  sib-supplied, 72
naming
  purpose of, 105
  in social identity, 236
Needham, R., 174
neighbors, settlement, 98–9
nephews, kinship role of, 119–20
newborns, 37; *see also* childbirth
Nheengatú (language family), 19
nieces
  kinship role of, 119–20
Nimuendajú, C., 23, 71
noise, tolerance for, 40

O'Laughlin, B., 59, 61
onchocerciasis (African river blindness), 18
Orellana (early writer), 18
ostracism, 40, 193
out-migration, 18
Owen, R., 175
ownership
  concept of, 57
  of land, 62
  see also property

pahkó-poná relationship, ambiguity of, 144
Papurí River, 83
parasites, 18

Index

parents
  and childbirth, 198
  role of, 117–19, 188–9
parents-in-law, 120
patronyms, 106
Peirce, C., 2
people, in Tukanoan classification, 227
pepperpot sauce, 33
permanence, in social identity, 235
personality, in social identity, 236
personal appearance, attention given to, 41
petroglyphs, 16
pets, 41
phratry
  definition of, 86
  and language distance, 171–4
  and language groups included in, 91
  and marriage making, 92–3, 94
  organization of, 88
  in traditional social structure, 73
Pirá-paraná River, 83
Pirá-paraná region
  map of, 14
  settlements of, 16
poison, fish, 42–3
political organization, 68
polyandry, 129–30
polygamy, 128
polygyny
  disapproval of, 128
  incidence of, 193
population
  acculturation of, 24
  decline, 19
  density, 17, 21, 69, 99–100
  impact of disease on, 18
  language group estimates, 87
power, ritual, 196
prefectura, 25
property
  individual, 63
  lending of, 65
  manufacture of artifacts, 64
  ownership of land, 62–3
  private, 212
  ritual, 63–4, 76
  secular communal, 63
Protestant missionaries, 23
  influence of, 224–5
  rivalry with Catholic missionaries, 219
  see also Summer Institute of Linguistics
puberty rites, 209; see also initiation ritual
Pūmanaka buro
  catechism program at, 222
  health and nutrition at, 58
  marriages at, 139
  people of, 26, 28–30

settlements intermarrying with, 140
  see also daily life
Pygmies (African society), 161

quarrels, 62
quiñapira (pepperpot sauce), 33

racism, 167
Radcliffe-Brown, A. R., 132
raiding, and control strategies, 100
rain forest, ecology of, 51; see also forest
rainy season, 13
ranking, in Tukanoan world view, 212
rapids, and river transportation, 16, 44; see
  also rivers
raudales (cataracts), 16
Raven, P. H., 28
reality, concept of, 9–11
rebirth, in Tukanoan cosmology, 209
reciprocity
  peasant patterns of, 57
  women as expression of, 187–8
  see also exchange
regionality, in social identity, 238
regional perspective, concept of, 5–8
Reichel-Dolmatoff, G., 5, 11, 13, 16, 21, 23,
  49, 87, 89, 96, 100, 151, 152, 153,
  156, 161, 177, 205, 207, 230
Reid, H., 17, 18, 149, 150, 154, 157, 162,
  240, 241
reincarnation, in Tukanoan cosmology, 209
relationality
  in social identity, 4, 232–3
  in Tukanoan public ritual, 234
residence
  patterns of, 28
  settlement, 77
  see also longhouse
respect, in parent–offspring relationship
  118–19
Rice, H., 23
rigidity, vs. fluidity, 8, 9
risk, in social identity, 231, 232
ritual
  associated with death, 200–1
  associated with river, 45
  function of, 208
  greeting, 98
  individuality downplayed in, 234
  in longhouse, 37–8
  male, 181–2
  male initiation, 234
  property associated with, 63–4, 76
  sex roles in, 183–4
  Yuruparí, 191
  see also symbolism
rivers

characteristics of, 16
and communication, 44–5
dangers of, 45
and fishing, 42–3
ritual associated with, 45–6
and social organization, 99
and transportation, 43
in Tukanoan classification system, 227
Rivière, P. G., 66
Rodríguez Lamus, L. R., 24
Rosaldo, M. Z., 130
Ross, E. B., 63
rubber boom, 22
rubber gatherers
dealing with Tukanoans of, 211
labor "recruited" by, 17
Tukanoans as, 216
see also caucheros
rubber industry, of Colombia, 215
Ruddle, K., 50, 54

Salesians (missionaries), 17–18
San José de Guaviare (town), 217
Sankoff, G., 175
Sapir, E., 166
Sapir, J. D., 168
savanna, 22, 51
Schneider, J., 186
Schultes, R. E., 153
seasons, markers of, 16
segregation, sexual, 141, 142, 181, 183, 193
Selby, H. A., 107, 127
self
concept of, 2
Tukanoan vs. Western, 3–4
see also individualism
servant–master relationship, Makú in, 163
servants
role of, 119
role of Makú as, 160
Serviço do Protação ao Indio (SPI), Brazilian,
25
settlements
clearing in, 31–2
importance of, 77
interaction between, 96–104
intermarrying among, 140
language groups of, 80
and local exogamy, 77
regional perspective on, 5
size of, 21
sex
in kinship system, 107
myths concerning, 115–16
in social identity, 2
sex roles
defined, 179

and domestic activities, 184–5
and food production, 182–4
and male and female sexuality, 189–92
of parents, 188
problems with research in, 180–1
relations between men and women, 181–2
of spouses, 185–8
shamanism, 195–7
birth in, 197–8
death in, 200–1
and hunting, 48
sorcery and disease in, 198–9
shamans, 66
ambiguity of, 196
curing by, 199
and food, 184, 189
as food intermediaries, 197
function of, 208
individualism of, 234–5
language of, 177
snuff taken by, 153
in Tukanoan classification, 230
and wahtía, 208
Shapiro, J. R., 194
Sharanahua (South American society), 194
Shavante (South American society), 194
sibling rivalry, 114
siblings, in kinship system, 120
sibs (clans), 37
exogamy of, 76
and linguistic proficiency, 176
and local descent groups, 72
meaning of, 75–6
names of, 72
ranking of, 72, 74–5
ritual property of, 76
system of, 71–2
sickness
attitudes toward, 37, 40
and food taboos, 54–5
and thunder and lightning, 205
Silverwood-Cope, P., 24, 28, 87, 107, 126,
149, 150, 151, 152, 153, 154, 156,
157, 160, 240
Singer, M., 2
Sirionó (South American society), 128, 194
Siskind, J., 63, 193, 194
sisters
in kinship system, 120
marriage exchange of, 126, 127, 129
sisters-in-law, 122
skin-changing, 209
slavery, 156–8
smoking, of fish, 43
snakebite
danger of, 48
thunder and lightning connected with, 205

Index

snakebite (*cont.*)
  victim, 37
snuff
  at festivals, 203
  shamans', 153
social identity
  balance in, 231, 232
  concept of, 2–5
  language as emblem of, 170
  language group in, 234
  language and speech as indicators of, 166
  maintenance in, 231
  moderation in, 231, 232
  naming in, 236
  permanence vs. transience in, 235
  vs. personal identity, 2
  regional orientation in, 238
  relationality in, 231–3
  risk in, 231, 232
socialization, 118
social structure
  kinship in, 102–3
  and language distance, 171–4
  and language group, 77–86
  and linguistic discreteness, 174–6
  and linguistic proficiency, 176–7
  phratry in, 86–96
  regional integration in, 96–104
  and residence, 69–71
  role of language and speech in, 165–71
  sibs (clans) in, 71–7
  traditional local group organization in, 73, 77
Sorensen, A. P., Jr., 6, 19, 20, 24, 82, 93, 95, 100, 101, 136, 168, 169, 171, 172, 173, 174, 177
Soto Holguín, Alvaro, 24
"soul food," 197, 202
Spanish language, 220
  ability to speak, 167
  and passing as white, 224
speech
  as badge of identity, 165
  value placed on correct, 169
  see also language
spirits
  "dead-people," 200
  of forest, 49
  see also wahtía
spouses
  ages of, 193
  behavior of, 141
  kinship relations between, 130–5
  see also marriage, sex roles
Spruce, R., 22, 23, 157
star girl, 205
Stoll, D., 219

Stradelli, E., 23
starvation, 58
Sternberg, H. O., 50
storage, food, 58
stratification, social, 163
subsistence, sex roles in, 183–4
Summer Institute of Linguistics (SIL), 20, 23, 87, 174, 175, 176
  and Colombian government, 219–20
  influence of, 224–5
swamps
  in Tukanoan cosmology, 49, 206
  in Tukanoan environment, 13, 16
swidden horticultural systems, 50
symbiosis, of servant–master interaction, 161
symbolism
  concerned with rivers, 46
  destruction–creation, 191
  of differentiation, 89
  of hunting, 47–8
  Makú in, 158–61
  sex roles in, 183–4
  of sib structure, 75–6
  see also mythology

taboos
  food, 47, 54–5
  incest, 130, 189, 200
  on mentioning names of dead, 105
taxonomy, 228
Tayler, D., 13, 16, 24, 236
technology
  canoe-building, 45
  fishing, 43
  hunting, 46
temperature, of Vaupés region, 16
terminology
  kinship, 106–8, 109–11
  simplified Bará kinship, 112
  zero generation, 90
theft
  changing attitudes toward, 65
  spirits and, 200
Tindale, N. B., 176
tipití, symbol of, 191
tobacco, 197, 203
Torres Laborde, A., 24
towns; see mission towns, Mitú
trade, and intersettlement dependence, 99
trade goods
  disagreements over, 62
  introduced by whites, 22
trance, and shamanism, 196, 208
transience, in social identity, 4, 235
transportation
  and extractive industries, 215
  and rainy season, 13

Index

regional perspective, 6
technology, 43–4
transsexuals, 2
tribe
   definition of, 7
   in traditional social structure, 73
tuberculosis, 18
Tukanoan speakers, 21
Tukano language, 175
Tupian (language family), 19
Turnage, L., 87
Turnbull, C., 161
Tuyuka (mud people or clay people), 229
Tyler, S. A., 108

uncles, kinship role of, 119–20
universe, Tukanoan, 1, 46; *see also*
   cosmology
uranium, 215

values, Tukanoan, and deculturation process,
   214
Van Emst, P., 157, 158
Vaupés region
   cultivation in, 51–4
   ecological setting for, 13
   language families of, 19
   map of, 14–15
   population density for, 17
Vaupés system, fluid boundaries of, 8
villages, population of, 69
visiting, importance of, 98

wahtía (spirits)
   characteristics of, 207
   encounters with, 208
   in Tukanoan classification, 229
Wallace, A. F. C., 28
Wallace, A. R., 22, 23, 77, 99, 136, 151,
   157
Wallis, E. E., 20
Waltz, N. E., 19, 20, 82, 96, 172, 173, 174
war chiefs, power of, 66
Ward, B., 166
warfare
   cessation of, 194
   and settlement patterns, 97
Warner, W. L., 176
weapons, for hunting, 46
Wheeler, A., 19, 20, 82, 96, 172, 173, 174
Whiffen, T., 22, 23, 71, 156
whites, 1
   discrimination by, 224

and headman, 67
relationships with, 61
Tukanoan view of, 213
see also missionaries, rubber gatherers
Whitten, N. E., Jr., 53
wife-getting procedures, 134
wives
   of headman, 67–8
   role of, 185–8
   see also spouses
Wilson, R., 168
Witoto (South American society), 132
Wittgenstein, L., 108
Wolf, M., 186
women
   crops tended by, 52
   and gardening, 54
   in horticultural societies, 180
   and hunting, 46–7
   in male-female dichotomy, 229
   and marriage stability, 194
   personal appearance of, 41
   pivotal position of, 145, 146, 185, 233
   solidarity of, 142
   status of, 192–3
   value of, 192
   see also bride, sex roles
world, outside
   Colombian government, 217–18
   and deculturation process, 211–15
   extractive industries from, 215–17
   homesteaders from, 217
   missionaries from, 218–23
   Mitú, 223–4
world, Tukanoan; *see* cosmology, Tukanoan
work
   attitudes toward, 40–1
   and sexual division of labor, 183, 184

xenophobia, 97

Yanomamö (South American society), 97, 99,
   127, 154
   interaction with other settlements of, 64
   and trade goods, 128
   women of, 192, 194
Yukuna (language group). 132
Yuruparí instruments, 190, 191
   origin of, 188
   sacredness of, 208
Yuruparí Rapids, 16

Zuidema, R. T., 174

CAMBRIDGE STUDIES IN SOCIAL ANTHROPOLOGY

General Editor: Jack Goody

1. The Political Organisation of Unyamwezi
    R. G. ABRAHAMS
2. Buddhism and the Spirit Cults in North-East Thailand*
    S. J. TAMBIAH
3. Kalahari Village Politics: An African Democracy
    ADAM KUPER
4. The Rope of Moka: Big-Men and Ceremonial Exchange in Mount Hagen, New Guinea*
    ANDREW STRATHERN
5. The Majangir: Ecology and Society of a Southwest Ethiopian People
    JACK STAUDER
6. Buddhist Monk, Buddhist Layman: A Study of Urban Monastic Organisation in Central Thailand
    JANE BUNNAG
7. Contexts of Kinship: An Essay in the Family Sociology of the Gonja of Northern Ghana
    ESTHER N. GOODY
8. Marriage among a Matrilineal Elite: A Family Study of Ghanaian Senior Civil Servants
    CHRISTINE OPPONG
9. Elite Politics in Rural India: Political Stratification and Political Alliances in Western Maharashtra
    ANTHONY T. CARTER
10. Women and Property in Morocco: Their Changing Relation to the Process of Social Stratification in the Middle Atlas
    VANESSA MAHER
11. Rethinking Symbolism*
    DAN SPERBER, *Translated by Alice L. Morton*
12. Resources and Population: A Study of the Gurungs of Nepal
    ALAN MACFARLANE
13. Mediterranean Family Structures
    Edited by J. G. PERISTIANY
14. Spirits of Protest: Spirit Mediums and the Articulation of Consensus among the Zezuru of Southern Rhodesia (Zimbabwe)
    PETER FRY
15. World Conqueror and World Renouncer: A Study of Buddhism and Polity in Thailand against a Historical Background*
    S. J. TAMBIAH
16. Outline of a Theory of Practice*
    PIERRE BOURDIEU, *Translated by Richard Nice*
17. Production and Reproduction: A Comparative Study of the Domestic Domain*
    JACK GOODY
18. Perspectives in Marxist Anthropology*
    MAURICE GODELIER, *Translated by Robert Brain*

285

19. The Fate of Shechem, or the Politics of Sex: Essays in the Anthropology of the Mediterranean
    JULIAN PITT-RIVERS
20. People of the Zongo: The Transformation of Ethnic Identities in Ghana
    ENID SCHILDKROUT
21. Casting out Anger: Religion among the Taita of Kenya
    GRACE HARRIS
22. Rituals of the Kandyan State
    H. L. SENEVIRATNE
23. Australian Kin Classification
    HAROLD W. SCHEFFLER
24. The Palm and the Pleiades: Initiation and Cosmology in Northwest Amazonia
    STEPHEN HUGH-JONES
25. Nomads of South Siberia: The Pastoral Economies of Tuva
    S. I. VAINSHTEIN
26. From the Milk River: Spatial and Temporal Processes in Northwest Amazonia
    CHRISTINE HUGH-JONES
27. Day of Shining Red: An Essay on Understanding Ritual
    GILBERT LEWIS
28. Hunters, Pastoralists and Ranchers: Reindeer Economies and Their Transformations
    TIM INGOLD
29. The Wood-Carvers of Hong Kong: Craft Production in the World Capitalist Periphery
    EUGENE COOPER
30. Minangkabau Social Formations: Indonesian Peasants and the World Economy
    JOEL S. KAHN
31. Patrons and Partisans: A Study of Two Southern Italian *Comuni*
    CAROLINE WHITE
32. Muslim Society
    ERNEST GELLNER
33. Why Marry Her? Society and Symbolic Structures
    LUC DE HEUSCH
34. Chinese Ritual and Politics
    EMILY AHERN
35. Parenthood and Social Reproduction: Fostering and Occupational Roles in West Africa
    ESTHER N. GOODY
36. Dravidian Kinship
    THOMAS R. TRAUTMANN
37. The Anthropological Circle: Symbol, Function, History
    MARC AUGE
38. Rural Society in Southeast India
    KATHLEEN GOUGH
39. The Fish-People: Linguistic Endogamy and Tukanoan Identity in the Northwest Amazon
    JEAN JACKSON
40. Karl Marx Collective: Political Economy of a Siberian Collective Farm
    CAROLINE HUMPHREY

41. Ecology and Exchange in the Andes
    DAVID LEHMANN
42. Traders without Trade: Responses to Trade in Two Dyula Communities
    ROBERT LAUNAY

*Published also as a paperback

287